A
HISTORY OF JEFFERSON COUNTY
WEST VIRGINIA

JEFFERSON COUNTY, WEST VIRGINIA.

LEGEND.

———	BOUNDARY LINES.
- - -	DISTRICT LINES.
+++	RAILROADS.
═══	AUTOMOBILE ROADS.
≡≡≡	RIVERS & CREEKS.
~~	SPRING STREAMS.
▓	Incorporated Towns.
▫	Unincorporated Towns.
✶	Points of Historical Interest.
○	Springs.

Miles.

WASHINGTON CO. MARYLAND

Potomac River

Pack Horse Ford
Pack Horse Road
Bedford
Scrabble / Terrapin Neck
Wild Goose
Rock Marsh Run
Rumsey Monument
Shepherd Town
Billmyers Mill Road
Money Tree
Morgan Spring
Old Fountain Rock
SHEPHERDS TOWN
Bakerton
Engles
Home of Gen. Darke
Duffields
Kearneysville
Reedson
N & W R.R.
Baltimore & Ohio R.R.
Kerneysville
Traveler's Rest
Paynes Ford

WEST VIRGINIA COUNTY LINE

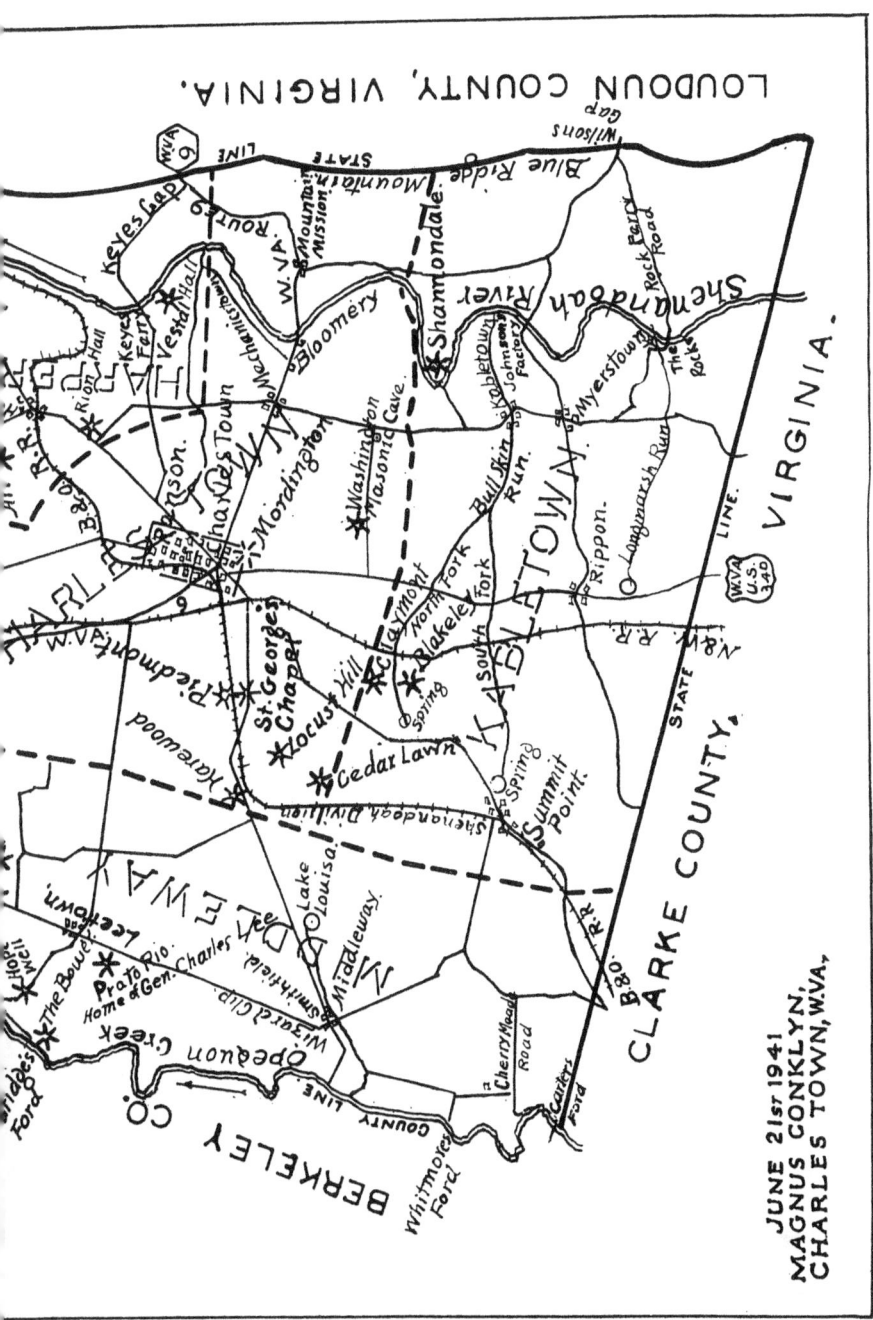

A History of Jefferson County West Virginia

1719-1940

Millard Kessler Bushong, A.M., Ph.D.

Professor of History and Government
Shepherd State Teachers College

HERITAGE BOOKS
2007

HERITAGE BOOKS
AN IMPRINT OF HERITAGE BOOKS, INC.

Books, CDs, and more—Worldwide

For our listing of thousands of titles see our website
at
www.HeritageBooks.com

A Facsimile Reprint
Published 2007 by
HERITAGE BOOKS, INC.
Publishing Division
65 East Main Street
Westminster, Maryland 21157-5026

Copyright © 1941 Millard K. Bushong

— Publisher's Notice —
In reprints such as this, it is often not possible to remove blemishes from the original. We feel the contents of this book warrant its reissue despite these blemishes and hope you will agree and read it with pleasure.

International Standard Book Number: 978-0-7884-2250-8

PREFACE

Since early childhood I have been interested in the history of my native county. Attempts to learn more about the historic region in which I lived were frustrated by the fact that no one had written a complete story of it. A few authors had depicted items of interest, but most of its past remained untold.

This was still the situation when I decided to further my education by working for the doctorate. At that time I conceived the idea of writing a history of Jefferson County as a dissertation. My adviser, Professor Charles H. Ambler of West Virginia University, realized the possibilities of a thorough study of a county so rich in history as Jefferson. With his consent and encouragement I began the writing of this volume. Because there is so much history connected with this vicinity before Jefferson County was formed in 1801, I have begun my study with the date 1719. In doing so, however, I have confined my work to what later became Jefferson County.

I am indebted to many persons for aid in my research and writing. Professor Charles H. Ambler has been constructively helpful in directing my research and in encouraging my work. His colleagues, Professors James M. Callahan, Oliver P. Chitwood, and Festus P. Summers, have rendered similar service. For valuable information concerning the early settlements in the Lower Shenandoah Valley I am obligated to Editor Clifford S. Musser of Shepherdstown, West Virginia. Colonel Robert L. Bates of Lexington, Virginia, gave the results of his research in connection with the Middleway neighborhood. Dr. R. B. Woodworth of Burlington, West Virginia, supplied useful information about the Presbyterian churches. Colonel Braxton D. Gibson and Editor Robert C. Rissler, both of Charles Town, West Virginia, furnished many helpful suggestions. Unusual courtesies which greatly facilitated my work were extended to me by Editor William B. Snyder of Shepherdstown, West Virginia, and officials of the Old Charles Town Library. Miss Eleanor Burr of Charles Town, West Virginia, typed the manuscript. Last but not least, members of my family deserve credit. My mother, Mrs. Frank Lee Bushong of Charles Town, West Virginia, and my sister, Mrs. George W. Dress, Jr., of Hagerstown, Maryland, aided materially by reading the manuscript a number of times and helping in every way possible. I am indebted to my brother, Attorney Lee Bushong, Jr., of Charles Town, West Virginia, for many valuable suggestions, as well as the financial assistance which made my research possible.

I have made a special effort to reduce errors to a minimum, but, for such as may have crept in, I ask the kind indulgence of the reader.

Millard K. Bushong

Charles Town, W. Va.
October 15, 1941.

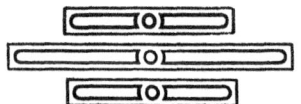

TABLE OF CONTENTS

CHAPTER		PAGE
1	NATURAL FEATURES	1
	Location	1
	Topography	1
	Geological Structure	1
	Climate and Water	2
	Agriculture and Industry	3
	Beauty of Harpers Ferry	5
2	EARLY DAYS	6
	Explorations	6
	Settlements	8
	Towns and Villages	15
	Churches, Ministers, and Schools	19
	The French and Indian War	24
	The Masons	25
3	THE REVOLUTION	27
	Companies of Soldiers	27
	The "Bee Line" March	27
	Robert Rutherford	30
	Other Events	30
	Revolutionary Generals	32
4	JAMES RUMSEY AND THE STEAMBOAT	37
	Early Life	37
	First Experiments	38
	Success	42
	The Rumseian Society	45
	Rumsey Goes to London	45
	Difficulties Abroad	46
	John Fitch, the Rival Inventor	48
	Other Inventions of Rumsey	50
	The Rumsey Memorials	50
5	ASPIRATIONS AND INCIDENTS, 1790-1800	53
	Early Newspapers	53
	The National Capital	54
	St. Clair's Defeat	55

CHAPTER		PAGE
	Harpers Ferry Armory and Arsenal...	55
	An Episode...	57
	Churches	57
	Education	60
	Dolly Madison's Wedding...	62
6	THE JEFFERSONIAN ERA...	64
	Jefferson Becomes a County...	64
	Diversions	68
	War of 1812...	69
7	THE NEW NATIONALISM, 1815 to 1840..	75
	Political Events...	75
	Harpers Ferry Armory and Arsenal....	77
	Churches	79
	Sunday Schools...	80
	Internal Improvements...	81
	The Iron Industry...	84
	Negroes and Slavery...	85
	Literary Activities...	86
	Towns and Villages...	87
	The Masons...	87
	Death of Lafayette...	88
8	THE EVENTFUL FORTIES...	89
	Politics	89
	Harpers Ferry Armory and Arsenal....	89
	Schools	90
	The Mexican War...	91
	The Forty-Niners...	94
	Newspapers	96
9	ANTE BELLUM DAYS, 1850-1861...	97
	Census of 1850...	97
	Politics	98
	Secession	101
	Harpers Ferry Armory and Arsenal....	103
	Churches and Schools...	105
	Attempt to Divide the County...	107
10	THE JOHN BROWN RAID...	109
	John Edwin Cook...	109
	Osawatomie Brown...	110

TABLE OF CONTENTS

CHAPTER		PAGE
	Attack on Harpers Ferry	114
	Attack on the Engine House	120
11	THE JOHN BROWN TRIAL AND EXECUTION	124
	Trial	124
	Execution	134
	Attempt at Escape by Cook and Coppoc	136
	Conclusion	140
12	THE CIVIL WAR	142
	Ten Companies	142
	Harpers Ferry in 1861	145
	The Year 1862	152
	Raid on Winchester and Potomac Railroad	153
	Capture of Harpers Ferry	155
	After Antietam	157
	Raids, Spring of 1863	163
	Skirmishes after Gettysburg	165
	Imboden Captures Charles Town	167
	Raids in Early 1864	168
13	THE CIVIL WAR (CONCLUDED)	170
	Skirmishes, July, 1864	170
	Shepherdstown vs. Sharpsburg	170
	Devastation by David Hunter	171
	Shenandoah Valley Campaign, 1864	176
	Mosby in 1864	181
	Skirmishes, Winter of 1864-1865	186
	John Yates Beall	187
	The End	187
14	VIRGINIA OR WEST VIRGINIA	190
	Formation of West Virginia	190
	Efforts to Obtain Jefferson County	194
	Attempts to Reunite with Virginia	195
	Virginia vs. West Virginia	198
15	RECONSTRUCTION	201
	Post-War Conditions	201
	Politics	203
	The County Seat Controversy	209
	Schools	215

CHAPTER		PAGE
	Miscellaneous Items	217
16	NEW INTERESTS AND OUTLOOKS	219
	Politics	219
	Schools	222
	Schemes	227
	Miscellaneous Improvements	233
	The Spanish-American War	234
17	THE RURAL FREE DELIVERY	236
	Wanamaker's Efforts	236
	Wilson Selects Jefferson County	237
	Developments	240
	Growth of System	242
18	THE NEW CENTURY	243
	Politics	243
	Modern Improvements	246
	Schools	249
	Moral Questions	253
	Newspapers	255
	The World War	256
	Miscellaneous Items	258
19	RECENT YEARS	260
	United States vs. United States Harness Company	260
	Another Treason Trial	261
	Politics	265
	Schools	267
	The Second World War	271
	Miscellaneous Items	271
	BIOGRAPHIES OF PROMINENT FORMER RESIDENTS	276
	FOOTNOTES	315
	BIBLIOGRAPHY	343
	APPENDIX A, ROLLS OF SOLDIERS	350
	APPENDIX B, THE FORTY-NINERS	397
	APPENDIX C, AFFIDAVIT OF JOHN AVIS	399
	APPENDIX D, LIST OF COUNTY OFFICIALS	402
	FOOTNOTES FOR APPENDICES	408
	INDEX	410

LIST OF ILLUSTRATIONS

	PAGE
Jefferson's Rock, Harpers Ferry	4
Pack Horse Ford, near Shepherdstown	6
Said to be the Oldest House in West Virginia	10
"Piedmont", near Charles Town	12
"Mordington", Formerly "Happy Retreat" the Home of Charles Washington	18
Ruins of St. George's Chapel, near Charles Town	21
"Travelers Rest", Home of Major General Horatio Gates, near Kearneysville	33
"Prato Rio", Home of Major General Charles Lee, at Leetown	35
James Rumsey	39
Model of Rumsey's Steamboat	44
The Rumsey Monument at Shepherdstown	51
"Harewood", Originally the Home of Samuel Washington, near Charles Town	63
Holl's Tavern, Charles Town	68
The United States Armory at Harpers Ferry in 1857	104
"Beall Air", the Home of Colonel Lewis Washington, near Halltown	111
Street Scene in Charles Town during the John Brown Trial	127
John Brown Leaving the Jail at Charles Town for His Execution	135
The John Brown Procession on the Way to the Gallows at Charles Town	137
John Brown Ascending the Scaffold at Charles Town	139
The John Brown Fort Today at Harpers Ferry	140
Harpers Ferry at the Beginning of the Civil War from the Maryland Side	143
The United States Armory at Harpers Ferry in 1861	147
Destruction of the Railroad Bridge at Harpers Ferry by the Confederates on June 15, 1861	149

LIST OF ILLUSTRATIONS

	PAGE
Ruins of Hall's Rifle Works at Harpers Ferry in 1861	151
Federal Troops on Camp Hill at Harpers Ferry in 1862	161
Jefferson County Courthouse at Shepherdstown, 1866-1871	205
Storer College at Harpers Ferry	216
Joseph McMurran, the First Principal of Shepherd College	223
John Stephenson Seminary at Charles Town	225
The Charles Town Public School, 1893-1912	226
Cartoon Which Appeared in the **Farmers Advocate** Opposing Shenandoah River Bridge	245
The Old Jefferson County Jail at Charles Town	248
Knutti Hall, Shepherd State Teachers College	250
St. Hilda's Hall for Girls at Ranson	252
The Charles Town Academy Just Before It was Torn Down	254
"Claymont Court", the Home of the Author, Frank R. Stockton, near Charles Town	259
The Jefferson County Courthouse at Charles Town	263
Shepherdstown High School	268
Charles Town High School	270
Harpers Ferry in 1941	272
The Charles Town Jockey Club	274

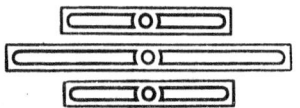

A
HISTORY OF JEFFERSON COUNTY WEST VIRGINIA

CHAPTER ONE
NATURAL FEATURES

LOCATION.

Jefferson County is located in the lower Shenandoah Valley in that part of West Virginia known as the Eastern Panhandle and is the farthest eastern extremity of the state. It is bounded by Maryland and Virginia and is contiguous to only one other West Virginia county, Berkeley, from which it was formed in 1801. On the north the Potomac River separates it from Washington County, Maryland, and on the east the Blue Ridge Mountains divide it from Loudoun County, Virginia. Another portion of the Old Dominion, Clarke County, bounds Jefferson on the south, while Opequon Creek is part of its western boundary. An arbitrary line and Rocky Marsh Run complete the encirclement on the west side. The county has an area of 212.41 square miles, a length of 24 miles, and a breadth of 12 miles.[1]

TOPOGRAPHY.

The Great Valley subdivision of the Appalachian Area includes most of Jefferson County. Extending from the Blue Ridge Mountains west to North Mountain, it is a broad, fertile limestone and shale valley, with limestone predominating. Its surface is rolling and marked by low hills and shale ridges. Rising from about 400 feet above sea level near the Potomac River to 600 near the mountains on the west, the Valley has an average elevation of from 400 to 450 feet.[2]

GEOLOGICAL STRUCTURE.

The present mountain and valley topography is due to erosion and not to rising and falling influences. The varied character of

1

the land depends on the nature of the rocks and the amount and rapidity of erosion, but it is also determined in large part by the character and changes of the original mountain formation. The rocks of the Great Valley are hard limestone, which are more or less resistant brittle masses that break into sharp folds. The Valley has been so greatly eroded that now only the upstanding edges of the strata are visible and these project along northeast-southwest lines as prominent features of the landscape.[2]

Most of the surface rocks within the Harpers Ferry region are of sedimentary origin, that is, they were deposited by water. Consisting of sandstone, shale, and limestone, they present great variety in composition and appearance. The materials of which they are composed were originally gravel, sand, and mud, derived from the waste of older rocks, and the remains of plants and animals which lived while the strata were being laid down. Thus some of the great beds of limestone were formed largely from the shells of various sea animals.[4]

At one time hardwoods consisting of white oak, red oak, hickory, poplar, ash, and black walnut, covered much of the land now included within present Jefferson County. As so much time has elapsed since the forests were cleared away, no definite data can be collected regarding original conditions. Civilization has made such inroads that only along Opequon Creek and the Shenandoah River are forests found today. Most of these trees are pines and inferior hardwoods.[5]

CLIMATE AND WATER

Although the county's climate is quite variable, it lacks the low temperatures of the more northern states in winter and the extreme high temperatures of the southern states in summer. Geologists claim that nearness to the seacoast probably gives this region a more moist and equable climate than districts farther inland. Frosts cease earlier in the spring and come later in the autumn, so that the growing season is of good length and fruit cultivation is less hazardous. Heavy snows of long duration on the ground in winter are exceptional.

With an average annual rainfall of 36 inches there is abundant moisture for all purposes, though in some years the rains

NATURAL FEATURES

are unequally distributed with troublesome results to crops. Heavy and destructive floods occur at times, but they are exceptions and attract unusual attention when they come.[6]

The Potomac and Shenandoah rivers meet at Harpers Ferry, where they are merged as one. The former descends from the northwest while the latter wends its way from the south. Numerous smaller streams, such as, Opequon Creek, Bullskin Run, Evitts Run, Furnace Run, and others, assure Jefferson County abundant water power.

Many fine springs, the most famous of which are those at Shannondale, are found in the county. Located five and a half miles south of Charles Town, near the Shenandoah River, Shannondale Springs was for many years a popular health resort. An analysis of the water there showed a temperature of 55° Fahrenheit and a content of sulphate of lime, carbonate of lime, and sulphate of magnesia.

Shannondale Springs first attracted public attention in the fall of 1819 and soon thereafter several buildings were erected. George Washington is said to have drunk from these waters while he was surveying in the vicinity for Lord Fairfax. Others prominent in early United States history, namely, James Monroe, Andrew Jackson, Martin Van Buren, Millard Fillmore, John C. Calhoun, Commodore David Porter, and General Duff Green, visited there. The resort declined in popularity after it had been plagued with disastrous fires. One in 1858 destroyed the hotel, and another, in 1909, did so much damage that Shannondale sank into complete disuse.[7]

AGRICULTURE AND INDUSTRY.

Fertile limestone land is Jefferson's main natural heritage. It is so far superior to other West Virginia counties in this respect that one can hardly believe it is in the same state. The rolling land is easy to cultivate. Consequently, in spite of the advance of industrialism in the United States, the county remains primarily agricultural. Farming, dairying, and orcharding comprise the chief pursuits. Wheat, corn, oats, potatoes, and alfalfa are the principal crops.

Nevertheless, there is a limited amount of industry in the

county. In the regions around Millville, Bakerton, Engle, and Kearneysville are limestone quarries. Ranson is the largest industrial center and contains garment, brass, harness, fertilizer, and cold storage establishments.

For a number of years the finest quality of natural cement was obtained from the region east of Shepherdstown. The Potomac Cement Company began operations about a mile east of that place in 1830 and until 1900 cement was produced. Much of it was used in the construction of Government buildings at Washington and of the locks of the Chesapeake and Ohio Canal.[3]

Although Jefferson County lacks the natural resources for which West Virginia is most noted, such as coal, oil, and gas, it possesses limited deposits of iron ore. For 100 years iron was mined at the Virginia Orebank, along the Potomac River four miles above Harpers Ferry. Operations began there in 1816. In 1839 a furnace was erected on the east side of the Shenandoah River, a mile below Shannondale Springs. Its ruins may still be seen near the stream now known as Furnace Run. The iron percentage of this ore is 50.8, which is fairly high for a brown hematite ore. Geologists state that there still appears to be a considerable tonnage available in the region.[9]

Jefferson's Rock, Harpers Ferry

BEAUTY OF HARPERS FERRY.

One of the county's most outstanding natural features is the beautiful view at Harpers Ferry, which is perhaps equal to any in America. The town is partly surrounded by mountains, and two rivers unite to flow through a gap. Picturesqueness is supplied by the useless bed of the old Chesapeake and Ohio Canal and the Baltimore and Ohio Railroad, which passes through a tunnel at the base of Maryland Heights. No wonder Thomas Jefferson, while standing on the high rock named for him, declared the "scene to be worth a voyage across the Atlantic".[10]

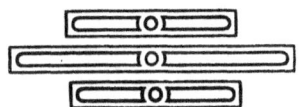

CHAPTER TWO
EARLY DAYS

EXPLORATIONS.

Slightly more than a mile east of Shepherdstown on the Potomac River is a place where the water may be easily forded. The banks slope gently down and a broad, flat rock extends across the bed of the stream. For many years this crossing was known as Pack Horse Ford. Later, it received the name of Boteler's Ford or Blackford's Ford from nearby property owners. For ages a great game trail crossed the river at this location and buffalo, deer, elk, and bear roamed in abundance. Large game trails generally follow natural pathways through the country.

Pack Horse Ford, near Shepherdstown

As might be expected, the Indian trails followed those made by the wild animals. One of them, the Warriors Path, led northward through the Shenandoah Valley to Winchester, where it divided. A branch crossed the Potomac River a few miles north of present Shepherdstown and another crossed it a mile below at Pack Horse Ford. Tradition tells of a fierce fight at the latter spot between the Delawares and Catawbas. The numerous arrowheads, tomahawks, and other implements of war which have been found there at various times indicate that such a struggle actually took place. According to this tradition, the northern Indians did not fare so well, for it is said that every Delaware except one was killed. He fled as far as the Susquehanna River,

EARLY DAYS

where he was overtaken by a pursuing Catawba and slain.¹

The first white man of record to look upon the Shenandoah Valley, of which Jefferson County is a part, was John Lederer, a German. Commissioned by Governor Sir William Berkeley to explore, Lederer made three distinct tours between March, 1669, and September, 1670. On his first expedition he is thought to have penetrated as far west as present Madison County, Virginia, where he reached the summit of the Blue Ridge Mountains. His second journey took him farther south, within the limits of present Campbell County, but his final trip is believed to have carried him to a point along the Fauquier-Rappahannock County border. From here he looked across present Warren County into the Shenandoah Valley.²

No more recorded explorations were made into the Shenandoah Valley until 1707, when Louis Michel, a Swiss, made a map of the country about the junction of the Shenandoah and Potomac rivers. In 1712, another Swiss, Christopher Baron de Graffenreid, trying to find desirable sites for future settlement, appeared along the Potomac River. He had made arrangements with Governor Alexander Spotswood of Virginia to bring a colony of Swiss into the undeveloped region. He apparently went as far west along the Potomac as the present counties of Hampshire or Mineral. A land dispute between the proprietors of Maryland and those of the Northern Neck of Virginia influenced de Graffenreid to look elsewhere.³

The energetic young governor of Virginia, Alexander Spotswood, took the next step in exploring the Shenandoah Valley. In August, 1716, with a number of followers he set out from Williamsburg to determine what lay beyond the Blue Ridge Mountains. It was believed then that the Great Lakes were just across the range. Spotswood and his party crossed the Blue Ridge at Swift Run Gap into the present borders of Rockingham County.

Entering the Shenandoah Valley, the adventurers proceeded to the west bank of a stream which they named "Euphrates". They then took formal possession of the country in the name of King George I of England. After a celebration consisting of firing salutes and drinking toasts, most of the party began the return trip. A few remained behind to make further explorations. To commemorate the event and to encourage other expeditions Spotswood later gave each of his party a miniature golden horseshoe. This was the beginning of the famous order of the "Knights of the Golden Horseshoe".[4]

SETTLEMENTS.

The date of the first settlement in the Shenandoah Valley is not definitely known. Evidence points to the possibility of a settlement at or near Shepherdstown in 1719. The New Castle Presbytery and the Philadelphia Presbyterian Synod records reveal the existence of settlers south of the Potomac River at that early date. On September 19, 1719, the records state that the Synod had received a letter from the people of "Potomoke, in Virginia," requesting that a minister be sent to them. It is not certain that this settlement was at or near the present site of Shepherdstown, but a review of the facts makes such an assumption logical.[5]

In the first place, the phrase "in Virginia" eliminates all possibility that Potomoke could have been "Pocomoke" or some other name that was identified with settlements in Maryland. Shepherdstown was frequently called "Potomack" and "Potomoke" may have been an earlier spelling of this name. Additional support to the above belief is furnished by the Donegal Presbytery record of June 22, 1745. It states that the Rev. Samuel Caven was appointed to supply the Potowmack, Opeckon, and Bullskin churches, all of which were probably close to each other. If the Potowmack congregation was the same as the earlier "Potomoke" congregation and had been located very far from the other two, it would have been impossible for the same minister to supply all three in that day of slow travel. Another record, under date of August 31, 1762, states that a Mr. McGanis was ordered to supply the churches at "Tuscarora and Potomack in Virginia." This indicates the proximity of "Potomack" to the Tuscarora church near Martinsburg.[6]

Since "Potomoke" was in Virginia and near churches in the Shepherdstown vicinity, it seems probable that the term must refer to a place at or near present Shepherdstown. The latter is nearest Pack Horse Ford and hence would be the first to be seen by settlers from Pennsylvania. It appears likely that these pioneers would have settled upon the desirable land near the ford

EARLY DAYS

rather than move further away where the land was no better, if as good.

The Potomoke request of 1719 was answered by the appointment of the Rev. Daniel McGill, who served this congregation for several months. His work was so satisfactory that he was asked to remain as the permanent minister. There is no evidence that he did so, as his name does not appear on the Presbytery records until June 6, 1721. On that date he was elected moderator of the Philadelphia meeting of the synod. The spread of Presbyterianism in the Potomoke vicinity is attested by the fact that in 1722 three ministers were sent into that field. The following year more came. Soon the names of the Rev. Hugh Conn, John Orme, William Stewart, and Jonathan Dickinson appear as ministers for the Potomoke region.[7]

If the assumption that "Potomoke" referred to a congregation near present Shepherdstown be accepted, then it can be stated that a settlement large enough to ask for and receive a minister existed in the Shenandoah Valley in 1719. This contradicts the generally accepted tradition that Morgan Morgan was the first white settler in the region. He is said to have established himself on Mill Creek, near Bunker Hill, Berkeley County, in 1726. As a matter of record, Morgan Morgan was a coroner in Delaware from 1726 to 1729, inclusive, and did not purchase Virginia lands until the early 1730's. Consequently, it would have been impossible for him to have settled on Mill Creek in 1726.[8]

In 1727 German settlers from Pennsylvania crossed the Potomac River at Pack Horse Ford and founded the town of New Mecklenburg, later renamed Shepherdstown. They had emigrated from the Rhine Valley to America because of intolerable conditions in the fatherland. The tyranny of autocratic rulers, devastation caused by numerous wars, and crop failures, all contributed to the exodus. Other factors in the mass movement were the cooperation of the British Government in providing transportation and the activity of shipping companies which sought cargo for their immigrant trade. Many of the unfortunates went directly to Pennsylvania and when the areas in the southern and eastern portions of that colony had been taken, they overflowed into the Shenandoah Valley and through the back country.[9]

After New Mecklenburg was settled, many tracts of land were

Said to be the Oldest House in West Virginia.
According to tradition, this house in Shepherdstown was erected in the early 1700's by Richard Morgan

EARLY DAYS

sold. On June 17, 1730, John Van Metre was assigned 10,000 acres in the fork of the Shenandoah, including the places called Cedar Lick and Stony Lick. In addition, his grant was to contain 20,000 acres not already taken up by Robert Carter and Mann Page, "or any other living in the fork between the Sd River Sherrando and the River Cahongaroota, & extending thence to Opeckon & up the South Branch thereof ...."[10] Isaac Van Metre obtained a grant of 10,000 acres lying between Carter's tract, the Shenandoah River, and Opequon Creek.

In 1731 the Van Metres sold portions of their land to Jost Hite and a group of associates. Part of Hite's grant was included in that which Governor Gooch patented to Thomas Shepherd on October 3, 1734, and which became the site of present Shepherdstown. The original town consisted of fifty acres from this tract. Later additions of 172 and 50 acres, respectively, furnished more room for the settlement.[11]

Jost Hite and his sons-in-law, George Bowman, Jacob Chrisman, and Paul Froman, with their families, came to the Valley in the fall of 1731 and settled near Winchester. Other pioneers in the neighborhood were: William Stroop, Thomas and William Forester, Israel Friend, Thomas Swearengen, Van Swearengen, James Froman, Edward Lucas, Jacob Hite, John Lemon, Richard Mercer, Edward Buckles, John Taylor, Samuel Taylor, and John Wright.[12]

At the time the Germans were establishing themselves at New Mecklenburg newcomers were appearing in the western part of Jefferson County along Opequon Creek. John Smith and Rees Smith, millwrights, were among these early pioneers and were greatly chagrined to discover that they were on land patented to the Van Metres in 1730. The difficulty was subsequently adjusted, for on August 20, 1734, Governor Gooch granted the Smiths 420 acres. This tract was located along both sides of a branch of Opequon Creek called Turkey Run. It included the entire course of the stream almost from its source to Opequon Creek, as well as the site of present Middleway.[13]

Only a few settlers began to obtain land in the vicinity of present Charles Town in the decade after 1730. Robert Worthington, Sr., a member of the Society of Friends, acquired a tract of 3,000 acres from the crown in 1730 and established a home on

Evitts Marsh. He named it "Quarry Banks" for his old home in England. It is now "Piedmont" and is in possession of the Briscoe family. In addition to being a farmer, Worthington engaged in business as a merchant and exporter. He was also active in promoting the settlement of the Lower Valley. He was the grandfather of Thomas Worthington, sixth governor of Ohio.

"Piedmont", near Charles Town

Edward Lucas, another Quaker, came to present Jefferson County from Bucks County, Pennsylvania, some time before 1740. He established his home on a plantation which he called "Cold Spring". He was the grandfather of Robert Lucas, eleventh governor of Ohio, and the great grandfather of Edward and William Lucas, both of whom represented the Valley District in Congress. Another descendant, Daniel Bedinger Lucas, was United States Senator-elect from West Virginia but was never seated.[14]

The settlement of Harpers Ferry began after New Mecklenburg and Smithfield, or Middleway, had received their first inhabitants. Exact details are lacking but the first person to reside at the confluence of the Potomac and Shenandoah rivers is supposed to have been a Pennsylvania Dutch squatter, named Peter Stephens. Because of its natural location the site of his abode was commonly referred to as "The Hole". It was not long before Stephens acquired the strange name of "Peter in the Hole".

EARLY DAYS

His family consisted of his wife and three children. His nearest neighbors were Billy Sheeler and a Squire Hamilton, each of whom lived about three miles distant. The operation of a few small boats, including a ferry business, occupied Stephens a part of the time.

Another character associated with Harpers Ferry's early history was Peter Hoffman, an itinerant trader who traveled between Baltimore and the Upper Valley. He became a good friend of Stephens and often stopped at "The Hole".[15]

The main character in this unfolding drama was an Englishman named Robert Harper. Historians disagree as to the date when he came into the Harpers Ferry region. Some claim it was as early as 1734 and others as late as 1747. However that may be, Harper, who had made an enviable reputation as a builder of churches and mills, was residing in Philadelphia when he received a call to the Lower Valley. This came from members of the Society of Friends who lived in present Frederick County, Virginia, and who wanted some mills constructed. It is not clear how they heard about the Philadelphia builder, but perhaps it was through their connections in the Quaker City. Harper accepted the position tendered him and set out on the southern journey.

On the way to Frederick County Harper spent a night at Frederick, Maryland. There he met Hoffman, the trader, who persuaded him to alter his course so as to include the road past "The Hole". Hoffman assured him that this route was not only shorter but offered more beautiful scenery than the one Harper had planned to take. In addition, the obliging acquaintance offered to accompany the Philadelphian as guide.

When the travelers arrived at the junction of the rivers, Stephens rowed them across to his home. Harper was so struck with the unexcelled beauty and grandeur of the locality that he purchased Stephens's holdings. The deed was transferred in the presence of Squire Hamilton who realized the questionable nature of the Stephens title and advised Harper to obtain a legal title from Lord Fairfax. The purchaser made a visit to "Greenway Court", the Fairfax home in present Clarke County, Virginia, and soon acquired undisputed ownership of the Stephens tract. Fairfax welcomed this opportunity to get rid of Stephens, who had caused him no end of trouble.[16]

Harper did not forget the real purpose of his southern trip. He soon contacted his Quaker employers with whom he arranged to devote two days a week to their work and the remainder to the development of his own property. Harper moved his family into Stephens's log cabin, which stood on the present site of Dittmeyer's Drug Store. His own time was spent in improving the road and ferry facilities, in building a grist mill for himself on the Shenandoah River, and in supervising the construction of other mills in the vicinity. Hoffman was engaged as his purchasing agent.

The winter of 1747-1748 was unusually severe. Deep snows and freezing weather lasted until the end of February. Unfortunately for the newcomers, both the Potomac and Shenandoah rivers went on a rampage in the spring of 1748 and drove the Harpers from their home to higher ground. Another freshet, in 1753, also inconvenienced them.[17]

In March, 1748, a surveying party led by James Genn, the county surveyor of Prince William County, laid off tracts in the Harpers Ferry region for Lord Fairfax. Two youthful adventurers, George Washington and George William Fairfax, were allowed to accompany the expedition. The party is supposed to have stopped at the river junction and to have surveyed Harper's lands. All previous leases and transfers had been made by stepping, measuring from the eye, and blazing the line-trees with a tomahawk. They were known as "tomahawk titles" and were naturally quite unreliable.[18]

In March, 1761, Harper obtained the right to establish and maintain a ferry across the Potomac to the Maryland shore. When a village later sprang up at the junction of the two rivers, it became known as "Shenandoah Falls, at Mr. Harper's Ferry". This name was retained until after the Revolutionary War. Subsequently, it was shortened to "Shenandoah Falls" and, finally, on March 24, 1851, the village was incorporated as "Harpersferry".[19] Harper died at his home on Shenandoah Street, near his ferry, in October, 1782, and was buried in the graveyard on the hill overlooking the beautiful view at that location.[20]

By 1760 other settlers had established homes on the land between the Potomac and Shenandoah rivers. Particularly was this true in the northern part of what is now Jefferson County. Joseph

EARLY DAYS
15

Darke moved his family from Bucks County, Pennsylvania, to the Shepherdstown vicinity about 1741. His first home here is supposed to have been a log cabin located about four miles east of the German settlement along the Potomac. His son, William, later lived a mile east of the present village of Duffields. Melchior Engle bought land from Lord Thomas Fairfax along Elk Branch about 1750 and built a stone fort around his house and spring, and eight years later James Hendricks moved from Pennsylvania to a spot three miles south of present Shepherdstown.[21]

TOWNS AND VILLAGES.

Before long Thomas Shepherd became active in making plans for the incorporation of the settlement at New Mecklenburg. He laid out fifty acres of his land into lots and streets and on November 12, 1762, presented a bill of incorporation to the Virginia House of Burgesses. For some undisclosed reason, the name was shortened to "Mecklenburg". The bill was given its first reading in the house on November 22 and its second the following day. After a third reading it was passed by the House of Burgesses on November 25, was approved by the Council of Virginia on November 30, and became a law by the governor's signature on December 23, 1762.[22]

Because of the dispute between Shepherdstown and Romney regarding priority, details of the progress of Romney's bill of incorporation are interesting. It was first presented and read to the House of Burgesses on November 18, 1762. It received its second reading on November 20 and after being amended was read a third time and approved by the council on December 17. The governor's signature was obtained on December 23, the same day that he signed the bill incorporating Mecklenburg. In the group of bills signed by the governor on December 23, Romney's bill is listed twentieth and Meckenburg's, twenty-first.[23]

Whether or not this technicality gives Romney the distinction of being the oldest town in West Virginia is left for the reader to decide. There is no doubt, however, that there was a settlement at New Mecklenburg several years before there was one at Romney. The latter town was not settled until 1734 or 1735.[24]

The fifty acres included in the site of Mecklenburg were divided into 96 lots, each 103x206 feet. The town extended as far east as the present location of the Norfolk and Western tracks and as far west as Shoe Lane. Rocky Lane is as far north as it went and Back Alley as far south. Eight lots comprised a square and intersecting streets were sixty-five feet wide. The first deed of the new town was recorded on July 21, 1764, at which time Thomas Shepherd and Elizabeth, his wife, transferred thirty-five new lots to others.[25]

Mecklenburg's original charter existed until 1793, when it was repealed and a new one granted. Thomas Shepherd was the town's sole trustee from 1762 until his death in 1776. From the latter date until 1793 no one seems to have been in complete authority. By act of the General Assembly on December 2, 1793, Mecklenburg received its second charter. In it the town was granted enlarged powers and duties, among which was that of selecting its own board of trustees. In April, 1794, the following trustees were elected: Abraham Shepherd, Henry Bedinger, 2nd, Conrad Byers, Jacob Haynes, John Morrow, Henry Line, and William Chapline.

The name of Mecklenburg ceased to exist officially after January 11, 1798. On that date, in response to a petition received the preceding December, the Virginia General Assembly passed an act changing the name to Shepherdstown, in honor of the town's founder. The act merely put into statutory form what had been the practice for a number of years, as the name of Shepherdstown had gradually become more popular than that of Mecklenburg.[26]

Shepherd's holdings were not limited to the 222-acre and 50-acre grants mentioned heretofore. On June 12, 1751, he had obtained a tract of 457 acres from Lord Fairfax adjoining his original purchase. He improved the latter by erecting in the center of Mecklenburg a stone house. This was intended as a dwelling for his family in time of peace and a place of refuge in time of war. When the Indians went on the warpath, neighboring families congregated within the stone walls of "Fort Shepherd", as it was properly called. The "fort" remained as it was constructed until 1812, when it was torn down. The original stones were used for a wall around the lot. A brick building, McMurran Hall of Shepherd State Teachers College, now occupies the site of the old stone fort. Among other properties belonging to Thomas Shepherd were a gristmill, sawmill, and a ferry.[27]

EARLY DAYS

Charles Town, Jefferson County's largest town and seat of government, was established in 1787 by act of the Virginia General Assembly. Prior thereto it was a small village of taverns, scattered houses, and perhaps a nearby mill or shop. Charles Washington, the youngest brother of George Washington, came to this locality in 1780 from Spotsylvania County and built a residence on the outskirts of the present town site, which he named "Happy Retreat". In September, 1837, the property was purchased by Judge Isaac Douglass, remodeled, and named "Mordington".[28]

On November 23, 1786, Charles Washington and several others petitioned the Virginia General Assembly to establish a town upon eighty acres of Washington's land in the county of Berkeley. The request was favorably received and the resulting bill given final approval on December 12. It was signed by the president of the Senate on January 4, 1787, and by the speaker of the House on January 7. As the governor's signature, apparently, was not required at that particular time in Virginia, the latter date may be accepted for the official establishment of Charles Town.[29]

The above paragraph contradicts the erroneous general impression that Charles Town was incorporated in October, 1786. The impression was due to a misleading heading in Hening's **Statutes of Virginia.** The page on which the act establishing Charles Town is found carries the date "October, 1786" but it does not say that this particular act was passed on that date. The same date appears at the top of all the pages containing acts passed at that session. It refers to the session which began on October 16, 1786, and ended on January 11, 1787.[30]

The act establishing Charles Town, originally "Charlestown", provided that the eighty acres on which it was located be laid out into half-acre lots, with intersecting streets, according to the discretion of Charles Washington. Government was vested in a board of trustees, with self-perpetuating powers, composed of the following persons: John Augustine Washington, Robert Rutherford, William Darke, James Crane, Cato Moore, Benjamin Rankin, Magnus Tate, Thornton Washington, William Little, Alexander White, and Richard Ransone. Erection of a sixteen-foot square dwelling, with a brick or stone chimney, entitled lot owners to all the rights of other freeholders in the state.[31]

The last important town in present Jefferson County char-

"Mordington", formerly "Happy Retreat" the home of Charles Washington

EARLY DAYS

tered by the Virginia General Assembly in this period was Smithfield, or Middleway, established January 15, 1798, upon the lands of John Smith, Jr., and William Smith. The act of incorporation named John Packett, Moses Smith, John Smith, Jacob Reese, Joseph Grantham, and John Grantham, Jr., as trustees.[32]

CHURCHES, MINISTERS, AND SCHOOLS.

The Potomoke Presbyterian Church has already been treated in connection with early settlements in Jefferson County. In 1740, or perhaps a year or two earlier, members of that denomination erected a building at the headspring of Bullskin Run, near Summit Point. However, it was not until November 25, 1771, that the land was deeded by David Castleman and wife to Isaac Larew, John Riley, John Oliver, George Hampton, William Rankin, and William McCormick, trustees. Although the house of worship was commonly known as the Bullskin Church, its ecclesiastical name was Hopewell. The latter name appears in the records of the Presbytery of Donegal as early as April 2, 1740, and is frequently mentioned thereafter.[33]

The Bullskin Church seems to have grown out of the preaching place for which the Rev. William Williams obtained a license in 1736. On September 22, 1737, Williams took the oath required of dissenting ministers in Orange County Court and declared his intention to hold meetings at his own plantation and that of Morgan Bryan. He took the same oath in the new county court of Frederick County on June 4, 1745. The Bullskin, or Hopewell, congregation continued to meet at Summit Point until about 1800. By that time the building had fallen into decay and it was decided to worship in the new union church at Smithfield, the title to which was held by the Lutherans. After April 24, 1819, the Hopewell name was changed to Smithfield. Services were continued until April 19, 1933, when the membership became so small that the Winchester Presbytery dissolved the church.[34]

Some time between the years 1763 and 1767 the old Potomac [Shepherdstown] Presbyterian congregation divided. One group decided to set up a separate church on Elk Branch, about seven miles south of Shepherdstown. The mother church had already been conducting services on Elk Branch and had erected a house of worship there on the stream at the Link Spring in front of the residence of the late James Burr Osbourn. It was a separate building from the blockhouse which had been erected there for protection against Indians.

The first mention of Elk Branch as a separate church appears in the records of Donegal Presbytery on April 11, 1769. Donegal had been formed from New Castle Presbytery in 1732. The first minister sent to the new organization was the Rev. Robert Cooper. Others who followed were: Messrs. Balch, Slemons, Vance, Craighead, Rhea, Lang, Hoge, McKnight, Thompson, Hunter, and McConnell. These were all supply pastors and served at irregular intervals.

The need of a regular minister prompted Elk Branch Presbyterians to ask for one in April, 1776. Following authorization by Donegal Presbytery, three commissioners, John White, John Wright, and James McAllister, extended a call to John McKnight, who was promised a salary of 132 pounds. Although McKnight received two other calls at the same time, he accepted in June, 1776, the one from Elk Branch. With seven ministers and four ruling elders officiating, he was ordained on December 3, 1776, as the first regular preacher of Elk Branch. Despite the fact that McKnight served its congregation for six years and was popular with his parishioners, he was not always paid his salary promptly. This was especially true in the time of the Revolutionary War when money became worthless. Consequently, in 1782 he left to accept a call from Marsh Creek [Gettysburg], Pennsylvania, and from that date until 1792 Elk Branch was served by supply pastors. In 1792 the congregation divided. One part joined the church under the Rev. Moses Hoge at Shepherdstown and the other united with the old Bullskin congregation in organizing a new church at Charles Town. In 1833, however, the Elk Branch church was reorganized.[35]

The first Lutheran church in the Shepherdstown neighborhood was organized in 1765, when nine persons met for that purpose. Among them were Henrich Budinger, Sr., Henrich Kuchas, Martin Endler, Philip Keller, Nicholas Hahn, and Martin Wohlfarth. They assembled in a private residence and, after singing a few hymns, listened to a sermon by one of their number. There is no evidence that the congregation erected a building before

EARLY DAYS 21

1795, but they may have had some sort of log structure. No resident minister served them until 1790, although occasionally one from Winchester, Hagerstown, or Frederick would hold services. Among the early preachers are recorded the names of Bauer, Wildbahm, and Nicodemus. The first records of this church are in German.[36]

What are perhaps the most interesting ruins in Jefferson County today, those of St. George's Chapel, had their beginning as a church in the later 1760's. The stone remnants of this once elaborate house of worship, located a mile and a half west of Charles Town, are still visited by sightseers. Its early history is closely associated with the name of Colonel Robert Worthington, Jr., who lived nearby and was a strong supporter of the Episcopal church.

Ruins of St. George's Chapel, near Charles Town

It was necessary for Worthington to travel ten miles to attend services in a church of his preference. The nearest one was located at the present village of Bunker Hill. As he and his neighbors were taxed for the support of the Episcopal Church, they felt they should not be made to suffer so much inconvenience. They therefore petitioned the House of Burgesses in November, 1769, for a division of Frederick parish. In reply, the burgesses passed an act establishing three smaller parishes, Frederick, Beckford, and Norborne. The latter was named for Norborne Berkeley, Virginia's popular colonial governor. The act made further provision for the resignation of the old vestrymen and the election of three new groups.[37]

According to the terms of the division Frederick and Norborne parishes were each to have a new church, the cost of which had already been defrayed by inhabitants of the old parish. The presumption is that a new church had already been erected in Norborne parish some time prior to November, 1769, at the expense of Worthington. Claims that Samuel Washington and James Nourse were active in its erection are false, as they did not settle in present Jefferson County until 1770, but no doubt they contributed to the support of the church after it had been built.

St. George's Chapel was a beautiful structure. The main building, which rose to a height of two stories, was constructed of native limestone. Two tiers of windows on all sides provided sufficient light and ventilation. The general plan of the floor resembled the letter T. A foundation two feet wide supported walls twenty-two inches thick and a roof made of sheet lead. Cedar wood was used in the window and door frames. High-backed pews of carved oak rested on a floor of imported tiles. An elegantly carved, elevated pulpit faced the main doorway, outside of which were massive stone steps. The large silver candlesticks along the sides of the interior added greatly to its appearance. At various times the structure has been known as Berkeley Church, the English Church, Norborne Chapel, and Trinity Chapel. Its ruins are referred to as those of St. George's Chapel. Services were held here until 1811 and possibly as late as 1817.

The Rev. Daniel Sturgiss, who was ordained in 1771, was the first minister of record at St. George's Chapel. He was followed in 1775 by John Hurt. The latter's successors prior to 1810 were: John Wilson, a Mr. Veasey, Bernard Page, William Heath, Emanuel Wilmer, and John Price. Samuel Washington acted for a time as senior warden and William Hancher was junior warden. Among the early worshippers were members of the Washington, Nourse, Davenport, Worthington, and Throckmorton families.[38]

Trinity Episcopal Church was established at Shepherdstown during this period of activity. Definite information of its organization is lacking, but a small stone building is supposed to have existed in 1769. Thomas Shepherd and Joseph Van Swearingen assisted in the movement. In Shepherd's will, probated in 1776, he requested that the lot on which the English [Episcopal] Church then stood be reserved for the sole use of the church and free from ground rents. As there are no records for the period between 1769 and 1840, it is difficult to determine who the early ministers were. A Rev. Mr. Sturgiss is said to have served the congregation about 1784 and in 1786 a man by the name of Stubbs succeeded him. The membership of the church was small.[39]

The Methodists were slower in gaining a foothold in present Jefferson County. It was not until 1776 that an itinerant Methodist preacher, Freeborn Garretson, held a service in Shepherdstown. Two years later the Sixth Annual Conference of the "unepiscopal" Methodists in America, held at Leesburg, Virginia, sent Edward Bailey to preach in the recently formed Berkeley Circuit. He was thus the first regularly appointed Methodist pastor of record for this region. Bailey was transferred to the Fairfax [Virginia] Circuit, and in 1779 John Tunnel and John Hagerty served the Berkeley congregations. These two men, along with Micajah Debuler, returned the next year. In 1781 Ignatius Pigman, Edward Morris, and William Partridge were preaching there, and two years later Moses Park and Thomas Humphries came.

The humble beginning of the above denomination in these parts bore fruit, however, for the first person to plant Methodism in the far northwest, Francis McCormick, was from this section. He was reared in present Jefferson County and converted in Charles Town.[40]

Members of the Reformed Church, who had been worshipping with the Lutherans in Shepherdstown, broke with them in 1782 over the custom of preaching in German. They objected to a continuation of this procedure and organized Christ Reformed Church directly across from the Lutheran meeting-place. Early Reformed ministers were a Mr. Bauer and Michael Slaughter.

The bells placed in Christ Reformed Church have an interesting history. They are three in number and are of different sizes. Cast in France, the oldest was made in 1732, another in 1798, but the date of the third is unknown. An unusual ceremony preceded the placing of the last bell. Before it was lifted into the tower, it was turned upside down and filled with wine. At the completion of the service each member of the congregation took a drink until the bell was empty. One of the participants stated later that a few persons felt a little tipsy.[41]

There is evidence that the early settlers at Shepherdstown were interested in education. It is asserted that by 1762 both a German and an English school were located there. The latter was for elementary and higher education and was taught by a Scotchman named Robert Cockburn. Its curriculum included the "three R's", as well as surveying and other studies. In 1773 a school on High Street is mentioned in a Berkeley County deed referring to Shepherdstown. Three years later a schoolmaster by the name of Kramle taught some of the town's children. Mention is made of another "pedagogue", the Rev. Robert Stubbs, as teacher of the Shepherdstown Academy in 1787.[42]

THE FRENCH AND INDIAN WAR.

The Lower Valley resounded to the tramp of soldiers during the French and Indian War. In the spring of 1755 part of Braddock's army passed by on its ill-fated expedition to Fort Duquesne. This was an attempt by the British to drive the French from the Ohio Valley and to help protect the defenseless settlers. The army set out from Alexandria in two divisions, one of which was to proceed westward by Winchester, Virginia, and the other by Frederick, Maryland. It was the former group which passed through present Jefferson County. It crossed the Blue Ridge Mountains at Keyes's Gap and the Shenandoah River at Keyes's Ford. According to tradition, some of the soldiers dug a well about a mile southwest of Charles Town.

The division that passed through this immediate vicinity left Alexandria on April 9 under the command of Sir Peter Halket, in charge of powder and cannon. The other part of Braddock's army, led by a Colonel Dunbar, left Alexandria on April 18 for Frederick, Maryland. At the latter place the officers decided to join their comrades at Winchester. Accordingly, the soldiers crossed the Potomac River at the present site of Williamsport and then went through what is now Martinsburg to Winchester.[43]

The French and Indian War aroused the patriots of this section. In 1755 Captain Richard Morgan organized a company of

EARLY DAYS

men at Shepherdstown, which he led to Fort Cumberland to join Braddock. Three years later Robert Rutherford of "Flowing Springs", near present Charles Town, recruited a company of rangers. After Braddock's defeat the whole border region was attacked by Indians and it was to meet this threat that "Rutherford's Rangers" were organized. George Washington had advised Governor Dinwiddie of Virginia to appoint Rutherford in command of the newly formed group. The rangers were to operate only in what was then Frederick County, Virginia, and were to fight in true Indian style. Braddock's defeat had revealed that it was necessary to abandon European military tactics in favor of fighting Indians in the Indian fashion.

Accordingly, Rutherford's men did not wear uniforms but used instead the picturesque garb of the frontiersman. To the hunting shirt with its long cape effect were added breeches, leggings, and moccasins. The weapons consisted chiefly of a rifle, shot pouch, hunting knife, and possibly a tomahawk. For the most part, the rangers operated in bands of twos and threes, although larger numbers were used when necessary.

One account states that the soldiers did not get off to what might be termed a "flying start". When they unexpectedly came upon a large body of redskins, they are said to have run away. This happened, however, when the men were still raw recruits. Reports state that they later became a highly efficient fighting group and performed valuable service in defending the frontier. It is perhaps significant that William Darke, later General Darke of Indian fame, served as corporal in the Rutherford Rangers.[44]

THE MASONS.

According to a widespread tradition, in 1754 George Washington presided as master over the first lodge of Free Masons to be assembled west of the Blue Ridge Mountains. The meeting-place is said to have been a large limestone cavern located about two miles south of the present site of Charles Town. The purpose of this meeting was the establishment of a lodge. A cave was selected so that the Masons would not be disturbed by curious onlookers. The belief that the cave may have been decided upon as the permanent meeting-place is strengthened by a deed filed in the Berkeley County clerk's office in September, 1773. By it a Mr. Davis conveyed to Samuel Washington and others, as trustees, a tract containing one and one-eighth acres of land on which the cave is located. Although regular meetings were not held in the cave, a Masonic celebration occurred in May, 1844. Assembling there in June, 1927, the Masons commemorated the historical significance of the cave.[45]

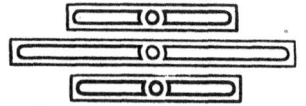

CHAPTER THREE
THE REVOLUTION
COMPANIES OF SOLDIERS.

Jefferson County was a part of Berkeley during the Revolutionary War and its efforts for the cause of independence are therefore closely associated with those of the mother county. It is difficult to distinguish between the soldiers recruited in what is now Jefferson and what is now Berkeley County. Nevertheless, it appears that at least seven companies of riflemen were obtained in present Jefferson County.

The commanders of these companies, together with the dates of their organization, were: Captain Hugh Stephenson, 1775; Captain William Brady, 1776; Captain Abraham Shepherd, 1776; Captain William Morgan, 1776; Captain George M. Bedinger, 1781; and two by Captain Henry Bedinger, 1781 and 1783. Three hundred privates are said to have enlisted at Shepherdstown, more than one hundred of whom were residents of the town. Of the latter, two-thirds died in active service.[1]

Because of its unusual response to the American cause, Shepherdstown is alleged to have furnished more officers and soldiers to the Continental army, in proportion to the number of inhabitants, than any other town in Virginia. At this time it contained about 1,000 persons, whereas, Charles Town probably had less than 100. This explains the importance of Shepherdstown as a mustering-place.[2]

THE "BEE LINE" MARCH.

When news of the battle of Lexington reached Shepherdstown, most of its able-bodied men sprang to arms. They drilled on a vacant lot behind the old Entler Tavern. The request of the Continental Congress for two companies of riflemen from Virginia found a ready response and they were soon being organized. General Washington recommended as heads of the Virginia soldiers Hugh Stephenson and Daniel Morgan, both of whom had commanded groups in Dunmore's War. Stephenson lived along Bullskin Creek within the limits of present Jefferson County, whereas Morgan hailed from Frederick County, Virginia.[3]

Much rivalry developed between the two companies. Each commander wanted to complete his group first and thus obtain the honor of leading the way. Stephenson organized his company at Shepherdstown and his rival chose Winchester. In spite of the fact that the volunteers were required to furnish their own equipment, recruits poured into both towns. Each man had to provide himself with an approved rifle, shot pouch, powder-horn, blanket, knapsack, and clothing. All recruits were required to be men of character. Both bodies were enrolled within a week.[4]

Difficulty in obtaining rifles of the desired quality delayed both companies almost six weeks. In this interval the Shepherdstown Committee of Safety appointed the following assistants to Captain Stephenson: William Henshaw, first lieutenant; George Scott, second lieutenant; and Thomas Hite, third lieutenant. Abraham Shepherd succeeded Hite when the latter declined to serve. The riflemen themselves selected Samuel Finley, William Kelly, Josiah Flagg, and Henry Bedinger as sergeants.

Finally, everything was ready for the long march to Boston. Both groups were anxious to get into the fray. It was agreed that Stephenson, who was the senior officer, would cross the Potomac at Shepherdstown and that Morgan would cross it at Harpers Ferry. They were to meet at Frederick, Maryland, and then proceed together to Boston.

Prior to their marching, Stephenson's men enjoyed a barbecue given by Colonel William Morgan at his home on June 10, 1775. The riflemen met at a large spring on Morgan's place and indulged in a patriotic song. In addition, they agreed that the survivors of their company would meet on the same spot, on the same date, fifty years later. When the appointed time came only five of the original ninety-seven were living. Of these only two, Major Henry Bedinger of Virginia and Major Michael Bedinger of Kentucky, were able to keep their pledge. The other three, Judge Robert White of Winchester, General Samuel Finley and William Hulse, both of Ohio, wished to attend but were too feeble

THE REVOLUTION

to do so. Nevertheless, the two survivors and many friends enjoyed an elegant dinner served by their host, Daniel Morgan. Afterwards they witnessed a military display.[5]

Stephenson's company set out from Shepherdstown on July 16 but failed to find Morgan's men at Frederick, as had been expected. The reason is that Morgan stole a march on his rivals, for he crossed the Potomac River on July 15 and hastened to Boston. According to the **Draper Manuscript**, he asked Stephenson to wait a few days in order that the two groups might march together. Stephenson did so only to learn later that Morgan had already left so as to have the honor of being the first to arrive at Washington's side. Although Stephenson's men often covered 30 to 36 miles a day in an effort to overtake their rivals, they were unable to do so. They reached Cambridge on August 11 and learned that Morgan's men had arrived just before them. In a "bee line" march they covered almost six hundred miles in twenty-four days. These companies were the first from the South to join Washington.[6]

The appearance of these frontiersmen at Cambridge is said to have caused a sensation among those already on hand. Washington galloped to meet his fellow-Virginians and with tears of joy grasped the hand of every man.

The newcomers were in sharp contrast with their surroundings. Dressed in homespun hunting shirts, in leather leggings and moccasins, and with a buck-tail in their hats, they were a strange-looking lot. No less curious were their weapons, which consisted of tomahawk, scalping-knife, and rifle. Each of Stephenson's men was further adorned with the immortal words of Patrick Henry, "Liberty or Death," embroidered upon the breast of the hunting-shirt.

In spite of their unprepossessing appearance, the Virginians proved themselves to be among the best marksmen in Washington's camp. Many persons marvelled at their ability to hit a mark seven inches in diameter at a distance of 250 yards, even while they were advancing. Other demonstrations of expert shooting were equally sensational.[7]

Both of the Virginia companies, along with the two from Maryland which arrived a few days later, were ordered to Roxbury. This position, about six miles from Cambridge, faced

Boston Neck. The British troops remained in Boston and after the battle of Bunker Hill no important engagements took place in the colonies for more than a year.

ROBERT RUTHERFORD.

About the time these riflemen reached Roxbury one of their neighbors was playing an important role in Virginia. He was Robert Rutherford of near Charles Town, who, as a member of the Virginia Convention of 1775 meeting in Williamsburg, helped to decide on her course in the Revolution. He was one of the seven delegates chosen by the Convention to reply to Lord Dunmore's proclamation demanding that Virginians either join the British army or be held as rebels. On December 13, 1775, he signed a declaration stating that the relations between England and Virginia were forever severed.

The committee then laid the foundation for the successful prosecution of the war for independence. To this end pardons were promised all slaves who had taken up arms in behalf of the mother country in response to Dunmore's proclamation promising freedom. These pardons were granted only on condition that those affected would resume their status as slaves.[8]

OTHER EVENTS.

In the North when the Virginians' one-year enlistment was about to expire, it was decided to organize a rifle regiment. Stephenson, who had been promoted to the rank of colonel, was selected by Washington to head the larger organization. Eight companies were raised for the regiment in the summer of 1776. When Stephenson died in August of that year, Colonel Moses Rawlings of Maryland succeeded to his command.[9]

A company of the rifle regiment was recruited by Captain William Brady, a resident of the Bloomery vicinity, near Charles Town. His subordinates were William Pyle, first lieutenant; his brother, Christopher Brady, second lieutenant; and Battail Harrison, third lieutenant.

Another company was raised by Captain Abraham Shepherd, assisted by Samuel Finley and Henry Bedinger. Most of the men came from the neighborhoods of Charles Town, Martinsburg,

THE REVOLUTION

and Stephens City. They left Shepherdstown in the fall of 1776 and went to reinforce the defenders of Fort Washington, near New York City. In spite of General Washington's advice to withdraw beforehand, Congress forbade him to abandon Forts Lee and Washington. Both were captured by the British and 3,000 Americans taken prisoners, among whom were members of Captain Shepherd's company. The inhuman treatment given the prisoners by their captors resulted in the death of an unusually large number. Within two months and four days over 1,900 had been killed or had died in prisons. Only a few of the patriots from Berkeley County lived to be exchanged.[10]

Late in the fall of 1776 Captain William Morgan recruited a company of volunteers to reinforce Washington's army at Morristown, New Jersey. Other officers were: William Lucas, first lieutenant; Edward Lucas, second lieutenant; George Michael Bedinger, third lieutenant; and Cato Moore, fourth lieutenant. The men enlisted for three months, but a request by General Washington for a slight extension was cheerfully granted. Early in March, 1777, this body, commanded by Colonel Charles Winston, was defeated by a superior force of the enemy at the battle of Piscataway in New York. Shortly afterwards, their term of service having expired, the volunteers were honorably discharged.

At home, in the spring of 1777, Colonel Samuel Washington resigned as county lieutenant of Berkeley, and Colonel Van Swearingen succeeded him. The position of colonel of the county militia, which had been Van Swearingen's, was filled by Philip Pendleton. Robert Carter Willis succeeded Pendleton as lieutenant colonel of the militia.

During the next few years Colonel Van Swearingen, as county lieutenant, received a number of requests from the Governor of Virginia to raise troops for Indian campaigns. Incited by the British, the savages were on the warpath along the frontier. They caused great distress among the settlers. Many of the appeals came in the summer and fall of 1777, and Berkeley County contributed its full quota.[11]

Although persons from Shepherdstown joined the American army after its defeat at Brandywine in 1777, no sizable group did so again until the spring of 1781. At that time Captain Henry Bedinger raised a body of forty-seven men and marched it to Albemarle Old Court House, the place of rendezvous. The group left May 14, arrived at its destination on the twenty-eighth, and was absorbed into the regular army.

About the same time George Michael Bedinger enlisted a company in Berkeley County and at Winchester. It was to be one of the companies in the new regiment that Colonel William Darke was organizing in Hampshire, Frederick, and Berkeley counties. The men marched to Yorktown but did not witness the surrender of Cornwallis, as their term of service had expired a few days before. However, Darke and many of the Berkeley men were present on that momentous occasion.[12]

Captain Henry Bedinger recruited a company in the winter of 1782-1783, but it did not see active service because of the advent of peace and subsequent disbanding of the American army.

In addition to furnishing soldiers, Berkeley County helped the American cause in other ways. As early as June 24, 1776, the Virginia Committee of Safety sent thirteen Highlanders to be kept there as prisoners, and in February, 1781, British prisoners were ordered from Winchester to Shepherdstown because of the scarcity of provisions in the former. The county supplied wagons, food, clothing, and other articles to the cause of independence. Shepherdstown was one of the centers of activity for the collection and transportation of supplies, as well as soldiers.[12]

REVOLUTIONARY GENERALS.

The story of the Revolution would be incomplete without mention of three unique figures in that struggle who lived in Berkeley County. Two, Horatio Gates and Charles Lee, are known to have resided within the limits of present Jefferson County, and the other, Adam Stephen, is thought to have done so. It is quite a coincidence that all three were born in Great Britain, were captains in the French and Indian War, were wounded in that struggle, were present at Braddock's defeat, were active in the cause for independence, were major generals in the American army, were deprived of their commands, and were neighboring plantation-owners.

Major General Horatio Gates (1729-1806) came to Berkeley County in 1772 and made his home at "Travelers Rest", which he had bought several years before. At the beginning of the Rev-

"Travelers Rest", Home of Major General Horatio Gates, near Kearneysville

olutionary War he was commissioned a brigadier general and a few months later and rose to the rank of major general. He received the surrender of Burgoyne at Saratoga on October 17, 1777. He was slated to receive Washington's post as commander in chief if the Conway Cabal had succeeded. It has not been definitely established that he was active in the plot, but he did not prevent friends from working in his behalf.[14]

In June, 1780, Gates was appointed to command all American troops in the South. At the battle of Camden, a few months later, he attacked Cornwallis but was disastrously defeated. The disappointment of Congress was so great that it appointed General Nathaniel Greene to succeed him and ordered an inquiry to be made. A war of words ensued between the angry Gates and the Continental Congress. He retired to his plantation and continued to live there until 1790, when he moved to New York, in which state he died.[15]

In 1775 Major General Charles Lee (1731-1782) came to Berkeley County to live. At the invitation of his friend Gates he purchased a large estate near the present village of Leetown, Jefferson County, which he named "Prato Rio". When he was commissioned a major general in the American army, he acquired an exaggerated opinion of his own ability and became critical of his superiors. At the battle of Monmouth he was severely censured by Washington for making an almost fatal retreat. A court-martial found him guilty and suspended him from the army. He returned to his Virginia estate in 1779 and spent most of his time criticizing Washington and Congress. He was stricken with fever on a visit to Philadelphia in 1782 and died shortly afterwards.[16]

Lee was an eccentric person. Among other proofs, his house is said to have had no partitions. By the use of chalk lines, one part was set aside as a kitchen, another as a bed room, a third as a library, and a fourth for harness, etc. To a surprised and inquisitive acquaintance, he defended the arrangement as "the most convenient and economical establishment in the world." "The lines of chalk which you see on the floor," said he, "mark the divisions of the apartments, and I can sit in any corner, and give orders, and overlook the whole, without moving my chair."[17] Additional proof of Lee's eccentricity is attested by the following

"Prato Rio", Home of Major General Charles Lee, at Leetown

quotation from his will: "I desire most earnestly that I may not be Burried in any Church or Church yard or within a mile of any Presbeturian or annabaptist Meeting House for Since I have resided in this country I have Kept So much bad Company when living that I do not Chuse to continue it when Dead."[18]

The third member of this remarkable trio, Major General Adam Stephen (? -1791), is said to have lived at "The Bower". on Opequon Creek, also near Leetown. A quarrel with Washington occurred at the battle of Germantown on October 4, 1777, when Stephen was charged with drunkenness. His troops collided with those of General Anthony [Mad Anthony] Wayne, and the authorities held Stephen responsible. After a court-martial he returned to his home in the country. In 1778 he laid out the town of Martinsburg on his own land.[19]

No doubt these three disappointed, disillusioned men found much comfort in each other's company, where they could criticize Washington to their heart's content. Tradition has it that shortly before his death Lee was entertaining his two soldier friends and after a few rounds of liquor, made the following toast: "The county of Berkeley is indeed to be congratulated. She can claim as citizens three noted major generals of the Revolutionary War. You, Stephen, distinguished yourself by getting drunk when you should have been sober. You, Gates, were cashiered for advancing when you should have been retreating, while your humble servent (sic) covered himself with glory and laurels and was cashiered for retreating when he should have been advancing."[20]

Brigadier General Edward Stevens (? -1820) was a Revolutionary officer, said to have been born near Leetown. Details concerning his early life are completely lacking, but he is supposed to have moved to Culpeper County. He was major of a battalion of riflemen at the battle of Great Bridge, near Norfolk, at the beginning of the war. In 1776 he was made colonel of the Tenth Virginia Regiment. After distinguishing himself at the battles of Brandywine and Germantown, he was promoted by Congress to the rank of brigadier general. He commanded a brigade at the engagements of Camden and Guilford Court House and was present at the surrender of Cornwallis at Yorktown.[21]

CHAPTER FOUR
JAMES RUMSEY AND THE STEAMBOAT

Most historians accept Robert Fulton, with his Clermont, as the inventor of the steamboat. Only a few mention John Fitch and James Rumsey and still fewer give the credit to Rumsey. But the fact remains that Rumsey successfully performed a public experiment at Shepherdstown with steamboats in 1787, twenty years before Fulton made his first successful trip.

EARLY LIFE.

Born at Bohemia Manor, Cecil County, Maryland, in March, 1743, James Rumsey was of Welsh ancestry. His father, Edward Rumsey, and his mother, Anna Cowman, were of good social standing, although of limited means. A large family, plus the inadequate income of a farmer, made it difficult for the father to give James a good education, yet the son acquired a considerable amount of useful information. He was particularly adept in the physical sciences and was a good mechanic and blacksmith.[1]

Details concerning Rumsey's early life are meagre. His personal qualities are best revealed through his letters. They disclose characteristics of honesty, industry, and perseverance. In appearance he was attractive and is said to have had a charm that endeared him to his friends.

Rumsey is reported to have served in the American Revolutionary army and is known to have lived in Baltimore prior to 1782. In that year he bought land at Sleepy Creek in present Morgan County, West Virginia, and became a partner of George Michael Bedinger in the milling business. He was ill-adapted for this and the next year he entered the mercantile business at Bath, now Berkeley Springs, West Virginia. In 1784 he, together with Robert Throgmorton, was the proprietor of a boardinghouse at Bath.[2]

FIRST EXPERIMENTS.

However, Rumsey's whole time was not taken up with his various vocations. He was deeply interested in water navigation and on September 6, 1784, showed a model of a mechanical boat to General Washington, then on his way to the Trans-Allegheny region for his sixth and last visit. Washington was greatly impressed with the boat and gave the inventor the following certificate of praise:

Certificate to Mr. James Rumsey.

I have seen the model of Mr. Rumsey's Boats constructed to work against stream; have examined the power upon which it acts;—have been an eye witness to an actual experiment in running water of some rapidity; & do give it as my opinion (altho' I had little faith before) that he has discovered the Art of propelling Boats, by mechanism & small manual assistance, against rapid currents;—that the discovery is of vast importance—may be of the greatest usefulness in our inland navigation—&, if it succeeds, of which I have no doubt, that the value of it is greatly enhanced by the simplicity of the works, which when seen & explained to, might be executed by the most common mechanics.—

Given under my hand at the town of Bath, County of Berkeley in the State of Virga. this 7th day of September, 1784.[3]

This model did not employ steam as motive power but used instead a kind of mechanical device. It is commonly believed that this was Rumsey's first attempt at a steamboat but he declares otherwise. Washington, too, in a letter to Thomas Johnson, says that the model was not that of a steamboat.[4]

The next step was to request the Virginia General Assembly for the sole and exclusive right to construct and navigate boats on the waters of that state for ten years. Rumsey's petition, under date of November 8, 1783, was granted and a similar one was shortly afterwards approved by the Maryland Legislature. Rumsey had intended to complete the mechanical boat, but, before he could do so, he became interested in steam navigation. According to his own statement, he made such progress in experimenting with steam engines that he postponed the mechanical boat.[5]

On November 10, 1784, Rumsey contracted with Dr. James

McMechen whereby the latter became his partner and was to continue as such only on condition that the inventor make a financial success of the steamboat. After Rumsey's death McMechen sued the executor for a share of the profits he claimed the inventor had obtained. Edward Rumsey, the executor, replied by showing that McMechen had not lived up to his part of the contract and, as a result, owed the estate 1,250 pounds as his share of Rumsey's expenses. This sum was not collected.[6]

JAMES RUMSEY

In the spring of 1785 Rumsey was appointed Superintendent of the Potomac Company, an organization formed to improve the navigation of the upper Potomac. George Washington was one of its principal instigators, its president, and the one who recommended Rumsey to the directors. Fortunately for the inventor, one of the superintendent's chief duties was to direct the building of canals around the most difficult parts of the river, and there were few qualified candidates. He presented a letter of recommendation from General Horatio Gates and on July 14, 1785, was chosen superintendent. He was to receive a salary of 200 pounds a year, Virginia currency, and an assistant.

The new superintendent had by no means an easy task. From the first he had difficulty in obtaining supplies necessary for the work. Then he was troubled with insubordination on the part of the laborers. This became so serious that it was necessary to discharge about one-half of the workmen. In spite of handicaps progress was made. The men worked during the summer of 1785 in the vicinity of Seneca Falls and Shenandoah Falls and succeeded in blasting and removing a number of boulders from the river. They then turned their attention to Great Falls, where they built a canal around the rapids.

Work was interrupted by freshets and floods, the approach of winter, and more trouble with the laborers. A large part of Rumsey's time was devoted to petty tasks, such as providing clothing and other supplies for the workers. Finally, because of insufficient pay, on July 4, 1786, he severed his connection with the company. His assistant, Richardson Stewart, became the new superintendent.[7]

Although handicapped by lack of money, Rumsey was now able to devote full time to his pet project. As early as July or August, 1783, he was thinking about constructing a steamboat. This is proved by a certificate dated July 4, 1788, and signed by John Wilson of Philadelphia, who had visited Bath, now Berkeley Springs. Wilson testified that Rumsey had mentioned steam navigation to him in a conversation in July or August, 1783. Another Philadelphian, Juliana Stewart, corroborated this by certifying that when Wilson returned to Philadelphia in the autumn of 1783, he mentioned Rumsey's steamboat.

Further proof of the inventor's early interest in steam navigation is supplied by Nicholas Orrick, one of his former associates in the mercantile business. He made oath on November 24, 1787, that in 1784 he had been on board a steamboat constructed by Rumsey, which, in a secret experiment, proved to be successful, though not to the inventor's entire satisfaction. Orrick also stated that Rumsey had previously informed him of his plans for a steamboat.[8]

On November 28, 1787, George Michael Bedinger, Rumsey's former partner in the milling business, added to the above evidence. He then made oath before John Kearsley, a justice of the peace in Berkeley County, that in or before the month of March, 1784, Rumsey had mentioned steam navigation to him and announced his intention to construct a boat which would run by steam. Furthermore, the inventor had mentioned some of the necessary machinery.[9]

Additional letters could be cited in the matter but there would be no point to this. The reason so much evidence has been given in establishing the approximate time of Rumsey's first thoughts about steamboats is, however, important. A little later it will be shown that his rival for steamboat priority, John Fitch and not Robert Fulton, claimed to have thought of steamboats first.

Actual work on the proposed steamboat began during the summer of 1785. It was then that Rumsey employed his brother-in-law, Joseph Barnes, to construct a boat for him near present Berkeley Springs. It was brought to Shepherdstown in the early fall. Barnes went to Baltimore and Frederick to obtain parts of machinery for the boat. In the month of December machinery was installed and the craft taken to Shenandoah Falls for experimental purposes. The forming of ice on the river interrupted the workmen's progress, and in January, 1786, the machinery was taken from the boat and stored in a cellar for the winter.

Rumsey had been dissatisfied with the first boiler and accordingly had a new one made. When he was ready to resume experiments in the spring of 1786, he found some defects in the new boiler's workmanship and was compelled to use the old one again. In the subsequent trial in April, 1786, the vessel moved against the current of the Potomac, but various kinds of trouble developed. The machinery was so imperfect that steam escaped and repairs were necessary. They were made at Great Falls, after which another trial was attempted. The boat was sent forward with powerful strokes until the repair work gave way and caused the escape of steam.[10]

While Rumsey was trying to improve the boiler for his steamboat, Barnes made an experiment with a mechanical boat constructed on the model exhibited in 1784, but it, too, was not successful. In a letter to Washington, dated September 19, 1786, Rumsey gave an account of this failure. He explained that his assistant, Barnes, made the experiment in his absence. Barnes had taken nine or ten persons aboard, which, together with the ballast, made a combined weight of about four tons.

Under this burden the boat moved upstream for 200 yards, but it did not perform satisfactorily. It was not as steady as it should have been, and the poles, or shovers, slipped along the bottom of the river instead of taking the desired hold. Sometimes a pole on one side of the boat performed satisfactorily, only to have one on the other side slip. A later experiment with this sort of craft was no more successful, and Rumsey realized that it would have to be improved or abandoned.[11]

Undaunted by the failures, Rumsey tried the steamboat again. Having equipped it with a new boiler, he experimented in December, 1786, but this time heat from the steam melted the soft solder used in the machine's construction and rendered it entirely useless. Repairs were no sooner made with hard solder, than drifting ice carried the boat away. The resulting destruction was equal to approximately half the expense of a new vessel.

Despite these losses and failures Rumsey was ready in September, 1787, for another trial. In the meantime he had repaired his boat and greatly improved the boiler. With a cargo of two tons, not including the machinery, the craft moved against the current of the Potomac at the rate of two miles an hour. But trouble again developed in the boiler with the result that quantities of steam escaped.

In spite of this setback, Barnes was enthusiastic about the new boiler, which, he declared, exceeded all others and could be made efficient. Although it held only twenty pints of water, it produced, according to Barnes, more steam than a 500-gallon boiler of the old type. He believed also that six bushels of coal were sufficient for a twelve-hour run. The machine weighed about 700 pounds and occupied no more space than four barrels.[12]

SUCCESS

The inventor was so confident of the success of his idea that he invited the public to witness a demonstration at Shepherdstown on December 3, 1787. On the appointed day a large crowd of townspeople and visitors gathered along the cliffs and shores of the Potomac River. Every class and color in the community was on hand. No doubt many came because of curiosity, others to cheer the efforts of the persistent inventor, and still others to make sport of "Crazy Rumsey". Among the spectators were Major General Horatio Gates, Major Henry Bedinger, Colonel Joseph Swearingen, Colonel William Darke, Captain Abraham

Shepherd, the Rev. Robert Stubbs, Philip Pendleton, John Kearsley, and Cato Moore.

At Rumsey's invitation several ladies entered the boat to witness the experiment at short range. They were Mrs. Abraham Shepherd, Mrs. Rumsey and her sister-in-law, Mrs. Charles Morrow, and a Mrs. Mark and her daughter, Ann, together with several others. In addition, Charles Morrow went aboard to take charge of the helm, and Dr. James McMechen accompanied him to assist with the machinery.

When Rumsey started the engine, the craft steamed upstream. The inventor proceeded in this direction for perhaps half a mile to the vicinity of Swearingen's Spring and then, turning around, went downstream. As he passed the enthusiastic onlookers, a great shout arose from those on shore. The boat continued to go up and down the river for two hours, after which it steamed back to the river bank.

The excitement produced by this successful experiment of the "flying boat" can hardly be imagined. As soon as the craft began its first trip up the river, General Gates became so excited that he took off his hat and exclaimed, "My God, she moves!" The average rate of speed was three miles an hour and many congratulations were bestowed upon the proud inventor as he stepped ashore after the experiment. It seemed that at last fortune had smiled on him.[13]

On December 11 Rumsey made another experiment which was more successful than that of December 3. With a load of three tons his boat made four miles an hour against the current of the Potomac. This was accomplished even though holes, covered with rags, were in the pipes of his machine. They had been caused by the freezing of water a few days before.[14]

As evidence of the success of these experiments Rumsey obtained certificates from several eyewitnesses whose oaths were made before two Berkeley County justices of the peace, John Kearsley and Cato Moore. Moses Hunter, clerk of the same county, attested to the status of the justices. Witnesses giving sworn statements of the success on December 3 were General Horatio Gates, the Rev. Robert Stubbs, Abraham Shepherd, William Brice, David Gray, Charles Morrow, John Morrow, and Henry Bedinger.

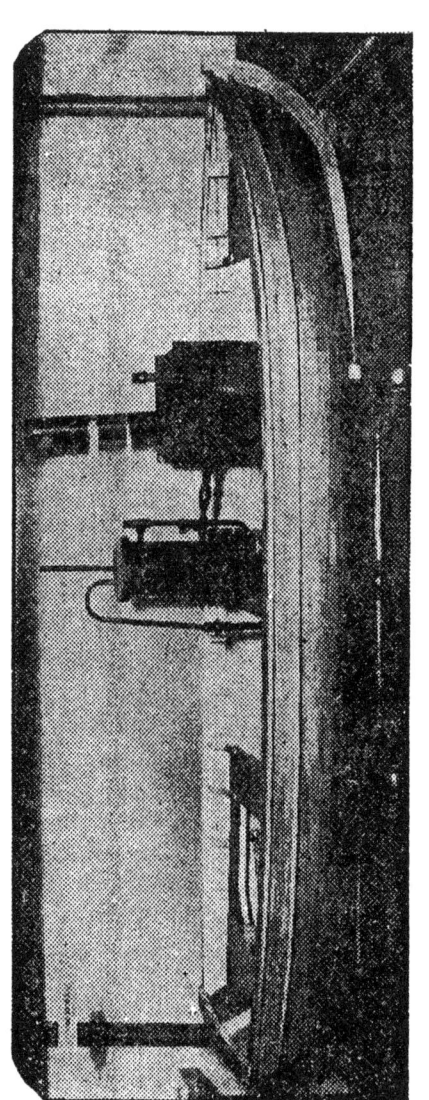

Model of Rumsey's Steamboat

The success of the second experiment, that of December 11, was substantiated by sworn certificates of Moses Hoge, Cornelius Wynkoop, John Mark, Benoni Swearingen, John Morrow, Joseph Swearingen, Charles Morrow, Thomas White, the Rev. Robert Stubbs, Abraham Shepherd, and Henry Bedinger. These affidavits are all included in a pamphlet entitled **A Plan Wherein the Power of Steam is Fully Shewn**, published by Rumsey in 1788.

THE RUMSEIAN SOCIETY.

Following the foregoing experiments Rumsey went to Philadelphia in the winter of 1787-1788. There he contacted a number of prominent citizens and showed them drafts and descriptions of his inventions. They were so impressed with the simplicity and utility of the various designs that they agreed to help him. Consequently, they formed on May 9 an organization known as the Rumseian Society and made Benjamin Franklin its president.[15]

The members of the Rumseian Society appointed a Committee of Correspondence to advertise their hero in distant places. They were especially interested in the boiler which, it was believed, would serve English as well as American needs. Then, too, they hoped that their protege might find financial aid in England, at that time the industrial and financial center of the world.

RUMSEY GOES TO LONDON.

It was in search of such help that Rumsey went to London in May, 1788, and took with him letters of introduction from prominent Philadelphians. Among them was one from Dr. Benjamin Rush to his friend, Dr. John Lettsom, a prominent London physician. Another was from Benjamin Franklin to Benjamin Vaughan. The latter became one of Rumsey's most loyal friends abroad and helped him considerably.

When the American arrived in England, he made contact with the firm of Matthew Boulton and James Watt, inventors and manufacturers of steam engines. He was anxious to form a partnership with these men, but when he learned of their proposition, he refused. Among other things, they demanded that Rumsey sever relations with the Rumseian Society, the organization that had sponsored his trip abroad.

Rumsey felt that he could not honorably accede to such a demand and when his counter-proposition was declined, negotiations with Boulton and Watt were broken off. He obtained a patent for his boilers and steam engines on November 6, 1788, and then tried to gain the support of wealthy Englishmen. Finally, he entered into an engagement with a man named Whiting, who agreed to help finance the building of a steamboat.[16]

DIFFICULTIES ABROAD.

In expectation of aid from his sponsor Rumsey built a steamboat at Dover, which cost 600 guineas. He then went to London where he learned that his backer had become bankrupt. In modern parlance or slang Rumsey was thus left "holding the bag". After using all the funds available from his Philadelphia friends as a first payment, he tried to borrow elsewhere. Finally, he managed to get 700 pounds, but he failed to reach an agreement with the new backers concerning ownership of his British patent. When they demanded the return of their loan, Rumsey was fortunate enough to borrow sufficient funds elsewhere.[17]

The inventor's troubles were not yet over. Since he was an alien, he could not have the boat registered in his own name and he had to use that of one of his backers. The latter suddenly decided to invest his money elsewhere and threatened to sell the craft if Rumsey did not raise sufficient money to pay him the debt. Fortunately for the inventor, this man had made himself liable for the engine, and Rumsey got the manufacturer of the machine to demand his money. The backer then agreed to wait for his money, and Rumsey had sufficient time to borrow from his friends, Vaughan and a man named Barclay. Thus the boat was saved but the experiment was delayed almost a month.

After having named his vessel **Columbian Maid,** Rumsey prepared to try her out. According to a letter from Rumsey, dated February 27, 1790, to his friend, Captain Charles Morrow of Shepherdstown, the trial was a failure. Among other things, the engine was so imperfectly constructed that practically the whole thing had to be rebuilt.

Additional delay and expense made his friends more dubious

than ever about success. He was still beset with financial troubles. One of his creditors failed and the assignees demanded payment. There was nothing to do but borrow again, and borrow he did. Another of his friends lent him enough money to pay the bill and thus saved him from a debtor's prison. Additional financial difficulties caused the inventor to hide from the sheriff for a while.[18]

On March 25, 1790, Rumsey formed another partnership, this time with Samuel Rogers and Daniel Parker. Again he made a bad choice, for again his partners failed and involved him to the extent of 300 pounds. With much difficulty Rumsey paid their obligations and thus again saved his boat. Meanwhile, he had trouble with the Rumseian Society which was on the point of deserting him.

When it seemed that the unfortunate inventor could no longer stall off his creditors, luck changed. He received a position superintending the construction of a canal in Ireland at a salary of ten pounds sterling a day. He seems to have performed the work creditably and after completing it returned to England. He had worked forty days and was thus able to face his creditors once again.[19]

Encouraged by preliminary trials Rumsey was in December, 1792, on the point of obtaining success for the **Columbian Maid**, but again unkind fate intervened. At the conclusion of a lecture, delivered on December 20, 1792, to the Society of Mechanic Arts in London, he became ill. The best medical assistance possible was soon at his side but he failed to recover. Shortly after nine o'clock the next morning at the Adelphi Hotel the inventor breathed his last. His body was interred in the churchyard of St. Margaret's, Westminster, the official church of the House of Commons. Here, Rumsey's remains lie under the shadow of Westminster Abbey, near the tomb of Sir Walter Raleigh.[20]

Several weeks later Rumsey's boat was tried out on the Thames River and performed satisfactorily with a speed of four knots an hour against wind and tide.[21]

An incident that was to prove significant is said to have occurred some time before the inventor's death. In one of Rumsey's letters he is supposed to have remarked about meeting a young man named Robert Fulton. The latter was in London about that time for the purpose of selling a torpedo boat to the British Government. He was not interested in steamboats then, and it may be that the alleged association with Rumsey turned his attention to them.[22]

JOHN FITCH, THE RIVAL INVENTOR.

Rumsey's experiments at Shepherdstown in 1787 were twenty years before Robert Fulton made a successful trip in his Clermont. When it is recalled that Fulton obtained his steam engine from a well-known firm in England and Rumsey had his made by unskilled laborers, the latter's achievement is all the more remarkable. His chief competitor, however, for the honor of inventing the steamboat was not Fulton but a native of Connecticut, John Fitch, who was a contemporary inventor.

According to Fitch's own statement, he did not get interested in steamboats until about the middle of April, 1785.[23] It has already been proved that Rumsey was thinking about steam as a means of propulsion as early as 1783. Neither, however, can claim priority in first conceiving this idea, for others had previously advanced the same thought.[24] It remained for Rumsey to put that thought into practice.

Fitch went to Philadelphia and in September, 1785, presented models and plans of his proposed invention to the American Philosophical Society. He succeeded in organizing a company to assist him in obtaining funds and then managed to acquire exclusive privileges in several states, among them, Pennsylvania and Virginia. He was beset with a number of insurmountable difficulties.[25]

When Rumsey issued several pamphlets after his successful public experiments in 1787, Fitch replied with a publication of his own. In it he attempted to discredit Rumsey and his invention but could not furnish satisfactory evidence that he himself had done as well. In **The Original Steamboat Supported** he failed to prove that he had made a successful experiment with steamboats prior to Rumsey's. Most of his claims are worded in such general terms that it is impossible to obtain any specific information from them concerning his success.[26]

The war of pamphlets was continued by Rumsey's friends

after he had gone abroad. In July, 1788, Joseph Barnes entered the contest by publishing a reply to Fitch's claims. He cited evidence that Rumsey had made several trials with his steamboat before 1787.[27]

Finally, Fitch became so dissatisfied with his method of propelling boats that he looked with favor on the method Rumsey used, that of jet propulsion. To learn more about it he in April, 1789, made a secret visit to Shepherdstown, but he was unsuccessful. In fact, he almost came to grief, for its people did not approve of his suspicious actions. Captain Charles Morrow, in particular, made it so unpleasant for the rival inventor that Fitch was glad to retreat across the Potomac to Sharpsburg. According to Major Henry Bedinger, only the influence of himself and a few other prominent citizens saved Fitch from bodily harm at Shepherdstown.[28]

In 1788 Rumsey's friends attempted to obtain from the Virginia General Assembly a continuation of the privilege granted him several years previously. A petition of the Rumseian Society on June 14 and one from Charles Morrow on November 26 asked repeal of Fitch's exclusive rights. Although the legislative committee reported in favor of repealing Fitch's privileges, the House of Delegates rejected the report. Thus both Fitch and Rumsey had exclusive rights for navigating steamboats on the rivers of Virginia.[29]

After the Federal Constitution became effective in 1789 Congress enacted its first patent law. Under it both Rumsey and Fitch applied for patents. Numerous delays ensued, but on August 26, 1791, the rival inventors each received a patent, which was signed by President Washington, together with Jefferson, Knox, and Randolph.

It was not until 1790 that Fitch appears to have reached any vestige of success with steamboats and then his craft was able to make only six miles an hour in still water! The Philadelphia inventor was greatly handicapped by the size and weight of his engine. A comparison with Rumsey's, as given by sworn affidavits, is interesting. Henry Bedinger estimated the weight of Fitch's apparatus at five tons and said it was so bulky that it left little room in the boat for anything else. In sharp contrast he declared Rumsey's entire machinery weighed about 500 pounds.

By affidavit William Askew placed his estimates a little higher. From observation and information he concluded that Fitch's machinery weighed seven tons, with a boiler capacity of 500 gallons. The same person estimated the weight of Rumsey's apparatus at more than 800 pounds.[30]

OTHER INVENTIONS OF RUMSEY.

Although Rumsey failed to obtain universal recognition as the inventor of the steamboat, he is receiving much credit for his associated inventions. While he was in England he acquired patents for several forms of boilers. One of them was for the first coil boiler. He receives most credit, however, as the originator of the water-tube boiler, which is extensively used today. This is the type of boiler employed for applying steam to stationary engines or turbo-generator units. The water-tube boiler is much more effective for this work than other types. It is best for large steam plants and those worked at very high pressure. Since the modern trend in engineering seems to be along this line, Rumsey's contribution becomes all the more important.

The highest tribute paid to Rumsey's genius is found perhaps in the fact that the water-tube boiler has been adopted by the navies of Great Britain and the United States. Still another form patented by Rumsey and now used is the vertical tubular boiler.[31]

THE RUMSEY MEMORIALS.

Rumsey's adopted state has been slow to pay tribute to his work. It was not until 1905 that the West Virginia Legislature appropriated $1,750 for the erection of a monument to the inventor. The act required the memorial to be placed on the banks of the Potomac River at Shepherdstown. It was erected under the auspices of a corporation chartered for that purpose. Largely through the efforts of George M. Beltzhoover, Jr., an organization known as "The Rumseyan Society" was formed and received its certificate of incorporation in April, 1906. The following officers were elected: Judge D. B. Lucas, president; George M. Beltzhoover, Jr., vice-president; and Harry L. Snyder, secretary. Subsequent appropriatons swelled the total to $13,625, which, along with donations, proved adequate for the purpose. At last, in

The Rumsey Monument at Shepherdstown

1915, a beautiful white granite column, seventy-five feet high, was placed on the lofty bluffs of the Potomac at Shepherdstown.[32]

A final tribute to Rumsey was the erection of a magnificent highway bridge across the river in 1939 to replace the one lost in the flood of 1936. The new structure has appropriately been designated "The James Rumsey Bridge."[33]

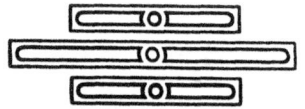

CHAPTER FIVE

ASPIRATIONS AND INCIDENTS, 1790-1800

EARLY NEWSPAPERS.

In the autumn of 1790 a Massachusetts printer, Nathaniel Willis, came to Shepherdstown to establish a newspaper. Willis, a former member of the Boston Tea Party of 1773, had previously published a newspaper in Winchester, Virginia. In November he set up a printing press in Shepherdstown and in the same month issued the first number of the **Potowmac Guardian and Berkeley Advertiser.** This was the first newspaper published in present West Virginia. The editor's son, Nathaniel Willis, Jr., delivered copies to the scattered subscribers. Mounted on a horse, with tin horn and saddle bags, he rode through the countryside. Incidentally, it was this same youth, who, in 1827, established the nationally-known **The Youth's Companion,** which was published continuously until September, 1929, when it was consolidated with **The American Boy.**[1]

Nathaniel Willis, Sr., continued publication of his newspaper at Shepherdstown for about two years, when he moved it to Martinsburg. He remained there until 1799 and then left to try his fortunes in the Territory of Ohio. At the new location, in Chillicothe, he founded the **Scioto Gazette,** which is still published.

Another newspaper, the **Imperial Observer: or Shepherdstown, Charles-town and County Advertiser,** was established at Shepherdstown in 1797. It was the second newspaper to be set up in present West Virginia. Philip Rootes and Charles Blagrove were the publishers and issued their first number on June 28, 1797.

Although Rootes and Blagrove's newspaper was short-lived, lasting perhaps less than a year, they made a distant contribution in another way, the publication of the first book to be printed in present West Virginia. This was a 332-page volume bound in calf-skin, entitled Christian Panoply, containing an apology for the Bible, in a series of letters to Thomas Paine, etc., by R. Watson, D. D., F. R. S., Lord Bishop of Landaff, etc., etc., (together with) An address to scoffers at religion by the same author and a brief view of the history evidences of Christianity, by William Paley, M. A. archdeacon of Carlyle. Shepherdstown. 1797. Printed by P. Rootes and C. Blagrove.[2]

THE NATIONAL CAPITAL.

About the same time that Willis was establishing his paper in Shepherdstown residents of that community were attempting to have the national capital located there. As a result of shrewd bargaining between Alexander Hamilton on one side and Thomas Jefferson and James Madison on the other, the seat of government was to be determined by President Washington, with certain restrictions. The capital was to remain in Philadelphia for ten years, after which it was to be established at some place along the Potomac, "between the mouth of the Eastern Branch and Connogocheague." In return for this concession Hamilton was promised Southern support for his assumption policy.

As soon as word of the agreement reached Shepherdstown, prominent residents became interested. On December 1, 1790, Henry Bedinger and William Good wrote the President a letter in which they outlined the activity of their fellow-townsmen in attempting to have the capital located in Shepherdstown. They pointed out that Sharpsburg, across the river in Maryland, was also willing to cooperate in an effort to get the desired trophy. At the time the letter was written subscriptions on the Virginia side of the river amounted to $20,662.67 and on the Maryland side to $4,837 and 475 acres of land. The land pledged lay directly between Sharpsburg and the river. In addition, the writers promised to furnish the President with a plat of the proposed site. This plat was enclosed in a subsequent letter and is now on file among the **Washington Papers** in the Library of Congress.[3]

Shepherdstown became a Federal post office site, the first in present West Virginia, on March 20, 1793, and Horatio Ross was the first postmaster. This office was established not long after the ones at Boston, New York, Philadelphia, and Baltimore.[4]

ST. CLAIR'S DEFEAT.

Trouble with the Indians in the Northwest Territory occupied President Washington in his first administration. After General Harmer had failed to achieve definite results, General Arthur St. Clair was ordered to head a punitive expedition against the redskins. On October 3, 1791, he led a motley array of two thousand men from Fort Washington at Cincinnati, Ohio, toward the Indian country.

The left wing of St. Clair's army was commanded by Colonel William Darke of near Duffields, in present Jefferson County. His youngest son, Joseph, was a captain in his father's regiment, and Major George Michael Bedinger of Shepherdstown led the Virginia Battalion.[5]

At a critical moment in the fighting St. Clair ordered Colonel Darke to charge the enemy with the bayonet. The charge was successful only momentarily, for the foe closed in again. Another charge was made by the brave Virginians and again the enemy retreated for a short while but came back stronger than ever. By this time the slaughter had become so terrific that Darke's command would have been annihilated but for the timely assistance by the right wing. His son, Joseph, had been mortally wounded in the fiercest of the fighting but the father managed to save him from capture.

The remnants of St. Clair's army retreated to Fort Jefferson, thirty miles from the scene of slaughter. There in a council of war Darke, although wounded, urged the expediency of another attack and said that the Indians would be flushed with victory and might be beaten. But as the army was in no condition for a renewal of the conflict, Darke was overruled. Major Bedinger did not take part in the battle as he had previously been sent back to Fort Jefferson with invalids. Captain Joseph Darke died on the way home and was buried along the route. Darke is credited with saving the entire left wing of St. Clair's army. As a reward for his services he was promoted to the rank of brigadier general and awarded 8,000 acres of public land in Ohio.[6]

HARPERS FERRY ARMORY AND ARSENAL.

In 1794 conditions in Europe threatened the peaceful security of the United States. Although President Washington had issued his proclamation of neutrality in the preceding year, rumors of war persisted in the United States. Secretary of War Timothy Pickering recommended that the Third Congress provide for additional weapons and authorize the regular manufacture of arms. By an act of April 2 Congress moved accordingly.[7]

The legislation authorized the President to direct the establishment of three or four arsenals for storing arms, with magazines, and gave him discretionary power to select the locations. It was expected, however, that the existing state arsenals of Springfield, Massachusetts, and Carlisle, Pennsylvania, would be used. In addition to arsenals, the act provided for a like number of armories, or arms factories. The sum of $59,000 was appropriated for repairing the existing arsenals and $22,865 for defraying the expense of the national armories for a year. In addition, $340,000 was to be applied to the purchase of arms, ammunition, and military stores.[8]

For one of the arsenals President Washington selected Springfield, which had been associated with the manufacture of small arms since 1776 and already contained a number of shops and warehouses. Harpers Ferry was his choice for the other site. In a letter to the Secretary of War dated September 16, 1795, he called attention to its water power and the fact that the necessary land could be obtained. In another letter to Secretary Pickering, dated September 28, 1795, he described Harpers Ferry as the most eligible spot on the whole river, "in every point of view." Among other letters was one to Tobias Lear, dated February 15, 1796, in which Washington deplored the fact that the arsenal had been "shamefully neglected".[9]

Although production at Springfield was started in 1795, the land at Harpers Ferry was not purchased until June 15, 1796. By a deed of that date executed by the heirs of Robert Harper the Government obtained title to 125 acres of land, located in the triangle formed by the Potomac and Shenandoah rivers. The next year, by a deed dated February 20, a tract of 310 acres was acquired from a man named Rutherford. The latter addition included a part of the land on which the town of Bolivar is now located. The construction of suitable buildings on the first tract soon began.

ASPIRATIONS AND INCIDENTS, 1790–1800

Actual making of arms at Harpers Ferry did not start until late in the year 1796 and was under the direction of an English Moravian named Perkins, the first superintendent. Prior to 1800 production was restricted to muskets, and only a small number of these were made.

Several things explain the absence of effectiveness in the product. First of all, Congress had limited the total number of employees in all the armories to one hundred. Then, too, a majority of the workmen were not gunsmiths. A third handicap was the effort to produce the French infantry musket, 1763 model, without sufficient machinery.[10]

AN EPISODE.

During the winter of 1798-1799, when war with France appeared imminent, a body of United States troops camped at Harpers Ferry. This small army was commanded by General Pinkney and had its quarters on the high ridge between Harpers Ferry and Bolivar. As a result, the ridge has since been known as "Camp Hill."

While the troops were stationed there an interesting episode is alleged to have happened. Toward the latter part of President John Adams's administration the bitter political feeling between Federalists and Republicans reached the troops at Harpers Ferry. A Captain Henry is said to have been a strong Federalist and a hater of Thomas Jefferson. According to the story, he took a detail of soldiers to "Jefferson's Rock", now a famous landmark, and ordered them to throw the rock over the mountain side. The part thus destroyed is believed to have been the one on which Jefferson had inscribed his name and from which he gathered data for the description of Harpers Ferry as recorded in his **Notes on Virginia.**

It is stated furthermore that a young Republican resented this action to such an extent that he challenged Captain Henry to a duel. But General Pinkney intervened at this point, arrested the would-be contestants, and thus prevented possible fatalities.[11]

CHURCHES.

During the decade of the nineties churches continued to expand. About 1790 the Methodist influence reached the neighborhood of Keyes's Ferry, near present Millville. A devout group of worshippers met at the home of Robert Goldsborough, a log structure about sixteen feet square. It was located on the eastern side of the Shenandoah River half a mile below Keyes's Ferry, opposite what was known as "Sheler's Spring". A year or two later the worshiping-place was moved to the dwelling of Robert Bogges, two miles to the northward and about half a mile above Halltown. When the Bogges family moved to the West, the congregation met at the home of the Rev. Thomas Keyes for many years.

Ministers preaching in this circuit in 1790 were Lewis Chasteen and Thomas Scott. The next year it was served by Lewis Chasteen and Valentine Cook, who were succeeded in 1792 by Thomas Haymond and in 1793 by William McLenahan and Thomas Lyall. The "charge" was then part of the Berkeley Circuit. Among some of its communicants were: Mrs. Elizabeth Allstadt, Thomas Keyes, Mrs. Mary Hall, the Douglass family, Samuel Williams, Rebecca McCrea, and Sarah and Mary Burnett.[12]

As indicated in a paper bearing date of June 24, 1791, and recorded in Martinsburg, Methodists organized at that time a congregation in Charles Town. George Hite was a trustee of their proposed building. Three years later Bishop Francis Asbury found a good house of worship and one local preacher there, but almost ten years passed before the Charles Town Methodist Church received a deed for its church property, which is dated January 9, 1803.[13]

The extension of Methodism to the Smithfield vicinity was evidenced by the erection of a church at that point prior to 1800. The structure was a plain, rambling brick building with a rectangular front concealing the roof. Subscribers to the church were Mrs. John Smith, Thomas Griggs, A. B. Davenport, James Grantham, John Fry and F. Hardesty.[14]

The first Baptists of record in what was later Jefferson County were fourteen persons, who, on April 24, 1792, organized a congregation at the home of Christopher Collins, located two miles northwest of Charles Town. The church was an offspring of the Buck Marsh [Berryville] Baptist Church and took the Biblical name of "Zoar", meaning "a little one". Its original members were Christopher Collins, Samson Marmaduke, William Talbot, Ann Moore, David Moore, Hannah Sullivan, Ann Collins, Elizabeth Riely, Sarah Simpson, Mary Ridgway, and four Negroes, Elisha, Suky, Phyllis, and Rachel. Three ministers from eastern Virginia, Andrew Broaddus, Lewis Lunford, and Henry Toler, furnished spiritual guidance. Christopher Collins was the new leader and church clerk.

A subscription for purchasing land and building a meetinghouse was started on February 14, 1795. At the same time the church expressed a desire that Collins be ordained as a regular minister. In February, 1798, its members seemed to be undecided whether to disband or to call Collins to the ministry. They finally agreed to continue their meetings and called him on April 8, 1798. With Elder Thomas Bridges and Absalom Waller assisting, he was ordained in November of that year. It was not, however, until June 13, 1801, that the church had its own building. It then purchased a house from Jesse Hall and formally named it "Zoar Meeting House". The building was of wooden construction and stood on the Charles Town-Duffields road, about two miles south of Shenandoah Junction. It was later replaced by a stone edifice.[15]

The first formal church organization in Charles Town was effected in 1792 by the Presbyterians. Its members had bought a lot in 1787 but apparently did not receive formal recognition until five years had elapsed. The first mention of the Charles Town Presbyterian Church in the records of the Lexington Presbytery, which then served this district, is on April 30, 1792. This was also the year when its congregation received a regularly ordained minister.[16]

Efforts of Charles Town Presbyterians to organize began with the purchase of a lot from Charles Washington in a deed dated February 17, 1787. They built a small church on this lot, which was located at the southwestern end of Charles Town on the Berryville road. Attempts to obtain a minister proved vain, but occasional services were conducted by the Rev. Moses Hoge who came to Shepherdstown in the fall of 1787. His work was supplemented in 1790 by that of the Rev. Robert Marshall who was sent to the region to serve congregations without pastors. During the winter of 1791-1792 Archibald Alexander ministered to the needs of the Charles Town and Bullskin churches. They had called the Rev. William Hill but when he became sick in Winchester, Alexander took his place.

By September 15, 1791, Hill had recovered sufficiently to preach his first sermon to the Bullskin Church, near Summit Point. He also held meetings at the homes of his parishioners and served in addition the Charles Town and Elk Branch churches. When the Lexington Presbytery met in Charles Town on May 28, 1792, Hill was examined for ordination. The following day he delivered a trial sermon and on May 30 he was ordained and installed as pastor of the united congregations of the Bullskin and Charles Town churches. His term of service at Charles Town lasted but seven years, for the Winchester Presbytery dissolved the pastorate on May 16, 1799. He continued at the Bullskin church until April 27, 1816, when that pastorate was dissolved that Hill might give his whole time to Winchester.

Although part of the Elk Branch congregation united with the Charles Town group in 1792, matters did not go so well for a while. After the departure of the Rev. William Hill the Charles Town congregation apparently was unable to support a minister. It was not until 1815 that the church was reorganized on a firmer basis.[17]

St. Peter's Lutheran Church in Shepherdstown laid the cornerstone of its first recorded building in August, 1795, in the ministry of the Rev. David Young. The brick edifice stood on a hill east of town opposite the German Reformed Church. Its bell is said to have been used in Marseilles, France, but was dismounted in the trying times of the French Revolution. Although 416 persons contributed $2,016 toward the structure, financial difficulties overtook them. In a petition to the Virginia General Assembly, dated December 4, 1798, they therefore requested permission to raise $1,000 by a lottery, so as to obtain sufficient funds to complete it. There is no evidence that the request was granted.[18]

EDUCATION.

In 1795 a movement was launched that resulted in the Charles Town Academy, an institution which, with interruptions, continued to offer instruction until 1905. In 1910 the building formerly used by it was sold to the Charles Town District Board of Education.[19]

The purpose of the Charles Town Academy, as revealed by its charter, was to provide a seminary of learning in which the Latin and Greek languages would be taught. In case of a demand, its curriculum could be expanded to include French, English, geography, astronomy, criticism, mathematics, and natural and moral philosophy. It was maintained by subscriptions and donations and administered by twelve trustees, chosen by the donors and authorized to select a principal.

By August, 1795, the eighty-one contributions aggregated 514 pounds, 18 shillings, or about $1,712. Accordingly, the subscribers met and elected the following persons to constitute a board of trustees: Philip Pendleton, Thomas Griggs, Thomas Rutherford, Sr., Gabriel Nourse, Christopher Collins, George Steptoe Washington, George Hite, Ferdinando Fairfax, George North, Edward Tiffin, Alexander White, and William Hill.

On August 10, following, the trustees received bids from John Young and Charles Fouke for the construction of a suitable building. They proposed a brick or stone structure, 40 feet by 20 feet, to cost 550 pounds, or about $1,833. Although the estimate was more than the total of the subscriptions, the trustees let the contract for building a structure on South Lawrence Street. The work was supervised by George Hite and William Hill.[20]

Apparently, the Board of Trustees did not meet again until April 3, 1797, when Fairfax Washington and William Hill were appointed to draw up certain rules and regulations and to prepare a petition to the Virginia General Assembly for a charter. The ensuing request, dated December 13, 1797, desired an act of incorporation so that the school could the better manage its own affairs. In response, the General Assembly passed an act of incorporation, dated December 25, 1797. The act retained all of the original trustees except Philip Pendleton, Christopher Collins, and George Steptoe Washington. In their stead were Elisha Boyd, John Dixon, and Samuel Washington.

On June 28, 1797, George Hite and William Hill reported the conveyance of a bond from Captain Samuel Washington for the lot on which the academy had been built. At a meeting of the trustees on February 3, 1798, they adopted a code of rules and regulations. One of the most important of these provided for the free education of youths who otherwise might be deprived of learning. This was permissible, however, only when the academy's treasury permitted. Although the majority of students paid tuition, this farsighted policy toward the poor is indicative of the later attitude of Jefferson County in respect to education of the unfortunate.

The first principal of the Charles Town Academy seems to have been William Hill, one of the trustees. Fragmentary records indicate that he headed it during the year 1798-1799 and was succeeded by John Mines some time in 1799.

A female seminary was established on the lot opposite the academy about the same time that the male school opened its doors. It was directed by Miss Angelica Collins, a sister of the Baptist minister, Christopher Collins.[21]

DOLLY MADISON'S WEDDING.

In 1794 an event of social importance occurred at "Harewood", the former home of Colonel Samuel Washington near Charles Town. It was the marriage on September 15 of Mrs. Dorothea Payne Todd, better known as "Dolly" Todd, to James Madison. Mrs. Todd's sister, Lucy, was the wife of George Steptoe Washington, son of Samuel Washington and at that time owner of "Harewood". Madison met his future bride at a boardinghouse in Philadelphia, where she had gone to live with her mother after the death of her first husband. Tradition relates that Aaron Burr told Congressmen, among them Madison, about the young widow's charms. The "Father of the Constitution" lost no time in obtaining an introduction. A recess of Congress provided a good opportunity for the marriage.

Although Dolly had been reared in a Quaker family and was accustomed to simple ways, the wedding was a cause of much celebration. Thomas Jefferson had offered his coach for the wedding-trip, and George and Martha Washington, friends of Madison, had expressed felicitous approval. On the wedding day a company of kinsfolk and friends gathered at "Harewood" to enjoy the feasting and dancing. Light Horse Harry Lee is said to have dashed up on one of his favorite horses just before the ceremony. The couple was married by the Rev. Alexander Balmaine, a relative of Madison from Winchester. The bridesmaids are reported to have cut the groom's Mechlin lace ruffles and divided them as souvenirs. After the ceremony the newly-weds journeyed to "Montpelier", in Orange County, to visit Madison's parents, but the approaching session of Congress necessitated their speedy return to Philadelphia.[22]

"Harewood", Originally the Home of Samuel Washington near Charles Town and Later the Scene of Dolly Madison's Wedding

CHAPTER SIX
THE JEFFERSONIAN ERA

JEFFERSON BECOMES A COUNTY.

In the autumn of 1800 petitions carrying hundreds of signatures asking for a new county were circulated in the southeastern part of Berkeley County. Sentiment had been crystallizing for several years, but it did not take definite form until the beginning of the new century. A few years before 1800 Charles Washington had promised to give the four corners of the public square in Charles Town for public buildings of the town and a new county, on condition that another county be formed. His death in 1799 prevented him from fulfilling his wishes in the matter, but they were carried out by his son, Captain Samuel Washington of Spotsylvania County, in a deed dated August 31, 1801.[1]

A petition dated December 5, 1800, and signed by 187 persons set forth the reasons for a new county. First, it claimed that Berkeley County, as then constituted, was so extensive that communication with its county seat, Martinsburg, was a matter of great expense and inconvenience to residents of the proposed county. Another cause was the large accumulation of legal business in the courts, which so congested them as to retard the administration of justice. Still another reason was the alleged jealousy between the upper and lower parts of the existing county. A fourth reason was the "plentiful" population in each part to assure financial support for two governments. The petition further proposed Opequon Creek as the dividing line. The new county was to be named "Richland" with Charles Town as its seat of government. The expense of erecting a courthouse and other public buildings was to be borne by popular subscription.[2]

To this petition the Virginia General Assembly responded on January 8, 1801, by passing an act for the division of Berkeley

County, but it did not grant the desired boundary which would have followed Opequon Creek all the way from Frederick County [Virginia] to the Potomac River. Instead, it established the boundary only from the Frederick County line to a bend immediately below "Wallingford's tavern", about half a mile southwest of Mt. Zion Church and later known as "Payne's Ford". From the bend of the creek below the ford the established line was located direct to Wynkoop's Spring near the Shepherdstown-Martinsburg turnpike. It then followed Rocky Marsh Run to the Potomac. Thus the region between Opequon Creek and Rocky Marsh Run was retained by Berkeley County. The other boundaries of the new division were the same as those which had formerly been the mother county's, or the same as today. The new county was named Jefferson in honor of Thomas Jefferson who was then Vice-President of the United States and President-elect.

The act further stipulated that the division should take place on October 26, 1801. After that date courts were to be held at the county seat by the justices of the new county on the second Tuesday of each month. They were to meet first at the home of Basil Williamson. The first sheriff was to be appointed by the governor, who at that time was James Monroe.[3]

Information on the origin of Jefferson County is pertinent. From 1772 to 1801 it was a part of Berkeley County; from 1738 to 1772 it was a part of Frederick; from 1734 to 1738, a part of Orange; and from 1720 to 1734, a part of Spotsylvania. It belonged to Essex County from 1691 to 1720, Old Rappahannock from 1656 to 1691, and Lancaster from 1652 to 1656. From 1648 to 1652 it was part of Northumberland County. Prior thereto, present Jefferson County helped comprise the Indian district of Chickacoan and was not a part of any of the eight original counties, established in 1634, the names of which were as follows: James City, Henrico, Charles City, Elizabeth City, Warwick River, Warrosquyoake, Charles River, and Accawmack.[4]

On November 10, 1801, Jefferson County officials assembled for the first time. Their meeting-place was the home of John Mines in Charles Town, formerly occupied by Basil Williamson. Bearing commissions from Governor James Monroe, dated September 26, 1801, the following justices of the peace took office:

William Little, Joseph Swearingen, Alexander White, John Briscoe, Richard Baylor, John Kearsley, George Hite, George North, Daniel Collett, Abraham Davenport, John Packett, Daniel Morgan, Jacob Bedinger, and Ferdinando Fairfax. Three others, William Darke, Van Rutherford, and Daniel Morgan, had been appointed justices, but there is no record of their having taken the oath of office.[5]

In colonial times and for many years after the Revolution, justices of the peace performed important county governmental functions. They constituted a court and exercised the powers now vested in the County Court. They tried cases, civil and criminal, heard chancery suits, provided for the settlement of estates, laid out roads, gave permission for the construction of mill dams, authorized the erection of bridges, and built courthouses, jails, and other public edifices. They usually appointed the clerk of the court, coroners, constables, captains of militia, and subordinate officers. They recommended to the governor persons for appointment as sheriff, county lieutenants ,and colonels of the militia. As they were a close corporation, they nominated their own successors.

After organization the justices of the new county installed the sheriff and other county officers. Under their direction, William Little, appointed by Governor Monroe, took the required oath and became the first sheriff. His deputies were Cyrus Sanders, Benjamin Stephenson, William Little, Jr., and John Sanders. The justices then appointed George Hite first county clerk. He was assisted in his official duties by William R. Lowery. John Baker was made deputy attorney for the commonwealth and William McPherson was recommended as county surveyor. After designating McPherson and Joseph Swearingen commissioners to meet representatives from Berkeley County to mark the common boundary, the court adjourned.[6]

The work of organization was continued the next day, November 11, when the following attorneys were admitted to practice: William McGuire, Edward Christian, Lewis Elsey, Matthew Whiting, John Dixon, Samuel Reed, Elisha Boyd, William Tate, and Hugh Holmes. George North was recommended for appointment as county coroner and five constables were selected, namely, Jacob Long, William Shope, John Grantham, Peter Martin, and

THE JEFFERSONIAN ERA 67

Christian Olliman.[7]

Thereafter the County Court had little business for several months. A few owners appeared before the justices in efforts to free Negro slaves. In February, 1802, it made more recommendations for appointments. Among others, it recommended Abraham Morgan for major of the First Battalion, Fifty-Fifth Regiment, Virginia Militia, and suggested Jacob Haines for captain. As efforts were made to raise funds for the county's public buildings, on February 10, the court requested Matthew Frame, Thomas Hammond, and David Humphreys to continue their service of soliciting.

On March 9, 1802, Jefferson County's first grand jury was empaneled. It was composed of the following persons: George Washington, foreman, Lawrence A. Washington, Leodorick Fry, Eli Phelps, Zacariah Buckmaster, Richard Hardesty, Nicholas Shall, Beverly Whiting, John Sheeley, John Lemon, Alexander Burnett, Samuel Wright, Jacob Moler, James Likens, Jacob Smurr, and Samuel Reed.[8]

Determined by present-day standards, justice, as then administered, was severe. For instance, on March 26, 1803, a Negro slave belonging to Robert Baylor was charged with stealing one vest pattern, two yards of calico, one and one-half yards of linen, and some thread. Although the prisoner protested his innocence, the court found him guilty as charged and ordered that he be burned in the hand and given twenty lashes on his bare back, in the presence of the court. The burn in the hand, which branded one as a criminal, was frequently inflicted at that period although it was sometimes administered with an iron barely warm.[9]

Construction of county buildings had started by December 14, 1802. On that date the court ordered the sheriff to pay John Young $100 for this purpose. On February 9, 1803, it ordered payment of a similar amount to Young. The last payment on the courthouse was authorized in April and the first court in the new structure convened on July 12, 1803. It was used until 1837 when a new and larger building was erected. On February 12, 1806, the court authorized the building of a new structure for a county jail. It was of brick and its construction was supervised by David Humphreys. In the following year the old jail was converted into the clerk's office.[10]

On June 9, 1807, Jefferson County was divided into two districts known as the "Northern" and the "Southern". The dividing line ran by the "Main road from the Loudoun line by Keyes', thence with Hite's road to Lee and thence with the main road by Robert's ford on the Opequon to the Berkeley line".[11]

The county justices regulated taverns or "ordinaries" in such matters as charges for meals, beverages, etc. Among the persons whom they licensed to operate taverns in the county in this period were: Henry Gilbert, Henry Garnhart, Casper Walper, Catherine Wiltsheiner, John Conaway, Henry Haines, John Anderson, John G. Unseld, Basil Williamson, John James, Christian Fouke, George Little, Jacob Alstadt, and Curtis Grubb.[12]

Holl's Tavern, Charles Town

Supposedly obtained by Samuel Holl from Henry Haines this old tavern was for many years a famous landmark. It was torn down in 1911.

DIVERSIONS.

At this period horse-racing was a popular form of amusement. Beginning at Charles Town about 1786, it became more prominent in 1808. Followers of the turf sport today will be interested in knowing that a "Charles Town Jockey Club" was organized to sponsor races at the county seat. A notice in the **Farmer's Repository,** September 2, 1808, announced that horse-racing would be held for three days the following month. The first day's purse was expected to be $100 and the second day's $60. On the final day the purse was to consist of the entrance fees and gate money of the first two days. Four horses were declared to be the minimum number of participants.[13]

A few weeks later Smithfield followed in the steps of Charles Town as it advertised horse-racing in November. The purses were only $40 and $20. The races were financed by private donations and non-subscribers were required to pay gate fees. Shepherdstown, too, was interested in racing, for in October, 1810, it announced a proposed meet.[14]

Entertainment of a different sort was provided in 1809, when Peyton Smith and Joseph Holmes, both members of prominent Virginia families, fought a duel across the Potomac River from Shepherdstown. Details of this incident vary but agree on attributing it to a quarrel over a trivial matter. Both were well-educated young residents of Winchester and devoted to each other. It is said that after a dispute over a card game, Holmes challenged Smith to settle the difficulty with pistols. At the appointed time the youthful antagonists met, and, in spite of the fact that Holmes was a poor shot, Smith fell mortally wounded. He died shortly afterwards in the Entler Hotel in Shepherdstown. Holmes is reported to have been so overcome at the result that he left Winchester and never returned. The prominence of both families and the large number of relatives in the neighborhood caused the duel to receive more than passing notice.[15]

Although early newspapers did not carry much local news, they formed the chief contact with the outside world and were eagerly read. On April 1, 1808, the **Farmer's Repository** made its first appearance at Charles Town. It was edited by Richard Williams and William Brown. The following year Williams became the sole publisher.[16]

WAR OF 1812.

In the Presidential election of 1808 a majority of the electorate of Jefferson County voted for James Madison. The vote was Madison, Republican, 110, C. C. Pinckney, Federalist, 62, and James Monroe, Independent, 45. The total vote seems small today, but this was twenty years before Jacksonian Democracy extended the suffrage. Then, too, the scarcity of voting precincts, no doubt, cut down the number of ballots. Roads were bad and communication and transportation of necessity slow and cumbersome.[17]

Before the new President was inaugurated opposition developed in the county to the continuation of Jefferson's policy of "peaceable coercion". The Embargo Act of 1807 was so unpopular in Shepherdstown and vicinity, which had considerable trade down the Potomac River, that on February 23, 1809, a number of citizens met in protest. Colonel Joseph Swearingen was called to the chair, and Captain Abraham Shepherd was made secretary. Between 200 and 300 persons vigorously denounced the act.[18]

Local feeling against Madison's administration continued to grow and in both the Congressional and state elections of 1809 Jefferson County gave majorities for the Federalists. The next year one Republican, Daniel Morgan, along with the Federalist, Rawleigh Morgan, was chosen for the General Assembly. In 1811 the Federalists came back stronger than ever, and the county gave all of their candidates substantial majorities. The antiadministration feeling continued into the succeeding year and again the county selected Federalists to represent it at Richmond. Data on the Presidential election of 1812 are not available, but, judging from the preceding election results, Madison's administration was none too popular.[19]

Despite its opposition to the Republican party, Jefferson County provided at least seven companies of volunteers for the American army in the War of 1812. The only available muster rolls are those of the companies commanded by Captains Joseph Grantham, George W. Humphreys, James Conn, and Presley Marmaduke, respectively. The company led by Humphreys is the only one which left a record of its activities.

War was declared on June 18, 1812, and by November of that year a company of over fifty men had enlisted at Charles Town and offered its services to the President. Its officers are not known but possibly Colonel Robert Lucas was its chief officer, as

THE JEFFERSONIAN ERA 71

he is credited with having formed a company about that time. In addition to this local company more than one hundred men from Jefferson County enlisted in the regular army.[20] In the navy Midshipman John Packett bore the county's laurels in the war. He was on the frigate, **Constitution**, later immortalized by Oliver Wendell Holmes as **Old Ironsides**, when she engaged the **Java** off the Brazilian coast in December, 1812. In recognition of his bravery the Virginia General Assembly on May 20, 1813, directed the Governor to thank him and awarded a beautiful sword to the midshipman. The sword was presented in Boston.[21]

The next year two more groups of volunteers were organized in the county. On February 24, 1813, Lieutenant Henry Swearingen enrolled a detachment of more than fifty men and led it from Shepherdstown toward the country's northern frontier, where a series of reverses had considerably lowered American morale. A short while later Lieutenant Otho W. Callis enlisted a similar number of men in Charles Town.[22]

In the spring of 1814 the number of local enlistments in the war was further augmented. In March Captain Joseph Grantham's company of the Fifty-Fifth Regiment, Virginia Militia, was called to the colors. Officers serving with him were: Braxton Davenport, first lieutenant; Richard Williams, second lieutenant; Thomas Briscoe, first ensign, and George Feaman, second ensign.[23] Two other companies of militia, called into service in April, 1814, were those commanded by Captain James Conn and Captain Presley Marmaduke.

After successfully defending Canada against invasion, the British decided to strike at the capital of the young republic. The regular American army was scattered and as the state militia had proved its inefficiency on numerous occasions, they were reasonably sure of capturing Washington. An expedition appeared at the mouth of the Patuxent River, in Maryland, on August 22, 1814. Captain Henry St. George Tucker of Winchester was then in command of a company of cavalry near Washington. As soon as he learned of the enemy's approach, he sent an urgent appeal for aid throughout the countryside. When news of the country's dilemma reached Charles Town, Thomas Griggs mounted a butcher's block in the old market house and appealed for volunteers. At the same time a drummer and a fifer were sent through the streets. In less than two hours over fifty men had enrolled.[24]

Using the rest of that day to get personal equipment in shape, the company left Charles Town the next morning for Harpers Ferry, where it planned to obtain rifles and ammunition from the Government armory. Besides the desired munitions, it acquired about forty recruits, among whom was Colonel James Stubblefield, the superintendent of the armory. On Wednesday, August 24, the men of the company embarked on two flour-boats. After an hour's voyage the company landed and elected the following officers: George W. Humphreys, captain; Thomas Griggs, first lieutenant; James L. Ranson, second lieutenant; Joseph Blackburn, third lieutenant; and Samuel Russell, ensign. At the same time it was reduced in number by a decision that work at the armory was too important to be interrupted. Therefore, Stubblefield and most of the other Harpers Ferry volunteers who were employees at the Government plant returned to the Ferry. However, a few Government workmen who insisted that they could best serve their country by remaining as soldiers were allowed to proceed down the river.[25]

After traveling down the Potomac quite a distance members of the company heard the sound of firing at Bladensburg, a few miles from Washington, where the Americans had chosen to make a stand. The ensuing retreat of the militia under General W. H. Winder has been referred to as "the Bladensburg races" because of the speed with which the Americans fled.

The Jefferson volunteers were too late for the fighting. When they reached the mouth of Seneca Creek, they saw the capital in flames. The British burned some of the public buildings in retaliation for the destruction of York [Toronto] by Americans the preceding year.

Captain Humphreys then decided to report to General Winder at Rockville, where that unfortunate officer had managed to collect his scattered troops. When Humphreys arrived there, his company was mustered into service on August 26 for thirty days. It joined General Walter Smith who commanded at Washington after the British withdrawal. A short entertainment at Georgetown by a prominent citizen, Washington Bowie, was scarcely over when the men were ordered to Greenleaf's Point. They pitched camp near the later site of the Naval Observatory and after a few monotonous days marched to a place known as the White House, several miles below Mt. Vernon on the Potomac.

There on September 2 the company joined Commodore David Porter and assisted him in defending the channel. He had placed three six-pounders on a bluff of the river and was waiting to harass two British ships. The vessels had captured Alexandria and were expected to pass by on the return trip. As the channel at this point was near the Virginia shore, they would be forced within easy rifle-shot. Captain Humphreys's men were posted in a woods.[26]

The hopes of the Americans were doomed to failure, for Commodore Porter had not mounted the guns properly. Consequently, when the enemy warships appeared on September 5, they had little difficulty in running the gauntlet. The three small cannon on the bluff inflicted slight damage, but the riflemen were able to cause casualties. They were so eager to get good aim that they threw caution to the winds and went down to the river shore in full view of the British. Effective fire from the ships soon silenced Porter's batteries and even leveled every tree within range.

From the heavy grapeshot of the British vessels the volunteers suffered most. One was killed and five were wounded, two of them seriously. David Harris of Shepherdstown was killed by grapeshot; David Humphreys had his right hand and arm shattered, which rendered amputation necessary; Hugh McDonald was dangerously wounded by grapeshot in the hip; and Richard Fielding, Thomas Steadman, and Lieutenant Joseph Blackburn were slightly wounded.

The remaining volunteers returned home and on September 24 were mustered out of service with pay for thirty days. Further demands for their services were ended by the Treaty of Ghent, which was signed December 24, 1814.[27]

News of the treaty of peace did not reach Jefferson County until February, 1815. As the Secretary of War was anxious to prevent financial loss to its farmers and millers because of the war's abrupt end, he notified Colonel Stubblefield by "pony express". At one time flour was selling as low as three dollars a barrel in depreciated paper money and huge surpluses of it and wheat had accumulated in the county. France was paying twelve dollars in gold for a barrel of flour, but the British blockade effectively kept American ports closed. As soon as word of the peace treaty was received in the United States, speculators attempted to obtain quantities of country produce at the existing low prices.

News of the cessation of hostilities spread rapidly through Jefferson County. Soon the farmers and millers gathered to learn the latest prices of their goods. Flour that had been selling for three dollars a barrel quickly advanced to ten. Even at such an advance, only a few were willing to sell. Many of them waited to see what the French agents would offer, for France had thousands of hungry soldiers to feed. Ability to supply them at substantial charges brought rejoicing in the county.[28]

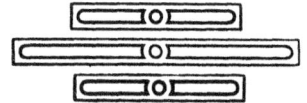

CHAPTER SEVEN
THE NEW NATIONALISM, 1815 TO 1840

At the end of the War of 1812 the United States entered a new era in which the old order changed and younger men took control of the ship of state. The first part of this period witnessed the death of the old Federalist party which failed to recover from its unfortunate part in the Hartford Convention. As a result, the Republican party remained in control until the Whig triumph of 1840. The impetus gained in the Era of Good Feeling sustained it against factional and sectional strife, but changes wrought by Jacksonian Democracy left wounds that refused to heal. Politics, internal improvements, extension of the right to vote, and slavery occupied most of the young nation's attention at this particular time.

POLITICAL EVENTS.

One of the chief local bones of contention in the new era was representation in the Virginia General Assembly. In a petition dated November 18, 1816, the people of Jefferson County asked that body to call a convention to change the state constitution so that the region west of the Blue Ridge Mountains would be fairly represented at Richmond.[1]

In spite of the decline of the Federalist party in the country at large, Jefferson County continued to elect Federalists. In the Congressional election of 1817 its candidate, Edward Colston, received 135 votes, or 14 more than the total of his two opponents, Daniel Morgan and Robert Bailey. In the race for members of the General Assembly George W. Humphreys and George Reynolds, both Federalists, defeated their Republican opponent, Braxton Davenport, by votes of 166 and 158 to 109.[2]

At an election held in April, 1830, Jefferson County residents were asked to voice their sentiments on the new state constitution, which a special convention had just completed. As the document gave more representation in the General Assembly to the Shenandoah Valley, it was expected to be overwhelmingly approved. A favorable result was considered so certain that only 296 voters went to the polls. Of these, 243 favored the constitution and 53 opposed it.[3]

Although results of some of the Presidential elections in the county are not available, in 1832 a majority of the voters opposed the reelection of Andrew Jackson. The vote was: Henry Clay, 362, and Jackson, 279. Of the four county precincts Clay carried Charles Town and Shepherdstown. At Middleway the vote was tied with 44 for each candidate, but Jackson obtained a slight majority at Harpers Ferry, where industrial laborers predominated. This election is indicative of the future, for the Whig party, successor to the National Republican organization, continued to control the county.[4]

An interesting counterpart to the election occurred on January 21, 1833, at the courthouse. At that time a meeting was held to determine the people's attitude toward South Carolina's defiance of President Jackson on the question of nullification. Although Jefferson's electorate had voted for Clay the preceding November, it strongly supported the Democratic President in his firm stand against allowing a state to nullify an act of Congress. Despite the fact that the day for the gathering was unfavorable, over 300 persons attended. A resolutions committee reported in favor of condemning the course of South Carolina and upholding that of Jackson. Able speeches by Andrew Hunter, John A. Thompson, and others helped, no doubt, to obtain an almost unanimous vote accepting the resolutions. A substitute measure supported by John Davenport and William Lucas received but small consideration. The Union sentiment was too strongly entrenched in Jefferson County to be dislodged so easily.[5]

The county showed much interest in the political questions which came to the forefront in 1834 when Jackson's war on the United States Bank stirred up the countryside. In his effort to destroy the power of the bank the President had the general support of the poorer classes but was opposed by the moneyed interests. At a mass meeting in the Jefferson County courthouse on January 20, 1834, over 200 persons listened to arguments condemning "Old Hickory's" policy. A large majority endorsed resolutions disapproving the removal of the deposits. An attempt to take a stand on the Force Bill, another controversial issue, was defeated because it was not in accord with the original purpose of the meeting. For some unknown reason an election was held in April on the bank question and the results showed that 275 of the county's voters favored restoration of the deposits and 21 opposed it.[6]

The newly organized Whig party emerged from the county elections in April, 1835, as the victor over the Republicans, now generally called Democrats. The Whig candidate for Congress, John R. Cooke, barely nosed out the Democrat, Colonel Edward Lucas, a resident of Jefferson, by a vote of 372 to 365. However, Lucas won by 123 votes in the whole district. The Whig majority in the House of Delegates race was more pronounced, for Thomas Griggs and Henry Berry obtained 411 and 396 votes to their opponents' respective totals of 387 and 310. In this contest the Democratic nominees were Samuel Cameron and Jacob Morgan.[7]

In 1836 Whig candidates swept the county. They not only carried Jefferson County's seats in the General Assembly but also maintained their advantage in the Presidential contest. Their ticket polled a total of 400 votes in November, whereas Martin Van Buren, the Democratic nominee, received only 269. Middleway was the only precinct to give Van Buren a majority.[8]

HARPERS FERRY ARMORY AND ARSENAL.

In 1817 the Government armory and arsenal at Harpers Ferry entered a new phase of its history when John H. Hall, an able inventor and gunsmith from Yarmouth, Maine, arrived. In 1811 Hall had been granted a patent for a breech-loading firelock, or flintlock pistol, and the following year he adapted the patent to the heavier charge of long arms. After several years of vain attempts to interest the Federal Government he had finally in 1816 received from it a contract for 100 rifles. The next year he continued his experiments at the Harpers Ferry Armory, and his success resulted in a contract in March, 1819, for 1,000 breech-loading flintlock rifles which would bear his name. He soon entered the Government employ as assistant armorer at Harpers

Ferry in order to insure quantity production and proper construction. Two buildings were erected for his use on an island in the Shenandoah River, about a quarter of a mile from the main plant along the Potomac. The new establishment became known as "Hall's Rifle Works".

Hall did more than merely patent the first breech-loading gun in the United States. He also designed and constructed a number of machines used in the manufacture of his rifle. Among them were some which made possible the interchangeability of parts. Colonel James Stubblefield, who had succeeded Perkins in 1810, was the superintendent during the armory's period of expansion.[9]

In an excellent account of Harpers Ferry in 1821 the armory appears as a group of thirteen buildings, eleven of them brick. The arsenal was part of the armory. A canal, a mile and a fourth long, led from a dam across the Potomac to the shops to supply water power. Hall's Rifle Works consisted of four buildings. Workmen numbering 250 produced about 12,000 stands of rifles and muskets annually.

Colonel Stubblefield concerned himself about the education of his employees' children. For that purpose four teachers were engaged for 200 pupils.[10]

Much excitement was caused by a murder committed at Harpers Ferry in 1830. Colonel Thomas B. Dunn, a strict disciplinarian, had succeeded Stubblefield as superintendent the preceding year. The severity of his rules offended several of the workmen and one of them, a young man named Ebenezer Cox, considered himself so unjustly treated that he sought revenge. Accordingly, on January 29, 1830, he went to the main office and shot Dunn through the heart. The resulting death caused Cox to be taken to the jail at Charles Town. After a fair trial he was found guilty, sentenced, and executed publicly on August 27.[11]

General George Rust of Loudoun County, Virginia, succeeded Dunn at the armory and served until 1837, when he in turn yielded the superintendency to Colonel Edward Lucas.

In 1837 the breech-loading arms produced at Hall's Rifle Works received favorable acclaim by a board of officers appointed by the Government to investigate various arms. After experimenting with other makes, the board reported that Hall's rifles were decidedly superior. Among the fine points of the Hall guns were those of long range, rapid reloading, and ability to resist wear. In fact, they could be loaded and discharged eight times a minute, whereas the ordinary rifle could be loaded and reloaded only twice a minute. The army found the Harpers Ferry rifle particularly adaptable for cavalry use.[12]

CHURCHES.

Church activity was evident in the county during the new era. After a lapse of twenty years the Charles Town Presbyterian Church awakened from its lethargy, and for the first time since 1797 it was represented at a meeting of the Winchester Presbytery in October, 1815. Its representative was Elder Thomas Likens. The organization thus revived continued as a permanent force.[13]

About the same time Trinity Episcopal Church, Shepherdstown, received new blood in the person of the Rev. Benjamin Allen. Prior to his ministry the church had been inactive the greater part of the time since its founding. Allen was a tireless worker and his enthusiasm became so contagious that the church grew strong, spiritually and financially.[14]

Shepherdstown Lutherans were also revived in this period. Fifteen years of factional strife and destitution had all but closed the doors of the old church. The bone of greatest contention was the question of whether the service should be in German or English. A succession of discouraged ministers ended in July, 1819, when the Rev. C. P. Krauth took over the pastorate. He conducted services in English during his eight-year ministry and the church was established on a sound foundation.[15]

Episcopalians in the Charles Town neighborhood decided to abandon the old St. George's Chapel and erect a new place of worship at the county seat. Since Jefferson County's organization in 1801 Charles Town had been growing in importance. In 1815 work was begun on the future Zion Church. Progress was slow and it was not until three years later that a congregation met within its walls for the first time. In spite of the unfinished interior, the bishop of the diocese preached and administered the rite of confirmation there on May 28, 1818. Fixtures from St.

George's Chapel were removed to Charles Town for the use of Zion's congregation. Pews in the new structure rented for an average of $31 a year.[16]

Elk Branch Presbyterian Church, one of the oldest in the county, was reorganized on December 14, 1833. The congregation, once active, had divided in 1792 when some of the members went to Shepherdstown and others to Charles Town. In 1829 erection of a small limestone structure, about half a mile from the old site, was begun. After this building was completed the congregation petitioned the Winchester Presbytery to reorganize their church. The petition, dated March 30, 1833, was granted.[17]

SUNDAY SCHOOLS.

Following the opening of the first Sunday School in Virginia in 1815 at Winchester, similar organizations were begun by November, 1819, at Shepherdstown, Charles Town, Harpers Ferry, and Leetown. The first of these was a union of Reformed, Lutherans, and Presbyterians, which began in Shepherdstown about 1816. The one at the county seat was opened on April 25, 1819, with an attendance of seventy-five. At a meeting held ten days before in the courthouse the ministers, S. Bunn, J. Matthews, Benjamin Allen, and W. C. Walton, were selected to manage the new venture. Designated laymen to assist were S. J. Cramer, Thomas Likens, R. Worthington, G. W. Humphreys, Charles Gibbs, A. Woods, R. Williams, and William Lock.[18]

In 1827 after the Sunday School movement had become general in the county a "Berkeley and Jefferson Sabbath School Union" was formed. The new organization was the result of an appreciation of advantages in increase, improvement, and permanency of Sunday Schools which could be obtained by mutual assistance and cooperation. No doubt the success of the American Sunday School Union, organized at Philadelphia in May, 1824, had its influence. Delegates from a number of schools in the two counties met in the Presbyterian Church at Shepherdstown on September 17, 1827. They elected Colonel John Strother moderator and then drew up a constitution.[19]

The combined influences of churches and Sunday Schools were doubtless partly responsible for an advertisement which appeared in the **Farmer's Repository** for February 21, 1821, which

said: "The Jail of Jefferson County will be for rent at July court next.
J. L. Ranson."

INTERNAL IMPROVEMENTS.

The people of Jefferson County shared in the current country-wide interest in internal improvements. On October 20, 1823, a large number of them met at the courthouse to appoint delegates to a meeting in Washington to consider the improvement of the navigation of the Potomac River. Among those in attendance were relatives of George Washington, the father of this enterprise. The following representatives were designated to attend the Washington meeting: Henry S. Turner, Hierome L. Opie, Braxton Davenport, Bushrod C. Washington, Daniel Morgan, John Peter, and Andrew Kennedy, but only the first three named were on hand. They were accompanied by William Butler and Richard E. Byrd, also of Jefferson County. The delegates met on November 7 in the hall of the Supreme Court at the Federal Capitol and launched the Chesapeake and Ohio Canal project.[20]

Almost two years later some of the county's residents became interested in the Cumberland Road and met in Charles Town on May 13, 1825. This road was begun in 1811 to connect Cumberland, Maryland, with Wheeling, Virginia. In 1825 it seemed likely that Congress would authorize its extension to the nation's capital, hence the renewal of interest on the part of Jefferson's alert people. At the Charles Town meeting of May 13 James M. Brown, the county's deputy surveyor, was authorized to lay out a direct route from the Loudoun County line at Keyes's Gap to Mill's Gap on North Mountain. Simultaneously, a committee consisting of Major Braxton Davenport, Colonel James Hite, Captain James Shirley, Major John Griggs, William Short, and Sebastian Eaty, was appointed to look after the county's interests.[21]

In 1830 Jefferson County laid the foundations for the fine roads which eventually marked its progress. On January 14 interested persons petitioned the Virginia General Assembly to pass an act incorporating a turnpike company to construct a road from Harpers Ferry to the vicinity of Middleway. The same year the Summit Point and Harpers Ferry Turnpike Company received its first charter. Sixteen miles of water-bound macadam soon stretched from Harpers Ferry to Middleway and fourteen miles of telford connected Shepherdstown and Middleway. As was the case with most early roads, these pikes were built by stock companies and toll was charged for their use. The usual rate was two cents a mile for a horse and buggy.[22]

By 1830 a stage line connected the county with Washington. Its stages ran from the capital to Leesburg three times a week and passed once a week on the canal route and twice by the turnpike on the Virginia side. They visited Harpers Ferry twice weekly and Charles Town once and returned by the same places. The fare from Washington to Charles Town or Harpers Ferry was four dollars and the trip was made in one day.[23]

The Chesapeake and Ohio Canal reached Harpers Ferry from Washington in November, 1833, seventeen years before it reached Cumberland, and its rival, the Baltimore and Ohio Railroad, arrived at the river junction in December, 1834. They had waged a battle that had impeded the progress of both. Following the meanderings of the Potomac westward from Georgetown, the canal was making an effort to reach the Ohio River and divert the western trade to its eastern terminus. The railroad, pushing westward from Baltimore, sought the same objective. Although the railroad lost the race to Harpers Ferry, it not only arrived in Cumberland, in 1842, ahead of its rival but by 1853 also reached the Ohio, an accomplishment the canal was never able to achieve.

Speed on the canal was slow, about nine miles an hour, but cheap transportation had at last arrived in the county. By the old plan of "wagoning" it had cost from eighty-five cents to $1.00 to send a barrel of flour to Georgetown and $1.00 to Baltimore. Now, thanks to the waterway, a saving of sixty cents on a barrel could be made on the carriage to Georgetown and sixty-six cents on a barrel to Baltimore. Since the canal did not extend to the Maryland city, it was necessary to transfer to the railroad at Point of Rocks. A saving of twelve cents a bushel on the transportation of wheat was equally helpful. It was now possible for passengers from Harpers Ferry to leave at five o'clock in the morning and arrive in Baltimore in the evening of the same day.[24]

On December 4, 1834, a Baltimore and Ohio Railroad train,

bringing nearly a hundred passengers, steamed into Harpers Ferry. It had left Baltimore at eight o'clock that morning and it reached the Ferry, eighty-two miles distant, at two in the afternoon. A few short stops were made en route.[25]

The Winchester and Potomac Railroad, which also benefited Jefferson County, began operation more than a year later. This line was thirty-two miles long and extended from Winchester to Harpers Ferry, where it connected with the Baltimore and Ohio. On March 9, 1836, the locomotive "Tennessee", with its two passenger cars, the "Pioneer" and the "Virginia", arrived in Harpers Ferry for the first trip to Winchester.

Amid shouts and cheers of spectators the train left the depot on the Island of Virginius. As both the engine and roadbed were new, no effort was made for a speed record. Arriving safely at the southwestern terminus at Winchester, the train was prepared for the return trip on March 14. Passengers were crowded into every available space, even on the tops of the cars, and with a load of flour the "Tennessee" puffed away.

Unfortunately, the high hopes of the enthusiasts were doomed to a temporary disappointment. At Cameron's Depot, now Aldridge, an accident marred the otherwise perfect trip. Some meddler had turned a switch, and, as a consequence, one car was derailed and another damaged. After an hour's delay, the procession resumed the journey to Harpers Ferry.[26]

The formal opening of the Winchester road did not take place until several weeks later. On the last day of March the locomotive and cars brought the committee of arrangements to Harpers Ferry, where the train took on board the president and a few directors of the Baltimore and Ohio. Then, with the borrowed engine, "Thomas Jefferson", attached to the "Tennessee" and fifteen cars, the procession got ready for the triumphant trip to Winchester. With the Harpers Ferry band aboard, the flag-bedecked train, after taking on several more guests along the route, reached Winchester about five o'clock in the evening. There an enthusiastic reception greeted the arrivals. The large crowd, which lined the railway for almost a mile, and salvos of artillery united to make the event outstanding. On a platform of freight boxes and casks at the depot President John Bruce of the road delivered an address, which was answered briefly by

Philip E. Thomas, President of the Baltimore and Ohio. Then the procession moved to the Virginia House for a banquet. As originally planned, the Winchester and Potomac would have followed a route by way of Middleway. When residents of that conservative community heard of the idea, they became greatly alarmed. Among other things, they feared that "the cars" would kill their cattle, sheep, and other livestock. They fancied also that sparks from the engine would burn their crops. Then, too, it was feared the noisy iron monster would disturb their peaceful slumbers. Much to the relief of Middleway's inhabitants the railroad was re-routed by way of Summit Point, five miles distant.[27]

The enlarging business life of the region was reflected in the need for a new courthouse. Work was begun on a building that was completed in 1837.[28] This was used until the Civil War, when it was partially destroyed. Hence, it was the structure in which John Brown and his associates were tried in 1859.

THE IRON INDUSTRY.

In response to improved transportation new industries emerged. In 1839, a new iron industry sprang up across the Shenandoah River, a mile below Shannondale Springs. Two men named Perdue and Nichols constructed a furnace along present Furnace Run, about a fourth of a mile from the river. They erected a large building for smelting operations and used its eastern portion for the reception of ore and coal. The western wing received the metal after it had passed through the furnace. The latter, located in the center of the structure, was blasted by air forced through a pipe near its bottom. Machinery, run by an overshot water wheel, forced air through the pipe to the furnace.

Ore was obtained in great abundance from the immediate vicinity and was located near the surface of the ground. Coal was made from wood taken from the thick forests in that part of the county. About three tons of pig iron were produced daily. As there were nearly fifty men employed at this time, numerous small buildings were erected nearby for their accommodation.[29] The furnace was operated until the outbreak of the Civil War, in which struggle the main buildings are supposed to have been burned by Union soldiers. Today the solitary reminder of this once-flourishing business is a large stone stack, which is used to house pigs.

NEGROES AND SLAVERY.

About 1818 the increasing free colored population began to be a problem in Jefferson County as elsewhere. Through no fault of their own they were virtually persons "without a country". They could not compete with white labor or with slave labor and were social outcasts. Unlike their brethren in bondage they had no master to provide them with the necessities of life nor kind mistress to look after them when sick. Humanitarians in Washington conceived the well-intentioned but impractical idea of transporting them to Africa. For this purpose they organized the African Colonization Society.

Generous masters had been freeing their slaves for some time in Jefferson County so that the number of free Negroes had risen to 354 in 1810 in a total population of 11,694. The number of slaves according to the same census was 3,488, or more than enough to do the work of the whites. As a result of much agitation the influence of the colonization society in Washington spread into the surrounding countryside.

A meeting was held in Charles Town on August 3, 1819, at the Episcopal Church to form a subsidiary colonization society. At the gathering, which was attended by many prominent persons, the proposed organization was effected, a constitution adopted, and officers elected. In general, the body was to raise funds to help the parent organization at Washington. The following officers were selected to head the county's society: Dr. Samuel J. Cramer, president; B. C. Washington, Adam Weaver, H. S. Turner, N. Craighill, J. T. A. Washington, and G. W. Humphreys, vice-presidents; John Marshall, secretary; and R. Worthington, treasurer.[30]

Evidence that the slavery controversy was affecting Jefferson County is furnished by a petition to the General Assembly, dated January 13, 1835. In it a group of slaveowners in the county requested that body to assist them in retaking runaway slaves. They stated that their position along the frontier near Pennsylvania rendered slave property insecure. The problem of recovering runaways in the Quaker State, where slavery did not exist, was attended with much difficulty. Complaining that its laws prohibited the recapture of a fugitive and that its citizens were hostile to such action, they also deplored the antislavery and abolition societies.

Remedies proposed for these alleged evils were increased rewards for apprehending runaways, the incorporation of a company to insure against loss of deserting slaves, and efforts to persuade Pennsylvania to enact laws requiring its magistrates to enforce the Federal Fugitive Slave Law. A final suggestion asked the General Assembly to obtain from Congress the power to form compacts with non-slaveholding states on the subject of retaking fugitive slaves. The General Assembly replied by passing an act on March 10, 1835, incorporating "The Virginia Slave Insurance Company" at Charles Town to insure against losses by the absconding of slaves.[31]

The high prices which slaveowners received for slaves is illustrated by a sale in Charles Town on June 15, 1835, when a large number of Negroes were sold at auction by the sheriff. One man was purchased for $1,200 after $1,000 had been offered as the first bid. A woman and four children went to the highest bidder for $1,950, and another woman and two children brought $1,126. Two boys, aged 14 and 16, sold for $615 and $790, respectively, whereas, two girls, aged 10 and 13, together brought $795. Many other slaves were disposed of and the above prices were not exceptional.[32]

LITERARY ACTIVITIES.

Broader influences during this era extended to the field of literature. As a result, the inhabitants of Harpers Ferry petitioned the Virginia General Assembly to incorporate "The Library Society of Harpers Ferry". The request bearing date of December 8, 1819, was not granted until December 15, 1820. The resulting library is said to be the first of record in present West Virginia.[33]

Following the example of Harpers Ferry, Charles Town became interested in a library society. Accordingly, on November 25, 1825, a group of its residents met at Hammond's Hotel and formulated plans for the organization of a similar group. Among them were the Rev. Alexander Jones, Robert T. Brown, John Yates, Andrew Kennedy, and Thomas A. Moore. There is no evidence that the Charles Town society was incorporated.[34]

In 1827 the county's leading newspaper, the **Farmer's Repository**, was bought by John S. Gallaher and merged with the **Virginia Free Press** as **The Virginia Free Press and Farmer's Repository**. Gallaher had been publishing the **Virginia Free Press** at Harpers Ferry since 1821. The name of the merged paper was shortened about 1831 to the **Virginia Free Press**, which was printed at Charles Town, except for the Civil War period, until 1916. During the greater part of this time it was published by the Gallaher family.

TOWNS AND VILLAGES.

A few new towns were created in this period. On December 7, 1825 residents of "Mudfort" in eastern Jefferson County petitioned the Virginia General Assembly for town status. They wished to be known henceforth as "Bolivar", in honor of Simon Bolivar, the South American patriot. An act which complied with their request was passed December 29 and appointed as trustees George Rowles, Dr. John R. Heyden, Robert Avis, John Graham, and Joel Downer.[35]

A year later inhabitants of an island in the Shenandoah River, at Harpers Ferry, petitioned the General Assembly that their settlement be established as the town of "Virginius". The act doing so was passed January 8, 1827, and appointed as trustees, Lewis Wernwag, Fontaine Beckham, Townsend Beckham, John S. Gallagher, and John G. Unseld.[36]

Jefferson County's largest town in 1820 was Shepherdstown with 1,441 persons. Harpers Ferry was second with 1,353, Charles Town was next with 1,049, and Smithfield was fourth with only 337. Ten years later, Harpers Ferry had 1,379, Shepherdstown 1,326, and Charles Town 1,118. Smithfield, now known as Middleway, had 303 and Bolivar 270. The county's population decreased from 13,087 to 12,956 in 1830.[37]

THE MASONS.

Following the lead set by Mt. Nebo Lodge No. 91, chartered at Shepherdstown in 1811, a similar organization was established at Harpers Ferry in 1818 and was known as Charity Lodge, No. 111. The date of its charter was December 15, 1818. In 1868 this body was consolidated with Eureka Lodge, No. 25, also of Harpers Ferry, to form Logan Lodge, No. 25.

One of the oldest Masonic organizations in the county still active is Triluminar Lodge, No. 117, which was chartered on December 24, 1819, at Bruce's Mills, now Brucetown, Frederick County, Virginia. It was moved in 1832 to Middleway, where it thereafter met regularly, with occasional interruptions. Its name means "three lights", and the dates of its meetings were fixed on the first Saturday evenings following the full moon of each month.

The first Masonic lodge in Charles Town was Livingston, No. 66, chartered January 16, 1839. It was afterward changed and chartered as Malta Lodge, No. 80, December 14, 1847.[38]

DEATH OF LAFAYETTE.

When news of Lafayette's death in May, 1834, reached Jefferson County, there was much mourning. In fact, gloom spread over the entire United States, and various communities vied with each other in ways of showing their grief. Shepherdstown's residents decided to hold a pretended funeral in which the imaginary remains of their hero would be laid to rest. Invitations were sent to Martinsburg, Charles Town, Middleway, and other communities, requesting participation of their militia companies in the procession to be held August 4, 1834. The program consisted of speeches praising Lafayette and comparing him with Washington, after which the pretended body was laid to rest. Following the firing of a salute, the companies of soldiers marched by the reviewing stand, on which was seated Governor Littleton W. Tazewell. The Middleway Blues, led by John F. Smith, was awarded a trophy as the best-drilled group.[39]

CHAPTER EIGHT
THE EVENTFUL FORTIES
POLITICS.

On the political front in Jefferson County Whigs continued to predominate. In the 1840 contest for seats in the Virginia General Assembly their candidates won in both houses. Although the Presidential race was closer, General William Henry Harrison, the Whig nominee, won by a margin of seventy-eight votes in a total of 1,258. His greatest strength centered in Shepherdstown and Charles Town, whereas Harpers Ferry and Middleway were Van Buren's strongholds.[1] Charles Town and Shepherdstown vicinities contained, for the most part, large landowners, while Middleway and industrial Harpers Ferry had many laborers.

A continuation of Whig power was indicated, though with varying majorities, in the elections of 1844 and 1845. In the Presidential contest the perennial Whig candidate, Henry Clay, received 725 votes, while his Democratic rival, James K. Polk, obtained 622. In the following year, when slightly more than half the total county voters participated in the Congressional and state elections, the Whigs nominated no candidate for Congress, and the Democrats had none for the General Assembly. William Lucas was elected to Congress and William F. Turner and Benjamin T. Towner were chosen for the General Assembly.[2]

The Presidential election of 1848 resulted in another triumph for Jefferson County Whigs. General Zachary Taylor obtained 738 votes, while the Democratic nominee, Lewis Cass, received 594. The Whig strength continued to be centered in Shepherdstown and Charles Town and the Democratic in Harpers Ferry and Middleway.[3]

HARPERS FERRY ARMORY AND ARSENAL.

The appointment of Major Henry K. Craig in April, 1841,

to succeed Colonel Lucas as superintendent marked the beginning of a new period at the Harpers Ferry Armory and Arsenal. The choice was in line with the recently adopted policy of substituting military for civilian heads of national armories. A desire to increase efficiency, to obtain properly qualified superintendents, and to have more direct control, prompted the War Department to request the change. It was also contended that the head of a national armory should have some knowledge of science, as well as of the construction and use of arms.

Major Craig, being an ordnance officer, substituted military discipline for the laxity which had heretofore existed at the plant. In addition, he compelled piece workers to labor as long as regular day workers. Prior to this time piece workers were allowed to labor whenever they chose. At the same time the ingress and egress of armorers and visitors were regulated by armed guards, and drunkenness was absolutely forbidden.

Employees rebelled against these innovations as an invasion of their rights and in 1842 a large number chartered a canalboat for Washington, where they presented their case to the President. Tyler received them cordially and after listening patiently to their complaints, advised them that they "must go home and hammer out their own salvation". The people of Harpers Ferry bitterly opposed the military superintendency until 1854, when it was abolished. Craig was succeeded in 1844 by Major John Symington.[4]

SCHOOLS.

An important forward step in connection with Jefferson County's schools was taken in 1846. On February 25 the General Assembly passed an act authorizing the establishment of free schools in several counties, among which was Jefferson. At the election on April 23 the county approved free schools by the overwhelming vote of 861 to 180. All four of its precincts returned majorities for the measure, but the Shepherdstown precinct vote was fairly close with 135 for and 110 against.[5]

Under the act patrons would find it cheaper to send their children to the public schools than the academies, even though a new tax system would be set up. Defects in the original act concerning taxation were remedied when on March 20, 1847, the

THE EVENTFUL FORTIES 91

General Assembly passed another act. By this measure commissioners were instructed to divide the county into districts and arrange for the election of boards of education. In addition, they were to provide suitable schoolhouses. Instruction was restricted to the three R's, and, where practicable, to English grammar, geography, history, moral philosophy, and other higher branches. Indigent children between 5 and 21 were to be taught free, and the charge for others was limited to fifty cents a quarter.

Before the act could be effective, it had to be approved by a two-thirds affirmative vote in an election set for June 3, 1847. The result was 74 more than the necessary two-thirds, but the total vote was small, 554 for, to 167 against. Three of the four precincts favored the act, and in the other, Shepherdstown, there was a tie vote. The estimated cost of the system for the first year was $10,000.

Thus, Jefferson has the distinction of being one of the first counties in present West Virginia to adopt a free school system. John Yates of "Walnut Grove", near Flowing Springs, is credited with having been active in establishing a public school on the Lemen farm near Shepherdstown.[6]

An interesting report of progress in the county's school system was made on December 28, 1848. It showed that the board had increased the number of school districts from 24 to 27 and had erected 13 new schoolhouses. Some of the latter were constructed of brick and stone and the others were of wood. Three more houses were under construction and four additional structures had been repaired and made suitable for use. Twenty-three schools with an enrollment of 1,100 were in operation. Seven teachers received $300 a year each, and sixteen others received $275. The branches of learning were reading, writing, arithmetic, spelling, grammar, and geography. Text-books were Comley's **Spelling Book,** Hazen's **First and Second Speller,** Walker's **Dictionary,** McGuffey's **Series of Readers,** Colburn and Pike's **Arithmetic,** and Parley's and Morse's **Geography.**[7]

THE MEXICAN WAR.

On November 18, 1846, William Smith, Governor of Virginia, appealed for the organization of ten volunteer companies of infantry to carry the Old Dominion's colors in the war with Mexico. The men were asked to serve until the end of the war unless discharged sooner.[8]

As soon as this request reached Jefferson County, efforts were made to enlist men for active service. Simultaneously, Major John F. Hamtramck of Shepherdstown and Captain John W. Rowan of Charles Town appealed to the volunteer companies which they headed. Later, Major John Symington of Harpers Ferry attempted to recruit a company of mounted men to serve with Rocket and Howitzer batteries. As this organization was intended to be a "crack" company, none but active, brave, and intelligent young men were accepted for it. The promised pay was nearly double that of other volunteers and the mounts and equipment were to be of the best. To discourage the timid, Symington advertised that this special group would operate constantly in advance of the others and that the hardest fighting could be expected.[9]

Although additional information concerning the Shepherdstown and Harpers Ferry companies is lacking, the **Spirit of Jefferson** kept a good record of events relating to the Charles Town organization.

Public meetings were held at the county seat on December 11 and December 21 to aid the company being raised there. Committees of prominent citizens solicited subscriptions to defray the expenses of the volunteers. Officers chosen on December 24 were: John W. Rowan, captain; John Avis, Jr., first lieutenant; Lawrence B. Washington, first, second lieutenant; and William McCormick, second, second lieutenant.[10]

Jefferson County was distinctly honored by the selection of Major John F. Hamtramck of Shepherdstown as colonel of the entire Virginia regiment. Hamtramck was well qualified for the position. He was a graduate of West Point, had been a sergeant in the War of 1812, and had served in the Northwest Territory where his father was an old Indian fighter. By a strange coincidence, he had fought under General [then Major] Zachary Taylor in the War of 1812.

Among the other officers of the Virginia regiment was Jubal A. Early of Franklin County. Early, the later famous Confederate general, was appointed major under Colonel Hamtramck.

Another later Jefferson resident, George A. Porterfield, who was defeated by a Federal force at Philippi, in present West Virginia, in the Civil War, served as adjutant of the regiment for a while.

On January 4, 1847, Captain Rowan's company prepared to leave Charles Town. A meeting was held in the courthouse, where the men listened to a parting address by Charles B. Harding. Then a letter from Mrs. D. Alexander was read informing the company's officers that she was sending a Bible to each of them. She had also given Captain Rowan an order in Richmond for a copy of the New Testament for each of the soldiers. The sixty-seven volunteers then proceeded to the depot, where they boarded a train for Harpers Ferry. There, they took passage on canal packet boats.[11]

At Richmond the volunteers of Rowan's company were quartered in the Union Hotel, and later John S. Gallaher, their state senator, presented them to the governor, who received them cordially. They were welcomed by residents of Richmond with much enthusiasm. A short while afterwards the company was selected by Colonel Hamtramck as one of the two Virginia companies to be organized as riflemen. In addition, it was honored by the appointment of J. Cunningham as fife major of the regiment and of James H. Baker as color bearer.

Additional men, some of whom were from southern Virginia, were from time to time placed in the Jefferson company. While waiting for ships at Old Point Comfort, part of the soldiers became sick, largely because of the wet and disagreeable weather. Three, Peter Bougher of Winchester, W. Kirk of Loudoun County, and W. Bryant of Richmond, died of fever.[12]

Finally, on February 22, Captain Rowan's company, along with two others, left Old Point Comfort in the barque **Exact** for Isabel, Texas. Colonel Hamtramck and his adjutant took the western route down the Mississippi. On the sea trip Captain Rowan was in command of the detachment, which consisted of his own men, a Captain Alburtis's company from Berkeley County, and a Captain Young's organization from Portsmouth.

The Jefferson and Berkeley men reached Texas in good condition and by March 12 were on the Brazos River, whence they crossed the border to Camargo. From there they went to Matamoros and then returned to Camargo. On April 14 they marched to a little place named China. Known officially as Company K, Virginia Regiment, Captain Rowan's company did not engage the Mexicans except for occasional clashes on scouting expeditions.[13]

The reason for this is that after General Taylor's decisive victory at Buena Vista the scene of fighting shifted to the south, where General Winfield Scott marched from Vera Cruz to Mexico City. Earnest efforts were made by the officers and men of the Virginia regiment to be transferred to a more active theatre, but the request was denied by General Taylor. Believing that another demonstration would be made on the northern frontier, he kept an army on duty there. The treaty of Guadalupe-Hidalgo, ending the war, was signed in February, 1848, but Captain Rowan's company did not return home until the first week in August.

Meanwhile, other soldiers from Jefferson County had seen hard fighting. Peter T. Duke, Nathan Hafer, and James Downing, all of Charles Town, participated at Cerro Gordo, Molino del Rey, Chapultepec, Churubusco, and in the capture of Mexico City.[14]

THE FORTY-NINERS.

The discovery of gold in California in 1848 had its repercussions in Jefferson County, Virginia. Reports indicated that there was sufficient gold for everybody, and in January, 1849, a company was formed in Charles Town to direct mining operations in California. It was a joint stock organization of eighty members, each of whom paid $300 into the common treasury. The constitution of this company provided that the Sabbath should be duly recognized and forbade any member from working on that day. Gambling was strictly prohibited and intemperance was discouraged. Regulation of the organization was vested in an elected board of directors of seven persons.[15]

Filling vacancies and collecting money from its members, the company continued to meet from time to time in Charles Town. On February 10 it selected the following officers: Benjamin F. Washington, president; Robert H. Keeling, first commander; Smith Crane, second commander; Joseph E. N. Lewis, third commander; Edward M. Aisquith, treasurer; Nathaniel Seevers, quartermaster; J. Harrison Kelly, secretary; and Dr. Wake Bryarly of Baltimore, surgeon.

THE EVENTFUL FORTIES 95

At the same time an effort was made to organize a company in Harpers Ferry. The number of persons in this group was not limited, as each member was to go on his "own hook". That is, there was to be no common pool, but each was to provide his equipment and supplies. From 500 to 800 adventurers were expected to go, and each was to pay ten dollars to a Colonel Whiting, who would act as guide. Whiting had been a Texas Ranger and his services were considered indispensable. His Harpers Ferry agent was George H. Furtney, who assured prospective members that the total individual cost would be unlikely to exceed $200. No additional information about this group was discovered.[16]

At a meeting of the Charles Town company held on March 3 at Sappington's Hotel the last payment of $190 was made. It was decided to increase the membership to seventy-five exclusive of the surgeon, and to set Tuesday, March 27, as the day of departure. The committee to purchase mules was to leave on March 6 and the one to procure wagons, on March 13.

True to schedule, the company left Charles Town on March 27. The route led through Cumberland and Brownville, Pennsylvania, to Pittsburgh, which was reached three days later. Cincinnati, Cairo, St. Louis, and St. Joseph, were passed in turn, and the long journey of 2,105 miles loomed before the adventurers.

A letter dated May 25 written 250 miles west of St. Joseph by one of the group reveals interesting facts. The men feared Indian attacks but up to that time had been unmolested. For a period of two weeks half of them had been sick, but at the time of this writing all had recovered except one. He was Joseph C. Young, of Poolesville, Maryland, who died on May 22 and was buried near Little Timber Creek. The writer does not give additional information concerning the place of burial. Several of the company had had narrow escapes from death. Noble Herbert's team had run off and thrown him under the front axle-tree. After holding on for a minute, he had let go, and one of the wheels had passed over his hair but did not touch his head. The writer described this incident as "a hair-breath escape".[17]

Other near-catastrophes were narrowly averted. When one of Daniel Fagan's mules became frightened and caused the saddle to turn, his team ran away and his foot became fastened in the stirrup. He was dragged thirty yards before the mules could be stopped. By a miraculous stroke of luck Fagan was not even bruised. A runaway team belonging to W. J. Burwell upset its passengers, Edward M. Aisquith and Thomas C. Moore, on the contents of the wagon, soft and greasy bacon.

The distance covered each day depended on the terrain and varied from 12 to 28 miles. The average was about 20 miles a day. Many other wagon trains, a large majority of which were headed west, were seen.

The company arrived at Sacramento in due time. Then several of its members went to San Francisco to obtain provisions which had been sent by sea. About this time by almost unanimous vote it decided to disband. Thereupon, the remaining money was divided equally among the survivors. Five, Thomas Washington, Joseph Young, Thomas Milton, James Davidson, and Noah Tavener, had died on the trip across the continent.

Before long many of the prospectors had spent all their money and set out to mine in small parties. Some of the men were fortunate enough to get the object of their hazardous journey, but many did not obtain the precious metal. After various adventures, too numerous and detailed to describe here, the remnants of the company returned home.[18]

NEWSPAPERS.

On July 17, 1844, appeared the first issue of the **Spirit of Jefferson**, a weekly newspaper established at Charles Town by James W. Beller. Except for the Civil War period, it has been published continuously since its first number came from the press, and today it is one of West Virginia's oldest newspapers. From the first it has supported the Democratic party.

The Shepherdstown Register was founded on December 4, 1849, when John H. Zittle edited the first issue.[19] For many years the paper was published by Harry L. Snyder. At his death his son, William B. Snyder, succeeded to the editorship and continues publication.

CHAPTER NINE
ANTE BELLUM DAYS, 1850-1861
CENSUS OF 1850.

In 1850 Jefferson County had a population of 15,357, consisting of 10,476 whites, 4,341 slaves, and 540 free Negroes. Harpers Ferry with 1,747 inhabitants continued to be the largest town, and Shepherdstown with 1,561 was still second. Charles Town had grown to 1,507 for a gain of 373 over 1840. Bolivar had almost doubled its population in the preceding decade, as it now had 1,054 compared to 536 in 1840. The general increase extended even to Middleway which boasted 446 residents in 1850, whereas ten years before it had only 350.[1]

In regard to social statistics, the county real estate was valued at $6,139,225 and personal property at $4,000,000, for a total valuation of $10,139,225. There were twenty-seven public schools, three private boarding schools, two male academies, and two female academies. The number of pupils attending all these places of learning totaled 1,165, and 1,000 of them were in public schools.

According to the census, three newspapers, the Whig Virginia Free Press, the Democratic Spirit of Jefferson, and the "neutral" Shepherdstown Register kept their 2,600 subscribers enlightened as to the course of events. In the number of churches the Methodists had six; the Presbyterians four; the Episcopalians three; and the Lutherans, Baptist, German Reformed, and Roman Catholic, one each. In addition, there were three Union churches. According to the report, no criminals were convicted during the preceding year. Laborers received 75 cents a day with board, or $1.00 without. A carpenter was paid $1.25 per day without board. The price of board to laboring men was $2.00 a week.[2]

POLITICS.

At the beginning of this decade, Jefferson County, like other parts of western Virginia, was influenced by questions of larger western representation in the General Assembly. Although the constitution of 1830 gave the General Assembly power, after 1841, to reapportion delegates to that body, it had failed to do so at its 1841-1842 meeting. Consequently, western Virginia remained greatly dissatisfied with the arrangement whereby the eastern portions continued to send more representatives to Richmond than they deserved, in proportion to population. Western Virginia, which included the Shenandoah Valley, with a total white population of 271,000, had thirteen senators and fifty-six delegates in the General Assembly, whereas the eastern part, with only 269,000 whites, had nineteen senators and seventy-eight delegates. The western part of the state favored the white basis, that is, representation proportioned to the number of white inhabitants only. The eastern region wanted representation to be determined on a mixed basis, that is, according to the number of white persons and slaves. As the easterners had large numbers of Negroes and the westerners comparatively few, representation on a mixed basis gave the former a big advantage.[3]

Throughout the decade of the forties eastern Virginia was able to defeat attempts to hold a constitutional convention. Not until that section realized it could control such a gathering did it resolve to hold one. Finally, it was proposed to hold a convention to meet on October 14, 1850, and Jefferson County proceeded to select delegates. In the election held on August 22 the people were presented with one slate of candidates favoring the white basis and another favoring representation on a mixed basis. The result showed an approximate majority of two to one for the white basis candidates, William Lucas and Andrew Hunter.[4]

Notwithstanding the fact that delegates to the convention met on October 14, they were unable to begin work because census data were not available. Accordingly, they adjourned to assemble on January 6, 1851. After many disputes on the basis of representation they finally effected a compromise. Representation in the House of Delegates was apportioned arbitrarily but approximately on the white basis of the census of 1850, and that in the

Senate was fixed arbitrarily so that the east obtained thirty senators and the west only twenty.

The west was pleased with the new constitution because of a provision which gave the Assembly power to reapportion representation in both branches upon the white basis in 1865 or thereafter by a referendum. If the lawmakers failed to act, the Governor was required at that time to submit the question of white or mixed basis to a popular referendum.

In return for these concessions, the east received constitutional guarantees which later proved to be as objectionable to the west as the basis of representation had been. A tax equivalent to that on land valued at $300 might be assessed on each slave over twelve years of age. Younger slaves were to be exempt from taxation. All property was assessed on its full and actual value except Negro slaves. The western farmer was thus taxed on the full value of his livestock, regardless of age, but the slaveowner paid no tax on his young Negroes and on other slaves only a tax based on a fixed value below the average market price. Among other provisions of the new constitution were the extension of suffrage to all males over twenty-one years of age and popular election of state and county officers.[5]

Because of the changes wrought by the new constitution, its ratification was effected with little or no opposition. At the election in Jefferson County held in October, 1851, the vote was 1,003 for ratification, and 67 against. At the same time the Whig party in the county continued to poll more votes than the Democratic organization. In the Presidential election of 1852 the Whig nominee, General Winfield Scott, led General Franklin Pierce, the Democrat, by 58 votes.[6]

In the Presidential election of 1856 dissension among the old Jefferson County Whigs threatened to disrupt the party. It had declined nationally and in 1855 many of its erstwhile supporters had changed to the American, or Know-Nothing, party. With the exception of the House of Delegates seats, this newly formed group carried the county in the elections of 1855. Many Old Line Whigs who did not favor Millard Fillmore in 1856 voted for James Buchanan. The exact figures for the result in the county are lacking, but Buchanan defeated his opponent by a small majority. In the state election of 1857 the Democrats were again successful.[7]

As the election of 1859 approached there was much political excitement. Ill-feeling between the North and South over the slavery question dominated local as well as national politics. Party labels were, however, somewhat confusing. The Democratic state ticket carried the county, but one Democrat, Colonel John T. Gibson, and one of the opposition party, John J. Locke, were chosen for the House of Delegates. In the Congressional contest Alexander R. Boteler of Jefferson County, an Independent, defeated his Democratic opponent, Charles J. Faulkner, 1,012 to 740. Incidentally, Boteler also won in the district with a vote of 6,619 to 6,450 for Faulkner.[8]

The Presidential election of 1860 found the county hopelessly divided. Support of Lincoln's candidacy was out of the question, for he had declared that the Government could not endure permanently half slave and half free. His views in opposition to slavery extension were too well-known and there were too many slaveowners in the county to expect them to vote for a man with such opinions. The Northern Democrats nominated Stephen A. Douglas, but his repudiation of the Dred Scott decision caused him to lose Southern support. Then, too, he had broken with Buchanan on the troublesome Kansas question. Finally, the candidacy of the Southern Democratic nominee, John C. Breckinridge, was unacceptable because of his views on secession. Up to that time Jefferson County had been a staunch supporter of the Union.

Since all three of the leading candidates were unacceptable to Jefferson County voters, there was but one alternative. It was to support the fourth nominee, John Bell. He had been chosen by the Constitutional Union party, a compromise organization composed mostly of Southern Whigs and Know-Nothings. Bell sought to avoid the slavery issue and ran on a platform committed to "the maintenance of the Union and the Constitution and the enforcement of the laws".

As a result of these conditions, the vote was Bell, 959, Breckinridge 458, Douglas 440, Lincoln 0. With the exception of industrialized Harpers Ferry, which voted for Douglas, every precinct in the county showed a majority for the Constitutional Union nominee. In view of the fact that Buchanan had carried the county in 1856 the Bell vote was significant. In spite of their

Southern ties and sympathies, the people of Jefferson County could not support the secessionist Breckinridge.[9]

SECESSION.

The strong sentiment for the preservation of the Union had thus been expressed on two separate occasions. In 1833, it will be recalled, the people of Jefferson County had manifested approval of President Jackson's firm stand against South Carolina's nullification procedure. This position had been reiterated by the county's voters in the Presidential election of 1860. Subsequent events gave added support to the contention that there was a very strong Union feeling in the county.

Three days before South Carolina passed her Secession Ordinance residents of Jefferson County on December 17, 1860, assembled for a mass meeting at the courthouse. Members of all political beliefs there joined in approval of a resolution which instructed their delegates to the General Assembly to support the proposed state convention. The General Assembly voted to call a convention to meet in Richmond on February 13. Delegates were to be chosen on February 4, at which time the voters were to determine for themselves whether or not important decisions of the convention would be final.[10]

The voters of Jefferson County took interest in the selection of delegates. Party lines were down and the chief issue was whether Union men or secessionists would be chosen. The overwhelming support given to those favoring preservation of the Union showed clearly how the citizens felt toward secession. Alfred M. Barbour, a former lawyer from Monongalia County, and Logan Osburn, the Union Conservative candidates, received 1,433 and 1,350 votes, respectively, while their States' rights opponents, Andrew Hunter and William Lucas, obtained 467 and 430. Thus Jefferson County sent two men to Richmond pledged to vote against secession. At the same time the proposed referendum was approved by the electorate by a vote of 1,424 for, to 394 against it.[11]

For the first few weeks of the Convention it looked as if Virginia might be saved for the Union. Of the 152 delegates elected, about 120 were opposed to secession at that time and about fifty of them were against it at any time. The outright secessionist strength was only about thirty persons, most of whom came from the Piedmont and Tidewater regions. At the other extreme, there were about fifty Unionist delegates, and most of them came from the Trans-Allegheny and Valley counties. The largest group, the moderates, came from the Valley and the upper Piedmont and Potomac counties. As they numbered about seventy they held the balance of power. In spite of efforts made by "fire-eaters" and radical Southerners, a Secession Ordinance was rejected on April 4 by the decisive vote of 85 to 45.[12]

Following President Lincoln's decision to relieve Fort Sumter, events favorable to secession moved rapidly. On April 12 the Confederates under General P. G. T. Beauregard opened fire on the fort. Three days later Lincoln issued a call for 75,000 volunteers to bring the Southern Confederacy to terms. Two days later, on April 17, the Virginia Convention adopted a Secession Ordinance by a vote of 88 for, to 55 against. The ordinance was to be effective when ratified by the people in their regular spring election, which came that year on May 23.

One of Jefferson's delegates at Richmond, Logan Osburn, remained true to his constituents and voted against secession, whereas the other, Alfred M. Barbour, did not vote at all. Barbour later signed the Secession Ordinance.

Meanwhile the Union sentiment in Jefferson County gave way to loyalty to Virginia, first and foremost. States' rights was too deeply bred in the hearts of the people to stand up before their second love, the Union. They loved the Union, but they could not fight against their own people. The thought of Federal troops crossing Virginia to coerce a sister state was also more than they could comprehend. State militia had already moved into the county and had captured the Government armory at Harpers Ferry.

Consequently, the local results of the referendum of May 23 on the Secession Ordinance were not surprising. The county approved the ordinance by a vote of 813 for, to 365 against.[13] The small size of the vote, in comparison with the Presidential vote of 1860, was supposedly due to the fact that many of the able-bodied men had joined the Southern army.

This change of attitude on the part of Jefferson's residents may best be explained by the words of Logan Osburn, one of its delegates to the Virginia Convention. In a statement to the newspaper press on June 13, he said:

> Gentlemen:—As I am about returning to Richmond, to resume my seat in the Convention, it may not be improper to give publicity to my present position.
> When I was a candidate for a seat in the Convention, I denied (in a Card which I published) the constitutional right of a state to secede from the Union; and regarded a resort to secession as a dangerous exercise of a very doubtful power, that could only be justified after every constitutional means had been exhausted, and failed. In conformity to those opinions, I have earnestly, (and perhaps obstinately) opposed the secession of Virginia.
> I voted against its ratification by the people. I regarded it as mischievous in its tendency and destructive in its consequences, to all our best interests, socially, politically, and commercially. My opposition was honestly entertained and frankly expressed. But my opinions have been overruled by a large majority of the freemen of my state. I therefore bow (from a sense of patriotic and public duty) in humble submission to their will, and acquiesce in their decision. My lot has been cast. I am a son of Virginia, and her destiny shall be mine. I will return to the Convention to aid in faithfully carrying out the provisions of the Ordinance, and to co-operate in all measures calculated, in my opinion, to bring our present difficulties to a successful termination.
> With great respect, I remain your friend, &c.
> Logan Osburn.[14]

HARPERS FERRY ARMORY AND ARSENAL.

The question of civil or military superintendents at the Harpers Ferry Armory and Arsenal was still causing trouble. The military group remained in control and continued its practices, much to the dissatisfaction of the workers. Colonel Benjamin Huger, later a Confederate general, succeeded Major John Symington as superintendent in 1851. During that year $252,088.69 was spent at Harpers Ferry, and 11,100 percussion muskets, along with 3,050 percussion rifles, were produced. In 1852 many of the employees at the plant bought their homes from the Federal Government. At the same time the United States made donations of land for religious, educational, and municipal purposes.[15]

The United States Armory at Harpers Ferry in 1857

ANTE BELLUM DAYS, 1850–1861

Largely through the efforts of Charles James Faulkner, Congressman from this district, a bill was introduced in the House of Representatives providing for the abolition of military superintendents at the national armories after July 1, 1854. The House Committee on Military Affairs in 1852 reported in favor of the change and cited a number of reasons why it was desirable. A select committee of the House made additional investigations and came to the same conclusion two years later.

Meanwhile, in March, 1854, a certain Major Bell was sent by the Ordnance Department to replace Colonel Huger in the superintendency. Faulkner continued the fight in the House and finally was rewarded with the passage of a bill reestablishing the civil superintendents. Although it passed the House with a majority of seventy votes, it obtained a majority of only two in the Senate. President Pierce's signature was soon forthcoming, and in January, 1855, Henry W. Clowe, a worthy mechanic, became the new civil superintendent. The appointment of a fellow-workman was of course gratifying to the laborers.[16]

In 1858, another change was made in the superintendency. That year Henry W. Clowe quarreled with the district's representative in Congress and was removed from office. His successor was Alfred M. Barbour, who was in charge when the armory was destroyed early in the Civil War.[17]

CHURCHES AND SCHOOLS.

In the summer of 1856 members of the Zoar Baptist Church changed their place of worship to the county seat and thus established the Charles Town Baptist Church. For a time after the removal to town they met in the brick schoolhouse but later held their services in the courthouse. Purchase of the entire block in which the present church stands was made in April, 1857, and a two-story brick building was begun. The lower room was first used in 1859, but the structure remained unfinished until after the Civil War. Dr. J. A. Haynes was pastor from August, 1856, to September 2, 1860, when he was succeeded by T. R. Shepherd.[18]

Another church building that had its beginning at this time was the one erected by the Uvilla Lutherans, the cornerstone of which was laid on August 28, 1856. Prior thereto, on June 4, a meeting was held in the union schoolhouse, where it was decided to erect a church at what was then called Unionville. The new structure was to be named Luther Chapel. Its building committee consisted of George Licklider, Adam Link, and John Ronemus, but they were forbidden to incur a debt in excess of $200 beyond the total subscriptions. The Rev. S. Smeltzer was pastor at that time.[19]

Jefferson County's free school system was subjected to a serious attack in 1856. For some time evidence of increasing dissatisfaction was noticeable, particularly in the Shepherdstown vicinity. In 1850 residents of that locality petitioned the Virginia General Assembly for financial aid to construct a building to house the revived Shepherdstown Academy. In the request they claimed that they furnished annually to the free school system about twice as much as was spent to maintain it in their town. Upon receipt of a petition from a fourth of the white male citizens, County Clerk Thomas A. Moore advertised that an election on the question of free schools would be held on the fourth Thursday in May, 1856. Some of the objections to the existing system were reputed mismanagement of commissioners, employment of incompetent teachers, improper use of school funds, and the fact that it was unjust to make one man pay for the education of another's children.

The friends of free public education rallied at the polls and won a decisive victory. All of the eight districts in the county favored the new system by a total vote of 975 for, to 202 against. The large majority showed that the people had changed considerably since 1848 in regard to their support of free schools, for at that time they were somewhat apprehensive of its success. They had previously voted 554 for, to 167 against, on the question.[20]

In this period of public school beginnings the first requisite of a teacher was that he be a disciplinarian. No pupil taught at public expense was expected to like school, and compulsion was considered the key to learning. Punishment was meted out to those who would not, or could not, learn their lessons. The following picture of an old-time schoolmaster, Peter Smith, who lived near Opequon Creek, is typical of that day and age:

Peter Smith is represented as having been a man of medium height, of a nervous temperament and of a thin and wiry physical make-up. . . . In directing his school he was a thoroughgoing autocrat. An unnecessary cough or a spit ball was a heinous offense. Indifference or inattention to school work was sufficient to evoke Smith's wrath. Once an assignment had been made it must be recited verbatim. His moods could never be foretold. With rod in hand he imposed the discipline of his school. Many of his pupils learned to prefer the school of experience to things academic. Conspiracies were often fomented against him by the older boys. But Peter had a genius for apprehending malefactors before mischief got under way. It made little difference who was punished so long as vengeance was done. . . .[21]

In spite of the progress made in developing a free public school system, it was some time before the academies lost their influence completely. Consequently, it is not surprising that the private schools continued in existence. On August 12, 1858, the **Virginia Free Press** carried an advertisement by J. P. Smeltzer and Webster Eichelberger announcing the opening of "Fairview High School" at Bolivar on September 2. Instruction was offered both sexes in modern and ancient geography, English grammar, mathematics, natural, moral, and mental philosophy, anatomy, chemistry, Greek, and Latin.

ATTEMPT TO DIVIDE THE COUNTY.

Near the close of this period Jefferson County was threatened with a division of its territory. On February 6, 1858, residents of the southern part of the county petitioned the General Assembly to change the boundary line so as to include them within the limits of Clarke County. They listed many reasons for such a change. They stated that they were nearer the courthouse of Clarke, in Berryville, than the one in Jefferson and that the roads leading to the Clarke County seat were macadamized, whereas those to Charles Town were "acceptable to very few of us". It was also pointed out that most of the petitioners worshipped in Clarke County, business calls were more frequent there, and their social relations were confined almost exclusively to it. Finally, they stated that because Clarke County was so small, it was desirable to increase its territory and population.

The proposed line of division was as follows: "Beginning in the road between the lands of Paul Smith and William A. Riely;—thence along the road towards Rippon, until it strikes the county road between Berryville and Charlestown;—thence a straight course to McPherson's Mill branch at the cross roads just below the mill—thence along said branch to its junction with the Shenandoah river;—and thence due east to the top of the Blue Ridge." Roughly speaking, this was a line from the headspring of Bullskin Run, south of Summit Point, to Rippon, then southeast to Longmarsh Run, following this stream to the Shenandoah River near Rock's Ferry, and due east to the top of the Blue Ridge Mountains. The petitioners were Hugh N. Pendleton, Thomas M. Isbell, Arthur M. Allen, Gordon H. Pendleton, John Rabb, H. W. Castleman, Mrs. Martha N. Davis, James B. Lewis, R. Hume Butcher, I. I. Williams, Amos Shepherd, and Edwin Hart.[22] An advance notice of the petition was posted at the front door of the courthouse in Charles Town in the first days of the November and December [1857] County Court term.

As soon as residents of the rest of the county learned of the contemplated dismemberment, they prepared to defeat it. For that purpose, they circulated a counter-petition, dated February 8, 1858, in which they stated opposite views. Among other things, they emphasized that when Clarke was formed it was known to be smaller than Jefferson. If it was too small, it could have been made larger then at the expense of Frederick, the mother county. The petitioners stated further that the proposed division, if consummated, would place the county seat of Jefferson, Charles Town, in one extreme of the county and hence it might justly be moved to a more central location.

These petitioners claimed also that reduction in the size of Jefferson County would make the tax burden upon the remaining part excessive. Apparently, taxes in Jefferson at that time were much higher than in Clarke. The concluding words of the petition offered the following solution to the tax burden: "It might be wise carefully to enquire into the propriety of turning over all Jefferson County into Clarke and thus ease ourselves of the free school tax and the tax for the support of the court and its officers and of the name of Jefferson". Although the annexation bill was reported, it was not acted upon by the House of Delegates.[23]

CHAPTER TEN
THE JOHN BROWN RAID

JOHN EDWIN COOK.

On the fifth of June, 1858, a stoop-shouldered, fair-haired, blue-eyed, young man of twenty-eight years alighted from a train at Harpers Ferry. He was a person of pleasing address and intelligent appearance. He gazed for a short time at the beautiful view before him and then directed his steps to the widow Kennedy's boardinghouse located on a quiet street not far from the United States Armory and Arsenal.[1]

The stranger was John Edwin Cook, a native of Connecticut. He was of good family, had studied law, and after a series of adventures had met John Brown in Kansas. Brown selected Cook as his advance agent to go to Harpers Ferry and spy on the land to determine when conditions were ripe for his contemplated slave insurrection.

Cook made his residence at the Kennedy boardinghouse and laid his plans. As Brown wished to know the number and location of all slaves within a radius of eight to ten miles of Harpers Ferry, it was necessary for Cook to obtain this firsthand information. This he got by posing as a book agent, historian, and prospector at various times and visiting the neighboring farmers. He also taught school for a while. With true Southern hospitality some of the people invited the attractive Northerner to share a meal with them. Little did they suspect that he was at the same time plotting to arm their slaves for rebellion.

Cook's well-laid plans suffered one setback. Mrs. Kennedy had an attractive daughter, named Mary Virginia, who came home from boarding school shortly after Cook came to the Ferry. In spite of his efforts to the contrary, Cook found himself falling desperately in love with the Southern girl. He realized that such a course might seriously interfere with his plans, but he could not get Virginia Kennedy out of his thoughts. Virginia, too, was attracted to the young Northerner, and on April 27, 1859, they were married. Cook kept his great secret from his bride, and, though she realized something was troubling him, she did not press him for enlightenment.[2]

Brown had instructed Cook to become acquainted with Colonel Lewis Washington of "Beall Air", near Halltown, about four miles west of Harpers Ferry near the Charles Town road. Washington was a great, great nephew of the illustrious George and possessed two trophies that Brown himself desired. One was a sword presented by Frederick the Great to General Washington with the message engraved on the blade, "From the oldest General in the world to the Greatest." The other was a brace of pistols given Washington by General Lafayette. For some strange reason, which perhaps as much as anything else reflected his deranged state of mind, Brown wanted these trophies to use in another struggle for liberty.

Several months before the attempted raid Cook met Colonel Washington in south Bolivar. The stranger introduced himself and asked about the relics. A request to be allowed to see them and also to engage Washington in a pistol-shooting contest was readily granted, but for a while Cook did not put in his appearance. Then, one day in September, 1859, he visited "Beall Air", partook of his host's hospitality, and made careful notes regarding the relics and slaves on the premises.[3]

OSAWATOMIE BROWN.

Meanwhile, another mysterious stranger had come to the vicinity. On July 3, 1859, an old man of venerable appearance, accompanied by three young men, alighted from a train at Harpers Ferry. After some inquiries the group went to Sandy Hook, a small Maryland village about a mile down the Potomac River, and engaged lodging with Ormond Butler. In reply to questions about themselves, they stated that they were prospecting for minerals believed to exist in the neighborhood of Maryland Heights. The old man introduced himself as Isaac Smith and his three companions as his sons.

The old man in this party was none other than John Brown, a

Beall Air, the Home of Colonel Lewis Washington, near Halltown

fanatical Abolitionist. Two of his companions were his sons, Oliver and Owen; the third was Jeremiah G. Anderson. Brown was born at Torrington, Connecticut, on May 9, 1800, of a prominent New England family. His father moved to Ohio when the boy was five years old and John grew to manhood at what is now Hudson in that state. He planned to enter the ministry but gave up this idea in favor of working in a tannery. He became interested in the abolition movement in 1835, and when several of his sons went to Kansas in 1855 Brown followed. He took an active part in the Kansas controversy, and in addition to helping slaves escape he began a career of murder and robbery.[4]

Probably the most despicable of his acts was that committed along Pottawatomie Creek on the night of May 24, 1856. With seven other men, including two of his sons, Brown then and there had his followers call from bed and kill three members of the Doyle family, John, William, and Drury. Nothing but the frantic pleas of the mother saved her youngest son, Johnny, a lad of fourteen years. Two other victims, Henry Wilkinson and William Sherman, were captured by ruse and quickly dispatched.

None of these men owned slaves. None had done any harm to Brown. None had offered any resistance. They were only Southerners who had moved to Kansas to establish new homes. The elder Doyle was killed because he would not claim the Negro as his equal. His two sons were dispatched because they had not reached their majority and hence were presumed to have their father's opinions. Wilkinson was a member of the Kansas Legislature opposed to the Free Soil Party. Sherman was a brother of Henry Sherman, the most hated proslavery member of the settlement.[5]

Brown not only had these men killed, but he also robbed them and took, among other things, several horses. It was not until three months later that the proslavery forces attacked Brown's camp at Osawatomie and killed his son, Frederick. Prior to his arrival at Sandy Hook he had conducted a raid into Missouri, which resulted in freeing slaves, stealing property, and killing a man named David Cruise. As a consequence of this latest outrage, President James Buchanan offered a reward of $250 for the arrest of Brown. The Governor of Missouri raised the amount to $3,000. Such, in brief, is the background of the apparently harmless Isaac

THE JOHN BROWN RAID

Smith, who was preparing to strike at Harpers Ferry.[6]

Since his outrages in Kansas Brown had changed his appearance by allowing his beard to grow. Thus he was rather effectively disguised for his proposed work. Further to disguise his plans and purposes he rented a farm belonging to the heirs of Dr. Booth Kennedy. This property was located in Maryland, about five miles east of Harpers Ferry, near Sample's Manor, and was known as the "Kennedy Farm". As it had an isolated location, it was ideally situated for Brown's purposes. The new tenants moved in and, to all appearances, were engaged in prospecting throughout the countryside.

Shortly mysterious boxes began to arrive. The credulous farmers were told that these contained tools necessary for the location of minerals. In order to allay suspicion, Brown opened an office at Chambersburg, Pennsylvania, where supplies were received by rail and then hauled by wagons to his retreat. Other points in the vicinity likewise served as places of deposit and removal, and on one occasion Henry Kyd Douglas of Shepherdstown, later famous as Stonewall Jackson's youngest staff member in the Civil War, assisted in transporting Brown's "tools".[7]

The boxes were taken to the Kennedy farm, where they were found to contain Sharp's rifles, pistols, pikes, and other supplies. Of all, these pikes, sharp blades fastened to the end of six-foot poles, were perhaps most prized by Brown, because ignorant Negroes who could not understand the mechanism of a firearm could use quite effectively the simpler weapon. These and other arms were accumulated at the farm in considerable quantities.[8]

In August, 1859, Secretary of War John B. Floyd received an anonymous letter from Cincinnati, Ohio, in which the writer apprised him of the existence of a secret association to liberate slaves in the South by a general insurrection. "Old John Brown" of Kansas was referred to as the leader. The rendezvous of the raiders was declared to be in the mountains of Virginia, and it was said the state would be entered at Harpers Ferry. The writer gave additional information that Brown had already left the North and would strike within a few weeks. He concluded his message by warning the Secretary of War that arms were already being distributed.[9]

Floyd doubtless considered this letter too fantastic for reality as there is no record of his having paid any attention to it.

In the meantime, Brown had been assembling his men. As it would not do for too many to be seen by the prying eyes of curious neighbors, he kept most of his followers indoors in the loft of the farmhouse. Twenty men, five of whom were Negroes, comprised the band. Work of the household was done by the leader's daughter, Annie, and his son Oliver's wife. All the cooking, washing, and scrubbing for the entire group was done without a complaint by these two faithful women.

ATTACK ON HARPERS FERRY.

Finally, the time for action arrived. Events had been planned to the last detail. Cook had met his leader from time to time and had furnished information obtained while he was traversing the country as a book-agent. Maps of the vicinity were drawn and carefully studied. The number of slaves on each neighboring plantation, the names of their owners, and other pertinent information were in the hands of the raiders.

As a consequence, Brown did not have the slightest doubt that the ignorant Negroes in the neighborhood would hail him as a savior and would rally around his banner. He had a thousand pikes with which to arm them. He had even organized a provisional government with himself as commander in chief of the armies and had adopted a constitution.

All of this had been accomplished without arousing the suspicions of any of the inhabitants of the peaceful town of Harpers Ferry. Their position was comparable to that of lambs grazing contentedly while the hungry wolf licked his chops in anticipation of pouncing upon his unsuspecting prey.

About eight o'clock on Sunday night, October 16, 1859, Brown and eighteen of his men left the farmhouse for Harpers Ferry. Three others, Owen Brown, Barclay Coppoc [or Coppie], and F. J. Merriam, remained behind to guard the headquarters of the raiders. A wagon loaded with crowbars, sledge hammers, pikes, and oil-soaked faggots was driven along the road. All of the men were heavily armed and ready for any emergency.

Brown had picked a good night for his villainous deed, as he

THE JOHN BROWN RAID

had learned that the Methodists were holding revival services at the Ferry and few people would be on the streets.[10]

The first person encountered by the raiders was William Williams, one of the watchmen on the railroad bridge. Before the surprised Williams could gather his senses, he was captured by a group of armed men and taken to the armory enclosure. Another watchman, Daniel Whelan, on duty at the Government plant, was also taken into custody. Part of the raiders remained with the prisoners, while another group went to Hall's Rifle Works and captured its watchman, Samuel Williams, the father of William Williams.

Leaving some of their own men in possession of the rifle works, the remainder of this group brought their prisoner back to the main body. These seizures were made about eleven o'clock and so far everything had taken place as planned. Not a shot had been fired and the raiders were in possession of the armory with its huge supply of arms, the rifle works, and the bridges across the two rivers. The telegraph wires had been cut and communication with the outside world severed.

About an hour later Patrick Higgins of Sandy Hook arrived on the railroad bridge across the Potomac to relieve Williams as watchman. When he was unable to find him, he called, and to his surprise two men confronted him with guns in hand and told him that he was a prisoner. One of the captors endeavored to conduct the prisoner to the armory, but the Irishman struck him a stunning blow with his fist and escaped to Fouke's Hotel. Several shots were fired at the escaped watchman, but none took effect.[11]

The express from Wheeling thundered into Harpers Ferry at midnight and was immediately stopped on the bridge by armed men. Conductor Phelps contacted the leader of the raiders, talked with him, and finally succeeded in having his train released at five o'clock. Phelps supposed that the arches or timbers of the wooden bridge had been cut and hence he was at first afraid to cross the Potomac. He gave the order, though, and the train moved slowly away. It reached Baltimore at twelve o'clock noon.

During this delay the passengers had remained in their seats, too frightened to move. A free Negro porter, Hayward Shepherd, employed by the railroad, walked to the bridge some time in the night and was ordered by the guards to halt. Shepherd was seized with a panic and did not stop. The resulting shot entered his body and caused his death the following day. Thus the first person killed in John Brown's raid was an innocent Negro porter.[12]

Meanwhile, Brown had sent a detachment into the country to capture prominent persons as hostages. One of these, Colonel Lewis Washington, was taken, along with several of his slaves. From his home were also brought the famous sword and pistols which Brown desired for moral effect. Then, about three o'clock in the morning the raiders went to the home of John Allstadt and made him prisoner, together with his eighteen-year old son and the Allstadt slaves.

These prisoners were brought in a wagon to the armory, where they met the leader of their captors. He introduced himself as "Osawatomie Brown of Kansas" and then arming his prisoners' slaves with pikes, he told them to stand guard over their masters.

A short while before daylight James Darrell, the bellringer at the armory, appeared on the scene and was captured. As the armorers came to work they, too, were surprised and made prisoners. Another local resident taken in the same manner was George W. Cutshaw, who had just escorted a lady across the river to a canal packet boat. About seven o'clock firing broke out between residents of the town and the raiders, and it soon became unsafe for anyone to appear on the streets. Thomas Boerly approached the corner of High and Shenandoah streets and discharged his gun at the raiders near the arsenal gate, when one of them crouching behind the arsenal fence shot him. The bullet inflicted a ghastly wound in his groin and he died a few hours later, the first white person killed by the invaders.[13]

News of the attack soon spread throughout the neighborhood. Before long companies of Virginia militia from Charles Town, Shepherdstown, Martinsburg, and Winchester were on the march to aid their friends whose homes were menaced. The Jefferson Guards of Charles Town, 100 strong, left the county seat at nine-thirty under command of Colonel John T. Gibson, assisted by Captain John W. Rowan. When they arrived at the scene, it was decided that they should cross the Potomac and take possession

THE JOHN BROWN RAID

of the bridge and thus cut off retreat of the invaders. After successfully accomplishing this, the Guards maintained a position around the armory wall. Captain Vincent Moore Butler arrived on the scene shortly afterwards with his crack company, the Hamtramck Guards, from Shepherdstown. Colonel Robert Baylor assumed command of the Jefferson volunteers and organized them into a battalion.[14]

In their search for arms citizens suddenly recalled that Government weapons had been removed from the armory to a safer place when danger of high water had threatened their ruin. The raiders did not know about these guns. With them the Virginians kept up a desultory fire all day Monday.

One militia company under Captain Henry Medler crossed the Shenandoah River and took position on the east side of that stream, opposite Hall's Rifle Works. Another group, under Captain Hezekiah Roderick, posted itself on the Baltimore and Ohio Railroad, northwest of the armory. These two organizations, with the help of persons who had taken possession of the Potomac bridge, had the insurgents completely surrounded in the armory. An attack on the rifle works was successful and the raiders there were driven into the Shenandoah, where they were exposed to the fire of Medler's men. All were soon killed except one, a Negro named John Copeland, who was captured.[15]

The main fight on Monday took place around the armory, where Brown commanded in person. He had expected reinforcements, and when a group appeared on the Maryland end of the bridge, he thought it was coming to rescue him. Realizing his mistake, Brown sent two prisoners, Archibald M. Kitzmiller and Rezin Cross, accompanied by two guards, to negotiate a truce.

Brown wished to retire, unmolested, across the Potomac. However, shots from the Gault House wounded both of these guards. One made his way to the armory, and the other, assisted by Kitzmiller and Cross, was taken to Fouke's Hotel, where his wounds were dressed. When Brown realized he would not be allowed to retire across the Potomac, he selected nine prominent prisoners as hostages and then withdrew into a small brick building, known as the fire engine house of the armory. The other captives remained in the armory guardhouse.

A short time before Brown retired to the engine house

another citizen, George W. Turner, was killed. He had come to town on private business and was passing down High Street, when a bullet from a Sharp's rifle struck him in the breast. Turner, a graduate of West Point, was one of the county's most prominent residents. He was the second white victim of the invaders' rifles. The third casualty was Fontaine Beckham, who was killed along the railroad, near a watering station. Being at the time mayor of Harpers Ferry, a county magistrate, and station agent for the Baltimore and Ohio, he, too, was a prominent person. Beckham's death so infuriated the civilians that they seized a prisoner, Thompson, and riddled his body with bullets. Miss Christina Fouke endeavored to save him but was unsuccessful.[16]

About three o'clock on Monday afternoon a party led by Captain E. G. Alburtis of Martinsburg attacked the raiders from the west end of the armory yard. They succeeded in releasing most of the prisoners from the guardhouse, but the attackers did not escape unscathed. They were subjected to a galling fire from portholes in the brick walls of the engine house. Among the casualties in this engagement were Samuel C. Young of Charles Town and Edward McCabe of Harpers Ferry. Young received a severe wound in the breast, which shattered his left arm, and McCabe was shot in the shoulder.[17]

William H. Leeman, one of Brown's men, tried to escape from the armory grounds by swimming or wading the Potomac. His intention was soon discovered, and he drew the fire from a group on a nearby hill. Wounded, perhaps to the point of death, he took refuge on a rock in the river. When a pursuer came upon him, he threw up his hands and pleaded, "Don't shoot!" The reply was a rifle shot, and Leeman fell into the water with his face blown away.[18]

On Leeman's person was found a captain's commission dated October 15, 1859, and signed by "John Brown, Commander in Chief" and "H. Kagi, Secretary of War" of Brown's provisional government. This commission is today a trophy in the residence later built on the site where Brown was hanged.[19]

Brown and his associates had planned to reorganize the United States Government with a new constitution entitled "Provisional Constitution and Ordinances for the People of the United States". This was presented, read, and adopted at a convention held in May,

THE JOHN BROWN RAID

1858, at Chatham, Canada. It provided for an amendment or repeal of the preamble and the principal articles of the Federal Constitution and also for a President, Vice-President, House of Representatives, and Supreme Court, but no Senate.

The following officers were elected to head the new government: John Brown, Commander in Chief; John H. Kagi, Secretary of War; Richard Realf, Secretary of State; George B. Gill, Secretary of the Treasury; Owen Brown, Treasurer; Osborn P. Anderson and Alfred M. Ellsworth, members of Congress. A number of printed copies of the Chatham Constitution were found among Brown's personal possessions at the Kennedy farmhouse. A copy of this document was preserved by Colonel John T. Gibson and is now owned by his daughter, Miss Susan G. Gibson of Charles Town.[20]

Toward evening Brown asked for volunteers from his prisoners to act as messengers to bring an end to the firing, which was endangering the lives of the captives, as well as those of the insurgents. In return, he promised no further firing on the part of his men. Israel Russel agreed to perform this hazardous undertaking, even though his friends on the outside might have mistaken him for one of the raiders and fired on him before he could have proved otherwise.

Like that of Kitzmiller's and Cross's earlier in the day, Russel's mission accomplished nothing but the escape of the emissary, who of course did not return to the armory. About eleven o'clock that night Brown tried to obtain a pledge from Colonel Shriver and Captain Sinn of the Frederick [Md.] troops for the safe conduct of his men and himself across the bridge. Sinn told the insurgent leader that no terms would be granted.[21]

In the meantime, Cook had been carrying out his part of the raid. He had taken leave of his pretty wife Sunday morning and helped lead the invaders in their first march on the Ferry. Then he had been sent across the Potomac bridge with the wagons, horses, and treasures stolen from the home of Colonel Washington. These were to be stored at headquarters. Accompanied by Thompson and Leeman, Cook deposited some of the arms and supplies in a schoolhouse between Harpers Ferry and the Kennedy farm. Along this road the three raiders captured Terrence Byrne, James Byrne, and Linn Curry, a schoolmaster. James Byrne and Curry were soon released, but the third prisoner was taken to Harpers

Ferry by Thompson and Leeman. Looking down from Maryland Heights later, Cook saw Brown's hopeless position, and he, accordingly, escaped temporarily into Pennsylvania.[22]

ATTACK ON THE ENGINE HOUSE.

On Monday while fighting was in progress Conductor Phelps carried word of the raid to Baltimore. Before long Washington authorities were informed. At noon on Monday Chief Clerk Walsh of the Navy Department inquired at the Navy Yard of Lieutenant Israel Green about the number of marines available for immediate duty. Learning that ninety were on hand, Walsh informed Green about the Brown raid. The marines were soon ordered to Harpers Ferry.[23]

Taking with them two howitzers, Green and his men left on the 3:30 train. At Frederick Junction he received a dispatch from Colonel Robert E. Lee, his senior officer, directing him to Sandy Hook, there to await Lee's arrival. At ten o'clock Lee, accompanied by Lieutenant J. E. B. Stuart as volunteer aide, arrived on a special train. From Sandy Hook the marines were ordered to proceed on foot. The armory grounds were entered through a back gate and at eleven o'clock the marines replaced the volunteers and militia within the grounds.

At 6:30 Tuesday morning, October 18, Colonel Lee ordered Green to select a detail of twelve men for a storming party. Choosing twelve more as a reserve, the lieutenant carried out the command. Stuart took a part of the marines to the front of the engine house and demanded Brown's surrender. He was authorized to promise the insurgents protection from the infuriated mob while President Buchanan was consulted. Brown replied with a counter-proposition that he and his men be permitted to come out of the engine house and given the length of the bridge to escape. At a signal from Stuart, followed by an order from Green, the marines assaulted the large doors of the engine house. As they were strongly made, tied on the inside with ropes, and braced with a fire engine, the sledge hammers used to break them down made little impression.[24]

Green then ordered his men to use a nearby ladder as a battering-ram. This was more successful, and in a short time a ragged hole appeared in the lower right-hand door. Green leaped through the opening and ran to the side of the fire engine, where he saw Colonel Washington, who pointed out Brown.

Quick as a flash the marine dealt him a heavy blow with his saber. Brown had just moved and did not receive the blow on his head, as Green had intended, but on the back of his neck. This cut stunned the old man, who fell senseless to the floor. While he was falling, Green gave him a saber thrust in the left breast. The point evidently struck something hard in Brown's clothing, for it did not penetrate but merely bent double. The obstruction is believed to have been the buckle of the belt supporting the sword stolen from Washington.

Although Green came through the engine house door unharmed, Private Luke Quinn, who followed him, was struck by a bullet and mortally wounded. A marine named Rupert received a flesh wound and had several of his upper teeth knocked out. By this time the marines were pouring through the door and making short work of the raiders. Of the latter two were killed instantly. At this juncture Green ordered his men to spill no more blood and they rounded up the remaining insurgents. The fight had not lasted over three minutes.

When the struggle was over, a curious sight presented itself. The prisoners whom Brown had held as hostages were huddled in the rear of the building. With the exception of Colonel Washington, who would not come out until he had covered his soiled hands with kid gloves, they were a pitiful lot. They had not eaten for several hours and were in constant dread of being shot. The bodies of one of Brown's sons and several other slain raiders lay near them. A detail carried Brown outside where he soon recovered consciousness. He was then taken to the paymaster's office and his wounds dressed. The next day, Wednesday, October 19, he was removed to Charles Town, the county seat, and turned over to the civil authorities. As his cuts were only flesh wounds, he recovered rapidly.[25]

Among other prisoners released with Colonel Washington were John Allstadt; Armistead Ball, master machinist of the armory; John E. P. Dangerfield, clerk; Benjamin F. Mills, master armorer; Dr. Murphy, paymaster; and John Donohoo, assistant railroad agent. In addition, there were several slaves who had been forcibly taken from their masters. None of these captives had been harmed during their period of confinement.

The insurgents did not fare so well. Of the twenty-two who comprised the original group, ten had been killed in the fighting, seven were captured, and five escaped. Those who escaped were Owen Brown, Charles P. Tidd, Barclay Coppoc, Francis J. Merriam, whites, and Osborne P. Anderson, Negro. The following persons were killed in the fighting: John H. Kagi, Jeremiah G. Anderson, William Thompson, Dauphin Thompson, Oliver Brown, Watson Brown, Stewart Taylor, William H. Leeman, whites, and Lewis S. Leary and Dangerfield Newby, Negroes. Those captured and taken to Charles Town for trial were: John Brown, Aaron D. Stevens, Edwin Coppoc, Albert Hazlett, and John E. Cook, whites, and John A. Copeland and Shields Green, Negroes. Cook and Hazlett, having escaped into Pennsylvania, were not captured for several days.

As has been noted, there were casualties among the defenders of the town. Hayward Shepherd, Thomas Boerly, George W. Turner, Fontaine Beckham, and Private Luke Quinn were killed. A slave named "Jim" who was hired to Colonel Washington was drowned while swimming the river, and one named "Phil", belonging to John H. Allstadt, died in the Charles Town jail from cold and fright. These two slaves had been captured and held by the raiders. In addition, the following were wounded: Samuel C. Young, Edward McCabe, Evan Dorsey, George H. Murphy, G. N. Hammond, Wilson Hooper, Clinton Bowman, G. W. Richardson, George Wollett, and Private Rupert of the marines.[26]

The greatest surprise to Brown was perhaps the fact that the slaves did not rise against their masters. He was so certain they would do so that he was prepared to arm a large number of them. He believed all that was necessary to repeat Nat Turner's insurrection of 1831 was a leader. To the last, he confidently expected a large band of armed slaves to march to his relief, whereas not a single Negro rose against his master.. Except those who accompanied Brown and those compelled to join him, the Negroes about Harpers Ferry cared as little for him as did the whites.

While on a scouting trip the Independent Grays of Baltimore came upon a schoolhouse about two miles from Harpers Ferry,

THE JOHN BROWN RAID

where Cook had stored arms. Among other things found there were 200 Sharp's rifles, several boxes of revolvers, and 1,000 pikes. Farther on, at the Kennedy farm, they discovered evidences of Cook's hasty departure and found more arms, as well as powder, maps, and miscellaneous articles. Items of special interest were copies of Brown's provisional constitution and letters from prominent Northern Abolitionists, including Gerrit Smith and Frederick Douglass.[27]

For several days following Brown's capture armed civilians scoured the countryside looking for suspects, and some innocent persons were arrested. Among them was G. W. Dilbard of Charlottesville, a stranger to one of the bands, but he was later released. B. C. Wyman of Madison, a delegate to the Presbyterian Synod meeting at Shepherdstown, was also taken into custody and then permitted to go on his way. Most of these unusual happenings ceased when Government authorities collected the rifles belonging to the armory.[28]

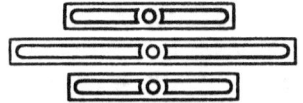

CHAPTER ELEVEN
THE JOHN BROWN TRIAL AND EXECUTION

TRIAL.

Governor Henry A. Wise arrived in Harpers Ferry on October 18 and insisted that the prisoners in the Charles Town jail be tried according to the laws of Virginia. Although much of the fighting had taken place on United States Government property, the question of Federal or state jurisdiction does not seem to have been raised. President Buchanan acquiesced in Wise's request and as the Jefferson County Circuit Court commenced its fall session on October 20, the wheels of justice soon began to revolve.

On October 25 the Magistrates' Court assembled for a preliminary hearing. It was composed of the following justices: Colonel Braxton Davenport, presiding justice; Dr. William F. Alexander, John J. Lock, John F. Smith, Thomas H. Willis, George W. Eichelberger, Charles H. Lewis, and Moses W. Burr. At this hearing were present the white prisoners, John Brown, Aaron D. Stevens, and Edwin Coppoc, and the Negroes, Shields Green and John Copeland.[1]

At ten-thirty o'clock on October 25 Sheriff James W. Campbell conducted the prisoners from the jail to the courthouse. Violence of any sort was prevented by a guard of eighty armed men. The sheriff read the commitment of the prisoners on the charges of treason and murder, after which the state's attorney asked the court to assign them counsel if they had none.

Upon being asked whether or not he had already obtained counsel, Brown replied:

> Virginians:—I did not ask for any quarter at the time I was taken. I did not ask to have myself spared. The Governor of the State of Virginia tendered me his assurance that I should have a fair trial, and under no circumstances whatever will I be able to attend a trial. If you seek my

THE JOHN BROWN TRIAL AND EXECUTION

blood you can have it at any moment without the mockery of a trial.

I have no counsel. I have not been able to advise with one. I know nothing about the feelings of my fellow prisoners, and am utterly unable to attend in any way to my own defence. My memory don't serve me. My health is insufficient, although improving. There are mitigating circumstances, if a fair trial is to be allowed us that I would urge in our favor But if we are to be forced with a mere form of a trial to execution, you might spare yourselves that trouble. I am ready for my fate. I do not ask a trial. I plead for no mockery of a trial—no insult— nothing but that which conscience gives or cowardice would drive you to practice.

I ask to be excused from the mockery of a trial. I do not know what the design of this examination is. I do not know what is to be the benefit of it to the Commonwealth. I have now little to ask other than I be not publicly insulted as cowardly barbarians insult those who fall into their hands.[2]

This outburst was evidently intended more for the Northern public than for the court at Charles Town. Brown overlooked the fact that he had been accorded every consideration it was possible for the authorities to give and that this tirade was uncalled for when they were merely trying to give him a fair trial. The court appointed Charles James Faulkner and Lawson Botts, two able attorneys, to defend the accused. In reply to whether or not these men would be acceptable Brown ignored the question but stated that he had sent for counsel. The other prisoners announced their acceptance of the proffered lawyers. After issuing an order to the press not to publish detailed testimony, as such would make it difficult to obtain a fair jury, the court adjourned.

The Circuit Court met that same afternoon with Judge Richard Parker of Winchester on the bench. The grand jury was called and was given a report of the preliminary examination. This body then retired with the state's witnesses and the next day, October 26, reported true bills against each prisoner. The indictment was written by Andrew Hunter, assisted by Charles B. Harding, the county's commonwealth attorney. Hunter had been appointed by Governor Wise to assist in the prosecution.

Four counts were listed against the prisoners. The first was treason against the Commonwealth of Virginia; the second was advising and conspiring with slaves and others to rebel, etc.; the third was the first degree murder of all five of the victims together; and the fourth was the murder of the three citizens separately.[3]

As the state was ready and Brown's outside counsel had not arrived, the court offered to assign for his defense his choice of the local bar. Brown conferred with Botts and replied that he wished to retain him and Thomas C. Green. Upon the court's request Green agreed to help the defense. Brown then arose and asked for delay because of the state of his health. He claimed a severe injury to one of his kidneys made him unable to go on with the trial. He was told that this question would be considered after he had been arraigned.

Some time was spent in selecting a jury, but late Wednesday, the following, most of whom were non slaveholders, were chosen: Isaac Dust, Jacob J. Miller, John C. McClure, William Rightstine, John C. Wiltshire, Joseph Myers, George W. Boyer, George W. Tabb, Richard Timberlake, Thomas Watson, Jr., Thomas Osbourn, and William A. Martin.[4]

Details of the trial are too numerous and tedious to be given here, and a resume must suffice. Brown was examined by Dr. Gerard F. Mason, a reputable Charles Town physician, who pronounced him perfectly able to stand trial. For moral effect upon his Northern friends the prisoner asked permission to recline on a couch during the trial. The request was granted. An attempt to have the prisoner plead insanity failed when he refused to do so. Every effort was made to see that the insurgent leader received the full benefit of the law. The trial began on Wednesday, October 26, and lasted through Monday, October 31.

On the afternoon of October 28, when some of Brown's witnesses failed to appear, the prisoner made a speech to the court, in which he claimed he had no confidence in his lawyers, Botts and Green. They then asked to be allowed to withdraw from the case, which request was granted. A young Boston attorney, George H. Hoyt, who had just arrived, volunteered to defend Brown if the court would adjourn until the following day. He would thus be given an opportunity to review the case. Botts of-

Street Scene in Charles Town during the John Brown Trial

fered Hoyt the use of his office and services in preparing the defense. The adjournment was made as desired.

The next day Hoyt appeared in court accompanied by two other defense attorneys, Hiram Griswold of Cleveland, Ohio, and Samuel Chilton of Washington, D. C. In refusing their request for additional delay, Judge Parker pointed out that Brown had caused the dismissal of his previous counsel and that it was not the state's fault that his new lawyers were unfamiliar with the case.

The examination of witnesses was concluded on Saturday, October 29, after which Harding delivered the opening argument for the prosecution. This was followed, on Monday, by speeches of the defense lawyers, Griswold and Chilton, and then Hunter concluded for the state. The jury conferred about half an hour and returned a verdict of guilty of treason and murder. The defense made a motion for arrest of judgment, which was refused the following day.[5]

When Brown was asked if he had anything to say why sentence should not be pronounced against him, he arose and replied as follows:

> I have, may it please the Court, a few words to say. In the first place I deny everything but what I have all along admitted,—the design on my part to free slaves. I intended certainly to have made a clean thing of that matter, as I did last winter, when I went into Missouri and there took slaves without the snapping of a gun on either side, moved them through the country, and finally left them in Canada. I designed to have done the same thing again, on a larger scale. That was all I intended. I never did intend murder or treason, or the destruction of property, or to incite slaves to rebellion, or to make insurrection.
>
> I have another objection, and that is that it is unjust that I should suffer such a penalty. Had I interfered in the manner which I admit, and which I admit has been fairly proved (for I admire the truthfulness and candor of the greater portion of the witnesses who have testified in this case),—had I so interfered in behalf of the rich, the intelligent, the so-called great, or in behalf of any of their friends, either father or mother, brother or sister, wife or children, or any of that class—and suffered and sacrificed what I have in this interference, it would have been all right; and every man in this Court would have deemed it an act worthy

THE JOHN BROWN TRIAL AND EXECUTION

of reward rather than punishment.

This Court acknowledges too, as I suppose, the validity of the law of God. I see a book kissed here which I suppose to be the Bible, or at least the New Testament. That teaches me that all things "whatsoever I would men should do to me I should do even so to them." It teaches me, further, to "remember them that are in bonds as bound with them." I endeavored to act up to these instructions. I say, I am yet too young to understand that God is any respecter of persons. I believe that to have interfered as I have done, in behalf of His despised poor, was not wrong but right. Now, if it is deemed necessary that I should forfeit my life for the furtherance of the ends of justice, and mingle my blood further with the blood of my children and with the blood of millions in this slave country, whose rights are disregarded by wicked, cruel, and unjust enactments, I submit. So let it be done!

Let me say one word further. I feel entirely satisfied with the treatment I have received on my trial. Considering all the circumstances, it has been more generous than I expected, but I feel no consciousness of guilt. I have stated from the first what was my intention, and what was not. I never had any design against the life of any person, nor any disposition to commit treason, or incite slaves to rebel, or make any general insurrection. I never encouraged any man to do so, but always discouraged any idea of that kind.

Let me say also, in regard to the statements made by some of those connected with me. I hear it has been stated by some of them that I have induced them to join me. But the contrary is true. I do not say this to injure them, but as regretting their weakness. There is not one of them but joined me of his own accord, and the greater part at their own expense. A number of them I never saw, and never had a word of conversation with, till the day they came to me, and that was for the purpose I have stated.

Now I have done.[6]

In view of the facts, the above speech cannot be given much credence. If Brown did not intend murder or rebellion, as he claimed, why did he collect 1,000 pikes and other arms for distribution to the slaves? Surely, these evil-looking weapons were not mere playthings sent all the way from the North to the Kennedy farm for no purpose at all. If he were trying to free the slaves as peaceably as he claimed, he did not need arms. Facts of his exploits in Kansas proved unmistakably that he caused murder to be committed, regardless of his denials that he never had any design against the life of any person. This speech, which was undoubtedly intended for its effect abroad, showed Brown in a worse light than ever, for it added lying to his other vices.

The court replied by sentencing him to be hanged on Friday, December 2.

The trials of the other prisoners proceeded in about the same manner as that of their leader, except that they did not take as much time. Edwin Coppoc was brought before the court on November 1, found guilty, and likewise sentenced to the gallows. Shields Green and John Copeland, Negroes, were subsequently found guilty, although the treason charge was dropped in their cases. The statute provided for "any free person" who committed treason, and since it was not definitely established that they were free, there was doubt concerning the application of the statute to them. The charges of murder and inciting slaves to rebellion could not be disposed of so easily.[7]

Cook, who had been captured in Pennsylvania and brought to Charles Town, was indicted on November 7 and tried the next day. Feeling against him was bitter on the part of the citizens because he had lived among them and had acted as a spy. Much to the surprise of everyone, except his attorney, he offered to plead guilty to all of the counts except treason and confessed the details of the raid. By thus throwing himself upon the mercy of the court he hoped to escape the inevitable death sentence. The court, however, overruled his plea, and Cook was required to stand trial. He had powerful connections, including his sister, wife of Governor Ashbel P. Willard of Indiana, who attended the trial with one of the best lawyers in Indiana, Daniel W. Voorhees, at that time Indiana's attorney general. Voorhees later distinguished himself as a United States Senator and was so eloquent that he was called "The Tall Sycamore of the Wabash".

As this gifted orator arose, the crowd in the courtroom listened attentively. He did not base his appeal on the letter of the law but took broader, higher grounds. He pictured the handsome youth before him as an adventurous prodigal, who had been enchanted by the fanatic, Brown. In his plea for mercy he mentioned the brokenhearted Virginia bride and the grief that would be caused the prisoner's distinguished relatives. It is said that when Voorhees had finished his speech strong men who had hated Cook were sobbing and that even the stern-visaged judge was crying. Nevertheless, the jury, after an hour's deliberation, found the prisoner guilty on all counts except treason. On November 10 he was sentenced to be hanged on December 16.

Brown's petition to the Virginia Supreme Court of Appeals at Richmond for a writ of error was refused on November 19 and with this rebuff the other prisoners' hopes also waned. Brown's plea was regarded as a test case.[8]

During the time between the end of the insurgents' trials and their executions Charles Town teemed with activity. A series of fires swept over the county, particularly in the rural regions, and many inhabitants attributed their losses to friends of the prisoners. One day five barns and outbuildings were set on fire by some incendiary near Charles Town. A noteworthy fact in this connection was that jurors at the recent trials seemed to be the principal sufferers.

Additional fires caused Colonel J. Lucius Davis, in charge of the troops at Charles Town, to seek reinforcements from Governor Wise. Volunteer companies poured in until over a thousand soldiers were on hand. Naturally, the town's limited facilities were taxed to the utmost to accommodate such an influx. Attorney Andrew Hunter's outer law office was turned into a kitchen for several companies. Other offices, as well as public buildings, became barracks and guardrooms. Townspeople accommodated many of the officers in their homes, and some of the more appreciative visitors sent gifts to their former hosts when the executions were over.

Among some of the out-of-town companies stationed in Charles Town and vicinity at this time were the following: Alexandria Riflemen, Alexandria Artillery, Mt. Vernon Guards, Richmond Howitzers, Morgan Continentals, Petersburg Artillery, Upper Fauquier Cavalry, Lower Fauquier Cavalry, Virginia Rifles, Petersburg Guards, Petersburg Grays, Wheeling Rifles, Wheeling State Fencibles, and the cadets of Virginia Military Institute. One of the members of the Richmond Grays was John Wilkes Booth, the later assassin of President Abraham Lincoln.[9]

All sorts of rumors filled the atmosphere. One said that an armed body of men was on its way from Wheeling to rescue the prisoners, which report caused Governor Wise to order 500 men from Richmond to Charles Town. Another rumor had it that a fight had occurred between would-be rescuers and defenders at "Underwood's Farm" in Clarke County. The people were thus kept in a state of great excitement and expected any moment to see a rescue attempt made. Mayor Thomas C. Green of Charles Town issued a proclamation requiring all strangers who could not give a satisfactory account of themselves to leave the community at once. Later, he addressed a notice to residents of the town in which he urged them to remain in their homes at night.

As might be expected, Brown received many letters from persons in all walks of life. Some of them urged him not to lose hope and promised to rescue him. Others contained checks from fifty dollars downwards. The huge task of reading these letters first devolved upon Andrew Hunter. One of them was written by a person who knew Brown in Kansas and reads as follows:

Chattanoga, Tennessee, Nov. 20, 1859.

John Brown:—Sir: Altho' vengeance is not mine, I confess that I do feel gratified to hear that you were stopped in your fiendish career at Harper's Ferry with the loss of your two sons. You can now appreciate my distress in Kansas, when you then and there entered my house at midnight and arrested my husband and two boys and took them out of the yard, and in cold blood shot them dead in my hearing. You can't say you done it to free our slaves; we had none and never expected to own one, but has only made me a poor disconsolate widow, with helpless children. While I feel for your folly, I do hope and trust you will meet your just reward. Oh, how it pained my heart to hear the dying groans of my husband and children. If this scrawl gives you any consolation you are welcome to it.

Mahala Doyle.

N. B. My son, John Doyle, whose life I begged of you, is now grown up, and is very anxious to be at Charlestown on the day of your executon; would certainly be there if his means would permit it, that he might adjust the rope around your neck, if Gov. Wise would permit.

M. D.[10]

THE JOHN BROWN TRIAL AND EXECUTION

Brown was not the only one to get letters for Governor Wise received his share. Piles of letters poured into his office at Richmond. They threatened, pleaded, and begged for the life of the insurgent leader. A score or more schemes were proposed to cheat the gallows. Although most of them depended on arms, some spoke of strategy and others of bribes. Threats of kidnapping the prisoner's prosecutors and holding their lives against his were made. Forces ranging from five men to 25,000 were declared organized for the rescue. The state executive did not yield to this tremendous pressure and refused to interfere with the course of the law. Even lower public officials were annoyed, as is proved by the following anonymous letter:

> New York City, Oct. 23rd, 1859.
> Clerk of the Court,
> Charlestown, Virginia
> Sir—You had better caution your authorities to be careful about what you (do) with Ossawottamie Brown; so sure as you hurt one hair of his head, mark my word—the following day, you will see every city, town, village south of Mason and Dixon's line in
> FLAMES!
> We are determined to put down slavery at all odds. Forcibly if it must, peaceably if it can. Believe me when I tell you, the end is not yet—by a long odds.
> All of us at the North sympathize with the
> MARTYRS OF HARPER'S FERRY[11]

As the day of execution drew near Brown appeared indifferent to his impending fate. He spent most of his time writing letters as a further means of helping the Abolition movement. He, no doubt, made thousands of new converts by the martyr air he assumed. His wife arrived at Harpers Ferry on December 1 and rode to Charles Town in a carriage. She was escorted by mounted soldiers detailed to guard her from intrusion of any sort. Upon her arrival at the county seat she went to the jail and spent four hours wih her doomed husband. The interview was witnessed by the sheriff, and after an embrace and a kiss, the unfortunate woman returned to the Ferry, where she awaited the reception of her husband's body the next day. She made a favorable impression on all who met her. Her companions were detained at Harpers Ferry while she made the trip to Charles Town.

EXECUTION.

On December 2, 1859, Brown prepared to leave the jail for the place of execution, about a quarter of a mile away. He first visited Copeland and Green and told them to stand up like men and not betray their friends. Saying he had no further use for the money, he handed each a quarter. He bade them farewell, visited the other prisoners, and took leave of his former associates.[12]

Apparently calm and cheerful, Brown came from the jail at eleven in the morning. The jail was at the corner of Washington and George streets where the United States Post Office is now located. His arms were pinioned and a military guard formed quickly about him to prevent rescue or injury to his person. Six companies of infantry and one troop of horsemen, along with Major General William B. Taliaferro and his staff, were in front of the jail. An open wagon was waiting at the door. In it was a pine box containing a fine oak coffin. After speaking to several persons whom he recognized, Brown took his seat on the box containing his coffin. He was accompanied in the wagon by his sheriff, James W. Campbell, his jailer, John Avis, and his undertaker, George Sadler. The procession moved out South George Street to the gallows, which were located in a field of the Rebecca Hunter farm on the southeast edge of Charles Town. The site is near the residence which Colonel John T. Gibson later erected on South Samuel Street. On his way to the scaffold Brown remarked to the undertaker, "This is a beautiful country—I never had the pleasure of seeing it before".

According to a reporter for a New York newspaper, Brown stooped and kissed a Negro child as he was leaving the jail, and the poet John Greenleaf Whittier wrote about the incident. As a matter of fact, no such occurrence could possibly have happened. The prisoner was so closely guarded that it was practically impossible for an outsider to get near him, least of all Negroes, who were said to have been scarce on the day of the execution. Then, too, Brown's arms were tied, which would make the task all the harder. As final proof, the jailer, John Avis, left a sworn statement, duly acknowledged, assserting that the incident never occurred. A copy of this affidavit may be found in Appendix C of

John Brown Leaving the Jail at Charles Town for His Execution

this volume. Perhaps Whittier was using his poetic license in the same way that he wrote the fantastic, but unmistakably false, tale about Barbara Fritchie at Frederick, Maryland.

Flanked by two files of riflemen in close order, Brown reached the gallows. Citizens were kept back at the point of the bayonet from taking any position except that assigned them, which was almost a quarter of a mile from the scaffold. Expressing disapproval that the citizens were kept so far away, Brown ascended the gallows. He thanked the sheriff and jailer for their kindnesses toward him, after which the cap was placed over his face and the rope around his neck. A pause ensued and at 11:15 the trap fell. As life departed from Brown's body, the only visible signs were a slight grasping of the hands and twitching of the muscles. The pulse did not cease beating until thirty-five minutes had elapsed, and then the body was cut down, placed in the coffin, and conveyed to Harpers Ferry. At the latter place, it was met by the sorrowful wife and then sent to North Elba, New York, for burial.[13]

In his will, written in the Charles Town jail on the day of his death, Brown directed that the proceeds of his estate be turned over to his wife, Mary A. Brown, and named Sheriff James W. Campbell as executor. By a codicil evidently penned shortly after the will was written the prisoner bequeathed a Sharp's rifle to Sheriff Campbell and also one to his jailer, John Avis, for their kindnesses toward him. Both the will and the codicil were witnessed by Andrew Hunter and John Avis.[14]

ATTEMPT AT ESCAPE BY COOK AND COPPOC.

After the leader's execution attention centered on the remaining prisoners. Nothing of any particular interest seems to have happened except a sensational escape attempt by Cook and Coppoc the night before their execution. They had planned to make the attempt the preceding night, December 14, but had postponed it because of the presence of Cook's relatives, Governor Willard and his wife. As they were leaving the following morning, Cook was afraid the escape would be linked with their departure. Nevertheless, he had urged Coppoc to make the effort. Coppoc preferred, however, that they make the attempt together and decided to wait until the following night.

The John Brown Procession on the way to the Gallows at Charles Town

The change in nights later cost them their lives. On December 14 the guard on duty at the angle of the prison wall most favorable for an escape was Charles Lenhart, a former Kansas Free State fighter. He had enrolled for service in the prison guards with the sole purpose of aiding the prisoners. Keeping in communication with Cook and Coppoc, he was able to inform them when he would be on duty.

The prisoners had obtained a Barlow knife from one of the jail guards on the pretense of cutting a lemon. A knife blade was acquired from Shields Green, a fellow-prisoner, and with it they made teeth in the blade of the Barlow knife. Using this weapon and a screw from the bedstead, they had worked for ten days making a hole in the wall of their room near a window. The plastering had been removed from that part of the room by a lunatic a short while after Captain Avis had taken charge of the jail and had never been replaced. Bricks from the wall were hidden under the bed and the hole near the window was concealed as much as possible. The prisoners worked on their shackles at night, underneath their bed-clothing, so that the sounds of filing would be muffled.[15]

At eight o'clock in the evening of December 15, while Jailer Avis was at supper, Cook and Coppoc removed their shackles, wrenched the loose bars from the window of their room and descended into the jail yard. They then mounted the jail wall, where they were discovered by a sentinel. Their friend, Lenhart, was not on duty this night, but instead a loyal Virginian, named Tom Guard, who fired at them. Realizing that they had been discovered, the disheartened prisoners dropped back into the yard and gave themselves to the jailer.

With the military much in evidence the executions were held on December 16. The Negroes, Green and Copeland, went to the gallows first, a few minutes past eleven o'clock in the morning. Two hours later Cook and Coppoc, exhibiting undeniable firmness, swung into eternity. The bodies of the Negroes were buried under the gallows but were later exhumed, while the remains of the white men were placed on board a train bound for the North.[15]

Another phase of this unusual drama began with the trial and execution of the two remaining prisoners, Aaron D. Stevens and Albert Hazlett. The Virginia General Assembly had authorized

John Brown Ascending the Scaffold at Charles Town

a special Circuit Court term for Jefferson County, which was to begin on February 1, 1860. Following a trial lasting three days Stevens was convicted, as was Hazlett about a week later. They were executed on March 16 and their bodies were sent to New Jersey for burial.[17]

CONCLUSION.

John Brown's Fort was the only one of the buildings in the old armory enclosure at Harpers Ferry left standing after the Civil War had ravaged the town. In 1892 it was sold to a company of Chicago men for removal and exhibition at the World's Fair the following year. It was rebuilt in Chicago and displayed to the public, but the venture was not successful. When the fair was over the building was sold for use as a stable, but Miss Kate Field, a noted actress and journalist, became interested in the relic and raised funds to purchase it. It was then removed to

The John Brown Fort Today
at Harpers Ferry

Harpers Ferry in 1895 and relocated on a site about two miles from the town, along the Shenandoah River. This spot was too inaccessible, however, and in 1910 the building was purchased and removed to the campus of Storer College at Harpers Ferry, where it may be seen today.[18]

The final act in the John Brown episode, as far as Jefferson County was concerned, occurred in July, 1899, when the bones of seven insurgents were disinterred at Harpers Ferry. They had been given a rude burial in a desolate spot near the banks of the Shenandoah River shortly after the raid took place. The disinterment was under the supervision of Dr. Thomas R. Featherstonhaugh and Captain E. P. Hall, both of Washington, D. C., assisted by the person who buried the bodies. The remains were sent to North Elba, New York, where on August 30 they were given a final resting-place near the grave of their leader.[19]

The monetary cost of the John Brown Raid to the State of Virginia was $287,459.10.[20] Much of this was for the equipment, transportation, and wages of the numerous militia companies. If the raid be considered one of the causes of the Civil War, as is sometimes claimed, its cost cannot of course be determined.

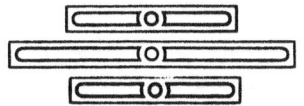

CHAPTER TWELVE
THE CIVIL WAR

Strategically located at the northern approach to the "granary of the Confederacy", as the Valley of Virginia has been aptly designated, Jefferson County saw considerable fighting during the Civil War. It was the natural gateway through which Confederate forces could strike at Washington, only sixty miles distant, or other parts of the North. If they failed in this they could retreat into the Valley and be partly protected by mountain ranges on both sides. Through the county passed the Baltimore and Ohio Railroad, and nearby paralleling the Potomac River on the Maryland side, ran the Chesapeake and Ohio Canal. Both were vital in the transportation of men and supplies for the defense of the Federal capital. Another factor which influenced events in the early days of the war was the United States Armory and Arsenal at Harpers Ferry. This was capable of turning out large quantities of arms, which, added to the thousands stored there, made it invaluable to warring parties.

TEN COMPANIES.

Since Jefferson County was overwhelmingly Southern in sympathy, it is not surprising that most of its young men of military age enlisted under the Stars and Bars. In all, the county contributed ten companies of infantry, cavalry, and artillery, aggregating approximately 1,600 men. There is no record of the organization of companies for the Union army, although a few scattered individuals joined the Federals. The five infantry companies, together with their commanders, were Company A (Jefferson Guards) of Charles Town, Captain John W. Rowan; Company B (Hamtramck Guards) of Shepherdstown, Captain Vincent M. Butler; Company G (Botts Greys) of Charles Town, Captain

Harpers Ferry at the Beginning of the Civil War from the Maryland Side

Lawson Botts; Company H (Letcher Riflemen) of Duffield's Depot, Captain James H. L. Hunter; and Company K (Floyd Guards) of Harpers Ferry, Captain George W. Chambers. All were components of the Second Virginia Regiment of the "Stonewall Brigade".[1]

The four cavalry companies and their leaders were Company A of Charles Town, Captain John H. Henderson; Company B of Charles Town, Captain Robert W. Baylor; Company D of Moler's Cross Roads, Captain John L. Knott; and Company F of Shepherdstown, Captain William A. Morgan. The first three belonged to the Twelfth Virginia Regiment, Rosser's Brigade, while the Shepherdstown company was attached to the First Virginia Regiment, Wickham's Brigade.

Jefferson County's one company of artillery, Chew's Battery, achieved distinction in its branch. It was organized in Jefferson County on November 11, 1861, by special authority of the Confederate Secretary of War. When first formed it was composed of thirty-three men and the following officers: R. Preston Chew, captain; Milton Rouss, first lieutenant; and J. W. McCarty and James Thomson, second lieutenants. Three pieces of artillery, a rifle gun called the "Blakeley", a howitzer, and a six-inch rifle gun, comprised the company's first armament. Upon the suggestion of Colonel Turner Ashby the whole command was mounted. Incidentally, this was the first mounted battery of flying artillery organized in the Confederate army. Its officers had received military training at Virginia Military Institute, where they were cadets, and consequently they were able to organize an efficient command.[2]

Chew's Battery served with Ashby's Brigade throughout Jackson's Valley Campaign in 1862, and after the deaths of Ashby and Jackson it was attached to Stuart's Horse Artillery. The membership grew until it reached a total of 197 men. Lieutenants Rouss and McCarty left the battery in 1862 to join the cavalry, and the vacancies were filled by James Thomson, first lieutenant, and James W. Williams and J. W. Carter, second lieutenants.

After Captain Chew's promotion to the command of Stuart's Horse Artillery in 1864, Thomson succeeded him as captain of the battery and E. L. Yancey became a second lieutenant. Promotions were in order again, for on March 1, 1865, when the Stuart

Horse Artillery was reorganized into five battalions of two batteries each, Chew became lieutenant colonel, Thomson was made a major, and Carter, a captain. It has been stated that Chew's Battery was engaged in more skirmishes and battles than any battery in the entire Confederate army.[3]

Even the surrender of General Robert E. Lee at Appomattox did not daunt Chew's Battery. When the contemplated surrender became known, the organization, along with the cavalry brigade of General Thomas T. Munford, cut its way through the Federal lines with its eleven guns in an attempt to join the forces of General Joseph E. Johnston in North Carolina. It was indeed not until news of the latter's capitulation reached this group that the artillerymen disbanded. However, in order to prevent their pieces from falling into Federal hands Chew's men buried them along the banks of the Staunton River. To mislead the enemy even more, the carriages and caissons were taken to a remote spot and burned. In 1903 an attempt was made with Colonel Chew's help to locate the guns, but nothing was found.[4]

HARPERS FERRY IN 1861.

Before Virginia passed her Secession Ordinance plans had been made to seize Harpers Ferry for the state. On the night of April 16, 1861, former Governor Henry A. Wise, John D. Imboden, Turner Ashby, Richard Ashby, Oliver Funsten, John A. Barbour, Superintendent Alfred M. Barbour of the Harpers Ferry Armory, and John A. Harman, plotted to move on the Ferry.[5]

The next morning Superintendent Barbour called the Harpers Ferry workmen around him. He told them that the place would soon be in possession of Virginia and that they would be paid high wages if they remained to work for the state. Some of the expert machinists later worked for the Union at Springfield, Bridesburg, and Washington, while others made guns at Richmond and Fayetteville, North Carolina, for the Confederacy.

Barbour's plea to the workmen proved costly to the Confederacy for it warned the Federal garrison at Harpers Ferry. Virginia passed her Secession Ordinance on April 17 and soon her militia were converging on the junction of the Shenandoah and Potomac rivers. The Federal garrison at this time consisted of

Lieutenant Roger Jones and forty-two regular soldiers of the Forty-Second Infantry. This small group had been sent from Carlisle, Pennsylvania, to guard the place after the superintendent had made an appeal on January 2. Jones realized the impossibility of trying to defend the Federal Government property with such a small force and so informed his superiors. At the same time he urged them to send reinforcements. He received orders to destroy the rifle works and abandon Harpers Ferry in case its capture became imminent.[6]

Barbour's plea to the workmen gave Jones all the information he wanted. Thousands of rifles and other arms were gathered in piles in a building. Trains of gunpowder were laid through and around them. Windows were opened to create a draft. Everything was ready to fire the whole plant and evacuate at a moment's notice. Nor had the garrison long to wait. On the night of April 18, about ten o'clock, a panting messenger rushed down the road to the village and reported to Lieutenant Jones that the Virginia militia was only a mile away. At the same time firing broke out between a group of loyal volunteers on Bolivar Heights and the vanguard of the attackers.

The order was immediately given to fire the buildings. The torch was applied and soon the rush and roar of flames told of the destruction being done. All of the garrison, except four who tarried too long, escaped across the Potomac River into Maryland. As the first of the 2,500 Virginians came upon the scene, they witnessed the destruction of a large number of arms. Nevertheless, about 5,000 completed muskets and 3,000 unfinished small arms were saved. This was due largely to the efforts of towns-people and workmen who arrived on the scene shortly after the flames had started and thus succeeded in checking their spread. Some of the employees had secretly wet several of the powder trains also. Although most of the armory and arsenal buildings were completely destroyed, the large workshops with their valuable arms-producing machinery were saved. This machinery was later dismantled and removed to Fayetteville, North Carolina, where it continued to produce arms, but this time for the Confederacy.[7]

On April 27, 1861, Thomas J. Jackson, later known as "Stonewall", who had received a commission as colonel of Virginia militia,

The United States Armory at Harpers Ferry in 1861

was ordered to Harpers Ferry to succeed Major General Kenton Harper. Shortly after Jackson arrived at his new post he proceeded to organize the untrained troops into an effective fighting force.

Realizing that if possession of Maryland Heights, across the Potomac from Harpers Ferry, remained in the hands of the enemy, it would be impossible for him to hold the town, Jackson seized that strategic location. Maryland Heights is much higher than any of the other mountain tops in the immediate vicinity and hence was of more military value than the others. From its top one could dominate both Loudoun and Bolivar Heights, as well as the town. Jackson's appreciation of the importance of Maryland Heights in connection with the defense of Harpers Ferry was borne out by subsequent events.[8]

When the Confederate capital was moved from Montgomery to Richmond, the authorities decided it would be more desirable to entrust the command of Harpers Ferry to an older and more experienced officer than the ex-professor from Virginia Military Institute. Accordingly, they appointed Major General Joseph E. Johnston to the command. He arrived on May 23.

Delay was experienced in effecting the change of commanders inasmuch as the Virginia authorities had failed to notify Jackson of the change. He, like a true soldier, replied that he did not feel at liberty to transfer his command to another without further instructions from Governor John Letcher or General Lee.[9] A communication from the latter cleared the situation and Jackson promptly yielded his command to Johnston.

Upon the organization of the Virginia troops into the First Brigade Colonel Jackson was appointed its commander. This brigade was composed of young men representing the best blood of the Confederacy. The Second Regiment in it was recruited chiefly from the counties of Jefferson, Berkeley, Frederick, and Clarke. It later achieved immortal fame as the "Stonewall Brigade".

After removing the arms-producing machinery from Harpers Ferry, Johnston decided to withdraw to Winchester, a more easily defended town. Accordingly, after burning the railroad bridge across the Potomac and several public buildings, the Confederates on June 16 moved out of Jefferson County.[10]

Destruction of the Railroad Bridge at Harpers Ferry by the Confederates on June 15, 1861

During the Confederate occupation of Harpers Ferry traffic over the Baltimore and Ohio Railroad continued. Although more than fifty miles of the company's main line were in Confederate hands, their government had adopted a liberal policy toward the railroad. With the exception of occasional interruptions traffic was permitted to continue. Even the seizure of a Federal officer, Brigadier General William S. Harney, from an eastbound passenger train late in April was followed by his subsequent release in Richmond.[11]

Traffic over the Baltimore and Ohio, consisting mostly of long eastbound trains loaded with coal, was particularly heavy at this time. On the return trip the westbound empty cars gave notice that soon more coal would be passing Harpers Ferry. The first restriction imposed by Jackson was that the unprecedented amount of night traffic must cease and that only regularly scheduled passenger and express trains would be permitted to operate. A short time later he required all freight trains to pass through Harpers Ferry in the daytime, between the hours of eleven and one.

Finally, the Confederate authorities, realizing that much of this coal was ultimately used for operating Federal ships in their merciless blockade of the Southern coast, ordered the railroad closed. Consequently, on May 22, 1861, Jackson commanded Captain John D. Imboden to seize the line at Point of Rocks and stop all eastbound trains, while Colonel Kenton Harper was doing likewise at Martinsburg. However, as early as May 14 an engine and cars had been seized at Harpers Ferry and communication with the West temporarily cut.[12]

A skirmish between a detail of Federal infantry commanded by Major William Atterbury and a number of Confederates on the Virginia shore took place at Harpers Ferry on June 14, 1861. As most of the firing was at long range across the Potomac and as the Federals were not equipped with long range rifles, they found themselves at a disadvantage. The Confederates made good use of the protection afforded them by the bridge piers, trestle-work, and buildings and thus offered poor targets. Finding that he was unable to inflict damage on the Southerners and that his own men were in danger, Atterbury ordered his detail to retire toward Sandy Hook.[13]

Ruins of Hall's Rifle Works at Harpers Ferry in 1861

No more important fighting occurred in Jefferson County until October 16, 1861, when a skirmish took place on Bolivar Heights between Federal troops commanded by Colonel John W. Geary and Virginians led by Colonel Turner Ashby. The Northerners had been engaged in removing a large quantity of wheat from Harpers Ferry to Maryland, when they received word that Ashby was approaching from the direction of Charles Town. Although the number participating was only about 450 on each side, a spirited engagement ensued. The Confederates had part of their force posted on Loudoun Heights, across the Shenandoah River, the better to enfilade the enemy in Harpers Ferry. Each side claimed the victory, but since both commanders retreated after slight losses, the skirmish appears to have been a draw. Ashby retired toward Charles Town and Geary across the Potomac. A few days later a body of Confederate cavalry entered the Ferry and burned A. H. Herr's flour mill, from which place the Federals had obtained their wheat.[14]

THE YEAR 1862.

The spring of 1862 witnessed Stonewall Jackson's famous Valley Campaign. Having defeated Major General N. P. Banks at Winchester and captured most of the Federal supply train, Jackson moved swifty against Harpers Ferry. This decision was made in full knowledge that the Union Generals McDowell, Fremont, and Shields were marching toward the Shenandoah Valley to cut off his retreat southward. As part of Jackson's plan, Brigadier General Charles S. Winder was ordered to pursue a body of Federals to Charles Town, where they had formed a line of battle in that section of the town known as "Potato Hill". On May 28 Winder with about 1,300 men met an enemy force of approximately the same size and after a fight of twenty minutes forced the Federals to flee. He was assisted at this time by Captain R. P. Chew, who, as a resident of Jefferson County, furnished valuable information about the surrounding country. Winder continued the pursuit to Halltown. With the Federals retreating toward their fortifications on Bolivar Heights, he then returned to the outskirts of Charles Town and established camp.[15]

Although the Union garrison had left Harpers Ferry at the enemy's approach, it was not long before Jackson moved up the

THE CIVIL WAR

Valley and the Federals reoccupied the place.

At the beginning of the war Daniel S. Rentch was appointed postmaster at Shepherdstown by President Jefferson Davis. Every time Union forces came to town this post office would close. On one occasion, when a rumor came that Federals were approaching, Jerome Dushane, the deputy postmaster, gathered the post office supplies in a big red bandanna and hid until the enemy retired. Later, when Dushane went into the army, he took with him about $10,000 worth of Confederate postage stamps.

The Southern post office at Shepherdstown flourished only a year. The Union people caused so much trouble for Postmaster Rentch that he was glad to close the office. The mail carrier at this time was William Crowl, who made three trips a week to Winchester, the headquarters for Southern mail. A private post office was maintained during the war by Albert Humrickhouse, who had a stage route between Shepherdstown, Winchester, and other points south. During the war he carried many letters. In addition to this, there were always messengers going back and forth, who conveyed an extra note or two.[16]

When it became evident that Jefferson County would be part of the Civil War battleground, the County Court directed that the valuable papers and records be removed to the interior of the state. Under the supervision of County Clerk Thomas A. Moore they were loaded on wagons and taken to Lexington, 160 miles southward. They were kept there until the end of hostilities, when they were brought back to the county. Had it not been for this foresight on the part of public officials, it is doubtful if any of the early records would have survived the subsequent destruction of the courthouse. The county records were thus preserved almost intact.[17]

RAID ON WINCHESTER AND POTOMAC RAILROAD.

An interesting incident concerning two Jefferson County young men occurred on August 23, 1862, in the Summit Point vicinity. Lieutenants George Baylor and Milton Rouss of Ashby's Cavalry commanded a party of thirty men which left camp at Mount Jackson to make an excursion into the Lower Valley. Avoiding the Federal garrison and pickets at Winchester, the group traveled at night until it reached Jefferson County. When the men arrived there, they decided to attempt to rob the Winchester and Potomac Railroad train between Summit Point and Wade's Depot. The distance between these two stations is only four miles and at each place were stationed eighty-five of the enemy. Thus, the Federals were only two miles distant in either direction from the selected spot of operations.[18]

After placing obstructions on the track, the Confederates waited for the next train due from Harpers Ferry. Within a short time the engine hove into view and soon came to a dead stop. The raiders entered the cars, made prisoners of eight soldiers on their way to Winchester to join their companies, and helped themselves to baskets of champagne and boxes of fruit. In addition to this, they obtained $4,000 in United States money, which had been consigned to the Union paymaster at Winchester, and the United States mail. In the latter were official dispatches from Major General John Pope to Brigadier General Julius White in command of Federal troops at Winchester.

Then the Southern soldiers decided to burn the cars, which were soon ablaze. The engine was given a full head of steam and sent rumbling toward Winchester with no one aboard. It was later ascertained that after performing a variety of antics along the rough roadbed, it came to a dead stop three miles from Winchester, completely exhausted. Although a few shots had been fired at the train before it stopped, the only one hurt was an agent of the Adams Express Company. He was badly wounded while attempting to escape. As if not satisfied with the damage already done, the Confederates destroyed the telegraph wire for a distance of more than 200 yards, just in time to prevent the completion of a message which was being sent over it.[19]

Leaving Lieutenant George Rowland in charge of the prisoners, Baylor and Rouss set out for Smithfield, or Middleway. On its outskirts they were mistaken by Federal pickets for Union troops and thus were able to capture three additional soldiers. When the attackers learned from their prisoners that there were fourteen more of the enemy in the town, they charged into Middleway and captured the surprised Federals. The latter did not have time to fire a shot. In addition to the soldiers, the raiders obtained seventeen horses, twenty revolvers, five carbines, eighteen saddles and bridles, overcoats and blankets. With the booty they proceeded directly to their company. They had traveled 175 miles in three days and been in the saddle for two nights.[20]

CAPTURE OF HARPERS FERRY.

After defeating Major General John Pope at the Second Battle of Bull Run, General Lee began his first invasion of the North. His troops crossed the Potomac River near Leesburg and singing "Maryland, My Maryland," set foot upon the old line state. It was expected that thousands of Southern sympathizers would join them, but in this the Confederates were disappointed. Only a few Marylanders cast their lot with the South at this time, although many volunteers from that state had already done so.

While the Confederate chieftain was in the neighborhood of Frederick, an important engagement was taking place at Harpers Ferry. Major General Stonewall Jackson had been ordered to march from Frederick to Martinsburg, capture it, and then proceed along the south bank of the Potomac to the Ferry.[21]

The advance guard, under Major General A. P. Hill, approached Martinsburg on the night of September 11, 1862. Finding that its garrison had retired to Harpers Ferry, Jackson entered the Berkeley County seat the next day and captured a few prisoners and a small amount of stores. The journey to the Ferry was quickly resumed and on September 13 Hill's division came in sight of the enemy entrenchments on Bolivar Heights.

From his knowledge of Harpers Ferry, obtained when he was in command there in the early days of the war, Jackson realized that to capture the place, it would be necessary to obtain control of both Maryland and Loudoun Heights. The task of dislodging the Federals from Maryland Heights was entrusted to Major General Lafayette McLaws. Coming through Middletown, Pleasant Valley, and Solomon's Gap, McLaws scaled the crest of the mountains and engaged the Union forces posted on the heights. After exhibiting a spirited defense, Colonel Thomas H. Ford, in command of the Federals, spiked his guns and retreated across the pontoon bridge into the Ferry.

Brigadier General John G. Walker was assigned the task of occupying Loudoun Heights, which he did after crossing the Potomac River at Point of Rocks. The planting of batteries on Loudoun Heights required much labor, as it was necessary for the Confederates to cut roads and then drag their guns up the steep slopes. Jackson established communication with McLaws and Walker on the morning of September 14 and then completed preparations for the attack. At night he sent troops to occupy the ravines along the Shenandoah River and also placed ten batteries of artillery across the river at the foot of Loudoun Heights. Thus was that avenue of escape closed.[22]

Promptly at dawn on the morning of September 15 a furious cannonade was begun by Jackson's batteries in the rear of Harpers Ferry, which were supported by those on Maryland and Loudoun Heights. At the same time the batteries which he had placed on the east side of the Shenandoah River at the foot of Loudoun Heights raked the Federals with a destructive enfilading fire. Although the Unionists on Bolivar Heights replied as well as they could, their leaders realized the futility of resistance and, after an hour's fighting, raised the white flag. The Federal officers unanimously favored surrender if reasonable terms could be obtained.

Unfortunately, the Confederates could not notify their most distant batteries of the capitulation for some time, and shells continued to fall upon the Federals. One of them struck Colonel Dixon S. Miles, the Union commander, in the leg and inflicted a mortal wound. The surrender was completed by Brigadier General Julius White, who had commanded the Martinsburg garrison before it fled to the Ferry. The terms were lenient, as the men were allowed to retain their overcoats and blankets, were permitted two days' rations, and were paroled.[23]

Jackson's capture of Harpers Ferry gave the South more than 11,000 prisoners, 73 pieces of artillery, 13,000 stands of small arms, and large numbers of wagons and other military supplies. That such an important victory could be accomplished with so little loss can be attributed to Jackson's brilliant strategy, more than anything else. He did not wait to carry out the details of surrender but hurried to join the main army at Sharpsburg. The junction was effected on the morning of the sixteenth. Major General George B. McClellan had found a copy of Lee's plans at Frederick and, acting with unusual swiftness, had driven the divided Confederate army back at South Mountain. Lee retreated

THE CIVIL WAR 157

to Sharpsburg, where he awaited Jackson's arrival. A. P. Hill was left at Harpers Ferry to complete the terms of surrender.[24]

A noteworthy achievement in connection with the siege and capture was that of Colonel B. F. Davis of the Eighth New York Cavalry. Realizing before the surrender that his force of 2,500 horsemen would be of no use in the forthcoming engagement at the Ferry and not having forage for his mounts, he requested permission of Colonel Miles to attempt escape by cutting his way out of the town. At a council the cavalry commanders decided to make the effort across the pontoon bridge over the Potomac and then take the route to Sharpsburg. On the night of September 14 they sallied forth and not only escaped the fate of those remaining in the town but also captured and destroyed an ammunition train belonging to Major General James Longstreet's corps. This was intercepted near Antietam Creek, shortly before Davis's troopers joined McClellan's army.[25]

In the preliminary movements relative to the siege of Harpers Ferry a sharp engagement took place between four companies of the First New York Cavalry and Company B of the Twelfth Virginia Cavalry. The encounter occurred on September 13 about a mile west of Charles Town. When the fighting was over, the Federals withdrew toward Halltown. The Confederates pursued them to the latter place and then joined Jackson for the siege of Harpers Ferry.[26]

AFTER ANTIETAM.

The indecisive battle of Antietam was fought on September 17, 1862. As George Alfred Townsend described it, "All day long the grim dogs of war tore at each other's throats until both were too exhausted to move". After the battles of South Mountain and Antietam thousands of Confederate wounded came into Jefferson County. Being closest to the scene of slaughter, Shepherdstown was transformed into a vast hospital. Every available shelter was thrown open to the Southern warriors, and even then there were not enough. After the supply of private homes proved insufficient, the town's six churches, the schoolhouses, the Odd Fellows' Hall, and the council room, were filled to capacity. Rough boards were thrown across the beams of the unfinished town hall and it was soon filled. Then it became necessary to use the stone warehouses in the ravine by the river and a dilapidated building known as the "old blue factory". Broken, mangled bodies were everywhere.[27]

After finding shelter for the injured came the task of dressing their wounds. Some of the Confederates had not received medical attention for several days, and the journey over the rough roads had aggravated their wounds. The scarcity of army surgeons was somewhat mitigated by the doctors of the town and countryside. Still it was some time before relief could be administered. Assisted by children, women of the neighborhood bathed the soldiers' wounds and helped in every way possible. Amputations by the hundreds were made and the piles of arms and legs reached enormous proportions. The task of feeding such an influx was met with undaunted courage by the townspeople and farmers. Food was generously distributed as long as it lasted. It has been estimated that from 2,000 to 3,000 sick and wounded soldiers were in Shepherdstown at this time.

Nor was this the end of the suffering. After the battle the retreating Confederates crossed the Potomac near Shepherdstown. A Federal battery was placed on the Douglas hill, opposite the town, and shells came screeching across the river. Soon pandemonium prevailed. Roads leading out of the place were jammed with wagons, ambulances, guns, caissons, horsemen, footmen, and civilians. The most pitiful picture was presented by the hundreds of wounded Confederates who were able to move.

They did not want to spend the remainder of their days in Northern prisons and therefore made every possible effort to escape. According to one account: "Men with cloths about their heads went hatless in the sun, men with cloths about their feet limped shoeless on the stony road; men with arms in slings, without arms, with one leg, with bandaged sides and backs; men in ambulances, wagons, carts, wheelbarrows, men carried on stretchers, or supported on the shoulders of some self-denying went to almost certain death. . . ."[28]

The retreat of the main Confederate army from Antietam was not as disorganized as the above description would indicate. On the contrary, it was conducted with admirable skill. Both sides rested on the day following the battle, and on the night of September 18 Lee's force recrossed into Virginia at Pack Horse Ford. General W. N. Pendleton was ordered to place a line of guns on

THE CIVIL WAR 159

the Virginia bluffs, but before he could prepare this line, Federal skirmishers crossed and captured four pieces of artillery. The loss so disgusted Jackson that he dispatched A. P. Hill to oppose the enemy. On the morning of September 20 Hill formed his troops on the north side of the present Shepherdstown-Moler's Cross Roads pike advancing northward and facing the ford. He then sent three brigades to the front but was unable to bring up his artillery because of the lack of time.

Union soldiers formed their lines on the high bluffs above the river, facing southward, where they awaited Hill's attack. While they were being assaulted on the front and on both flanks, the order came to withdraw. The attempted retreat soon developed into a rout and each Federal tried to save himself, as best he could. Some of the soldiers tried to escape by the ravine, others were driven back northward over the precipitous bluff and killed or mangled, while still others were shot crossing the river. The bluffs over which some of them fell are at places from fifty to eighty feet high. The following quotation is taken from Hill's official report of this phase in the fighting: "Then commenced the most terrible slaughter that this war has yet witnessed. The broad surface of the Potomac was blue with the floating bodies of our foe. But few escaped to tell the tale".[29]

The 118th Pennsylvania Volunteers, known as the Corn Exchange Regiment, suffered the greatest losses in this fighting. According to its own figures, the organization had 269 killed, wounded, or missing, out of an original total of 739.[30]

The above engagement, known as the battle of the Cement Mill, or Blackford's Ford, was fought by the Confederates without cannon. But it was just as well, for seventy enemy pieces on the Maryland side, in their inability to find the range of their opponents, poured volley after volley into the struggling mass of Union troops endeavoring to escape by the ford.

McClellan spent the following weeks resting his men on the battlefield of Antietam, whereas Lee went into camp near Bunker Hill. Comparative inactivity existed in this section until October 16, when Brigadier General A. A. Humphreys led about 6,500 Federals across the Potomac River and advanced toward Kearneysville. Simultaneously, a force under Brigadier General W. S. Hancock crossed the river at Harpers Ferry and moved toward Charles

Town. These maneuvers were made with the idea of screening the activities of McClellan's main army, which was traveling from Sharpsburg to Harpers Ferry. The attacks were so sudden that Confederate pickets, extending from North Mountain to the Shenandoah River, were cut off from their comrades. Engaged in picket duty from Engle's Hill to the Shepherdstown road, Company D, Twelfth Virginia Cavalry, fought a sharp skirmish with the Federal advance. The engagement occurred near the intersection of the Uvilla and Charles Town roads and was south of this point in Rocky Lane. Although it yielded no decisive results, the Confederates made their way through the enemy's lines and joined their regiment.[31]

Humphreys's advance guard progressed as far as Middleway, but his main body stopped a short distance south of Kearneysville. Confederate forces under Major General J. E. B. Stuart, which had been destroying the Baltimore and Ohio Railroad in this vicinity, were composed of Major General Fitzhugh Lee's and Major General Wade Hampton's brigades of cavalry. In addition, there was a body of infantry. Stuart had been making his headquarters at "The Bower", the home of A. S. Dandridge near Leetown.

In the evening of October 16 the Confederates attacked and, after heavy fighting, forced the enemy to withdraw. The retreat was continued the next day to a point on the Shepherdstown-Duffields road known as the Forks, where the Federal brigade of Major C. S. Lovell made a determined stand. Despite the fact that the Unionists felled trees across the road to impede their opponents' artillery and cavalry, they were forced to retreat and later crossed into Maryland.[32]

Driving before it Confederate cavalry under Colonel T. T. Munford, General Hancock's force of infantry, cavalry, and artillery, advanced on October 16 from Harpers Ferry toward Charles Town. About a mile from the county seat at a place known as the Old Fair Grounds the Southerners had posted a section of Chew's Battery under Lieutenant J. W. Carter and two guns of the Richmond Howitzers under Captain B. H. Smith. The Federal batteries were located a quarter of a mile away on an eminence known as Butler's Hill. Although the Confederates stopped the enemy's advance for several hours, the defenders were finally forced to retire. Union troops then took possession of Charles Town and remained

Federal Troops on Camp Hill at Harpers Ferry in 1862. This is now the Site of Storer College

there until two o'clock the next day, when they returned to Harpers Ferry. McClellan arrived in Charles Town shortly after it was taken by Hancock's forces and assumed charge of operations.[33]

About a week later, on October 24, Colonel Silas Colgrove of the Twenty-Seventh Indiana Infantry sent an expedition of seventy-five men from Sharpsburg to Shepherdstown to capture Confederate guerrillas. Led by Captain William Cogswell, the Federals crossed the river in boats a mile above the town, traversed the remaining distance, and entered Shepherdstown. They shot and killed Redmond Burke, a famous Confederate scout, and then captured his two sons. Four others, named Leopold, O'Brien, Hipsley, and Rentch, suspected of being too active in the Southern cause, were also taken prisoners. After searching the town for arms, the Unionists returned to Sharpsburg.[34]

On the morning of November 9, 1862, Brigadier General John W. Geary with 2,500 infantrymen left Bolivar Heights to make a reconnaissance in the direction of Rippon. After Lee's retreat from Sharpsburg, Harpers Ferry was abandoned by its Confederate garrison and allowed to fall into Federal hands. McClellan concentrated practically his whole army around the Ferry, placed a strong garrison there, and used the spot as his base for the next two months. Geary's expedition was sent out to determine the relative strength of enemy forces in the neighborhood. Encountering a small detachment of the Twelfth Virginia Cavalry at Charles Town, the Federals drove this before them and, advancing to Rippon, came upon the Confederate camp. The latter soldiers were forced to retire before overwhelming numbers and were driven almost to Berryville. Having accomplished the object of his reconnaissance, Geary returned to Bolivar Heights. In his official report he gives a vivid picture of the devastation and destitution wrought in the Lower Valley by the numerous skirmishes.[35]

Leaving Bolivar Heights on December 2 and returning four days later, General Geary led another expedition to ascertain the force and location of Confederates in the Lower Valley. With about 4,000 men he advanced toward Charles Town and a short distance east of that place met Company B of the Twelfth Virginia Cavalry. After a sharp contest the Southerners were compelled to retreat. The other companies of the Twelfth Virginia Cavalry made a furious charge on Geary's cavalry [Cole's Battalion] about a mile west of Berryville but withdrew after driving the Federals back. Geary then entered Winchester unopposed, as the Confederates retreated southward down the Valley Pike. He remained in that town one day and then returned to Harpers Ferry by way of Bunker Hill, Middleway, and Charles Town.[36]

On Christmas day a group of the First New York Cavalry under command of Lieutenant Isaac D. Vermilyea left Martinsburg to make a reconnaissance to Charles Town. Arriving at the latter place, it encountered a force of the Twelfth Virginia Cavalry, and in the ensuing fight drove the Confederates out of the town and captured two prisoners, one of whom was a son of Andrew Hunter of Charles Town.[37]

RAIDS, SPRING OF 1863.

Growing tired of the dull routine of camp life at New Market, where their brigade was then stationed, several Jefferson County cavalrymen in the early part of the new year, 1863, decided to visit the Lower Valley. Although their commander, Brigadier General William E. Jones, refused them permission, they feigned sickness and were sent to the hospital at Harrisonburg. When the medical authorities found out that there was nothing seriously wrong with the soldiers, they allowed the "patients" to stay with nearby friends but ordered them to report occasionally at the surgeon's office for examination. The group was composed of Lieutenant Milton Rouss, Lieutenant George Baylor, John Chew, Billy Manning, Charlie Henderson, Charlie Crane, John Yates, John Coleman, George Crayton, Billy Gibson, Upshur Manning, Joe Crane, and "Duck" English. The men left Harrisonburg, crossed the Massanutten Mountain to Luray, passed through Front Royal, and on February 12 arrived at Summit Point.

At the latter place they learned that twenty-one members of the Twelfth Pennsylvania Cavalry had just left for Middleway, and they decided to pursue the Federals. At that time Union troops occupied Winchester and daily sent out scouting expeditions into the surrounding country. Unconscious of danger until it was too late, the Unionists were overtaken at Middleway and driven from the town. They left behind some of their number, killed, wounded, or captured.[38]

Unfortunately for the Confederates, they returned to Summit Point with their prisoners and then went to Locke's Shop, where they stopped to have Rouss's horse shod. This proceeding was suddenly interrupted by the unexpected appearance of a body of Federal cavalry from the direction of Charles Town. In order to allow their comrades time to escape with the captured prisoners and horses, some of the Confederates made a dash against the advance column of the enemy. The dash was so successful that the Federal advance was thrown into confusion. As the Confederates were unable to make the captured Union horses jump fences, these horses and prisoners were recaptured by the Unionists. Three of the fleeing Southerners, George Baylor, Upshur Manning, and John Coleman, had the misfortune to have their horses stumble, with the result that all were taken prisoners.[39] Baylor was removed to Fort McHenry and later to Fort Delaware, from which prison he was subsequently exchanged.

Another daring raid on the county was made a few months later. On May 12 Captain R. P. Chew and Lieutenants G. B. Philpott and John W. Carter led forty-five Confederates from their camp near Harrisonburg to Charles Town. Arriving near the latter place on the night of May 15, they tied their horses in a woods close to the home of George Tate. Dismounting, the raiders went to the courthouse and the Carter House, where Captain George D. Summers's company of Federal cavalry was quartered. After a brief resistance from the enemy the raiders captured 53 prisoners and 75 horses. Summers escaped because he was not present when the attack was made. With their prisoners and booty the Confederates started on the return trip to Harrisonburg.

At daylight they halted at Piedmont, in Fauquier County, to rest their horses. Two of them who lived in the neighborhood went to see friends. On the way, they met two men in Confederate uniform, and full of pride, recited their achievement at Charles Town. Their discomfiture may be conceived when the supposed Confederates turned out to be "Jessie Scouts", or disguised Federals. The latter drew their revolvers and, capturing the unsuspecting raiders, bore them off to headquarters. The Federals ascertained from these prisoners where the main body of raiders was and sent a regiment of cavalry to intercept it.

The attack was so sudden that the Confederates were taken completely by surprise. At the first Union volley five Federal prisoners were killed. The panic-stricken Southerners were so intent on saving themselves that they had no time for anything else. Their rout was complete. The Unionists recaptured all of the prisoners and booty taken at Charles Town and also seven Confederate prisoners. Philpott himself, followed by eighteen Federals, had a narrow escape, but the ability of his horse to leap fences enabled him to outdistance his pursuers.[40]

While Lee was making his second invasion of the North, in the summer of 1863, Harpers Ferry was in possession of Union forces. Company B of the Twelfth Virginia Cavalry was assigned the task of watching the enemy's movements in this section. Having obtained permission from their commanding officer, Lieutenant George Baylor and S. Hammon on the night of June 30 with forty men attacked the Federal cavalry picket reserve in Bolivar. Avoiding the outer picket by following the bank of the Potomac to Bolivar Heights, the Confederates entered the rear of Bolivar. There they found the objects of their quest asleep and succeeded in capturing one officer, nineteen men, and twenty-one horses. One Union soldier was killed in the fighting and the others were brought back to the Confederate camp. Upon the Federal withdrawal from Harpers Ferry the next day Southern troops occupied the town.[41]

SKIRMISHES AFTER GETTYSBURG.

After the Confederate defeat at Gettysburg on July 3, 1863, Lee's battered army retreated southward with the enemy in close pursuit. A Federal detachment seized Maryland Heights on July 7 but did not cross the Potomac River until a week later. On July 14 members of the First Connecticut Cavalry under Major Charles Farnsworth encountered at Halltown Company B of the Twelfth Virginia Cavalry under the command of Colonel A. W. Harman. Although the Federals captured their opponents' advance squadron, they made the mistake of pursuing the others too far. Because of this lack of caution Farnsworth and twenty-five men were taken prisoners by the Confederates after a brief skirmish. This achievement was partially offset by the fact that the

Union cavalry captured seven Confederates, among them Harman.[42]

The following day, July 15, an engagement occurred near Halltown, when the First Maine Cavalry under Colonel C. H. Smith was ordered to advance from Halltown toward Charles Town. After proceeding nearly a mile, the Federals met Confederate pickets and drove them in the direction of the county seat. Fighting soon became general and after two hours with no great advantage on either side, the Unionists withdrew to rejoin the command at Halltown.[43]

The same day Federal cavalry arrived at Shepherdstown and, driving off a small enemy force, encamped. The next day, July 16, they left Shepherdstown and advanced as far as Kearneysville At the latter place they were met by mounted forces from the Confederate brigades of Brigadier General Fitzhugh Lee and Colonel John R. Chambliss. The fighting was brisk, and, although the Unionists fought stubbornly, they were steadily driven back until within a mile of Shepherdstown. As the ground was not suitable for the effective use of cavalry, the men on both sides dismounted. The Federals retired to a strong position in Butler's Woods, near the residence of Colonel Alexander R. Boteler. There they repulsed all efforts to dislodge them and there they remained until midnight, when they withdrew in the direction of Harpers Ferry.

An attempt by the Eighth Pennsylvania Cavalry commanded by Colonel Pennock Huey to proceed from Harpers Ferry to Shepherdstown to reinforce the Union troops was unsuccessful. At Moler's Cross Roads Huey's men were delayed three hours by Company D, Twelfth Virginia Cavalry, under the command of Major John L. Knott. When the Federals did arrive at their destination, about dark, it was too late to be of any assistance.[44]

In a skirmish at Middleway on September 15 between the First New York Cavalry under Captain Abram Jones and a smaller Confederate force, the Federals captured eleven prisoners.[45]

A few miles east of Summit Point at the "White House" place on October 7 occurred a skirmish between a Northern troop under Captain George D. Summers and a Southern force led by Major Harry Gilmor. Gilmor had been on a reconnoitering expedition in the neighborhood and, after vainly pursuing a small enemy group, stopped for a rest at the "White House" farm. He was suddenly attacked from the direction of Summit Point by Summers's troops, with that officer at their head. This rashness proved fatal, however, for Gilmor took careful aim and shot Summers through the head. The Federals were so disorganized without their leader that a Confederate charge sent them flying back to Summit Point. Gilmor's men captured eighteen, killed four, and wounded three of their opponents.[46]

IMBODEN CAPTURES CHARLES TOWN.

About the middle of October 1863, General Lee ordered Major General John D. Imboden to go to Berryville and to meet there General J. E. B. Stuart. Together they were to attack both Harpers Ferry and Charles Town. Imboden's brigade was then encamped in Rockingham County. Late in the evening of October 17 the Confederates arrived in Berryville, where they learned that Stuart had been unable to cross the Shenandoah River because of high water. Although Imboden's command alone numbered less than 1,000 men, he decided to act without Stuart. He modified his plans, however, so as to include only the capture of Charles Town.[47]

Having learned from a scout the size of Charles Town's garrison, Imboden ordered the advance. In the early morning of October 18 the Confederates surrounded the town with batteries. The Ninth Maryland Infantry Regiment under Colonel Benjamin L. Simpson had fortified itself in the courthouse, jail, and other nearby buildings in the heart of the town. To Imboden's demand for unconditional surrender, Simpson replied, "Take us if you can". An artillery barrage directed against the courthouse forced the garrison into the street, where their commander vainly tried to rally his men. Finding that it was impossible to maintain discipline over his panic-stricken troops, Simpson, with several other officers, broke through the Confederate lines and escaped by means of the Duffields road. After a short skirmish at the eastern edge of town, the remaining Federals threw down their arms and surrendered.

With barely time to hustle their 434 prisoners and captured supplies out of town, the Southerners were attacked by a Union relief force from Harpers Ferry. During the retreat to Berryville they were harassed by the Federals. The Confederates fell back slowly, and as they contested every foot of ground, they had to be driven from the numerous hills along the way. They would defend one position for a while and then fall back to another, where they would hinder the Union advance again. Finding that Imboden was escaping with his prisoners and supplies, the pursuers gave up the chase at sundown about two miles from Berryville.[48] A Federal court of inquiry convened at Simpson's request to investigate his losses at Charles Town exonerated him.[49]

RAIDS IN EARLY 1864.

Major Harry Gilmor and a small group of Confederates on the night of February 11, 1864, made a raid on the Baltimore and Ohio Railroad at Brown's Shop, between Kearneysville and Duffields. After having placed obstructions on the track, the raiders waited for the Baltimore Express, which approached from the direction of Harpers Ferry. As soon as the train stopped, it was boarded, and the passengers, many of whom were Federal soldiers, were made prisoners. Although the Southerners had hoped to obtain a large sum of money reported to be in the baggage car, they were doomed to disappointment. The expressman, who had the key to the safe, escaped while the train was slowing down.

About this time Gilmor heard that some of his men were robbing the passengers, and, according to his own account, he threatened to shoot any of them found doing so. He also claims to have restored some of the property to its owners. The raiders were unable to carry off their prisoners, for they perceived that an eastbound troop train from Wheeling was approaching. Scarcely having time to reach their horses, the Confederates left the scene in great haste, and, although the Federals scoured the countryside, the raiders escaped. Returning to camp, they had little to show for their trouble.[50]

There is no doubt that many of the passengers were robbed and that Gilmor's men were unjustified in thus infringing upon the rights of private citizens. Upon receiving reports of this action, General Robert E. Lee condemned it and ordered Gilmor to be tried by court-martial. The latter was to determine whether or not he had exercised due diligence in restraining his men from unlawful acts. After examining all of the evidence, the court decided that Gilmor was innocent.[51]

On the morning of March 10, 1864, a group of about fifty Confederates of Lieutenant Colonel John S. Mosby's command of partisan rangers but under the direct leadership of Lieutenant A. E. Richards attacked Federal pickets at Mechanicstown. Mistaking the enemy for their own men, the Union soldiers did not realize their error until they had received a volley at close range. The attackers killed and wounded several of the Federals, took prisoners, and then rode toward Kabletown. They were pursued by a small force of Union cavalry under Major Jerry A. Sullivan, but in the subsequent fighting three of the Federals, one of whom was Sullivan, were killed. The Confederates then crossed the Shenandoah River at Sampson's Ford and rejoined their command.[52]

Another raid by Mosby's men, this time led by that daring commander himself, occurred on June 29 at Duffield's Depot on the Baltimore and Ohio Railroad. A Confederate force of about 500 broke through the Union lines near Charles Town and attacked a company of infantry stationed at Duffields. The raiders captured about fifty prisoners and a large amount of stores. In addition, they interrupted communication between Federal troops along the railroad by cutting the telegraph line. After destroying the soldiers' quarters, Mosby's men eluded enemy forces sent to intercept them and escaped with much booty.[53]

CHAPTER THIRTEEN
THE CIVIL WAR (CONCLUDED)
SKIRMISHES, JULY, 1864.

When Lieutenant General Jubal A. Early was making his Shenandoah Valley campaign as part of a demonstration against Washington in the summer of 1864, Jefferson County again became a scene of much fighting. On July 3 a force of Confederates under Major General Robert Ransom attacked the enemy commanded by Colonel James A. Mulligan at Leetown and drove them as far as Shepherdstown. At the same time the Federals were forced to evacuate Martinsburg and fall back upon Shepherdstown. There they collected their defeated forces preparatory to crossing the Potomac River into Maryland.[54] These troops crossed the river and traveled to Maryland Heights, where they reinforced the garrison already on hand.

On the next day, July 4, a strong body of Confederates approaching from the direction of Charles Town attacked the Federal position on Bolivar Heights and forced the defenders to fall back to the riflepits near Camp Hill. There they succeeded in holding off the attackers until evening, when the Union commander, Brigadier General Max Weber, decided to evacuate Harpers Ferry and move his troops to Maryland Heights. This was done and several hours later he was joined by Major General Franz Sigel and the soldiers which had been engaged in the previous day's fighting at Leetown and Martinsburg. Maryland Heights was continually used as a Federal signal station. Although there was much skirmishing in this immediate vicinity, the Confederates withdrew on the evening of July 7 and thus allowed their opponents to reoccupy Harpers Ferry the next day.[55]

SHEPHERDSTOWN vs. SHARPSBURG.

An interesting side show of the Civil War in Jefferson County

THE CIVIL WAR (CONCLUDED)

was the struggle between Shepherdstown and Sharpsburg. These two towns, separated by the Potomac River, are only three miles apart, but they were jealous of each other. During the first half of the Civil War this hatred took shape in raids and counter-raids, plundering and defending canalboats, as well as arresting and counter-arresting citizens and strangers. Gradually, the amusement of pelting each other with musket balls at long range declined in popularity, for it was not fatal enough. As the residents of Shepherdstown pursued this private war with greater persistence, they gained on their rivals across the river.[56]

At this point an idea suggested itself to a certain Captain Sowders of Sharpsburg. He conceived the plan of mounting two old six-pounders, which the town possessed. These were of Revolutionary or 1812 memory and had been planted as street-posts in the Maryland town. The ammunition for the cannon consisted of bags of nails and scraps of iron in every shape and size. The would-be artillerists then hauled their implements of destruction to the river bluff opposite Shepherdstown. They used neither a friction nor a percussion fuse but lighted the guns with a cigar. The resulting explosion, witnessed by the Marylanders in nearby gullies and behind rocks, produced the desired result. As soon as the nails and iron began descending upon the frightened Shepherdstown inhabitants, they proposed a truce highly favorable to the Marylanders.

Occasionally it was necessary to wheel the battery into position on the bluffs again, for the Virginians sometimes grew lax in their observance of the truce. The mere presence of Sowders's Battery was generally sufficient to bring about a repentance of sins. One day, however, the victors left their guns on the bluff, unwatched, and retired home to celebrate. When they returned to the scene of action, they were greatly chagrined to discover that their opponents had snatched the guns in the night and carried them away. Thus, the warfare settled back into its original status.[57]

DEVASTATION BY DAVID HUNTER.

In the course of the Civil War various acts were committed by both sides against the rights of private citizens. This generally consisted of false arrest and imprisonment, robbery, commandeering of property, and infringements of a like nature. Sometimes they were excused on the grounds of military necessity, but, for the most part, were condemned by higher authority. Broadly speaking, officers of each side tried to respect private property in the enemy's country. However, two notable exceptions to the foregoing statements were found in the persons of Major General David Hunter and his successor in the Valley, Major General Philip H. Sheridan, both of the Federal army. Each committed so many unnecessary and inhumane acts against citizens that an unbiased observer would not hesitate to denounce them.

After Hunter had made a raid into Virginia in 1864 and had burned Virginia Military Institute, as well as Governor John Letcher's home at Lexington, Lee ordered Lieutenant General Jubal A. Early to move against him. Early was unable to catch Hunter who retreated into West Virginia. Nevertheless, the Confederates continued northward down the Shenandoah Valley. Early crossed into Maryland and defeated General Lew Wallace at Monocacy on July 9, 1864, and then made a demonstration against Washington. He later returned to the Valley, almost to Winchester. A blemish on the Southern ledger in this campaign was the burning of "Falkland," the home of Montgomery Blair, Lincoln's Postmaster General. This was said to have been done in retaliation for the burning of Governor Letcher's home by Hunter. Early denied that he ordered the destruction of Blair's home but claimed it was justified.[58]

General David Hunter was appointed Union commander in the Lower Valley and continued his career of devastation. One of his first acts there was to issue an order at Harpers Ferry to Captain William F. Martindale to burn the dwellinghouse and outbuildings of Andrew Hunter in Charles Town. Andrew, a first cousin of the Union general, had served as one of the prosecutors in the John Brown trial. Implicit directions were given Martindale that nothing should be taken from the house except the family.

It is perhaps needless to add that on July 17, 1864, these orders were carried out to the letter, for the women of the household were even refused permission to save their clothing or family portraits from the flames. To add to the desolation, the Union

THE CIVIL WAR (CONCLUDED)

cavalry camped on the beautiful grounds of the estate and thus ruined its natural beauty. Andrew Hunter was taken prisoner, held for a month, and then discharged without trial or explanation. At the time of his imprisonment he was wearing a gold ring that years before had been given to him, as an evidence of affection, by his "Cousin David".[59]

It might be mentioned here that the destruction of this home, as well as the others, was of no military value whatsoever.

"Fountain Rock", the beautiful home of Alexander R. Boteler located a mile southwest of Shepherdstown, was laid in ashes two days later. This spot subsequently became the site of the Morgan's Grove Fair Grounds. Colonel Boteler, who was a member of the Confederate Congress, and his wife were away while their home was being destroyed. The members living at "Fountain Rock" then were his widowed daughter, Mrs. David Shepherd, her three children, the eldest five years old and the youngest eighteen months, and another daughter, Miss Helen Boteler. A squad of about a dozen Union soldiers led by Captain Martindale rode up to the house and said they had orders to destroy all the buildings. In spite of the pleas that the inmates be allowed to save their own personal property, Martindale remained unmoved and ordered his men to begin their unsoldierly task.[60]

While some of the Unionists plundered the house of silver, spoons, forks, cups, and whatever they fancied, others got straw from the barn and carried it into the building. Furniture was piled on the floors, sprinkled with kerosene brought along for the purpose, and set on fire. Only a few articles were saved. Miss Helen Boteler, a devoted student of music, begged in vain for her piano. While the fire was making headway in the adjoining room and the smoke rolled about her, she seated herself at this instrument, struck a few chords, and sang Charlotte Elliott's hymn, "Thy Will Be Done". By this time the flames had crept closer and she calmly closed the piano, locked it, and went outside.

One by one the barn and other buildings were ruthlessly given the torch. Within a short time a few piles of stones, charred embers, and smoking ruins were all that remained of this once beautiful mansion. From an historical standpoint, the greatest loss was that of Colonel Boteler's library, which contained many fine pictures and rare manuscripts illustrating the early history of this part of Virginia. All of this was lost to posterity because of the intense ruthlessness of General David Hunter.[61]

From "Fountain Rock" the Federals rode into Shepherdstown and then out again on the Duffields road to "Bedford", the old colonial home of Edmund J. Lee, a first cousin of the famous Southern general. Meanwhile, they had been preceded to "Bedford" by several persons who took a short cut across some fields. Lee was absent in Clarke County, but his wife, Henrietta Bedinger Lee, and two young children, Harry and Nettie, awaited the coming of the Federals. Mrs. Lee had been sick in bed but arose and dressed when she received word of the impending doom. Martindale had evidently obtained wine at the Boteler home, for when he appeared at "Bedford", he was partly intoxicated. He roughly ordered the family to vacate.

The distressed wife and mother endeavored to persuade the Union officer to change his mind. She told him that it was her own home, an inheritance from her father, a Revolutionary soldier. Surely, she reasoned, the Federal army was not warring on women and children. Her pleas availed nothing, however, and she saved only a few personal belongings. The Negro servants were loyal and helped her to carry out some of the parlor furniture and other household goods. As at the Boteler home, straw, kerosene, and matches began the destruction of her home and outbuildings. The sick woman could only stand a short distance away, lean on relatives for support, and watch nearly everything she owned go up in smoke. In a few days the family joined Lee in Clarke County but later returned to Shepherdstown to live.[62]

Mrs. Lee's indignation was so great that on the following day she penned a scathing rebuke to General Hunter. Because of the incisive language used so forcibly, it is here reproduced in its entirety.

Shepherdstown, Va., July 20, 1864

General Hunter:

Yesterday your underling, Captain Martindale, of the First New York Veteran Cavalry, executed your infamous order and burned my house. You have had the satisfaction ere this of receiving from him the information that your or-

THE CIVIL WAR (CONCLUDED)

ders were fulfilled to the letter, the dwelling and every outbuilding, seven in number, with their contents, being burned. I, therefore, a helpless woman whom you have cruelly wronged, address you, a Major General of the United States Army, and demand why this was done? What was my offence? My husband was absent—an exile. He has never been a politician or in any way engaged in the struggle now going on, his age preventing. This fact your chief-of-staff, David Strother, could have told you.

The house was built by my father, a Revolutionary soldier, who served the whole seven years for your independence. There was I born; there the sacred dead repose. It was my house and my home, and there had your niece, Miss Griffith, who lived among us all this horried war up to the present moment, met with all kindness and hospitality at my hands. Was it for this that you turned me, my young daughter, and little son out upon the world without shelter? Or was it because my husband is the grandson of the Revolutionary patriot and "rebel", Richard Henry Lee, and the near kinsman of the noblest of Christian warriors, and greatest of generals, Robert E. Lee? Heaven's blessing be upon his head forever! You and your Government have failed to conquer, subdue, or match him; and disappointed rage and malice find vent on the helpless and inoffensive.

Hyena-like you have torn my heart to pieces! for all hallowed memories clustered around that homestead; and demonlike, you have done it without even the pretext of revenge, for I never saw or harmed you. Your office is not to lead, like a brave man and soldier, your men to fight in the ranks of war, but your work has been to separate yourself from all danger, and with your incendiary band steal unaware upon helpless women and children, to insult and destroy. Two fair homes did you yesterday ruthlessly lay in ashes, giving not a moment's warning to the startled inmates of your wicked purpose; turning mothers and children out of doors, your very name is execrated by your own men for the cruel work you give them to do.

In the case of Mr. A. R. Boteler, both father and mother were far away. Any heart but that of Captain Martindale (and yours) would have been touched by that little circle, comprising a widowed daughter just risen from her bed of illness, her three fatherless babies—the eldest five years old—and her heroic sister. I repeat, any **man** would have been touched at the sight but Captain Martindale! One might as well hope to find mercy and feeling in the heart of a wolf bent on his prey of young lambs, as to search for such qualities in his bosom. You have chosen well your agent for such deeds, and doubtless will promote him.

A colonel of the Federal Army has stated that you deprived forty of your officers of their commands because they refused to carry out your malignant mischief. All honor to their names for this, at least! They are **men,** and have human hearts and blush for such a commander! I ask who that does not wish infamy and disgrace attached to him forever would serve under you? Your name will stand on history's pages as the Hunter of weak women, and innocent children; the Hunter to destroy defenceless villages and beautiful homes—to torture afresh the agonized hearts of widows; the Hunter of Africa's poor sons and daughters, to lure them on to ruin and death of soul and body; the Hunter with the relentless heart of a wild beast, the face of a fiend, and the form of a man. Oh, Earth, behold the monster! Can I say "God forgive you"? No prayer can be offered for you! Were it possible for human lips to raise your name heavenward, angels would thrust the foul thing back again, and demons claim their own. The curse of thousands, the scorn of the manly and upright, and the hatred of the true and honorable, will follow you and yours through all time, and brand your name infamy! infamy!

Again, I demand why have you burned my house? Answer as you must answer before the Searcher of all hearts; why have you added this cruel, wicked deed to your many crimes?

Henrietta B. Lee[63]

SHENANDOAH VALLEY CAMPAIGN, 1864.

Such unprovoked acts aroused Early to retaliation. He sent Brigadier General John McCausland with two brigades of cavalry and a battery to Chambersburg, Pennsylvania, the nearest distinctly Northern community that could be reached. McCausland was ordered to demand $100,000 in gold or its equivalent in currency, as partial compensation to the victims of Hunter's ruthlessness. In default, he was to burn the town. The residents either could not, or would not, raise the money and on July 30 the town was burned. At least they were given an opportunity to save their homes by raising the stated sum of money. No such alternative was offered the families of Andrew Hunter, Alexander R. Boteler, or Edmund J. Lee.[64]

In August Major General Philip H. Sheridan succeeded Hunter

THE CIVIL WAR (CONCLUDED)   177

as commander of Federal troops in the Lower Valley. Having determined to attack him, Early, on August 21, ordered Lieutenant General R. H. Anderson to advance by way of Summit Point. At the same time Early planned to proceed from Bunker Hill to Middleway and then toward Charles Town. Anderson found his advance delayed by Brigadier General Wesley Merritt's cavalry at Berryville and Brigadier General J. H. Wilson's at Summit Point. Although Anderson finally succeeded in forcing both Merritt and Wilson to fall back, he was delayed too long to take part in the fighting around Middleway.[65]

Meanwhile, Early's attack along Opequon Creek had been successful. Forcing the enemy's cavalry pickets along the creek to retire quickly, he pressed at once against the Federal Sixth Corps. This part of the army had been camping at Welch's Spring, on the Charles Town-Middleway turnpike about two miles from the county seat. As soon as the Union commanders learned that their cavalry at Middleway had been attacked and driven off, they made ready for battle. Because of the sudden appearance of the Confederates, the Federals were almost taken by surprise. They found it necessary to bring up their reserves at once and in the ensuing engagement at Cameron's Depot [Aldridge's] were driven toward Charles Town. In spite of the fact that they had suffered severe losses, they remained on the field until midnight, when they retired to Halltown. Sheridan had decided to draw in Merritt and Wilson and concentrate his forces in front of Halltown, which he thought could be more easily defended. During the night of August 21 the Southerners camped about two and a half miles from Charles Town.[66]

In the engagement at Cameron's Depot Early had planted his cannon on the hill around the house of John R. Flagg and formed his battle lines north and south of this point. The center of Sheridan's lines was "Locust Hill", the home of John B. Packett, which was somewhat east of Early's position. As much fighting and cannonading took place about this house, it is not surprising that the brick structure received many bullet-holes, a large number of which may be seen today. Many Federals were killed and wounded in the immediate vicinity. During part of the engagement the house was occupied by its owners and some of their relatives, but when the shelling became so heavy, they escaped across the fields from the Union lines to Charles Town. Luckily, none of these refugees were struck while they were making their dangerous way to safety.[67] Other famous estates which also witnessed fighting in this engagement were "Harewood", "Sulgrave", "Tuscawillow", and "Cedar Lawn".

While Early was driving Sheridan back along the Charles Town-Middleway road on August 21, another engagement was taking place on his extreme left, in the vicinity of the Leetown-Charles Town turnpike. In cooperation with the general attack on Sheridan's lines around Charles Town, Major General L. L. Lomax with his cavalry was ordered to protect the left flank of the Confederate force under Major General Robert E. Rodes. Lomax entrusted the duty of protecting the extreme left to Major Harry Gilmor with two Maryland battalions and the Nineteenth and Twentieth Virginia regiments of Jackson's Brigade.

Gilmor dismounted his cavalry on the Charles Town-Leetown road and awaited a charge. This was near the house then owned by a certain Mrs. Daniel and now in possession of John J. Eby. The Federals made a valiant charge against the Confederate position but were repulsed. When Gilmor's cavalry charged it penetrated the enemy's line to his reserves and captured some prisoners. A brigade of Federal cavalry then attempted to outflank Gilmor by moving around his left, but that officer so maneuvered the two Maryland battalions that they repulsed the attack with heavy slaughter.

This attack was made by Duffie's Brigade led by the Twelfth Pennsylvania Cavalry with a Colonel Bell in command. The latter officer was killed while bravely leading his charging troops. After the Union soldiers had retreated from this assault, their artillery opened on the Confederates, who were in a woods. Although none of the latter were killed by these shells, many were wounded by the flying fragments of shell and falling limbs of trees. The Federals then attacked again. This time the position held by the two Virginia regiments received the brunt of the assault, but again the attack failed and the Federals were forced to retreat after leaving behind some prisoners.[68]

On the next day, August 22, Early found that the enemy had retreated on all fronts to Halltown, where Sheridan had strongly fortified himself. A few minor skirmishes convinced the Confed-

THE CIVIL WAR (CONCLUDED) 179

erate commander that Sheridan's position was almost impregnable, so, leaving part of his troops to face the Federals at Halltown, he took the main body northward to Shepherdstown. A series of unimportant skirmishes had been taking place for several days in that vicinity, but it was not until August 25 that engagements of greater magnitude were fought.

On that date between Leetown and Kearneysville Early's infantry came upon Wesley Merritt's and J. H. Wilson's divisions of Union cavalry commanded by Major General T. A. Torbert. The latter, assuming he had only horsemen to deal with, attacked vigorously, and, although he forced the Confederates back at first, he soon found himself getting the worst of this encounter and, accordingly, withdrew. Early even succeeded in cutting off Major General George A. Custer's brigade, but by putting forth great effort this body managed to escape to Shepherdstown. There it took part in another fight later in the day. Early's lack of cavalry in this particular engagement prevented his following Custer at once.

Early followed up his success at Kearneysville by pushing on to Shepherdstown. Although the Federals made another stand near the latter place, on the Charles Town road, they were again forced to withdraw, this time along the road to Halltown. Their First Brigade, while fighting the Confederates along the above road, discovered itself cut off by another force of the enemy which had marched across the country and had begun assailing its flank. The Federals then found it necessary to send the Second Brigade in order to enable the First to retire across the Potomac. The latter brigade under the leadership of Custer effected its escape and crossed the river at Pack Horse Ford.

The Confederates, after having thus disposed of their opponents, spent the night near Shepherdstown. On the next day, August 26, Early withdrew his infantry to Leetown, for he had decided to resume his former position west of Opequon Creek, near Bunker Hill. The Confederate withdrawal from Shepherdstown was accompanied by a minor skirmish with the First United States Cavalry, which temporarily took possession of the town after the Southern infantry had left.[69]

In the meantime, things had not been going so well with Anderson, who was confronting Sheridan before Halltown. That

Confederate leader had been greatly weakened when Early took some of his troops to Shepherdstown. Consequently, when Major General George Crook, reconnoitering on August 26, assaulted Anderson's lines near Charles Town, he was able to break them, capture prisoners, and force Anderson to retire.[70] After this engagement the latter general withdrew to Stephenson's Depot in order to cooperate with Early in resuming the former Confederate position near Bunker Hill.[71]

After Early's infantry had crossed to the west side of Opequon Creek, his cavalry under Fitzhugh Lee and Lomax remained near Shepherdstown. On August 28 while Lomax's horsemen were near Leetown, they were attacked by a similar branch of the Federal army commanded by Merritt and were driven to Middleway. Lomax had sent Gilmor to reestablish his picket line at Leetown, as he had been told that there were but 200 of the enemy at this place.

While Gilmor was attempting to carry out these orders, he found himself considerably outnumbered and was thus forced to retreat in great haste. The pursuit was kept up until the defeated Southern cavalrymen were forced to join their infantry across Opequon Creek. Fitz Lee retreated toward Brucetown and Lomax in the direction of Bunker Hill. Federal troops then occupied Middleway, where they burned several barns and houses. Among the unfortunate residents thus to lose their property were Mrs. Ariana Hughes, Mrs. Ruth Ringer, Miss Mary Moore, and Dr. William O. Macoughtry.[72]

The next day, August 29, Major Generals Stephen Ramseur and John B. Gordon were sent by Early to drive the Northern cavalry back, for it had advanced across Opequon Creek. Early also moved up his artillery, and after brisk cannonading across the creek, accompanied by heavy fighting, the Federals were forced out of a fortified position through Middleway to a place nearly three miles from Charles Town. Their cavalry had also been compelled to retreat. After this successful venture, Early withdrew his main force across Opequon Creek and left the cavalry east of the stream. In the late afternoon the Federals were reinforced and, driving ahead the small group opposing them, advanced again to the water's banks. Thus, a second time the Confederate cavalry was driven back across the stream. At dark the Northern soldiers returned to their camp near Charles Town.[73]

It was a short time after these engagements in the late summer of 1864 that Early's army in the Lower Valley was greatly weakened by the withdrawal of Anderson's force. The latter consisted of Major General Joseph B. Kershaw's infantry and Major Wilfred E. Cutshaw's artillery and was needed to aid Lee in the desperate struggle before Petersburg. The Southern general evidently realized what effect this withdrawal would have upon Early's chances for future success. In a dispatch to Anderson he stated that he thought that without Kershaw's division, Early's forces would be insufficient to meet successfully his numerically superior opponents in the Valley. Only the dire necessity for replenishing his rapidly diminishing lines with additional troops to defend the Confederate capital forced Lee to take such a step. Consequently, when Sheridan assumed the offensive in September, Early was in no condition to do more than attempt to retard the advance as much as possible.

Nevertheless, Early's activities in the Lower Valley had not been for naught. In threatening the defenses of Washington, he forced Lieutenant General U. S. Grant to dispatch part of his army to aid in the capital's defense. By holding the Opequon line for weeks, Early had caused great apprehension in nearby Maryland and Pennsylvania. In addition, he had succeeded to a remarkable extent in interrupting traffic over the Baltimore and Ohio Railroad and the Chesapeake and Ohio Canal, important arteries of communication with the West.[74]

MOSBY IN 1864.

Several of Lieutenant Colonel John S. Mosby's men under Lieutenant Joseph Nelson were suddenly attacked at their temporary camp at Myers's Ford, near Myerstown, by a body of Independent Scouts led by Captain Richard Blazer. These Scouts consisted of 100 picked men entrusted with the sole duty of watching and, if possible, capturing Mosby's rangers. They had served in suppressing guerrilla bands in West Virginia and had been brought along to win fresh laurels in the Valley. They were well-armed, brave, and well-led. The date of this attack was either September 4 or 5, for Blazer reports the affair as having taken place on the former date, whereas Mosby says it occurred a day later. Mosby broke camp near Hillsboro and, leaving part of his command at Myers's Ford under Nelson, took six men, crossed the Shenandoah River, and started to reconnoiter near Charles Town. His men left at the ford apparently were resting, with no thought of a possible attack. Meanwhile, Blazer's scouts, seeking Mosby, had left Charles Town, found their quarry's deserted camp at Hillsboro, and given chase. They finally came upon the unsuspecting rangers at the ford, on the east bank of the river. Being wholly unprepared for a defense, Nelson's men fled in all directions, although they did succeed in inflicting a little damage on their attackers. The latter, however, were more successful and, in addition to killing and wounding several rangers, also captured a small number. Mosby reported that with the six men he took on the reconnaissance to Charles Town, he captured twenty-five prisoners, two ambulances, and eighteen horses, and thus partially offset Blazer's success at the ford.[75]

Although the whole Lower Valley was in possession of Union forces, in the autumn of 1864 occurred Mosby's "Greenback Raid", one of the most successful in this section. Information had reached the bold Confederate leader that a train carrying forty-two Federal paymasters had left Washington over the Baltimore and Ohio tracks. The money was intended for Sheridan's army. As Mosby's men were an independent command, they received no regular salary from the authorities at Richmond, and the prospect of stopping this train appealed greatly to them. Accordingly, sixty-five or seventy of them crossed the Shenandoah River at Castleman's Ferry on the night of October 13 and moved toward Bunker Hill. They had decided to stop the train at a cut in the railroad between Duffields Depot and Kearneysville, at a spot a mile west of Shenandoah Junction.[76]

With a Jefferson County resident, James G. Wiltshire, showing the way, the rangers arrived at the chosen spot and prepared to stop the train. A detail of twenty men was entrusted with the work of pulling up the rails. This plan had to be abandoned because of the difficulty in finding a crowbar. Instead, it was decided to raise the entire track. Strong fence rails were used and the men soon had one side of the track raised some distance above

THE CIVIL WAR (CONCLUDED)

the level of the roadbed. As the railroad was double-tracked, both lines were torn up. A short time before, the rangers had disturbed only one track and were greatly chagrined to witness a train go thundering past on the track that remained untouched. Unknown to Mosby, the train he was attempting to rob had passed this point in safety before his command reached the railroad. However, luck was with him, for two Federal paymasters had missed the train and were compelled to take the next one. While the men were waiting for the object of their raid, they were startled by their guard's sudden announcement, "The Yankees are coming!" Running for their horses, the troopers were astonished to receive no rain of bullets. Closer examination revealed that the guard had been frightened by a sow and her pigs running through the dry autumn leaves. Thoroughly disgusted, the raiders resumed their former positions, while Mosby swore at the guard and threatened to send him back to the regular army, a thing greatly dreaded by all the rangers.[77]

Soon the clear autumn air was pierced by a distant rumble between two and three o'clock on the morning of October 14. Presently a locomotive's headlight came into view as a fast westbound train approached. A grinding noise resounded as the wheels struck the broken track, and the engine tumbled over into the other track. Although the engine was completely wrecked, the ten coaches did not receive much damage and the passengers escaped with a general jolting.

As soon as the train stopped, Mosby's men went through the cars. One of the rangers, J. West Aldrich, was doing this when he noticed a dark object between two seats. Further examination revealed it to be General Ruggles, one of the Union paymasters. A little later Aldrich's foot struck an object on the floor. He picked it up and it proved to be a paymaster's strong box containing more than $100,000. In the meantime, another Confederate, Charles H. Dear, had captured General Moore and $68,000 additional. As most of the money was in greenbacks, this name was given to the raid.

Mosby ordered the passengers out of the cars so that he might set fire to the wooden coaches. A little difficulty arose when a group of westbound German immigrants refused to leave their seats. An interpreter explained that as these Germans had purchased through tickets, they were determined to remain aboard until the end of the line was reached. Mosby then gave vent to his impatience by ordering his men to scatter newspapers, located in a corner of the coach, in the aisle and to "burn the d—d Dutch up if they didn't disgorge and leave the car". It is perhaps needless to add that when the flames spread through the wooden coach, these immigrants poured out like hornets after a small boy has disturbed their nest.

As many Union soldiers were not far away, the rangers determined to leave. In the light of the burning train they put their prisoners, who were Federals on furlough, behind them on horseback and departed. Before long they had placed the Shenandoah River between them and the scene of the raid. Agreeing to meet the following day at Bloomfield, in Loudoun County, the command divided. At the appointed time and place the money was divided among the men; Mosby alone refused to take a share. Each raider thus received about $2,000. Shortly after the raid the men showed their appreciation of their leader by presenting him with a thoroughbred horse, named "Croquette," which they had purchased at Oatlands, Virginia. The Federal paymasters were sent to Richmond as prisoners of war and another drama in Mosby's career was ended. For a time greenbacks were plentiful in northern Virginia.[78]

With two commands like Captain Blazer's Independent Scouts and Colonel Mosby's Partisan Rangers operating in the same region, on opposite sides, a clash was inevitable. Especially was this certain when Blazer's organization had no other purpose than to track down Mosby. The Confederate leader refused to be diverted from his main purpose, that of harassing Sheridan's army and communications. However, when Sheridan's troops had gone into winter quarters and active operations had ceased between the main armies in the Valley, Mosby had some time to devote to Blazer. Setbacks in two skirmishes with the Scouts had made Mosby's men unusually anxious to even the score.

Armed with specially procured long-range Spencer rifles to "clean out Mosby's gang", Blazer's men scoured the country. The Confederate rangers likewise left camp to put an end to "Old Blaze", as they called the rival leader. Mosby himself was unable to go on this expedition because of sickness but divided his

THE CIVIL WAR (CONCLUDED)

command into two groups containing eighty men each led by Lieutenants William Chapman and Adolphus [Dolly] Richards. Two advance scouts reported to Richards that Blazer's men had been seen in the Kabletown vicinity and to that section went the Southerners. In the meantime, Blazer learned that Richards was in the neighborhood and he started out to seek the Confederates. For a time the two commands traveled around in circles, while each sought the other.[79]

On November 18, 1864, Richards halted his men near the road along which he knew Blazer was coming and waited for his adversary. His position was on the George Harris farm directly south of a strip of timber adjoining the road from Myerstown to Myers's Ford. The Confederate leader intended to conceal his men in the woods and then burst forth suddenly on the Federals, so that the latter's advantage of long-range rifles would be minimized. The attempt at surprise, however, was frustrated by one of Richards's men who had imbibed too freely of whiskey. As soon as he saw the unsuspecting enemy approach, he dashed out of the ranks, fired his pistol, and thus exposed the Confederate position.

Blazer's men came rapidly forward and then halted at a stone fence seventy-five yards away. Richards thought the Union troopers intended dismounting behind this protection and then using their rifles to advantage. As his men had only pistols, such a contest could have but one end. Furthermore, the Southern soldiers would have difficulty in charging over the stone wall to attack. To entice the Federals into the open, Richards ordered Harry Hatcher, commanding Company A, to fall back a short distance over the hill. Blazer immediately thought this pretended retreat to be real and ordered his men to charge. This command was fatal. Before Blazer could recover from his surprise, he was attacked by Richards's whole group. Pistols were used with deadly effect and soon the remnants of the Independent Scouts attempted to cut their way out. The leader and those of his men who survived the first onslaught started a headlong retreat out of the woods and on to the Myerstown road.

Blazer was splendidly mounted and led four pursuers a lengthy chase toward Rippon. One of the rangers, Syd Ferguson, drew away from the others and continued to gain on the figure in blue. He did not know that his quarry was Blazer, but the blue uniform was enough to invite pursuit. Ferguson had already emptied his two pistols so when he drew abreast of the fleeing Federal, he arose in his stirrups and struck Blazer a tremendous blow on the head. The man tumbled to the ground on a spot not far from the home of Daniel Heflebower, near Rippon. Ferguson did not stop but continued following other fleeing blue-coats. When the pursuit was over, he returned and, dismounting, examined the stunned Federal leader. He soon found out that Blazer was "playing possum", and he made the prisoner accompany him back to the main body.

This engagement was one of the most destructive cavalry fights on record, in proportion to the numbers involved, approximately eighty on each side. Richards had one man killed, Hudgin, and seven slightly wounded, whereas, Blazer's loss was twenty-four killed, twelve wounded, and sixty-two captured, including himself. Only five of the Independent Scouts escaped to report the annihilation of Blazer's command.[80]

SKIRMISHES, WINTER OF 1864-1865.

The latter part of the year witnessed a few more skirmishes in Jefferson County. Lieutenant George Baylor of Charles Town had a brief engagement with Federal pickets at Keyes's Ford on November 22 in which his small group took several prisoners. Later, he led an expedition against the camp of the Twelfth Pennsylvania Cavalry, which was stationed at Charles Town. Accompanied by thirty men of Company B, Twelfth Virginia Cavalry, this bold Jefferson County native succeeded on November 29 in slipping through the Union lines. Arriving in town, the Confederates completely surprised the sleeping enemy, and they killed and wounded eleven, and captured twenty-seven prisoners and thirty-seven horses. Baylor reported a loss of one man killed and one seriously wounded. The slain Confederate was his brother, Robert W. Baylor, Jr., a lad of seventeen years.

An entirely different picture of this engagement was given by the Federal commander, Captain Nathaniel Payne. In his official report he numbered the attacking force at 200 and claimed his losses as less than Baylor reported. Baylor offered a possible explanation of this discrepancy. He suggested that perhaps Payne

THE CIVIL WAR (CONCLUDED) 187

was afraid of Sheridan's threat to throw into disgrace Federal officers who could not clear the country of guerrillas. For this reason he may have minimized the enemy's gains in this engagement.[81]

On February 3, 1865, a party of Confederates crossed the Shenandoah River at Keyes's Ford and derailed a train on the Baltimore and Ohio Railroad. Two groups of Federals sent out by Colonel M. A. Reno from Charles Town to intercept the guerrillas mistook each other for the enemy and fired, but, fortunately for them, only one man was wounded. The leader of one of these bodies, a Lieutenant Guild, was arrested and dismissed by his superior officer for the miscarriage of plans.[82]

JOHN YATES BEALL.

On February 24, 1865, John Yates Beall, a native of Jefferson County, was executed at Governor's Island, New York, on the charge of being a Confederate spy and guerrilla. This young Southerner had endeavored to support the Stars and Bars in many different ways. He had served in the army, had been wounded at Bolivar Heights, and later had organized a group to prey on Federal commerce in the lower Chesapeake Bay. He was captured, exchanged, and recaptured. An effort to free Confederate officers imprisoned on Johnson's Island, in Lake Erie, failed when his crew mutinied. On December 16, 1864, he was found in civilian clothes at Niagara and was later taken to Governor's Island. Many efforts were made to save him from the gallows, but all failed. His remains were sent to Charles Town and buried in the churchyard of Zion Episcopal Church.[83]

THE END.

The final skirmish in Jefferson County during the Civil War was caused by an expedition led by a native, Captain George Baylor. Baylor was elected captain of Company H of Mosby's men on April 5, 1865, in Loudoun County and shortly afterwards was ordered to lead a scouting expedition into Jefferson. With a group of about fifty well-mounted men he prepared for the trip. His rangers had been commanded to disband for the night and meet the next morning at Snickersville, in true Mosby fashion. In accordance with orders, his company assembled the next day, April 6, and set out for Charles Town. Having learned the whereabouts of the Loudoun Rangers, a body of Federals from Loudoun County, Baylor determined to try to capture them.[84]

Although it was necessary to pass through Federal lines to reach the Loudoun camp at Keyes's Switch [Millville], this was done successfully and the Confederates prepared for an attack. A sudden charge into the camp of the unsuspecting enemy and a few shots enabled Baylor's men to capture almost the whole force. This was done in spite of the fact that the Federals outnumbered the attackers two to one. The total number of captures resulting from this raid was sixty-five prisoners and eighty-one horses, together with their equipment. Several of the Unionists were killed or wounded, whereas Baylor had only one man wounded. Enemy infantry nearby attempted to intercept the raiders, but before they could get ready, the Confederates had crossed the river at Keyes's Ford and escaped into the surrounding hillsides.[85]

Meanwhile, the tottering Confederacy was swiftly approaching its doom. Grant had forced Lee to evacuate both Petersburg and Richmond, and on April 7 the Confederate leader asked for terms. The generous reply of the Federal commander made surrender only a matter of days. As soon as word of the impending capitulation reached Jefferson County, there was great rejoicing among the Union troops stationed here. One camp was at Kearneysville and a squad from it decided to celebrate. Accordingly, the soldiers went to Shepherdstown and directed their way to the home of "Uncle" Jordan Norris, the Negro sexton of Trinity Episcopal Church. Routing him out of bed on the night of April 7 and refusing him permission to dress, the soldiers told him to accompany them to the church. Clad only in a nightshirt the old Negro did as he was told.

When this strange group arrived at the church, the sexton was made to climb up into the belfry. His captors ordered him to ring the bell loud and long to celebrate the Union victory and threatened him with death if he stopped ringing without their permission. It is needless to add that "Uncle" Jordan rang that bell as it had never been rung before. While he was going strong, his tormentors locked the door on the outside, threw the key into the grass, and rode away. When they reached Walper's Cross

Roads, about four miles distant, they could still hear the pealing of the bell on the midnight air.

Although nearly everyone in Shepherdstown was awakened by the ringing, only a few persons ventured out. One of them, Dr. Charles W. Andrews, the Episcopal minister, went straight to his church and finally got inside. He made his way to the belfry and then witnessed a most unusual sight. He saw the poor old Negro, tired and perspiring freely, with his nightshirt flapping in the breeze, ringing the bell for all he was worth. Only after a convincing argument could the minister persuade his faithful sex-- ton to release the rope. The terror-stricken victim of the Federal joke could hardly believe that there were no soldiers waiting below to shoot him. It is said that to the day of his death this son of Africa never afterward had any use for "Yankees".[86]

With Lee's surrender to Grant on April 9, 1865, military operations in Jefferson County ended. The majority of Mosby's command, led by Colonel William H. Chapman, surrendered at Winchester on April 21 and were accordingly paroled. That indomitable leader himself, along with the remainder of his band, received the same liberal terms given to Lee and Johnston and surrendered on May 8.[87]

CHAPTER FOURTEEN
VIRGINIA OR WEST VIRGINIA
FORMATION OF WEST VIRGINIA.

While the people of Jefferson County were helping the South in the Civil War, a new movement was taking place in northwestern Virginia. Jefferson County did not interest itself in this movement and was not in sympathy with it. Yet a new state was being formed that was eventually to include Jefferson County and thus sever its geographical ties with the Old Dominion. To understand the course of events, it is necessary to review the steps in the formation of the State of West Virginia.

The grievances which people of western Virginia had against those in the eastern part of the state had not been entirely satisfied by the Constitutional Convention of 1850-1851. The mountaineers still remained in the position of an oppressed minority. Among other things, Negro slaves under twelve years of age were not then taxed by Virginia and those above that age were taxed on nominal values. Meanwhile, the property of western Virginians was taxed on its full value. Slavery was almost nonexistent in the northwest region. Since some provision had been made by the Convention of 1850-1851 to eliminate the unfair representation of westerners in the General Assembly, that question subsided. However, another sore spot that still existed was the fact that the northwest received only a small share of money spent by the state for railroads and public buildings.[1] Inasmuch as public expenditures for free schools were inadequate to provide for the education of the poor, the annual expenditure for the State University at Charlottesville was a source of dissatisfaction in the northwest.

The chasm thus produced was still further widened when on April 17, 1861, the Virginia Convention voted 88 for, to 55 against secession. That part of the state now included in West Virginia sent 47 delegates to the Secession Convention at Richmond. Of these, 32 voted against secession, 11 for it, and 4 did not vote. Two of those who did not vote later signed the ordinance, as did also two of those who had voted in the negative. Most of those who cast ballots in favor of secession did so in protest against Lincoln's call for troops to coerce the Southern states. Thus, there was an overwhelming sentiment in western Virginia against the course the state had taken.[2]

The minority delegates returned to their constituents to oppose the rising tide of secession. John S. Carlile of Harrison County was desirous of forming a new state and largely through his efforts a convention was held on April 22 at Clarksburg. The most important result of this meeting was the determination to invite every county in northwestern Virginia to send delegates to a convention to meet in Wheeling, May 13-15, 1861. This was subsequently known as the First Wheeling Convention. At that time and place 436 delegates from 27 counties met and denounced the Virginia Secession Ordinance. Jefferson County was not represented at this gathering, although its neighbors, Berkeley and Frederick, were. A majority of those assembled favored proclaiming a new state at once, while others wanted to reorganize the Virginia government on a loyal basis. Further action was postponed until the result of the state's referendum on secession was known. In the event this was favorable to secession, another convention was to be held on June 11.

The referendum was held on May 23. Meantime, other events had happened so fast that the state went overwhelmingly for secession. The vote in western Virginia alone, however, was about 44,000 against, to 4,000 for secession but was not accurately and fully determined. Accordingly, the plans for the second convention went forward and it, too, met at Wheeling, June 11-25. This time about 100 delegates from 34 counties were present. Even Jefferson County had a representative, George Koonce. He had remained loyal to the Union and had been a member of the volunteers who opposed the entrance of Virginia militia into Harpers Ferry at the beginning of the Civil War. For this he was forced to leave the county immediately and he did not return to Harpers Ferry until it fell into Federal hands again. His appointment was irregular in that Secretary of War, E. M. Stanton, a personal friend, asked Koonce to be present at the Wheeling Convention to look out for the interests of the Lincoln administration. Whether he was chosen at an election or mass meeting is not certain.[3]

On June 19 the Second Wheeling Convention adopted an ordinance for the reorganization of the state government on a loyal basis. The next day Francis H. Pierpont was, on motion of Daniel Lamb, unanimously elected governor of the Reorganized Government of Virginia to serve until such time as a regular election could be held, and other state officials were chosen. The new executive convened the Virginia General Assembly to meet in extra session on July 1, 1861. At this meeting the vacant places of R. M. T. Hunter and James M. Mason in the United States Senate were filled by the election of Waitman T. Willey and John S. Carlile, respectively. Although efforts were made to have this assembly form a new state, it was decided that such action should proceed from a constituent assembly rather than a legislature.

In an adjourned session of the Second Wheeling Convention, held August 6-21, the initial step in the dismemberment of Virginia was authorized. An ordinance for this purpose, passed on August 20 by a vote of 48 to 27, provided for the formation of a new state out of a portion of the territory of Virginia. The name of the proposed state was to be "Kanawha". Thirty-nine counties, all west of the Alleghenies, were to be included within its confines. On October 24 voters were to approve or reject the dismemberment ordinance and to elect delegates to a convention authorized to make a constitution for the new state.[4]

At the ensuing election in October [1861] the dismemberment ordinance was ratified 18,408 to 781, and delegates to West Virginia's First Constitutional Convention were elected. Assembling on November 26 at Wheeling, this convention laid the framework for the new state's government. Because of disturbed internal conditions, many counties were not represented. Enough delegates were on hand to enable a constitution to be framed, however. Among the first changes was the substitution of "West Virginia" for "Kanawha" as the state's name.

One of the most vexing problems in this connection was the boundary. After much discussion it was decided that the new state would include forty-four counties and, in addition, those Eastern Panhandle counties which favored the new constitution. The desire for the Panhandle district, which included Jefferson County, was undoubtedly caused by the fact that the Baltimore and Ohio Railroad traversed the Panhandle. Framers of West Virginia believed that as Virginia had been hostile toward this means of communication, it might continue that policy at the close of the war. It was freely admitted that the welfare of West Virginia was largely dependent on the railroad. As the best way to protect the carrier, and also the state's well-being, was to include the territory which it traversed within West Virginia, the Eastern Panhandle was desired. The importance of the railroad for the defense of the Federal capital and for the transport of troops and supplies were other considerations.[5]

The referendum on the West Virginia constitution was set for April 3, 1862, but because of disturbed internal conditions, many districts and counties did not vote. Most of them were in the central, southern, and eastern portions of the proposed state. Polls were taken, however, where conditions permitted. Of the total number voting, 18,862 favored the constitution and only 514 opposed it.

The next step in the new state movement was to obtain the consent of the Virginia Assembly to the formation of West Virginia. This was necessary to fulfill the conditions of the Federal Constitution relative to the formation of new states. Accordingly, Governor Pierpont convened the legislature of the Reorganized Government. This met at Wheeling and on May 14 passed an act giving the consent of "the Legislature of Virginia" to the formation and erection of the "State of West Virginia".

The bill for the admission of West Virginia passed Congress on December 11, 1862, and was on December 21 sent to President Lincoln, who signed it on December 31. But admission was conditional upon the new state's acceptance of an amendment providing for the gradual abolition of slavery. This was approved on February 17, 1863, by a convention. As an overwhelming majority favored the amended constitution in a referendum, the results were sent to the President, who issued a proclamation under which, West Virginia, on June 20, 1863, became the thirty-fifth state in the Union.[6]

The chief point raised in connection with West Virginia's formation was whether or not Virginia's Reorganized Government had the right to consent to the formation of the new state. As both Congress and the President regarded this government as the only legal one in the state, the question was settled for the time being. Later the United States Supreme Court accepted the formation and admission of West Virginia as a fact and did not question the action of Congress in this direction.[7]

EFFORTS TO OBTAIN JEFFERSON COUNTY.

Jefferson County did not vote on the West Virginia constitution at either time it was submitted. By legislative act, however, it was authorized to hold such an election on May 28, 1863. At the election to determine whether the county would be part of West Virginia or would remain in the Old Dominion those persons in control had things pretty much their own way. Federal troops were in possession of Jefferson County at that time.[8]

In the first place, the West Virginia advocates did not inform the voters about the proposed election. Many persons were ignorant that the question of a change of states was before them, and it was not until weeks later that they heard about the election. Those in control opened polls at only two precincts in the entire county, Shepherdstown and Harpers Ferry. Both of these voting-places were on Jefferson's northern border. The election commissioners could not qualify under the laws of Virginia for occupying such an office. At the time the election was held Jefferson County was subjected to strict military regulations. For weeks at a time persons were confined to their own premises and at times under no pretext, however urgent, were they permitted to pass the Federal lines.[9]

As the entire West Virginia movement was on the basis that only loyal persons counted, those who could not fulfill the requirements of a voter's test oath were barred from casting their ballots. This of course eliminated an overwhelming majority of Jefferson Countians. In view of all the attending circumstances, then, it is not surprising that those persons in control were able to engineer the returns so that they obtained a vote favorable to their interests. As certified to Governor Pierpont, the vote at

Shepherdstown was 196 for, to 1 against becoming part of West Virginia, and at Harpers Ferry it was 52 for, to 1 against. Thus, a total vote of 248 for, to 2 against annexation to West Virginia was declared to be a "full and free expression of the opinion of the people".[10]

Nor is this the whole picture. Among the papers of Colonel Alexander R. Boteler of near Shepherdstown is a list of those who cast ballots at that precinct in this election. According to the account, at the time the polls were closed, eighteen persons had voted in favor of subjecting the county to the jurisdiction of West Virginia and one had voted against. Colonel Boteler stated further that four of the eighteen were illegal voters. Thus, the remainder of the 196 ballots reported to have been cast at Shepherdstown in favor of West Virginia must have been added after the polls closed if Colonel Boteler was correctly informed.[11]

As the number of legitimate voters in the county in the Presidential election of 1860 was 1,857, it can be seen what a small proportion of the electorate was represented in the important question of becoming part of West Virginia.[12]

The returns were sent to Governor Pierpont, who, believing them to be genuine, on September 14, 1863, certified the election results to Governor Arthur I. Boreman of West Virginia. By an act passed November 2, 1863, the West Virginia Legislature then included Jefferson County within the confines of the new state. Unwilling but helpless, the people of Jefferson had no alternative but to submit to West Virginia's jurisdiction.[13]

Thus the matter stood until the end of the war. With the downfall of the Confederacy went the chances of the return of Jefferson County to Virginia. The age of hate which followed Lincoln's assassination was not a proper time to expect justice. Radical politicians like Thaddeus Stevens and Charles Sumner dominated the national scene and almost succeeded in removing President Johnson from office by impeachment proceedings. His successor, Ulysses S. Grant, became a mere tool in the hands of Radical politicians and failed to continue his generous policy, displayed at Appomattox, toward the South.

ATTEMPTS TO REUNITE WITH VIRGINIA.

After the war a controversy arose between Virginia and

West Virginia over the status of Jefferson and Berkeley counties. As the new state had obtained Berkeley in the same manner as Jefferson and at practically the same time, the position of the two counties was similar. Virginia based its claim for restoration on the fact that these two counties were not named in the act of Congress providing for West Virginia's admission. It contended that the transfer was thus never legally completed. Accordingly, the Old Dominion declared the counties in question to be part of its Seventh Congressional District, whereas West Virginia asserted they were part of its Second District. The Federal Commissioner of Internal Revenue examined the two claims and then transferred the disputed area to the Second Collection District of West Virginia.[14]

Naturally, with such a dispute raging a contest would arise for the seat in Congress from the district occupied by the two counties. The chairman of the House Committee on Elections, Henry L. Dawes of Massachusetts, took the position that Berkeley and Jefferson counties had not been legally annexed. He maintained that Congress had admitted West Virginia into the Union with a fixed boundary line. As this boundary line did not then include Jefferson and Berkeley and as Congress had never given its consent to a change in boundary, the House committee reported that the transfer had not been legally consummated.[15]

When the inhabitants of Jefferson County realized that there was still a ray of hope concerning their remaining in Virginia, they laid plans for carrying on the fight. A large majority of them had no desire at all to be included in West Virginia, for their interests, ties, customs, and whole life were more closely bound to Virginia. They had few things in common with western Virginians and were separated from the northwest by the Allegheny Mountains. On the other hand, they were a part of the Shenandoah Valley, which extended south into the Old Dominion. They could see no reason at all why they should be included in a new state, against their wishes, just because the Baltimore and Ohio Railroad passed through their county.

Assuming that they were still part of Virginia, residents of Jefferson County met on September 2, 1865, at the Carter House in Charles Town to appoint delegates to a convention in Winchester. The convention was to nominate a candidate for

Congress from the Seventh Congressional District of Virginia. The county selected forty-seven delegates to represent it. A committee of five reported several reasons why it considered that Jefferson County should belong to Virginia. Among other things, the members cited the opinion of the House Committee on Elections, which favored Virginia.[16]

By issuing a proclamation directing the arrest of any persons attempting to hold such an election, Governor Boreman frustrated an effort to hold one on October 12 to choose delegates from Jefferson County to the Virginia General Assembly. At the same time he had Federal troops, then stationed in the county, aid civil authorities to prevent the election from being conducted.[17]

Not disheartened by this setback, the people met on November 18 in Charles Town. Andrew Hunter and William H. Travers were appointed a committee to present petitions to Congress and the Virginia General Assembly. Containing a statement of reasons why the county should still be considered part of the Old Dominion, these requests asked the Assembly to repeal the act ceding Jefferson County to West Virginia. At the same meeting the citizens appointed two persons from each magisterial district to canvass the county for signers and contributions of money. The names of more than 1,200 white male citizens, two-thirds of the electorate, were obtained for the petitions.[18]

At the same time the Radical government at Shepherdstown was circulating a petition. The county seat had been removed from Charles Town to Shepherdstown by an act of the West Virginia Legislature passed January 26, 1865. This petition asked Congress to allow Jefferson to remain in West Virginia. To procure signers the Radicals argued that if the county remained in Virginia, the Baltimore and Ohio Railroad would move its tracks, bridges, stations, and other equipment across the Potomac River into Maryland. They claimed that Jefferson County would thus be deprived of that means of communication.

Nor did the Radicals stop here. Fearing that they might lose Jefferson to Virginia, they seriously considered the formation of a new county out of Jefferson and Berkeley to be known as "Shepherd County". This division was, roughly, to include that territory on the north side of the Baltimore and Ohio Railroad between Harpers Ferry and Opequon Creek.

In contemplation of the proposed change Shepherdstown and Scrabble waged a contest for the county seat. Shepherdstown claimed the honor on the basis of seniority, while Scrabble based its contention on the grounds of its loyalty and central location. When some of the politicians objected to the unusual name of Scrabble, supporters of that place suggested that it be changed to "Chapline City".[19]

In response to the petition from Jefferson County the Virginia General Assembly on December 5, 1865, withdrew its consent to the transfer of Jefferson and Berkeley counties to West Virginia. When it was ascertained that a fair vote of the people had not been obtained in those counties, an almost unanimous vote of both houses on the repeal was procured. The fact that Congress had not consented to the transfer also carried weight. Governor Pierpont of Virginia, now having removed his Reorganized Government to Richmond, referred the whole question to Congress and asked it to decide.[20]

Resolutions were immediately introduced in Washington asking the consent of Congress to the annexation of Jefferson and Berkeley counties to West Virginia. In the House of Representatives the resolution was referred to the Committee on Judiciary, whereas in the Senate it was given to the Committee on Territories. On December 20 the Senate committee reported in favor of West Virginia and on January 10, 1866, the House committee did likewise. The lower body passed this resolution on February 6 by a vote of 113 to 24, while the Senate approved it a few weeks later by the decisive majority of 32 to 5. As such overwhelming numbers favored the joint resolution transferring the two counties to West Virginia, the attitude of President Johnson did not matter.[21]

VIRGINIA vs. WEST VIRGINIA.

To test the constitutionality of the transfer Virginia then took the matter to the United States Supreme Court. For this purpose it employed two able attorneys, Judge Benjamin R. Curtis of Boston, a former United States Supreme Court member, and Andrew Hunter of Charles Town. The attorney general of the Old Dominion, Thomas R. Bowden, assisted them. On the other

VIRGINIA OR WEST VIRGINIA 199

side, West Virginia obtained Reverdy Johnson of Maryland and Benjamin H. Stanton of Ohio. A resolution of the Virginia General Assembly had named Johnson as one of the Old Dominion's lawyers, but since he had voted, as a Senator from Maryland, to transfer the territory to West Virginia, he did not serve.[22]

The case was opened on May 6, 1867, and the final argument was heard on May 9. Virginia filed a bill for the recovery of Jefferson and Berkeley counties. West Virginia demurred, that is, admitted the facts but said that Virginia had no case. As grounds for its demurrer, West Virginia contended principally that Virginia was not then a state in the Union but by reason of the action of Congress had been declared a territory. As such, it was not permitted to sue. The new state also claimed that as the election had been held in the two counties and the results certified by Governor Pierpont, that certificate was final and conclusive. The argument of Judge Curtis for Virginia was said to have been unusually good. One of the justices, who disagreed with him, declared it the ablest he had heard in twenty years' service on the bench.

When the Supreme Court reassembled for the December term, one of the justices, James M. Wayne of Georgia, had died. Thus, only eight were left. This was especially unfortunate then, for the vote on the Virginia-West Virginia suit was divided, four to four. Justices Salmon P. Chase, Robert C. Grier, Noah H. Swayne, and Samuel F. Miller voted in support of West Virginia's demurrer. On the other hand, Justices Nathan Clifford, Samuel Nelson, David Davis, and Stephen J. Field voted to dismiss it. Thus, nothing definite was determined. The situation was further confused by an act of Congress passed in July, 1866, which diminished the number of justices to seven and provided that no vacancies should be filled until the court was reduced to seven.[23]

There is no telling how long the deadlock would have lasted if Congress had not passed an act reconstructing the Supreme Court and increasing its membership to nine. As Justice Grier had resigned, President Grant thus had two appointments to make. He responded in 1870 by naming William Strong and Joseph Bradley.

Virginia's attorneys immediately urged a re-argument and decision of the case. Although the reopening was set for the first

Thursday in December, 1870, it was postponed until February 7, 1871, because of the illness of Chief Justice Chase. Attorney General Taylor of Virginia assisted Curtis and Hunter at this time. West Virginia employed Charles J. Faulkner to aid Stanton and Johnson.[24]

In February, 1871, the halls of the Supreme Court echoed again with the arguments, pro and con, of the distinguished counsel. This time Faulkner seems to have made an unusually impressive speech. On March 6, 1871, after several weeks of great suspense for the people of Jefferson County, the court's decision was made public. By a vote of six to three the justices had decided that the allegation of fraud was not sustained and that the question of jurisdiction had been determined by the people of Jefferson and Berkeley counties at the polls on May 28, 1863. In other words, the counties were awarded to West Virginia.[25]

Naturally, the people of Jefferson were greatly dejected with the decision. They were unable to understand how a tribunal supposed to render justice could uphold the small poll taken in the county, under such unusual conditions, on that fatal day in May, 1863. Nevertheless, they realized that the decision was final and they accepted it as well as could be expected. Reluctantly, some of the county's newspapers inserted "West" in front of the "Virginia" which they had been carrying at the top of their columns.

For a long while, however, many Jefferson County people refused to admit that they lived in West Virginia. Even today a few tell strangers that they reside "in Virginia, near Winchester". Antagonism toward the new state has been manifested by the large number of high school graduates preferring colleges in the Old Dominion to those in their own state. In recent years this trend has partly subsided and the younger generation looks more favorably toward West Virginia institutions, particularly the State University and Shepherd State Teachers College.

These same ties to Virginia also exist in religious circles, for many of the Jefferson County churches still belong to Virginia synods and associations. Perhaps at some future day they, too, will transfer their allegiance to West Virginia. Time alone will tell.

CHAPTER FIFTEEN
RECONSTRUCTION

POST-WAR CONDITIONS.

When the war-weary, dejected Confederate soldier returned to his Jefferson County home after Appomattox, he found conditions vastly different from what they had been four years before. Instead of the prosperous, well-stocked farms with their cultivated fields, he saw a great common overgrown with grass and weeds. Fences were gone and heaps of blackened ruins denoted the former location of comfortable houses or commodious barns. The happy, smiling faces had become careworn and sad. Instead of working contentedly in the fields, former slaves flocked around the towns and villages, spent their time in idleness, and dressed in gaudy clothes. With their branches shot away the trees had assumed a gaunt and spectral appearance. Extreme destitution seemed to prevail everywhere.[1]

Charles Town, the former county seat, had also changed. In place of the stately courthouse where the John Brown raiders were tried only the walls remained. The erection of a fort in the yard for protection against Confederate raids and use of the structure for a stable had left their marks. The town's market house was in ashes. The familiar faces which formerly conducted the county's public affairs had been replaced by those of opposite political beliefs.

In other parts of the county the Charles Town scene was duplicated. Harpers Ferry no longer resounded to the cheerful work of hundreds of employees at the armory and arsenal. Most of the buildings were in ruins and the only national work being done was the repair of broken guns. This was supervised by Daniel J. Young, ordnance agent and ex-foreman of the rifle factory. A large portion of this town and its twin village, Bolivar, had been burned by various troops to prevent occupation by the enemy. The soldiers had destroyed mills, ruined schoolhouses, and even used churches for stables.[2]

In February, 1865, the county seat was moved to Shepherdstown as a war measure so that it might enjoy the protection furnished by Federal soldiers stationed along the Baltimore and Ohio Railroad. This was done by an act of the West Virginia Legislature passed January 26, 1865. Legislation enacted on February 15, 1866, fixed Shepherdstown as the permanent county seat. Political control had passed into the hands of Radicals, who seemed more interested in perpetuating themselves in office than in looking after the best interests of the county. A Board of Supervisors had assumed the functions of the old County Court and was the chief local governing agency.[3]

One of the greatest county problems was that of the Negroes. Their newly-bestowed freedom had not been followed by proper instruction and care. Because they were unable to comprehend their new condition, the Negroes would not work. Instead, they passed their time in idleness and looked to the Government for support. Thus, there arose a serious labor shortage, for there were few able-bodied persons to begin the tremendous task of reconstruction. Sometimes former masters were required to take their ex-slaves and pay prescribed wages. This worked a hardship on the farmer, who could scarcely support his own family.

The crying need of the hour was Northern labor and Northern capital. Money was required to reestablish banks, stock and improve farms, and rebuild mills and factories. Land was cheap. Good farms where the fences had been destroyed could be bought for $25 an acre. Land whose buildings and improvements had not suffered as much from the ravages of war brought $40 an acre.[4]

Trouble in religious circles arose in July, 1865, when the minister in charge of the Berkeley Circuit of the Methodist Episcopal Church, South, excluded from worship all former Confederate sympathizers. The only way to remove this ban was to fulfill degrading conditions. When the presiding elder learned what had happened, he visited the circuit and closed the church against the minister. Simultaneously he directed the laity to assemble and hold prayer meetings. William Rush, the sheriff, then intervened and gave notice that the minister would hold services as usual, whereupon the presiding elder threatened Rush with arrest for violating the peace. How this unusual contest ended is not certain, but as no more mention is made in contemporary newspapers, it was probably settled to the satisfaction of those concerned.[5]

In 1867 the two divisions of the Methodist Church in Shepherdstown disputed over the ownership of the church building and parsonage. Instituting suit in the Circuit Court, the Methodist Episcopal Church received a favorable decision. This was obtained in spite of the fact that only 17 of the 221 members belonged to this branch and they had paid only $400 of the original construction cost of $7,000 to $8,000. In Charles Town a similar quarrel was settled when members of the Methodist Episcopal Church, South, retained the buildings but had to pay the other faction $575 and court costs.[6]

In spite of all the hardships it suffered during the period of Reconstruction, Jefferson County helped its less fortunate brethren in the lower South. By April, 1867, it had given an estimated $10,000 worth of corn, flour, bacon, woolens, and money to relieve suffering in former Confederate states. Donations like this in times when the county itself was none too prosperous is indeed commendable.[7]

POLITICS.

The first regular election in Jefferson County after the end of hostilities was held on October 28, 1865. For reasons best known to those in authority, the county's former eight precincts were reduced to seven townships. Shepherdstown had two voting-places, Chapline and Shepherd, while Charles Town, Harpers Ferry, and Bolivar retained one each. Middleway was included in the new Averill Township and Kabletown was within the limits of Osborn Township. The vote in this election was small because former Confederates and their sympathizers were excluded from the polls. Nevertheless, the county's electorate returned a majority of 100 for most of the Conservative party candidates.

It was a different matter when the Radical Board of Supervisors met in November at Shepherdstown to certify the results. In order to keep their organization in power they threw out votes until their own candidates were ahead. Claiming various irregularities, they discounted the entire Charles Town vote. As the former county seat had given large majorities for Conservative candidates, this was especially convenient for the Radicals. For instance, Ephraim B. Hall, the Radical nominee for judge of the Circuit Court, received only one vote there, whereas John W. Kennedy, his Conservative opponent, obtained 266. The Radical candidate for the State Senate, Joseph A. Chapline, did better, for he procured nine votes, while his opponent, O. D. Downey, obtained 256. Other Conservative candidates received substantially the same majorities at Charles Town.[8]

Such maneuvering of ballots by the supervisors produced the desired result. The vote was changed and the figures so revised that the entire Radical ticket was elected. Consequently, the following were declared elected: Ephraim B. Hall, judge of the Circuit Court; Joseph A. Chapline, State Senate; George Koonce and Charles H. McCurdy, House of Delegates [West Virginia]; and William Rush, sheriff. The Board of Supervisors responsible for the change consisted of Alexander Fossett, Ehud Turner, Daniel Cameron, Dr. James Logie, John W. McCurdy, and Truman W. Potterfield. The Board's president was Alexander Fossett. The clerk was Joseph A. Chapline.[9]

Another farcical election was held in the county the next year. The Board of Registrars had reduced the normal 1,800 electorate so much that the total vote in this election on May 24, 1866, was only 368. Dominated by Radicals, the West Virginia Legislature passed a constitutional amendment disfranchising all Southern sympathizers. In the subsequent referendum the state approved the amendment by a safe majority. Figures for this election in the county differ slightly in various newspapers, but the amendment seems to have been approved by a vote of 208 to 160.

Again, irregularities occurred at Charles Town, the only precinct whose returns were described in detail. With voting lists reduced from nearly 500 to 22, only 17 of the latter availed themselves of the privilege. According to one report of the results, eleven voted for the disfranchising amendment and six against it, whereas another states that twelve voted for and five against it. This is unimportant, except that eight of the registered voters affirmed afterwards that they cast ballots against the amendment and seemed indignant that these results did not appear in the official tabulation. John J. Sanborn received a total of seven votes for magistrate in Charles Town and Charles Warner obtained the same number for constable. Both were Radicals and both were declared elected. A peculiar fact in connection with this election is that of the small number who voted, eight or nine were elected to official positions and two others already held office.[10]

By June, 1866, the new Jefferson County courthouse was completed in Shepherdstown. Intended originally for a town hall, it was offered to the county for a courthouse by its owner, Rezin D. Shepherd, a descendant of the town's founder. Consideration was nominal, but the lease was conditional upon Shepherdstown's retaining the county seat. The donor also gave funds for completing the building and a lot for the jail. Prior thereto, the Board of Supervisors had met in an office over the store of W. A.

Jefferson County Courthouse
at Shepherdstown, 1866-1871

Chapline and the Circuit Court in the African Church at Shepherdstown.[11]

Additional difficulty with disfranchisement appeared when Governor Arthur I. Boreman of West Virginia, with legislative consent, appointed a three-member board of registrars for each county. Persons who desired to vote were required not only to take a test oath but also to prove that they were qualified to take such an oath. Thus, county registrars were given autocratic powers to regulate suffrage. In 1867 notices were served on Jefferson residents with Conservative leanings, which required them to appear within a limited time to give satisfactory proof of being qualified to vote. Otherwise, their names were scratched from the registration lists. These notices were generally served on persons living in remote sections of the county, who often found it impossible to appear at Shepherdstown within the prescribed time. Many of them had cast ballots in three or four previous elections.[12]

An example of "taxation without representation" is furnished by a statement made by the West Virginia Auditor concerning the counties' tax assessments for 1866. Jefferson paid in taxes $37,003.24, which was only a thousand dollars less than Ohio County with the large city of Wheeling. This amount was $7,477.73 more than that of Berkeley County and $4,000 more than twelve other counties combined! At the same time only about 300 of the county's 1,800 former voters were permitted to cast ballots.[13]

Trouble with the registration of properly qualified voters continued to plague the county. On the day fixed for listing voters, September 7, 1868, no registrar appeared in Charles Town. Consequently, many persons were compelled to return home without having given their names. At a subsequent registration held in Shepherdstown on October 5 prospective voters were put through a regular ordeal to have their names entered on the rolls. Even persons of unquestioned loyalty were cross-examined.

Citizens whose right to vote was indisputable were refused registration because they favored restoration of the county seat to Charles Town. Others were denied the privilege because they had "sat in a convention of which Frank Beall was a member". Some of the most respected residents of the county were called one at a time before the Board of Registrars in an effort to ascertain how they were going to vote in the forthcoming election.¹⁴

Such corrupt practices could not continue forever. Voters lost confidence in the Radical party, and in the election of October, 1868, the Conservatives, now called Democrats, emerged victorious in all of the contests but one, the judgeship of the Circuit Court. In that race Ephraim B. Hall, Radical, obtained 155 votes in the county, while E. Pendleton, the Democrat, received 134. Again, the vote of Charles Town Township was thrown out, this time because the registration books were not signed. Irregularities were said to have existed also in Chapline Township. In Averill Township the books were not signed and did not have the place and date of the election.¹⁵

In the Presidential election of 1868 Ulysses S. Grant's popularity and the Radical machine combined to give the Republican candidate 203 votes in the county, to 120 for the Democratic nominee, Horatio Seymour. As usual, Charles Town's vote was excluded, and not even the fifteen registered voters were allowed to express their choice for President.¹⁶

Another injustice was legislation by the state on December 23, 1868, consolidating four of the largest townships into two. Charles Town and Osborn were in 1869 and thenceforth to be known as Grant Township, while Harpers Ferry and Bolivar were to be united as Bolivar Township. The act provided further that the supervisor-elect of Bolivar and the same official from Osborn would serve for the consolidated townships. Thus, the supervisors who had been elected from Harpers Ferry and Charles Town, under the previous set-up, would not be allowed to serve, and the Radical majority on the Board of Supervisors would remain with the reduction in membership from seven to five. Claiming that George H. Turner could not qualify under the new law, the Board refused to seat him, and thus three Conservative supervisors were legislated out of office.¹⁷

Much excitement was created when the Radical Board of Supervisors advertised the public sale on June 5, 1869, of the former courthouse and jail at Charles Town. These buildings had been in a state of disrepair since the war, but the lots occupied by them were among the most valuable in town. The sale of this property would have materially reduced Charles Town's chances of ever again becoming the county seat. The decree by the Board of

Supervisors appointed Samuel Ridenour special agent to conduct the sale. When residents of Charles Town heard about the proposed sale, they employed William Crow and David Howell to represent them in the matter. An examination of the deed transferring the lots from Charles Washington's son, Samuel, to certain persons revealed the fact that the land had not been transferred to the county but to the inhabitants of Charles Town. In event the property ceased to be used for the purpose designated, it was to revert to the heirs of the original donors. Accordingly, a bill applying for an injunction to prevent the sale was drawn up by John W. Kennedy and Richard B. Washington and on June 1 laid before Circuit Judge Joseph A. Chapline. After examining the bill, Chapline granted the application and issued an order stopping the sale.[18]

In October, 1869, the Radicals elected their candidate for the State Senate and obtained one of the county's two seats in the House of Delegates. A large majority of the voters, especially in Grant Township, was still denied the right of suffrage. That district, embracing approximately one-third of the county, contained the names of only forty-one registered voters. Of these only eleven cast ballots. Charles Town was no longer a precinct, and voters registered there were required to go to Kabletown to vote. Of the eleven persons exercising this right, seven were Radicals, three were Conservative Democrats, and one was a Liberal Republican. Of the seven Radicals voting four were elected to office.[19]

The October, 1870, election resulted in an overwhelming victory for Conservative candidates. They were successful in every contest in the county except for the office of recorder. In that race James D. Feaman, Radical, defeated a man named Barry, 508 to 459. In the same election a young Harpers Ferry native, E. Willis Wilson, was chosen for one of the county's seats in the House of Delegates. Wilson, a Conservative, later served as Democratic Governor of West Virginia from 1885-1890. He was the only native of the county to achieve that distinction in West Virginia, although Jefferson County supplied four governors for the State of Ohio, Edward Tiffin, Thomas Worthington, Jeremiah Morrow, and Robert Lucas. Thomas Brown, who resided in the county for a few years, served as Governor of Florida.[20]

THE COUNTY SEAT CONTROVERSY.

Encouraged by recent successes at the polls, the Conservatives undertook the removal of the county seat from Shepherdstown to Charles Town. In December, 1870, they circulated a petition asking the West Virginia Legislature's consent. This request asserted that the county seat had been moved to Shepherdstown in the war, without any consultation or consent of the county's residents. It stated further that Charles Town was entitled to be the seat of government as it had been since the county's organization in 1801 and it possessed a much better location than its rival. It was near the geographical center of the county and enjoyed the advantages of a railroad and the convergence of the main county roads.

On the other hand, Shepherdstown was declared to be on Jefferson County's northern boundary, "inaccessible to travel, and subjecting to great inconvenience eight-tenths of the people of the county". As a final argument, the petition stated that the property in Charles Town still remained and could be reoccupied at less expense than that required at any other convenient point.[21]

The Board of Supervisors answered this challenge by meeting on December 21 and adopting a resolution petitioning the West Virginia Legislature against removal of the county seat to Charles Town. At this time the Board consisted of the following members: John R. Ray, Shepherd Township; J. J. Ramsburg, Averill; Hezekiah Roderick, Bolivar; J. H. Haines, Grant; and Ehud Turner, Chapline. In the Board's counter-petition the supervisors stated that two-thirds of the county's voters would be opposed to the change, a complete set of buildings had been erected in Shepherdstown, and a turnpike to connect Shepherdstown with other prominent places in the county was being constructed. In addition, they asserted that taxes were already too high and the expense of moving the county seat would be too great.[22]

Once the movement had begun, it was not allowed to stop. On January 21, 1871, a large and enthusiastic group of citizens met at Lee Hall in Charles Town to take steps necessary to have the county seat changed. Thomas C. Green stated that a bill would soon be presented to the West Virginia Legislature asking that five persons be authorized to spend a sum, not exceeding $10,000, for the construction of a courthouse at Charles Town. The bill was also to provide for the desired change in the seat of government. A committee of five was appointed to bring the matter before the Legislature and set forth reasons for the removal. Its members were Thomas C. Green, Logan Osburn, Joseph Starry, James W. Glenn, and Dr. J. V. Simmons.

A bill for the removal was introduced in the Legislature and passed by the House of Delegates on February 3 by a vote of 38 to 17. In the State Senate George Koonce of Jefferson County attempted to defeat passage by introducing a bill referring the subject to a vote of the people. The proposed question to be submitted to the electorate was, "Shall the county seat be removed to Charles Town or any other place?" As can readily be seen, the object was to stir up a number of claimants for the county seat and by thus dividing the opposition defeat the efforts of Charles Town and retain the seat of government at Shepherdstown.

Although Senator Koonce made no progress with his efforts, the illness of Senator Oakey Johnson prevented the sponsors of the bill favoring Charles Town from obtaining a majority vote in the State Senate. Finally, Johnson resigned, thus creating a vacancy, and on February 23, 1871, the county seat bill passed the upper house by the narrow margin of eleven votes to nine. William H. Travers of Charles Town telegraphed the good news home.[23]

This new act repealed the acts changing the county seat and locating it permanently at Shepherdstown. It provided that the county seat would cease to be at Shepherdstown thirty days after the date of passage and that it would be located in Charles Town. The act also appointed five commissioners, Logan Osburn, James H. Moore, John G. Cockrell, David Howell, Jr., and John J. Locke, to carry out its provisions. These persons were to make temporary provisions for courts and public officers, contract for the use of buildings, and certify necessary expenses to the Board of Supervisors. The latter officials were to pay bills from the county treasury. The courthouse at Charles Town was to be repaired, but not more than $10,000 could be spent.[24]

Other favorable legislation was an act restoring Charles Town,

RECONSTRUCTION 211

Osborn, Harpers Ferry, and Bolivar as separate townships. The Governor was given power to appoint township officers until an election could be held.[25]

Unwilling to yield without a fight, the Radicals at Shepherdstown made plans for opposing the county seat removal. With Senator Koonce and Delegate C. E. Stubbs present, the Board of Supervisors met on February 28 in special session. They seem to have attempted to prevent Supervisor J. J. Ramsburg of Averill Township from attending by notifying him of the meeting too late. Alert Charles Town residents, however, dispatched a special messenger to inform Ramsburg in time. Three of the supervisors, John D. Staley, Ehud Turner, and Hezekiah Roderick, voted to seek an injunction to prevent the county seat change as provided by the new act. They were opposed by J. H. Haines, the representative from Grant Township, and J. J. Ramsburg.

The injunction sought was based upon the ground that the recently passed act removing the seat to Charles Town was contrary to the Code of West Virginia. Another reason claimed was that the Legislature had no power to remove the county seat of any county. Thomas Van Swearingen and H. H. Blackburn represented the Board in this matter.[26]

Additional friction developed at a meeting of the supervisors on March 14 in Shepherdstown when the president, John D. Staley, refused to recognize the Board's two new members, Logan Osburn and Rezin Cross. Thomas Van Swearingen, as counsel for Staley, Roderick, and Turner, stated that he would resist any effort to seat them. Andrew Hunter replied by showing that the appointment of Osburn and Cross was in accordance with the provisions of the state constitution. As Staley continued to ignore the new members, Haines and Ramsburg refused to vote, although they believed the appointment of Osburn and Cross to be valid. Staley, Roderick, and Turner then voted against the appointment of Osburn and Cross, after which they supported a motion to adjourn.

Then an unusual act occurred. Even though the other four supervisors voted against adjournment, Staley announced the motion carried. Taking C. H. Trayor, the clerk, and the keys of the record case along with them, Roderick, Turner, and Staley left the room. The other members appointed Osburn temporary chairman and George H. Turner temporary clerk and, with the malcontents out of the way, these supervisors were able to get something accomplished. They ordered that the counsel employed to obtain the injunction be instructed to proceed no further and that the permanent clerk of the Board appear at the next meeting and produce the records. They voted to hold the next meeting on April 11 in Hooff's Hall at Charles Town.[27]

The matter then went to the courts. The plaintiffs, nine residents of Shepherdstown and vicinity, sought an injunction to prevent the five commissioners named in the act from discharging the duties imposed upon them. The application was first made to Judge Hoke of the adjoining judicial circuit, and, when he refused to act, it was presented to Judge Edwin Maxwell of the State Supreme Court of Appeals, who granted the injunction. The case was argued on March 27 at Martinsburg before Judge Ephraim B. Hall. Andrew Hunter, Thomas C. Green, and William H. Travers appeared for the commissioners named in the act, while Charles J. Faulkner, H. H. Blackburn, and Thomas Van Swearingen represented the Radical supervisors.

The chief argument made by counsel for the commissioners was that the parties plaintiff were private citizens and in no way entitled to represent the county officially, except in common with all the people of the county. Consequently, they were declared not competent to bring and maintain the suit. Another point made was that the act in question had been properly certified, authenticated, and enrolled as a law of the state and that the judiciary had no power to ascertain whether the Legislature had conformed to the requirements of the constitution in passing it. Finally, it was pointed out, even if the foregoing contentions were erroneous, the act in question was passed in full accordance with the constitution.[28]

Attorneys on the other side displayed tact and ability in making the most of a bad case. The argument, for both sides, lasted from ten o'clock in the morning until nine at night. Deciding in favor of the Radical supervisors, Judge Hall not only overruled the points made by the commissioners but even stated that he believed the Board of Supervisors to be the only body competent to discharge provisions of the act. As this decision would prevent the commissioners named by the Legislature from acting, they appealed to the State Supreme Court of Appeals.

Meanwhile, Jefferson County had two boards of supervisors, each of which was meeting in a different town, claiming to be the legal one, and transacting business. Three members of the old Board, Staley, Roderick, and Ehud Turner, assembled on March 28 in Shepherdstown, while Haines and Ramsburg, of the old body, met with Osburn and J. J. Kern, the new appointees, on April 11 in Hooff's Hall at Charles Town. Kern appears to have succeeded Rezin Cross from Harpers Ferry.

Logan Osburn continued acting as president **pro tem** for the Charles Town group and George H. Turner remained the temporary clerk. The commissioners appointed in the act leased suitable buildings for the county's use. With the Board of Supervisors using rooms on the west side, Hooff's Hall was also the home of the Circuit Court. The recorder's office was located in Hunter's Row, the third door west of the Carter House, while the adjoining office to the west was occupied by the circuit clerk. Hunter's Row was on East Washington Street, directly opposite the courthouse in Charles Town.[29]

Being perplexed as to which board should examine and certify the county's delinquent tax lists for 1870, Sheriff T. W. Potterfield wrote the state auditor for an opinion. The reply, dated April 17, 1871, was that the state department would recognize the lists certified by the board of supervisors established by the legislative act of February 23, 1871. In other words, it would recognize the Charles Town body as the proper one until an adverse opinion should be handed down by the State Supreme Court of Appeals.[30]

More trouble arose when the supervisors meeting in Charles Town received a notice to appear before Judge Hall at Martinsburg on May 8, 1871. There they were informed that Roderick, Staley, and Ehud Turner would apply for information in the nature of a writ of **quo warranto**. Such a writ would require the supervisors at Charles Town to show by what authority they were acting as the county's regular board. An injunction was also sought to prevent them from so acting. The same counsel, Blackburn, Van Swearingen, and Faulkner, represented the Shepherdstown body, while Andrew Hunter continued to appear for the Charles Town group. The judge issued a rule against the Charles Town body requiring it to show at the next Circuit Court term by what authority it was exercising the functions of the Board of Supervisors. He, however, refused the injunction.

The injunction concerned the question about the constitutionality of a legislative act authorizing the Governor to appoint two supervisors and his power under the law to fill a vacancy on the board. Judge Hall concluded that the Board of Supervisors had the right to judge the qualifications of the executive's appointees. Their action was declared to be subject, however, to supervision by the Circuit Courts. The judge also ruled that since one of the Governor's appointees had resigned under the law in question, the state executive could not fill the vacancy. He was emphatic in asserting that this refusal to grant the injunction did not in any way settle the question that the acts of either lawmaking body in Jefferson County were legal and valid.[31]

Finally, the West Virginia Supreme Court of Appeals rendered its decision. On August 18 and 19, 1871, telegrams were received by William H. Travers announcing that the state's highest tribunal had reversed both of Judges Hall's rulings. It was decided that the act transferring the county seat to Charles Town fulfilled all of the legal requirements and hence was valid. The decree preventing the commissioners from performing their functions was reversed and the bill dismissed.[32]

Backed by the Supreme Court ruling, Charles Town partisans on August 31 moved the circuit clerk's and recorder's records from Shepherdstown. With Judge Thayer Melvin of Wheeling on the bench, the fall term of the Circuit Court opened on September 12 at Charles Town after an enforced absence of ten years. As the courthouse walls were still standing, the authorities decided to rebuild on the same lot and awarded contracts to this effect. The work was completed by December 17, 1872, at a cost of $18,500, but additional expense, for refurnishing, increased the total to $21,179.18. The jail was finished July 22, 1873.[33]

The final act in this unique drama occurred on September 14-15 in the Jefferson Circuit Court, meeting at Charles Town. Both elements of the Board of Supervisors had been prevented from acting in their official capacities. The order against the Osburn group was issued by Judge Maxwell of the State Supreme Court of Appeals and against the Staley body by Judge Stuart of the Second Judicial Circuit. An appeal had been taken by the Staley men, the argument for which was to be held in January, 1872. By that time, however, the office of the supervisors would have expired. The Osburn clique employed Attorneys Green and Hunter to argue in the Jefferson Circuit Court for a dissolution of the injunction against them. Charles J. Faulkner, this time alone, opposed them. Judge Melvin decided that Osburn's supervisors held their office according to law and that the injunction should be dissolved. Thus, with the contest finally won and being free to perform its functions, a full Board met on October 2 at Charles Town.[34]

SCHOOLS.

The deplorable situation into which the county's public school system had fallen after the Civil War is disclosed in a report made in 1867 to the State Superintendent of Schools by Joseph Barry, county superintendent. Complaining that there was too great a disproportion between the amount collected and that spent by the state in the county, Barry said that the school tax annually yielded about $10,000, only $4,000 of which returned to Jefferson. Another difficulty was the fact that any person participating in school affairs was excluded by law unless he could take an oath that he had never been disloyal. As there were whole districts in the county where scarcely a person could take this oath and where no Radical teacher would dare to appear, schools could not be organized.

Barry reported that he had tried to establish schools even though such action meant evading this law and that his action was denounced by ultra-loyalists in his own party. He said that in whole districts not a person would undertake the duties of a school officer of any kind. Consequently, he added, "I have few schools, few teachers, low funds, and little courage to encounter the bigotry and stupidity that I meet every day while trying to prosecute my duties".[35]

In the Civil War the United States War Department assigned property on Camp Hill in Harpers Ferry to the Freedmen's Bureau for the use of schools. The idea attracted attention of benevolent persons in other parts of the country who made liberal donations.

Storer College at Harpers Ferry. These Buildings are Mosher Hall and Anthony Memorial Hall

Finally, John Storer of Maine left an endowment for a college to educate freedmen. Harpers Ferry was selected as the site and on October 2, 1867, with two teachers and nineteen freedmen present, the institution opened its doors. The Federal Government gave four large houses and lots on Camp Hill, and the school thus occupies a site, the view from which is perhaps unsurpassed from any campus in America. The first principal, the Rev. N. C. Brackett, a minister of the Free-will Baptist denomination, which supported the school, worked unceasingly to place the institution on a firm foundation. Later known as "Storer College", it was for many years the only institution in West Virginia offering an academic education to Negroes.[36] Dr. Henry T. McDonald is its present head.

MISCELLANEOUS ITEMS.

In pursuance of an act passed on December 15, 1868, by Congress the Government property at Harpers Ferry was sold on November 30 and December 1-2, 1869. The armory had been discontinued, even for repair purposes, after the war and the town suffered a great decline. Although interested persons made repeated efforts to have the rifle factory reestablished, they were unable to accomplish anything. At the sale Captain F. C. Adams of Washington, District of Columbia, bought the old armory grounds and the site of Hall's Rifle Works for $206,000. The purchaser, who was given two years to make payment, was supposed to represent a company of Northern capitalists. Most of the houses and lots in other parts of the town were sold to citizens at high prices. The Federal Government made generous donations of lots to religious, charitable, and educational organizations. The property sold aggregated a value of $294,444.50.[37]

Harpers Ferry did not witness the expected "boom". In spite of the incorporation of The Harpers Ferry Water Power and Manufacturing Company, the organization did not establish any plant. Adams's company was later revealed to be a fraudulent concern whose real purpose was to sue the Baltimore and Ohio Railroad. In order to have any grounds at all, the promoters had to buy the old Government property through which the railroad ran. After much litigation in which the carrier was successful, the property reverted to the Government. The conspirators had never paid for their purchase but had merely prevented other buyers from acquiring the valuable water-rights at the Ferry.[38]

Efforts of the Government to find a satisfactory purchaser for its Harpers Ferry property were unsuccessful until October, 1884, at which time Thomas H. Savory bought land along both rivers and erected pulp mills.[39]

On March 31, 1870, male taxpayers in the county voted 626 to 388 in favor of a $250,000 bond issue for a new railroad. Charles Town, Shepherdstown, and Kabletown were overwhelmingly for the project, while Harpers Ferry, Bolivar, and Middleway were just as bitterly opposed. On August 23, 1870, the Board of Supervisors carried out the county's wishes by voting to subscribe the $250,000 in bonds. Delay intervened and it was not until April 2, 1872, that the printing of the bonds was authorized. Known then as the Shenandoah Valley Railroad, the carrier later became part of the Norfolk and Western system.[40]

On September 30 and October 1, 1870, the Shenandoah River went on a rampage and flooded the lower sections of Harpers Ferry. Because of the sudden onrush of waters, some of the residents did not have time to leave their homes along the river, and, consequently, several lost their lives. In addition, considerable property damage resulted.[41]

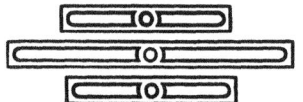

CHAPTER SIXTEEN
NEW INTERESTS AND OUTLOOKS

POLITICS.

In the elections of 1872 the Democrats continued in power in West Virginia. The new constitution, which was framed the same year, proved acceptable to Jefferson County residents by a vote of 1,684 for, to 894 against, at an election on August 22. Several months later the county's electorate voted 770 for, to 539 against, to supplant their Board of Supervisors with a County Court. In accordance with the people's wishes the State Legislature on December 21 approved an act reestablishing the County Court.[1]

In the Presidential election of 1872 voters were in a dilemma. The reform element of the Republican party, the Liberal Republicans, broke away from the "standpatters" and nominated Horace Greeley, influential editor of the New York **Tribune.** In spite of the fact that Greeley had been an implacable foe of slavery and had denounced Confederates as traitors and rebels, the Democratic party endorsed him. As was expected, the regular Republicans renominated President Ulysses S. Grant. Distasteful as it was to vote for Greeley, Jefferson Countians did not like to support Grant and thus endorse a continuance of his radical administration. Choosing what they considered the lesser of two evils, they cast 1,472 ballots for Greeley and 985 for Grant.[2] Grant's vote was large for a strong ex-Confederate county, but it must be remembered that the age of carpetbag governments had not yet passed and other Southern communities were electing Republicans. Then, too, since the Civil War many Northerners had come to Jefferson County to live.

With the reorganization of the County Court on February 17, 1873, the record under the Board of Supervisors was scrutinized. The cost of this experiment in county government may well be understood by a few figures. In 1853 private property of the county, both real and personal, amounted to $10,000,000, and the levy for expenses, including the support of paupers, was less than $9,000. Twenty years later, after the losses of war and the abolition of slavery, assessments amounted to less than $8,000,000. Yet under the reckless and extravagant management of the boards of supervisors the annual levy had risen to $80,000. The sheriff's salary alone was greater than the entire amount formerly spent for all county purposes. The assessor's office received a salary equal to one third of what had formerly been spent annually for all county purposes.[3]

Evidence that the West Virginia Legislature was looking more favorably toward Jefferson County is furnished by the fact that on January 11, 1873, it passed a bill providing that the State Supreme Court of Appeals would meet in Charles Town. As soon as word was received that its first session would be held in August, members of the local bar began to plan for a suitable library. A Library Association was organized and a room obtained. By giving their individual obligation for its safety and preservation, the lawyers acquired the library of Justice Bushrod Washington, formerly of the United States Supreme Court. Besides this, they contributed many of their own books and reports.[4]

As this was an inadequate provision for the Supreme Court of Appeals, the County Court was asked to supplement the work of the bar. It replied by appropriating $4,000, which was used to purchase reports and other works of permanent value, but it required that the books so bought remain the property of the county. Local attorneys were compelled to pay into the county treasury interest at six per cent on this appropriation for the privilege of using the law library. This arrangement was not reciprocal, for their own books could be used by the county and all of its courts free of charge. By the time the State Supreme Court of Appeals came to Charles Town the law library had 1,600 volumes.

With Judges Alpheus F. Haymond, James Paull, John S. Hoffman, and Charles P. T. Moore present, the state's highest tribunal met for the first time at its new location on August 6, 1873, in the Jefferson County courthouse. Appeal cases from

West Virginia counties east of the Alleghenies were to be tried in Charles Town. The other two meeting-places of the court at this time were Charleston and Wheeling. The tribunal continued to hold sessions at Charles Town until 1912 when it was decided that thereafter its sessions would be conducted only at the state capital.[5]

Thomas C. Green, one of Jefferson County's ablest lawyers, was appointed in 1875 to fill a vacancy on the State Supreme Court of Appeals caused by the death of Judge James Paull. Elected in 1876 and re-elected in 1880, Judge Green served on the bench until his death in 1889, when he was succeeded by Daniel B. Lucas of near Halltown.[6]

An organization that was formed primarily for the social and economic betterment of farmers but which later played an important part in politics was the Grange or Patrons of Husbandry. It was an outgrowth of a commission appointed by President Johnson to investigate conditions in the South after the Civil War. The first Grange in West Virginia was organized at Summit Point, Jefferson County, in June, 1873, and the next year the West Virginia State Grange held its first annual session at Charles Town. Other lodges were formed at Rippon, Leetown, and Shenandoah Junction in Jefferson County. The one at Shenandoah Junction was reorganized in 1904 and continued to meet until 1928, when its functions were taken over by the Jefferson County Farm Bureau. Among persons active in the Grange movement were Robert W. Baylor, C. H. Knott, M. W. Burr, Isaac Strider, and Daniel B. Lucas.[7]

Elections in the county for the next few years caused no great amount of interest, for Democrats were in overwhelming control of local politics. At an election on August 19, 1876, to determine the voters' attitude toward redistricting the county, 678 persons favored seven districts, while 359 desired five. At that time the seven districts were Bolivar, Charles Town, Harpers Ferry, Middleway, Osborn, Potomac, and Shepherd. A few months later in the Presidential election of 1876 Samuel J. Tilden carried every township in the county to defeat his Republican opponent, Rutherford B. Hayes, by a total vote of 2,023 to 975. At an election held the following year to determine the permanent location of West Virginia's state capital voters gave their neighbor, Martinsburg, 1,340, Charleston 328, and Clarksburg 41.[8]

In Jefferson County the Presidential contest of 1880 was a repetition of that of four years before. General Winfield S. Hancock, the Democratic candidate, carried every one of the fourteen precincts for a total of 2,025 votes. James A. Garfield, the Republican nominee, obtained 1,018, while James B. Weaver, the Greenback-Labor candidate, received 45 votes.[9]

Two years later one of the county's most brilliant natives, William L. Wilson, was elected to Congress. Although making a national reputation as a statesman, he was defeated in 1894 after having served six terms in the House of Representatives. In spite of his defeat in the district, he received a large majority in the county. Consequently, his defeat and other national losses brought great dejection to the Democrats. Shortly after the election a prominent Jefferson County Republican had the following conversation with an equally prominent Democrat:

"How do you feel now, Mr. Wiltshire?"

"I feel like Lazarus," savagely retorted the Wilson supporter.

"How's that?" said the Republican, with a grin.

"Been licked by dogs," replied Wiltshire.[10]

SCHOOLS.

No sooner had the county seat been moved from Shepherdstown than progressive residents of that place organized a "Classical and Scientific Institute". This was incorporated on January 12, 1872, as Shepherd College, and the first term under this new title began September 2. The building formerly used as the courthouse was leased from Shepherd Brooks for the institution. In order to induce West Virginia to locate a normal school there, its trustees offered the building to the state free of charge. The offer was promptly accepted and in 1873 the transfer was consummated. The school's principal, Joseph McMurran, continued to be its guiding hand until 1882. The modern version of this institution, known as Shepherd State Teachers College, is continuing the work of its ancestor in training teachers of this region.[11] Dr. W. H. S. White is its present head.

By 1873 the public school situation in the county had greatly improved since the years immediately following the Civil War.

Joseph McMurran, the First
Principal of Shepherd College

This was due largely to the efforts of the efficient county superintendent, William L. Wilson, who was elected to office in October, 1871. Better teachers had been engaged and their salaries were being paid more promptly than ever before. The people as a whole had become more anxious for the improvement of public schools.[12]

Under the influence of prominent Grangers the Jefferson County Agricultural College was begun in 1874 and incorporated by an act of the West Virginia Legislature passed January 19, 1875. According to the charter, the school was to be located at Leetown and was to offer the usual collegiate course of studies, with special emphasis on sciences pertaining to agriculture. It was to be under the control of seven directors chosen by the stockholders. The incorporators were Robert W. Baylor, Daniel B. Lucas, Hiram Showman, James H. Grove, and Thomas C. Green.[13]

Because of the failure to sell enough stock, the opening of the college was postponed. A committee from the school and the Grange went to Washington in an effort to get Congressional aid, but this effort likewise failed. In 1877 the Grangers succeeded in having the State Legislature pass a bill giving to the school such revenue as might come to the state in the future from the sale of public lands.

Unfortunately for the college, one of its influential backers, Daniel B. Lucas, was about this time appointed a member of the Board of Regents of the State University. He then shifted his support to the institution at Morgantown with the result that the Jefferson County Agricultural College project collapsed. After he resigned from the Board of Regents to enter the State Legislature, Lucas used his influence to have the lawmakers give all of the funds appropriated for agriculture to West Virginia University. A strong resolution objecting to this was passed by the State Grange. When Judge Lucas severed relations with the University because of his opposition to coeducation, he regretted his support of the Morgantown school.[14]

When Daniel B. Lucas became a member of the Board of Regents, one of his friends, another Jefferson Countian, Henry St. George Tucker Brooke, was appointed to the faculty of the State University. Professor Brooke was the first professor of the newly organized West Virginia University Law School.

In 1881 a new school law became effective in West Virginia. Boards of education consisted of a president and two commissioners, to be paid $1.50 each per day, but for only four days a year. They appointed three trustees for each sub-district and these trustees appointed the teachers. The boards were compelled to order a levy sufficient to run the schools for four months at least.

At that time Jefferson County had forty-eight teachers. The amount received from the state school fund for 1881 was $4,120.20, a decrease of over $500 from the preceding year. In fact, the state funds had been getting less and less. In 1884 the county paid into the state treasury for school purposes $9,774.41, but only $3,608.15 found its way back into the county. Some confusion resulted when the County Court in 1881 changed the number of magisterial districts from seven to five. The school districts were required by law to be composed of the same territory as the magisterial districts.[15]

Teachers' salaries varied in the different districts, most of which operated schools for a term of nine months. In 1887 Shepherdstown District paid $40 a month for nine months to teachers with first-class certificates, Kabletown $35, Charles Town $33, Harpers Ferry $33, and Middleway $30. Figures for lower grade certificates are not available, but several years before Shepherdstown District paid $30 and $25 a month, for nine months, to holders of second and third-class certificates, respectively.[16]

In 1887 the county's teachers adopted a new idea which proved a forward step in public school work. This was a schedule of grades in which pupils were to do a specified amount of work each year, advance from grade to grade, and finally graduate. The idea was worked out and tested by a West Virginian, Dr. Alexander L. Wade, a teacher and former superintendent of Monongalia County. Prior to this, pupils, particularly in the rural schools, had lost much time by going over the same subjects year after year without any definite schedule.[17]

Meanwhile, a good private school for girls had been opened in Charles Town. In the fall of 1882 the Rev. Charles N. Campbell, a former teacher of the Charles Town Academy, conducted a

John Stephenson Seminary at Charles Town

boarding and day school in the western part of town known as "Mt. Parvo Institute". It continued as such for two years when it moved to a different location in Charles Town and became known as the

"John Stephenson Seminary". Stephenson, who had been a resident of the county seat, had bequeathed land and a sum of money for establishing such an institution. Although the money was worthless after the Civil War, the land remained. Funds for a building were raised by forming a stock company, and the cornerstone was laid on June 12, 1884. Opening that fall and closing in 1917, the seminary was most of this period under the direction of Dr. Charles N. Campbell. At his death in 1905 it was conducted by his widow, Mrs. Laura Winder Campbell.[18]

In 1893 a large brick building constructed in the "boom" years shortly before was sold to the Charles Town District Board of Education. That fall a new principal, Wright Denny of Amelia

The Charles Town Public School, 1893-1912

County, Virginia, entered upon his duties as head of the Charles Town Graded School and served until his retirement in 1939. The school occupied the original building until its present quarters were provided in 1912.[19]

An accurate account of the public school situation in the county at the close of the century is furnished by a report made in 1899. At that time there were seventy-three public schools attended by 3,778 pupils, but 1,730 children of school age did not attend or were not enrolled. The cost of educating those who availed themselves of the privilege was $7.88 per capita, and the total value of all taxable property in the county was $6,444,236. The county superintendent's salary was $200 a year and that of the best qualified teachers was $328. Only seven counties in the entire state exceeded the rate paid to local teachers.[20]

SCHEMES.

Hidden treasure, a term seldom used in Jefferson County, came to the forefront in the fall of 1872. At that time the people of Shepherdstown, in particular, were greatly excited over the report that a stranger had dug up $62,000 at the base of an old tree located on the Shepherdstown-Duffields road about two miles north of the former and subsequently known as the "money tree". There seems to be undeniable proof of the truth of the following account:

In the summer of 1863 while Federal troops were in this region a quartermaster belonging to a New York brigade placed about $65,000 in gold and greenbacks in a small tin or metal box. The box and its contents were then put into a wooden container and buried at the base of a large oak tree along the road near the home of Wesley Myers. This money had been intended for distribution to Federal soldiers stationed in the vicinity. The officer reported at headquarters that he had been robbed by Confederates, but his story was not believed. An ensuing court-martial convicted him of stealing the money and, when he refused to offer any other explanation concerning the loss, he was sent to prison.[21]

Rumors about hidden money in the vicinity spread throughout the countryside and although many attempts were made to find it, none were successful. No one knew where to look. Shortly after the war a young man appeared in Shepherdstown and told residents that he had been a soldier in a New York cavalry regiment. Stating that he desired to visit nearby battlefields over which he had fought, the stranger took long walks in every conceivable direction. It was noticed, however, that he always carried with him an implement for digging. Subsequent watching revealed the fact that he walked up and down different roads in the Shepherdstown vicinity and anxiously scanned every tree near the roadside.

This unusual behavior was continued for more than a week. Finally, one evening he gave up in disgust and declared his intention to return home. Calling aside the gentleman with whom he was staying, the stranger told the truth about his visit. In the course of his remarks he revealed himself as the clerk and intimate friend of the Federal officer who had buried the money. He said that he had been unsuccessful in his quest and that the former quartermaster would join in the search as soon as the prison term was completed. Leaving Shepherdstown the following morning, the stranger was not seen again until September, 1872.[22]

On the latter date two well-dressed, fine-looking men stepped from a train at Keedysville, Maryland, about five miles northeast of Shepherdstown. Telling curious villagers that they were former New York soldiers revisiting old battlefields, they obtained a horse and buggy. They spent some time looking at the country around Antietam and one of them was recognized as having been the unsuccessful treasure-seeker. They then crossed the Potomac River and went to the old cement mill below the town. After conversing with the superintendent, they drove to Shepherdstown and out the Harpers Ferry road. They were not seen again until the next morning, about daylight, when they returned to Keedysville with a small box and boarded an eastbound train.

Later that same morning Wesley Myers discovered that immense piles of dirt had been thrown up from the root of a large oak tree standing by the roadside. Investigating the scene with several workmen, he noted that a wagon had been near the fence in the night and that three or four wagon-loads of earth had been taken from around the roots of the tree. One of the men discovered a place from which a box, about 15x24 inches, had been removed. Decayed portions of this were scattered all about the opening. The story of the hidden money was then revived, and many persons came to view the spot. A curious fact about the treasure was that for several years ploughs had passed over the exact place where the treasure was buried without once revealing it to the farmer.

For a number of years the money-tree guarded its empty storehouse. About the close of the century a fierce storm twisted the top off and left but a fragment. The tree did not die, however, but sprouted new branches and continued to grow. Decay set in to such an extent that when a storm on June 27, 1914, struck the tree, every limb but one was broken. A short while later, on July 13, more damage was done when the stump caught fire from some burning brush in the vicinity.[23]

A scheme of a different sort appeared in the spring of 1874 when by a vote of 11 to 3 the County Court refused to issue licenses for the sale of intoxicating liquors. In order to circumvent the decision Raleigh Domer obtained a license from the Washington County, Maryland, authorities to sell whiskey at Bridgeport, across the Potomac from Shepherdstown. Building a scow, he placed a shanty containing a bar upon it. After maneuvering his scow across the river to within a few inches of the West Virginia shore, he threw down a gangplank and got ready for business. As Maryland claimed the whole river under its jurisdiction, Domer figured that he was within his rights. In case West Virginia authorities should get too curious, he was ready at any moment to cut the hawser and glide further out into the stream.

The enterprising businessman, however, soon found that he could not evade the law. Everything worked well until August 1, when Sheriff Jacob Marker of Washington County, armed with a bench warrant, visited the makeshift bar. One of the proprietors, a man named Neil, was captured, and Domer was hauled into court at Hagerstown and fined $100 for selling liquor without a license. His license was for selling at Bridgeport and Bridgeport was not construed as including the Potomac River.[24]

The year 1890 was one of numerous "booms" in Jefferson County. Several years before, James D. Butt, a former Harpers Ferry resident, had endeavored to interest non-residents in business in that town, but something always happened to thwart his plans. In later attempts to attract foreign interests to the county Kearneysville paved the way. In February, 1890, it was announced to residents of that vicinity that A. J. Morris & Company of Avondale, Pennsylvania, had bought from B. S. McIntire eighteen acres of land north of the Baltimore and Ohio Railroad at Kearneysville. The new owners announced their intentions to quarry limestone rock for commercial purposes.[25]

Other towns were not far behind. In May a group of Charles Town promoters received a charter for the Charles Town Mining, Manufacturing, and Improvement Company. The incorporators were R. Preston Chew, Forrest W. Brown, Frank Beckwith, W. F. Lippitt, T. C. Green, B. C. Washington, and A. W. McDonald. Two weeks later Harpers Ferry announced the organization of the Harpers Ferry Mining, Manufacturing, and Improvement Company. Names of the incorporators were not listed, but they included thirteen residents of the river town and four of Washington, District of Columbia. In November a new town named Bakerton sprang up at Oak Grove schoolhouse. The Washington Building and Lime Company had bought forty-five acres of land in that neighborhood and was developing the limestone deposit there. At the same time the old Virginia Ore Bank, a mile northeast of Bakerton, was operating after fourteen years of idleness.[26]

Even the settlement at Moler's Cross Roads had visions of a great "boom". The cause of these high hopes was the supposed discovery of coal oil on the farm of R. D. Lamar in that region. In December Lamar stated that for the past month he had noticed a greasy scum on the surface of a small pool of water in a ravine near his home. Although he did not pay any particular attention to it at first, he later made an investigation. He skimmed some of the oil from the surface of the water, which was later identified in Shepherdstown as coal oil.

The excited farmer stated that it seemed to ooze from the ground and that the leaves lying around in that locality were saturated with it. He announced his intention to call in experts to determine whether or not the substance was likely to be found in paying quantities. As nothing more was done toward developing the discovery, the "oil boom" collapsed. Later, it was revealed that neighbors had sprinkled coal oil in the ravine to play a joke on Lamar.[27]

By far the greatest plans were made to transform Shenandoah Junction, located at the crossing of the main line of the Baltimore and Ohio and the old Shenandoah Valley Railroad, into a "teeming, thriving, large industrial city". With the Baltimore and Ohio running east and west and the Shenandoah Valley, now the Norfolk and Western, extending north and south, Shenandoah Junction was declared to have almost unsurpassed rail facilities.

The "boom" had its origin in the fall of 1890 when Colonel Charles T. Hood swooped upon the quiet village and began to acquire options on nearby land. He was successful in obtaining over a thousand acres in an almost perfect square at prices ranging from $100 to $250 per acre. This land extended for nearly a mile and a half each way on both sides of the railroads.

Then the promoter told the curious natives that The Antietam Manufacturing and Land Improvement Company was at the head of the scheme. With capital stock of $1,000,000, divided into 10,000 shares of $100 each, a purchaser could receive a paid-up certificate for $100 by paying only $50 on a share. The officers of the company, which was chartered by West Virginia, were B. R. Hutchcraft of Knoxville, Tennessee, president; W. F. M. McCarty of Hagerstown, Maryland, vice-president; Edward M. Mealey also of Hagerstown, treasurer; and Coleman Rogers, secretary.[28]

As the astonished villagers listened, Hood unfolded his company's plan for the transformation of Shenandoah Junction into "Antietam City". In other words, the company was, according to Hood, going to construct:

> . . . a solid, compact town, with first-class modern conveniences. The streets are to be wide avenues well macadamized and paved, with a fine sewerage. Gas and electric light plants will be provided for illuminating purposes. Waterworks are to be constructed upon the Holly system. The supply will be taken from the Potomac River, and conducted to the new city by a pipe line about five miles in length. . . .
> The Antietam Company says it will put up a mammoth steel plant with a capacity of 300 tons of merchantable steel per day, the value of which per diem at the mills will be $12,000. It is designed to employ 2,500 laborers, most of them skilled workmen, with a daily pay roll of $5,000. A

second plant will be an associated industry for working up a part of the steel output—150 tons a day—into a new product called Russian sheet steel, an article designed to take the place of tin in many of the domestic and business uses, and to which it is said to be superior. It is expected this enterprise will employ at the start 1,000 men. The third industry will be a plant for processing . . . all sorts of iron pipe, plates, etc. About 500 men will be required for this work. In addition to the above industries a number of lesser ones have been already secured . . . a hotel to cost $35,000 is to be built at once.

The company claims that in the near future it will have a thriving town of 20,000 inhabitants.[29]

The end of this dream came a few months later when the options expired and no efforts were made to renew them. The company claimed it was unable to place the stock on account of the unsettled state of affairs.[30]

Still the people of other sections of the county entertained high hopes of new developments. Capitalists representing a $2,000,000 concern were interested in the land lying on the southwest side of Bolivar. It was reported that iron ore of the finest quality and marble equal to that of New Hampshire had been discovered there in large quantities. Immense manufacturing plants were expected to begin operations. In another section of the county incorporators of the Summit Point and Berryville Railroad Company effected an organization and ordered a preliminary survey to be made. In Charles Town work was being done on a $12,000 three-story brick office building to be used as offices for real estate agents and others.

Shepherdstown was just a little behind the other county towns with its "boom". In January, 1891, a charter was issued to the Shepherdstown Mining, Manufacturing, and Improvement Company formed for the purpose of developing the town's resources and improving its business. The incorporators were George M. Beltzhoover, W. N. Lemen, A. S. Reynolds, E. I. Lee, and G. T. Hodges.[31]

Charles Town obtained another organization when the Charlestown Manufacturing and Development Company was incorporated to manufacture iron and promote real estate sales. The incorporators were B. D. Gibson, William Campbell,

NEW INTERESTS AND OUTLOOKS

Gerard D. Moore, T. Percy Mallorie, and J. F. Engle.

About this time residents of the county seat were beginning to spell the name of their town as two words. This was done so as to avoid confusion with Charleston, the capital of the state. It was not until December, 1911, however, that the United States Post Office Department spelled the name as "Charles Town".[32]

Most of these bubbles burst within the subsequent years. Charles Town's "boom" did bring a few substantial industries to the county seat that resulted in the later development of the town of Ranson. Except for a few cases, however, most of the dreams vanished into thin air. Persons who invested savings in these fantastic schemes realized their mistake too late. Evidences of this unique period of the county's history may still be seen in the large buildings erected to furnish offices for which there was no need.

MISCELLANEOUS IMPROVEMENTS.

In July, 1874, Charles Town completed a new town hall to replace the one destroyed by Federal soldiers in the Civil War. The new structure was named the Charles Washington Hall and was erected on the site of the old building at a cost of $10,000. It was described as, "spacious, well-ventilated, well seated and lighted, and combines very fine stage and scenic advantages".[33] For many years it served as a place for public entertainment and market house, after which it was converted into offices and stores.

Results of the county's $250,000 bond issue for the Shenandoah Valley Railroad were evident, when, on January 1, 1879, a locomotive steamed into Shepherdstown from the south. This marked the completion of the road across the county. Exactly one week later directors and other railroad officials formally celebrated the occasion as the dawn of a new era. Shepherdstown was, however, somewhat disappointed with later results. In addition to furnishing its share of the county's subscription, it also raised $8,000 extra on condition that railroad shops would be erected and maintained there. Some insignificant repair shops were kept there for a few years, after which they were torn down.

In reply to protests of indignant residents concerning the lack of good faith, Superintendent Joseph Sands of the road laughed and told them to be satisfied to smell the smoke as the trains went by.[34]

An improvement in the field of journalism was the establishment in February, 1885, of the **West Virginia Democrat** at Charles Town by D. S. Eichelberger and Everett W. Bedinger. In 1887 the paper passed into the hands of James M. Mason, Sr., who edited it until 1890. In the latter year R. W. Morrow obtained control and changed the name to the **Farmers Advocate,** by which it is known today. For a time it represented the interests of the Farmers' Alliance, an organization similar to the Grange.

In 1890 important steps toward improving the county's roads were taken. Henry Shepherd constructed four miles of macadam at his own expense from his home, "Wild Goose Farm", to Shepherdstown. The same year the Harrison County system was adopted in Jefferson. The principal change involved was that of having supervisors appointed to spend the money on roads, instead of requiring each man to work out part of his taxes, as had formerly been done.

The change resulted in so much improvement of the county roads that some of them became as good as turnpikes. This made the turnpike users dissatisfied, and on January 30, 1899, the County Court appointed a committee to inquire into the value of the stock ownership of various turnpikes in the county. By acquiring control of stock and by other means the local authorities were able to make all roads, except one, free in 1903.[35]

The first telephone in Jefferson County was installed in the office of **The Shepherdstown Register** on December 14, 1898, by the Maryland Telephone Company. The same day the company installed one at the Entler Hotel. Rates for the new convenience were $24 a year for business purposes and $18 for residential.[36] Charles Town did not get telephones until the Winchester Telephone Company installed them some time later.

THE SPANISH-AMERICAN WAR.

When the United States went to war with Spain over the Cuban situation, Jefferson County contributed its share of volunteers. On April 27, 1898, Company I, West Virginia Infantry [National Guard], left Charles Town for Charleston, the state's

NEW INTERESTS AND OUTLOOKS

mobilization point. Before leaving their armory, the soldiers were addressed by Colonel R. Preston Chew. Officers of this group were as follows: J. M. Pyne, captain; O. A. Prier, first lieutenant; T. P. Earnshaw, first sergeant; J. D. Walker, quartermaster sergeant; A. C. Glaize and A. F. Dunlap, sergeants; J. W. Clegg and D. A. Painter, corporals; and C. B. Glaize, trumpeter.[37]

On May 25, 1898, Governor George W. Atkinson appointed officers to recruit a volunteer regiment in West Virginia. State Senator H. C. Getzendanner of Shepherdstown received a commission as captain with authority to enroll a company in his native community. Dr. N. McK. Wilson had charge of the recruiting office at Shepherdstown, Frank Manning, Jr., at Charles Town, and W. H. Leach at Keller's. As Stephen B. Elkins, Jr., and H. H. Emmert, who were non-residents of the county, were appointed first and second lieutenants, respectively, for the company, they recruited men from other counties.

On June 28 Captain Getzendanner's company of twenty-seven men camped at Morgan's Grove and awaited orders to proceed to Charleston. These came two days later and the capital city was reached after an uneventful trip. This body became known as Company M, Second West Virginia Infantry.[38]

When hostilities came to an end on August 12 neither of the Jefferson groups had reached Cuba. The First West Virginia Regiment spent some time in camp at Chickamauga, Georgia, and Knoxville, Tennessee, while the Second Regiment encamped at Middletown, Pennsylvania, and later at Greenville, South Carolina. At Greenville the Second Regiment was discharged on April 10, 1899. This is said to have been the last volunteer regiment in the United States to be mustered out of service and Sergeant H. R. Fayman of Shepherdstown, the last soldier to receive his discharge.[39]

CHAPTER SEVENTEEN
THE RURAL FREE DELIVERY

Contrary to popular belief, the Rural Free Delivery system did not originate in the mind of William L. Wilson of Charles Town. There is unmistakable evidence that almost five years before President Grover Cleveland appointed Wilson Postmaster General, John Wanamaker, as Postmaster General in President Harrison's cabinet, had been thinking about rural free delivery. However, Wanamaker did not actually experiment with delivery of mail to farmers and Wilson did.[1]

WANAMAKER'S EFFORTS.

John Wanamaker's ideas regarding rural free delivery are stated in a book by Cushing Marshall entitled, **The Story of the Post Office, the Greatest Government Department in All Its Phases,** and published in 1893. This book was thus in circulation before Wilson became Postmaster General. Wanamaker favored "the rural free delivery, that is to say the free delivery by carrier in towns, villages, and even farming communities not at present enjoying it. . . . I do say that we can extend free delivery, and that, too, pretty fast, into the country more and more".[2]

It was Wanamaker's idea to begin his experiment in small towns first and then gradually extend the system so as to include outlying farms. One of his earliest recommendations to Congress was in this connection, and on October 1, 1890, that body passed a joint resolution embodying his plan. He was authorized to test in small towns and villages the practicability and expense of the free delivery system then enjoyed exclusively by larger cities. In response to Wanamaker's declaration that no person should be penalized for living in the country and that he believed

THE RURAL FREE DELIVERY 237

the Post Office Department should deliver mail to those to whom it was addressed, Congress appropriated $10,000 for the experiment.[3]

Between February 1 and September 3, 1891, Wanamaker tried out his plan in communities varying from 300 to 3,000 persons in population. There is no evidence that he experimented in communities smaller than 300, or in agricultural districts. The success of these trials made it clearer than ever that delivery of mail could be extended into sparsely settled regions. By working with the National Grange, National Farmers' Congress, and State Farmers' Alliance, the Postmaster General got more support for his plan. On January 5, 1892, Representative James O'Donnell of Michigan introduced "A Bill to Extend the Free Delivery System of Mails to Rural Communities". This bill carried an appropriation of $6,000,000 but failed of passage. Even an amendment appropriating $100,000 to be used in "experimental free delivery in the country as distinct from cities and towns" was rejected.[4]

WILSON SELECTS JEFFERSON COUNTY.

Nothing more was done until a month before Wanamaker retired from office, when Congress consented to spend $10,000 for experimental rural delivery. This bill was proposed by Representative Thomas E. Watson of Georgia and became a law on March 3, 1893. Although $20,000 more was granted on July 16, 1894, Wanamaker's successor, W. S. Bissell, did nothing with the money. Bissell was, in turn, succeeded on April 4, 1895, as Postmaster General by William L. Wilson, who served the remainder of Cleveland's second administration. Wilson, too, agreed with his predecessor that the proposal was impracticable but added that if Congress made the money available for the fiscal year 1897 he would attempt the experiment. Congress replied by appropriating another $10,000 on June 9, 1896, which, added to the previous amounts, made $40,000 available.[5]

Forty-four routes were accordingly selected in various localities in twenty-nine states. The idea was to conduct a general experiment to determine how the system would work under diverse conditions. Wilson chose his native county, Jefferson, as the place of the first trial. On Sepetmber 17, 1896, Colonel Thomas B. Marche, chief clerk of the free delivery system of the Post Office Department, arrived in Charles Town to arrange the details. A meeting attended by several prominent residents was held in the city council room in Rouss Memorial Hall and the proposed system was discussed. It was the unanimous opinion of this gathering that the experiment be given every chance to succeed.

Three carriers were desired to contract for the delivery of mail until the following July 1. They were to operate from the Charles Town post office and to receive a salary of $200 each for their work until July. Captain George H. Flagg, postmaster, was requested by Colonel Marche to select the carriers. Among the persons present at the meeting, in addition to Captain Flagg, were Colonel H. B. Davenport, Samuel J. Boyd, S. Howell Brown, Robert Chew, William Beall, Colonel R. P. Chew, Colonel John T. Gibson, George W. Washington, Gustav Brown, and George W. Haines.[6]

When October 1, 1896, the day designated for the experiment, arrived, five routes were established. Three men were to operate from Charles Town and one each from Halltown and Uvilla. The carriers from the post office at the county seat were Harry C. Gibson, Route No. 1; Frank Young, Route No. 2; and John W. Lucas, Route No. 3. Those from the Halltown and Uvilla post offices were I. Keyes Strider and Melvin T. Strider, respectively. On the specified day these men set out on their respective trips and, as was generally expected, they were gladly received by the farmers along the way. Each carrier averaged about twenty miles a day on horseback.

There is no official record of which one is entitled to the honor of being the first rural free delivery carrier in the United States. The Post Office Department merely lists all of them as having carried the mail on October 1, 1896. However, Harry C. Gibson always maintained that he carried mail, unofficially, for several days in the preceding August and September. He said that he did this to get acquainted with the work and to find out how long it would take him to make the rounds.[7] In addition to delivering mail to the farmers, he claimed that he also carried letters from them to the post office. Gibson remained in the service for twenty-one years. His original satchel used in carrying mail is on exhibit at the Post Office Department in Washington. Charles A. Johnson and A. Vernon Garney, clerks in the Charles Town post office, assisted the carriers in packing the bags.[8]

Postmaster General Wilson followed up the Jefferson County experiment by addressing an appeal to the farmers being served that they place boxes for the reception of mail. Thus, the carriers would not lose time in reaching residences some distance off the main roads. Gibson reported that at one time he had to open and shut sixty-three farm gates in delivering the mail on his route. At another time he was savagely attacked by two large dogs on the premises of one of his patrons. The placing of mailboxes along the roadside would remove these difficulties.

At the end of a month Postmaster Flagg rendered a report showing the extent of the service operating from the Charles Town post office. Its three carriers had delivered to eighty-seven families 1,167 letters and cards, as well as 1,059 newspapers and packages, for a total of 2,226 pieces. In addition, they returned for posting fifty-nine letters. Patrons receiving service were loud in its praise and were eager for its continuance. Prior to this, it was no unusual thing for them to lose a full half-day from their work to drive to town for expected mail or to send a letter or package.[9]

Jefferson County was the first but not the only community in which rural free delivery was tried at this time. A short while after the beginning of experiments there similar ones were conducted in other states. In all, fifteen routes were put into operation in various parts of the country in the month of October, 1896. Others were established, so that on June 30, 1897, when the fiscal year was ended, the service had grown to eighty-two routes operated from forty-three post offices in twenty-nine different states.

Not all of the reports concerning these experiments were as favorable as the ones from Jefferson County. The dead of winter had set in before the work got fairly under way, and all sorts of difficulties were encountered by carriers traversing rough country roads. Officials entrusted with inauguration of the service were not always as cooperative as they might have been. Some of them disliked the innovation because it took them away from their regular work, thus hindering their probable promotion.[10]

DEVELOPMENTS.

As a consequence of these discouraging reports, the new service was not well-known when Perry S. Heath became First Assistant Postmaster General in March, 1897. In fact, Heath was greatly surprised when he learned that a trial was actually being made of rural free delivery. Nevertheless, he took charge of the administrative division to which the experiment belonged and determined to pursue his duties in a thorough manner. Behind him he had the favorable reports of agents in charge of the work and the overwhelming endorsement of farmers throughout the country. Evidence that Congress was pleased with the results is furnished by an appropriation of $50,000 for rural free delivery in 1898.

Some opposition was still furnished by various fourth-class postmasters and star-route contractors who were afraid of being displaced by the new routes. In spite of this, experiments proceeded according to schedule. Finally, Postmaster General Charles Emory Smith, appointed by President William McKinley, developed the idea of putting the service to a test of practicability by extending rural delivery over an entire county. He wanted it to supersede all other service, with a balance sheet of profit and loss being kept. The plan embodied the following four lines of investigation: (1) the extent which rural free delivery would supersede fourth-class post offices and star-routes; (2) whether it could be used as a channel through which to extend to the farmer all other postal facilities, as money orders, etc; (3) its effect on postal revenues; and (4) its net cost to the Government as compared with that of the old system.[11]

In accordance with Smith's idea plans were made to conduct the first experiment with rural free delivery throughout an entire county, instead of on a few routes in a county. Carroll County, Maryland, was chosen with Westminster as the distributing point. On December 20, 1899, the trial was made. Postmaster General Smith ordered sixty-three minor post offices and thirty-five services by star-route contractors and mail messengers to be discontinued, all in one day, and rural free delivery substituted in their place.

The service started with four two-horse postal wagons operating throughout the countryside. They were equipped with all the appliances of a traveling post office, each with its clerk empowered to issue money orders, register and deliver letters, and cancel stamps on letters collected. In addition, the wagons supplied mail at designated points to twenty rural carriers, for whom cross routes were laid out. In this way all the territory embodied in the order was brought within easy reach of the mails and 387 of the county's 453 square miles were covered.[12]

The results of these experiments were stated by Postmaster General Smith as follows:

> Rural delivery has now been sufficiently tried to measure its effects. The immediate and direct results are clearly apparent. It stimulates social and business correspondence, and so swells the postal receipts. Its introduction is invariably followed by a large increase in the circulation of the press and of periodical literature. The farm is thus brought into direct daily contact with the currents and movements of the business world. A more accurate knowledge of ruling markets and varying prices is diffused, and the producer, with his quicker communication and larger information, is placed on a surer footing. The value of farms, as has been shown in many cases, is enhanced. Good roads become indispensable, and their improvement is the essential condition of the service. The material and measurable benefits are signal and unmistakable. . . .
>
> . . . The disposition to leave the farm for the town is a familiar effect of our past conditions. But this tendency is checked and may be changed by an advance which conveys many of the advantages of the town to the farm.[13]

In the subsequent development of the rural free delivery system in Jefferson County it was necessary to abolish several of the smaller post offices. Notwithstanding all the admitted benefits of the new project, many persons preferred the old way of handling the mail. Those living in the Leetown neighborhood, in particular, were indignant in July, 1903, at the proposition to abolish their office. They also disliked the way rural free delivery was handling their mail. Their carrier left Kearneysville at seven o'clock in the morning and thus much of the important mail for the Leetown neighborhood would remain at Kearneysville until the next day. Some of the residents refused to put up boxes and went to Kearneysville for their mail and thus partly defeated the principal idea of rural free delivery. A representative sent to Washington to obtain a revocation of the order closing the Leetown office was unsuccessful.

Bardane was more fortunate. Its office was slated to be closed on July 31, 1903, but its residents managed to get the postal officials to reconsider the order. Consequently, the office was retained. The objections which arose from time to time were eventually adjusted so that most of the patrons gladly accepted the new system.[14]

GROWTH OF SYSTEM.

From the humble beginnings sketched here rural free delivery has grown by leaps and bounds. Figures for the year 1939 disclose that there were 32,839 routes in operation, which covered a total of 1,392,657 miles. The annual cost had reached $91,141,653. The estimated number of families being served on June 30, 1939, was about 7,708,000 or 28,650,000 individuals. Carriers were better paid and service faster than in horse and buggy days. Few persons suspected that the first experiment in Jefferson County in 1896 would result in an extension of rural free delivery such as the above figures indicate.[15]

Thus, because its foremost resident was Postmaster General, Jefferson County received the honor of witnessing the first experiment in rural free delivery. But for this fact, it is doubtful if the honor would have fallen to the county.

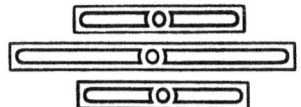

CHAPTER EIGHTEEN
THE NEW CENTURY

POLITICS.

The fall elections of 1900 marked the birth of a new era in Jefferson County. In the Presidential contest William Jennings Bryan received the largest majority ever given to a Democratic candidate up to that time. This may have been due partly to Bryan's personal appearance at Morgan's Grove on September 6, where a large number of persons were held spellbound by the silver-tongued orator. The Democratic nominee obtained 2,729 votes, while his opponent, President William McKinley, received 1,207. This large majority was indicative of the increasing Democratic strength in the county, which resulted in Jefferson's always being considered "safe" for followers of Thomas Jefferson and Andrew Jackson.[1]

The new era in local politics was caused by the election of J. Davis Billmyer of Shepherdstown as sheriff of Jefferson County. This was a departure from the custom of the past thirty years when the "old Sheriffalty" party had been retained in office. For a long time the offices of sheriff and deputy sheriff had been confined to a close circle of politicians, which included some of the county's leading residents. As one of the number would serve as sheriff and four years later become a deputy, he thus complied with the state law that a sheriff could not succeed himself. As so often happens when the same political group remains in office too long, the sheriff and deputies did not perform their duties properly. In order to obtain votes they grew lax in forcing taxpayers to meet their obligations to the county. For many years a real settlement of the taxes had not been made. As a result, the county sometimes had scarcely enough money to pay its expenses.

When Sheriff Billmyer came into office the County Court insisted upon an audit of the accounts of the former sheriff and deputies. When the delinquent officials were called upon to meet their financial obligations, they were unable to do so. Consequently, one of the most disastrous financial crashes known in this section for many years occurred. Four or five of "the clique" were forced into bankruptcy, and several of their best friends suffered serious financial losses by endorsements. To the new sheriff goes much of the credit for collecting this money due the county. By using tact, as well as firmness, he obtained gratifying results in his thankless task.[2]

The Prohibitionists put forward a ticket in the "off-year" election of November, 1902. Addressing an audience in Charles Town a few days before the election, one of their speakers, William R. Irvin of Pennsylvania, made the mistake of eulogizing John Brown in the course of his remarks. By the time he realized the blunder a vast majority of his listeners had left the hall. As is generally the case with third parties, the Prohibitionists did not poll a heavy vote.[3]

When the West Virginia Legislature convened on January 11, 1911, the House of Delegates chose Charles M. Wetzel of Jefferson County as speaker.[4]

The Presidential election of 1912 in the county was a repetition of those of former years. Woodrow Wilson obtained 2,525 votes, while his Republican opponent, President William H. Taft, and the Progressive nominee, Theodore Roosevelt, received 993 and 150, respectively.

At the same election an attempt to have a bond issue to build a bridge across the Shenandoah River at the Bloomery, two miles southeast of Charles Town, was defeated by a vote of 1,860 against, to 1,254 for. At the same time the Prohibition Amendment was ratified, 2,036 to 1,297. An attempt on July 10, 1913, to have the Charles Town District voters approve a $35,000 bond issue for the Shenandoah River bridge was defeated, 539 against, to 336 for.[5]

A curious complication existed in county political circles in 1914 when the Republicans tried to elect their candidate for county surveyor. In the absence of numerical strength they resorted to strategy. One of the Republicans, John Strother of Charles

Cartoon Which Appeared in the "Farmers Advocate" Opposing Shenandoah River Bridge

Town, ran in the Democratic primary. A short time before the primary election it was discovered that he was a Republican, but it was too late to prevent him from obtaining the Democratic nomination. Although he was nominated along with the Democrats, the committee of that party refused to certify him for the November election and his name was omitted from the ticket. Whereupon, the Republicans nominated him and put his name on their ticket. As the Democrats had no candidate for county surveyor, it appeared certain that Strother would win. However, A. S. Dandridge of near Leetown offered himself as a Democratic candidate to save the day. By asking voters to write his name in the Democratic column, Dandridge defeated Strother, 1,292 to 999.[6]

Woman's suffrage was not acceptable to conservative Jefferson County voters when the question was raised at the November, 1916 election. The vote for the proposed amendment was only 733, whereas 2,243 persons cast ballots against it. At the same election Democratic candidates received their usual large majorities.[7]

MODERN IMPROVEMENTS.

Electric lights became a certainty for Shepherdstown when on May 4, 1901, its voters approved a $4,000 bond issue for installing a plant. The vote was 159 for, to 21 against. On March 11, 1902, the town council formally accepted its new electric light plant from the Jacob G. Schaff Company.[8]

In March, 1902, Shepherdstown became greatly excited over the possibility that the main line of the Baltimore and Ohio Railroad would be rerouted through that place. The reason given was a desire to eliminate heavy grades at North Mountain and between Martinsburg and Harpers Ferry. The new route was to be a cut-off from Cherry Run by way of Shepherdstown to Harpers Ferry, a distance of thirty-two miles. For legal reasons, railroad officials planned to call the route the "Cherry Run and Potomac Valley Low Grade Freight Line".

Surveys were made, rights-of-way obtained, and everything was ready for actual construction of the cut-off. In spite of elaborate promises of something definite, no actual rails were laid. As time passed Shepherdstown still lacked Baltimore and Ohio facilities, and it became evident that nothing more would be done toward completing the project. Finally, the truth leaked out. The railroad had been staging a big bluff and had never intended to construct the cut-off. The whole idea was merely an attempt to block a rival railroad from acquiring eastern connections with Washington in territory already served by the Baltimore and Ohio.[9]

In August of the same year plans for an electric railway to serve this region were disclosed. A charter was granted to the Charles Town, Berryville, and Winchester Street Railway Company, which organization was to build an electric road to connect those places. It was proposed to use the county roads for the trolley lines, and it was expected that sufficient power could be obtained from the Potomac and Shenandoah rivers. The company's capital stock was $500,000 and its incorporators were S. M. Patterson of New York, George S. Eyster and F. S. Harrison of Halltown, and R. P. Chew and W. O. Norris of Charles Town.

Like so many similar ideas in the history of the United States this electric railway never materialized. However, in 1906 a dam was built across the Shenandoah River near Millville and a generating plant was constructed. Thus, electricity with its attendant advantages soon extended over a large part of the county.[10]

By June 3, 1903, all of the county's turnpikes except one had become free. The lone exception was that between Summit Point and the Clarke County line, with its tollgate in Virginia. In December, 1902, the collection of tolls ceased on the Shepherdstown-Halltown pike, and on June 3, 1903, the Charles Town-Kabletown and the Charles Town-Harpers Ferry roads were made free. Thus, important steps were taken toward the county's eventual ownership of all its roads.[11]

An indication of the fine roads Jefferson County boasted in 1909 is furnished by the fact that in December of that year it was awarded a prize of $500 for having the second best county roads between New York City and Roanoke, Virginia. A contest offering $4,000 in prizes for good roads was sponsored by the New York **Herald** and the Atlanta **Journal.** Mercer County, New Jersey, received the first prize of $1,000 in the 500 mile stretch.

Reports issued in 1910 and 1911 showed that the county had approximately 320 miles of roads and led all West Virginia counties in the matter of improved road mileage. Jefferson had 168 miles of improved roads, Ohio County was second with 155 miles, while Berkeley had only 65 miles.[12]

In July, 1919, the County Court voted to accept state and Federal aid in the construction of Class A roads. As a result of this cooperation, the county rebuilt the Harpers Ferry turnpike and three miles of the Berryville turnpike. About this time West Virginia inaugurated the present system of state highways and took over the construction and maintenance of Jefferson's main roads.[13]

Efforts were launched to establish a new town when on October 15, 1910, an election was held to determine the will of voters toward incorporating "Ranson". This settlement had grown up in the northern limits of Charles Town largely because of a few small industries. Qualified voters within the bounds of the proposed town cast sixty-nine ballots for incorporation and only two against. Application was made to the Circuit Court of Jefferson County for a certificate of incorporation, and on October 18, 1910, the town came into official being.[14]

A much-needed enlargement of the courthouse was begun on March 29, 1910, when the County Court opened bids for the construction of an annex. A large part of the money for this improvement was already at hand, so it was unnecessary to levy a special tax. The annex was placed behind the old building in Charles Town, directly adjoining it, and was soon completed.[15]

A step toward improving the appearance of the courthouse grounds was taken in June, 1914, when an unsightly iron "cannon" was removed. Several years before a request had been

The Old Jefferson County Jail at Charles Town. It Was Torn Down in 1919 and a New Post Office Building Was Erected on This Site in 1922

THE NEW CENTURY 249

made of the Federal Government that it furnish some historic old cannon as an ornament for the space in front of the courthouse. A huge old iron cylinder, weighing eight tons, was donated and sent to the county seat. At much expense this cylinder was transported to the courthouse and mounted on rough wooden blocks. Having no historical significance whatsoever and never having been finished as a cannon, the piece of iron was such an eyesore that the County Court was glad to sell it to a junk man. This was the county's last attempt to grace the courthouse lawn with cannon.[16]

By March, 1919, a new county jail had been completed and was ready for occupancy. Prior thereto prisoners had been kept in the same building in which the John Brown raiders were confined. The new building was constructed on a lot directly behind the courthouse annex, on the site formerly known as "Lawyers' Row". The old jail lot was later purchased by the United States Government, on which in 1922 it erected an attractive post office building.[17]

SCHOOLS.

In the fall of 1900 a new institution of learning in Jefferson County known as "Powhatan College for Young Women" opened its doors. Under the direction of Professor S. P. Hatton of North Carolina the school occupied the large hotel building constructed in north Charles Town in the "boom" days of the preceding decade. After weathering all sorts of vicissitudes, Powhatan College went into bankruptcy and closed its doors at the end of the 1913-1914 session.

Shepherd College received a valuable addition to its physical equipment when on May 2, 1904, it moved into a beautiful new building. This was constructed to replace the one destroyed by fire several years before and was named "Knutti Hall" in honor of J. G. Knutti, the school's principal when the new building was completed.[18]

About the same time the Episcopal Diocese of West Virginia established a school in Jefferson County. Purchasing a tract of land on the east side of the Shenandoah River, about four miles southeast of Charles Town, the church erected an industrial school for mountain children. Some of the things taught there were

Knutti Hall, Shepherd State Teachers College at Shepherdstown

THE NEW CENTURY 251

weaving, harness and shoe-repairing, soap-making, cooking, dairying, and dress-making. For a while academic work was also given, but this phase was later turned over to the county's public school system. The Rev. Richard Trapnell of Charles Town had charge of the boys for a time. At present this school is operating under the more familiar name of the "Mountain Mission".[19]

Evidence of the decreased interest in private academies was disclosed by the fact that in the summer of 1905 two of the principals resigned because of insufficient patronage. One of them had taught at the Charles Town Academy and the other at the Jefferson Academy at Middleway. Public schools and state institutions offering free education made it difficult for private schools to survive.[20]

A report of the State Superintendent of Schools for the year 1910 showed that Jefferson County's record was not particularly impressive. Of the 3,654 white children of school age only 2,135, or less than 58 per cent, were enrolled. Of the Negro children of school age, only one in three was in school. With an average cost of schooling per pupil of $14.18, the county spent only $196.36 for furniture and apparatus and $694.36 for permanent school improvements. The average cost of schooling for each pupil in the state was $16.57.[21]

Two years later things took a turn for the better. On February 23, 1912, the Harpers Ferry District Board of Education awarded a contract for the construction of a new high school building at the Ferry. It was opened on January 27, 1913, and the schools of Harpers Ferry and Bolivar were consolidated. In March, 1912, the Charles Town Board awarded a contract for a new high school building at the county seat, and it was completed the following fall on the site of the old Charles Town Academy. Each of the new buildings cost approximately $36,000 and each was later used exclusively for an elementary school.[22]

In the fall of 1915 a new preparatory school was opened in Ranson under the direction of Miss Maria Pendleton Duval. Known as "St. Hilda's Hall for Girls", it occupied the old Powhatan College building. In 1921 another structure was added and named "Peterkin Hall". The school flourished for a time but closed its doors in the economic depression which followed

St. Hilda's Hall for Girls at Ranson

the stock market crash of 1929.[23]

MORAL QUESTIONS.

Much excitement was caused in January, 1906, by the efforts of a group of Washington sportsmen to organize a "Metropolitan Turf Exchange" or "bookie" at Harpers Ferry. They planned to rent quarters in which to congregate from time to time to bet on horse races throughout the country. Messages giving results were to be furnished by telegraph. It was asserted that in addition to town quarters the sportsmen desired to operate the Rattling Springs hotel as a club-house.

Immediately persons interested in the moral welfare of Jefferson County sprang into action. Ministers united with laymen to hold mass-meetings at Shepherdstown and Charles Town in which they vigorously protested against the proposed turf exchange. As a large number of prominent residents were arrayed behind the ministers, the County Court announced that it would not license the new project. Accordingly, its promoters moved to other fields.[24]

In 1909 Shepherdstown was the only large municipality in Jefferson County that dispensed with its liquor saloons by a vote of the people. Charles Town with ten barrooms led in the number of dispensaries. Two of Harpers Ferry's saloon-keepers left the business, but the town still had two. At that time a saloon-keeper was required to pay $1,000 annually for a state license.[25]

In the summer of 1911 the controversial liquor question burst forth anew. A special election was held in Charles Town on May 4 to determine whether or not saloons should be licensed there for the ensuing year. The whiskey advocates won by a vote of 276 to 212, and it seemed as if the county seat would retain its ten barrooms. Declaring that their opponents had bought a large number of votes, the prohibitionists took the fight to the County Court.

At the subsequent hearing on June 5 on the question of granting licenses each side presented able arguments. Attorney Forrest W. Brown was employed by the liquor interests and former Judge Frank Beckwith by the opposition. Ministers, educators, and other prominent citizens joined the fight against licensing

The Charles Town Academy Just Before It Was Torn Down in 1912 to Clear the Site for the New Charles Town Public School Building

saloons. One of the no-license petitions was signed by 2,000 voters, while another carried the names of over 1,800 women.[26]

Meeting the following day to announce its decision, the County Court stated that by a vote of three to two it had voted against granting the licenses. Consequently, after July 1, 1911, for a time, there were no liquor saloons in the county.

About a year and a half later, on January 6, 1913, in spite of the protests of 3,000 petitioners, the County Court licensed four saloons in Charles Town and three in Harpers Ferry. Again Attorney Brown represented the liquor interests, whereas Attorneys Frank Beckwith and Frank L. Bushong argued the prohibition side. The saloon question was removed by West Virginia's prohibition law, which became effective on July 1, 1914.[27]

NEWSPAPERS.

The first issue of **The Independent**, Jefferson County's youngest weekly newspaper, appeared in January, 1907, in Shepherdstown under the editorship of Clifford S. Musser. As **The Independent** is the only Republican journal in the county, it, quite naturally, receives its greatest support from members of that party. However, the work of Mr. Musser in historical research and the publication of his findings have caused this newspaper to be highly valued by persons interested in history. The editor continues to use **The Independent** as a means of giving the public the benefit of his widespread research.

One of the county's oldest publications passed out of existence on March 16, 1916, when the **Virginia Free Press** printed its last issue. Established at Harpers Ferry in 1821 by John S. Gallaher, it was in 1827 moved to Charles Town and consolidated with the **Farmer's Repository**. It remained in the Gallaher family until 1911, when W. W. B. Gallaher sold it to William Campbell. The new owner published it for a time and then sold it to Clayton L. Haines of the **Spirit of Jefferson** and Robert C. Rissler of the **Farmers Advocate**. As two weekly newspapers were sufficient for Charles Town, these rival editors discontinued the **Free Press**. For a number of years it had been Whig in politics, then Constitutional Union [in 1860], and finally Democratic.[28]

THE WORLD WAR.

The county's normal pursuits were disturbed when on April 6, 1917, the United States declared war on Germany. President Woodrow Wilson's efforts to avert the catastrophe and Germany's unrestricted submarine warfare campaign are too well-known for repetition here. In order to raise an army of sufficient strength Congress on May 28 passed the Selective Service Act, and in accordance with its provisions all male Jefferson Countians between the ages of 21 and 31 were registered.

At that time 1,129 persons, composed of 882 whites and 247 Negroes, listed their names with the registrars. The local draft board consisted of J. William Rider of Halltown, and Captain H. C. Getzendanner and Dr. William Neill, both of Charles Town. When order numbers of the registrants were determined by the national lottery in Washington, it was disclosed that the first number, 258, was held by Harry T. Underwood of Middleway and the second number, 458, by Hugh S. Moler of Engle.

At the registration held in 1918 for men between the ages of 18 and 45 there were listed in Jefferson County 1,662 persons, composed of 1,347 whites, 314 Negroes, and one Chinaman.[29]

At least one county soldier, Sergeant Major John H. Quick of Charles Town, was cited for bravery in the World War. He was awarded the Distinguished Service Cross for heroic service in France. Prior thereto, in the Spanish-American War, he had received a Congressional Medal of Honor. On June 16, 1918, Quick volunteered and assisted in taking a truck-load of ammunition and materials into the town of Bouresches, France, and thereby relieved a critical situation. To do this, it was necessary for him to travel over a road swept by artillery and machine gun fire.[30]

Of the 548 men enrolled in Jefferson County for the World War thirty lost their lives. Five of these, Wade H. Jackson, Joseph W. Perks, Clarence C. Grove, William J. Geary, and one Negro, Solomon Johnson, were killed in battle. The following six died overseas from natural causes: John D. Cockrell, Harry N. Walker, Fayette B. Souders, William H. Link, Roy Wageley, and a Negro, Martin Snyder. The other deaths occurred from diseases in hospitals in this country. These victims were:

THE NEW CENTURY

Howard Allen, Perry Dunn, Harry Feagans, Ira M. Derr, Wilmer Miller, Thomas C. Reinhart, Marvin W. Henry, Bernard B. Hoke, James C. Webb, Daniel Newcomer, Harold W. Steadman, and Rudolph Cromwell. The following Negroes belong to this group: William W. Summers, George Carr, Luther Robinson, James Thornton, Barbour Boggerson, and Jesse Price.[31]

Jefferson County assumed more than its share of the financial burdens imposed by the war. Figures for all of the loans are not available, but the Second Liberty Loan allotment of $235,000 was readily subscribed by the county's seven banks. In the third loan residents were asked to raise $173,700 and instead they subscribed $274,800. The total number of local persons participating in this latter subscription was 1,077. The Red Cross allotment in 1918 was $2,500, and over $11,000 was given. For the fifth loan, which was the Victory Loan, the county raised over $300,000 to "finish the job".[32]

A study of figures concerning the cost of registration and enrollment of soldiers in West Virginia counties is interesting. Many Jefferson County officials performed the registration work without pay, as did the exemption board. The entire cost of registration and enrollment of the county's first quota, fifty-six men, was $174, or an average of $3.11 each. This figure compares favorably with those of other counties in the state. In Berkeley County, for instance, the amount was $9.76 for each man, in Kanawha, $23.86, and in Taylor, $32.41. Clay was the only county in the state where no pay was asked by anybody connected with the registration or exemption board.[33]

A large home-coming celebration for the returning doughboys was staged on September 25, 1919, in Charles Town. People turned out in great numbers to welcome the soldiers and to witness a parade. The latter consisted of the Powhatan Band, World War soldiers, Civil War veterans, various county fraternal organizations, and all kinds of gaily decorated floats. After the parade the crowd assembled in front of the courthouse, where it witnessed further exercises. In addition to this, the day's program included athletic events, dancing, and a lunch furnished by ladies of the town for the soldiers.[34]

MISCELLANEOUS ITEMS.

Evidence that the Civil War had not been forgotten in Charles Town is supplied by an order passed in 1902 by the town council which forbade the presentation of the play **Uncle Tom's Cabin** within the town's limits. The ordinance remained until 1933 when it was deleted in a recodification of Charles Town's laws.[35]

Francis Richard Stockton, noted novelist and short-story writer, died on April 20, 1902, at his home, "Claymont Court", near Charles Town. This mansion was originally the home of Bushrod Corgin Washington, a great nephew of General George Washington, and was built about 1820. The author, better known as Frank R. Stockton, moved to "Claymont Court" about 1899 from New Jersey and during his residence here wrote **Kate Bonnet** and **The Captain's Toll-Gate**. His most famous short-story, **The Lady or the Tiger**, was not written in Jefferson County, however.[36]

On April 13, 1906, a group of workmen discovered a cave under the center of Charles Town, only a block and a half from the courthouse. The laborers had been excavating and quarrying rock for a new livery stable to be erected on Liberty Street. Further investigation revealed a subterranean passage leading northward between two ledges of rock. A little distance beyond was a large lake of clear water. Years afterward this natural curiosity was developed and advertised as the "Lakeland Caverns", but today it is not commercialized.[37]

The Census of 1910 gave Jefferson County a total of 15,889 persons, exactly forty-six less than it had ten years before. Reasons for the decline were the general drift of population from the country to the city, the suspension of work at the quarries near Kearneysville, and the migration of Negroes to Maryland and Pennsylvania. There were 12,390 whites and 3,499 Negroes in the county. Charles Town continued to be the largest settlement with a population of 2,662. Shepherdstown was second with 1,070, Harpers Ferry third with 766, and Middleway fourth with 765. Bolivar brought up the rear with 687 inhabitants.[38]

"Claymont Court", the Home of the Author, Frank R. Stockton, near Charles Town

CHAPTER NINETEEN
RECENT YEARS

UNITED STATES vs. UNITED STATES HARNESS COMPANY.

Much excitement was caused in Jefferson County in June, 1921, when trouble arose between the Federal Government and the United States Harness Company of Ranson. The latter organization was formed at the end of the World War to dispose of surplus leather and harness supplies belonging to the army but located at the company's plant in Ranson. Its officials had contracted on September 3, 1920, with the Government to recondition, in some cases, and sell this surplus material upon a profit-sharing basis. The sale was advertised for June 15 at Charles Town, and at the appointed time a large number of dealers assembled to bid on the estimated $25,000,000 worth of harness and leather goods.[1]

Before the sale began army officers arrived in Charles Town and with legal advisers prohibited it from being held. President Warren G. Harding, acting on advice of Attorney General Harry M. Daugherty, had ordered the War Department to declare the contract null and void and to stop the sale. A Congressional committee on war expenditures had made a long report on the subject of the deal in which officers of the Ranson company were charged with breach of faith with the Government and with criminal conspiracy to enrich themselves at its expense.

A few weeks later, on July 15, a force of fifty United States soldiers with thirty army trucks arrived in Charles Town to take possession of the property of the United States Harness Company. Establishing camp on the Charles Town Horse Show grounds, the soldiers moved to the A. D. Goetz harness factory, where the harness was stored. When officials of the company communicated with Washington, they were advised to close the factory, lock all doors, and have the employees stand on the outside. In the meantime, the soldiers had loaded one truck. However, after the doors were locked they made no more attempts to remove the harness. There the matter stood until Attorney Forrest W. Brown obtained an injunction from Circuit Judge J. M. Woods of Martinsburg to prevent the soldiers from interfering with the harness company's property. The soldiers, who had been standing guard around the factory, then retired and the matter was taken into the courts.

The Federal Department of Justice took the question before the Federal courts, and on July 28, 1923, a grand jury at Elkins returned an indictment against the United States Harness Company, four of its officers, and three other interested persons. The indictment charged conspiracy to defraud the Government in connection with the contract for the disposal of surplus harness of the War Department. The matter was finally settled in January, 1924, when the defendants were acquitted by the United States District Court at Parkersburg. Judge D. L. Croner took the case out of the jury's hands and ordered a verdict of acquittal.[2]

ANOTHER TREASON TRIAL.

The distinction of witnessing two of the few treason trials ever held in the United States came to Charles Town in the spring of 1922, when, after sixty-three years, it was the scene of its second treason trial. West Virginia coal miners charged with treason and murder for engaging in warfare with state and Federal troops in Logan and Mingo counties were brought to Jefferson County on a change of venue. Public sentiment was such in the southern part of the state that they could not get a fair trial there.

In general, the dispute was over an attempt to unionize mine workers in the southern West Virginia coal fields. The mine operators were determined to stop this at all costs and for that purpose hired private guards and detectives. Some of these officers used force to break up union meetings, prevent non-union members from attending, and intimidate employees in other ways. Trouble had broken out in 1912 in which many were killed on both sides. When the national coal strike occurred in 1919, a mob of union miners of the Kanawha region swept toward the non-union fields of Logan County. Although they were turned aside from their objective, the question was not settled. When the operators opposed efforts to unionize the Williamson coal fields a short time later, more disorder followed. The state declared martial law in Mingo County.[3]

Early in August, 1921, miners assembled at Marmet, within a short distance of the state capital. From 2,000 to 3,000 well-armed men began a march to Logan to "get" Don Chafin, Logan County sheriff, and before long one of the largest industrial insurrections in American history was under way. The mob was disbanded at Madison, Boone County, by Frank Keeney, president of District 17, United Mine Workers of America. It reassembled, however, several days later when state police raided and disarmed miners at Sharples on the ground that they were moonshiners. Within twenty-four hours an army of 6,000 heavily armed men was marching toward the Logan County border. A week of bloodshed, terror, and actual warfare followed when Logan County mobilized its forces. The bloodiest fighting occurred at Blair Mountain and Sharples.

As the state officials were unable to cope with the situation, Federal troops were ordered to the scene. After airplanes had dropped messages on the miners telling them that Federal soldiers were in control, the invaders hid their arms in the mountains and departed. Definite information concerning the number of casualties is not available, but several were killed and wounded on each side.[4]

The first trial was set to begin on April 24, 1922, at the spring term of the Jefferson Circuit Court. A day or two before, Charles Town was flooded with hundreds of newcomers. Miners, operators, attorneys, witnesses, reporters, and many other persons composed the influx. State headquarters were at the Jefferson Hotel, while the miners and their friends chose the Palm Hotel. Local attorneys engaged in these trials were Prosecuting Attorney John T. Porterfield, Forrest W. Brown, and George M. Beltzhoover, Jr., for the state, and James M. Mason, Jr., for the defense. Other lawyers participating were John Chafin, A. M. Belcher, and C. W. Ozenton, for the state, and H. W. Houston. T. C. Townsend, Charles J. Van Fleet, L. P. Hager, L. F. Fulton, and Samuel Montgomery, for the defense.

Twenty-four persons were indicted for treason against West Virginia. William Blizzard, the alleged field generalissimo of the miners, was tried first. With Judge J. M. Woods of Martinsburg on the bench Blizzard's trial began on April 27 and lasted until May 27, when, after being out five hours, the jury brought in a verdict of not guilty.[5]

The second trial was that of Rev. James E. Wilburn, who was charged with the murder of a Logan County deputy sheriff in the attempted armed march. It began on June 13 and lasted until June 23, when he was found guilty of second degree murder.

The Jefferson County Courthouse at Charles Town Which Was the Scene of Two of the Few Treason Trials Held in the United States

His son, John, also indicted for the same killing, was likewise found guilty of second degree murder, on August 12. The next trial, that of Walter Allen, indicted for treason, began on August 29 and was completed on September 16, when he was found guilty.[6]

The next defendant, C. Frank Keeney, mine union president, also indicted for treason, was not brought to trial until October 23. In the middle of the testimony Keeney's lawyers asked for a change of venue on the ground that prejudice in the county rendered a fair trial impossible. This contention was upheld by Judge Woods on October 31, and the prosecution submitted the venue question to the State Supreme Court of Appeals. When the latter body met, on November 14, it affirmed Judge Woods, and Keeney's trial, as well as that of the other defendants, was removed to Berkeley Springs, in Morgan County. After legal skirmishing there another change of venue took the trials to Greenbrier County.

A good example of present day justice is furnished by the subsequent lives of the three men convicted at such great expense at Charles Town. The two Wilburns were sentenced by Judge Woods to eleven years each in the state penitentiary and Allen was given ten years. Governor Ephraim F. Morgan commuted the sentence of the Wilburns to five years each and they were pardoned by Governor Howard M. Gore after they had served but three years. Allen "jumped" his bail while an appeal was pending in the State Supreme Court of Appeals.[7]

The transformation wrought in Jefferson County during the miners' trials can scarcely be imagined. Charles Town was once again in the spotlight and received publicity throughout the nation. John L. Lewis, president of the United Mine Workers of America, was on hand, as was Governor Ephraim F. Morgan of West Virginia, and other state officials. A strange sight for this community was the hundreds of miners who filled the streets, hotels, and loitering-places of Charles Town. All eyes were on the courthouse, where the trials were conducted.

The reaction of the county's residents to this invasion of outsiders was interesting. Charles Town was divided into two hostile camps; one group sympathized with the operators and the other with the miners. Persons who had been friends for years drifted apart on this struggle between capital and labor, heretofore almost unknown in Jefferson County. Much ill-feeling was caused between residents of the town. Many persons were interested in the courthouse scenes, where able counsel argued. Women who had never before brightened the Circuit Court room with their presence took their knitting and even their lunches, that they might not miss any of the proceedings. Nevertheless when the trials were removed to Morgan County, the inhabitants of Jefferson were relieved. For the most part, they had become tired of the controversial question and were glad to have it taken away.

POLITICS.

Progressive residents of Charles Town attempted in 1921 to have the county seat's name changed to "Charles City". So much trouble had been experienced by local businessmen and others in having their mail go to Charleston, the state capital, that it was thought a change of name would benefit everyone. Despite their efforts in this direction, the town's residents on May 26, 1921, voted 850 to 129 against the change. Women, who had received the right to vote in 1920, turned out in large numbers to cast ballots against "the progressives". As a result, Charles Town retained its original name, and the confusion of mail with Charleston still annoys inhabitants of the Jefferson County town.[8]

Not in the least discouraged by this reverse, other "progressives" in the county seat attempted to obtain a sewerage system for that municipality. In the first election held for the purpose on March 19, 1925, proposing a $100,000 bond issue, they lacked seventeen votes of the necessary three-fifths majority. The vote was 421 for, to 310 against. An effort made more than a year later proved successful. On April 13, 1926, Charles Town's residents approved a $65,000 bond issue for a sewerage system by the vote of 575 for, to 275 against. The project was completed in due time.[9]

The Presidential contest of 1928 was one of the closest held in Jefferson County since the Civil War. For once a large number of Democratic voters did not endorse their party's nominee, Alfred E. Smith. Feeling against the former New York Governor was bitter, and one old-line Democrat after another announced his intention to support the Republican candidate, Herbert C. Hoover. As the election day drew near, it seemed that only a miracle could save Jefferson County for the Democrats, and party men "worked like beavers" to ward off the defeat threatening to break the county's Democratic precedents.

When the battle was over, it was disclosed that Smith had carried the county but by a greatly reduced majority. Whereas four years before, John W. Davis, whose first wife, Julia McDonald, was a Jefferson Countian, had obtained 2,511 more votes than President Calvin Coolidge, Smith received only 262 more than Hoover! The vote for the Democratic candidate was 3,312 and for the Republican 3,050. Other Democrats, Matthew M. Neely and J. Alfred Taylor, fared better, although they, too, failed to obtain the normal party majorities. For United States Senator Neely received a majority of 1,688 and for governor Taylor was given 1,605 more votes than his Republican opponent.[10]

In the Presidential election of 1932 Jefferson County voters turned against President Hoover and gave Franklin D. Roosevelt the largest majority ever accorded a Democratic candidate up to that time. As is generally the case, bad business conditions reacted against the administration in power. The Great Depression was at its worst when the voters went to the polls in November, 1932. Roosevelt carried all of the county's twenty-two precincts for a total of 5,350 votes, while President Hoover received only 1,506. Other Democratic candidates were given majorities only slightly smaller than that given the Presidential nominee.[11]

In compliance with the Democratic platform of 1932 the new administration set machinery in motion for repeal of the Prohibition Amendment. At a special election held in Jefferson County on June 27, 1933, the electorate ratified the repeal amendment by a vote of 1,939 for, to 1,017 against. Only two precincts, Duffields and Mt. Hope, remained faithful to the dry cause. That the result was a foregone conclusion is attested by the fact that only about one-fourth of the voters went to the polls.[12]

The Presidential contest of 1936 attracted no more than ordinary attention and President Roosevelt was given another large vote, but the campaign in 1940 aroused more interest. Considerable speculation developed concerning the reception of a third term for President Roosevelt by conservative Jefferson Countians.

The delicate foreign situation, coupled with benefits obtained by the county under the New Deal, caused most Democrats to disregard their conservatism and support their nominee, although the latter did not fare as well as he had in 1936. Roosevelt carried twenty-two of the county's twenty-three precincts for a total vote of 5,240. The Republican candidate, Wendell L. Willkie, had a majority in only one voting-place, Upper Shepherdstown, but he received 2,265 votes in the county. Democratic nominees for the United States Congress and governor obtained more votes in the county than President Roosevelt.[13]

SCHOOLS.

Crowded conditions in the Charles Town public school building forced the Board of Education to take steps to remedy the situation. Accordingly, in April, 1922, it purchased the Timberlake property on West Congress Street. This was used as a high school building for seven years.[14]

A few weeks later Shepherdstown District was compelled to establish a high school. Shepherd College had formerly provided a high school there, but a new order of the State Board of Education discontinued a high school in connection with the college. An election was held on May 6, 1922, on the question of establishing a high school at Shepherdstown, and the vote was 239 for, to 91 against. The college offered the use of a building until the public school officials could construct one.[15]

In the succeeding years efforts to obtain a new high school building for Shepherdstown District met with much opposition. At an election on July 12, 1924, on the proposal to issue $40,000 in bonds for such a purpose, only 245 voted for the project, to 276 against it. A three-fifths majority was required to carry the issue. At an election on September 13 the bond issue was defeated, 391 against, to 294 for. A third attempt, held on November 5, 1927, likewise failed. Every precinct in the district voted against the proposition, and the final results were 498 against, to 287 for a bond issue. Finally, in the Presidential election of 1928 residents of Shepherdstown District voted in favor of a $40,000 bond issue for a new high school building. With every precinct except Duffields favoring the proposition, the vote was 856 for the issue, to 286 against it.[16]

Shepherdstown High School

Not to be outdone, residents of Charles Town District at the same election voted 1,487 to 568 in favor of a $100,000 bond issue for a new high school building. In addition, they approved a $25,000 issue for a new structure for Negro children. Credit for the overwhelming majority given the high school project goes mainly to Dwight P. Hurley, principal of Charles Town High School. When Mr. Hurley entered upon his duties in the fall of 1926, there was little or no sentiment for a new building in Charles Town, although every informed person realized the need for one. By working industriously on the new high school project, he was able to achieve the desired goal.

Harpers Ferry District's voters also considered the question of a new high school building at the election of 1928. Hopes of public school officials there were frustrated, however, when only 833 favored a bond issue and 813 opposed it. A proposition to unite with Charles Town District in constructing a joint high school building was even more unpopular, with only 157 Harpers Ferry District voters in favor, to 1091 against the plan.[17] As a matter of fact, since the three towns needed new buildings, it had been suggested that all unite in constructing one large consolidated plant at a central point in the county. Petty jealousies, along with the necessity of traveling long distances, caused this proposal to be frowned upon in all three districts.

Charles Town and Shepherdstown soon completed their new buildings, but it was not until June 13, 1929, that Harpers Ferry District voters approved a $112,500 bond issue for the construction of a high school. The vote in this election was 607 for, to 64 against. The building was first used in the 1930-1931 school session.[18]

In a scoring of the state's public schools released in November, 1930, by the West Virginia Department of Education Jefferson County, with an average of 88.66 per cent, ranked third among the fifty-five counties. Ohio County was first with 101.73 per cent and Brooke was second with 96.23 per cent. Berkeley County was sixth with 79.03 per cent, while Morgan was twentieth with only 70.28 per cent.[19]

For the four-year period, 1934-1937, Jefferson County led all of the counties in the state in the percentage of high school graduates attending a college or university. More than half of the

Charles Town High School

county's high school graduates, or 52 per cent, enrolled in institutions of higher learning. Monongalia County, with 41 per cent, was second and Gilmer, with 40 per cent, was third. Pleasants County had the lowest average in the state, for only 6 per cent of its high school graduates went to college. The average for the entire state was 22 per cent.[20]

THE SECOND WORLD WAR.

In the summer of 1940 a new crisis confronted the American people. War had broken out in Europe in September, 1939, and Germany had scored amazing successes in its struggle with the Allies. In rapid succession Adolph Hitler's armies swept over Austria, Czechoslovakia, Poland, Denmark, Norway, Holland, Luxemburg, Belgium, and France. Realizing the inadequacy of the American army to meet this new threat, Congress on September 14 passed a peacetime Selective Service Act. On October 16, the appointed day, 1,968 Jefferson County residents between the ages of 21 and 35, inclusive, registered for military service.

At the national lottery in Washington number 158, which was held by Lester L. Bush of near Charles Town, was the first one chosen and number 192, held by Edward Clarence Cummings of Harpers Ferry, was the second. Those persons appointed to the Jefferson County Draft Board were Arthur Glover of Charles Town, George McKee of Shepherdstown, and Gilbert Perry of Harpers Ferry. Attorneys Lee Bushong, Jr. and Forrest A. Brown were appointed Government appeal agent for the county and a member of the district appeal board, respectively. Practically all of the county's physicians were asked to assist in examining registrants.[21]

MISCELLANEOUS ITEMS.

An unusual honor came to Charles Town in September, 1920, when Samuel Walter Washington and Henry Harrison Cooke were selected as Rhodes scholars from West Virginia. Mr. Washington is a direct descendant of George Washington's brother, Samuel. Both men were graduates of Virginia Military Institute and both continued their education at Oxford University in England for three years, as provided in their scholarships.[22]

Harpers Ferry in 1941

Bolivar came into the limelight in the fall of 1923 when its policeman, Arthur Littleton, arrested the German ambassador, Dr. Otto L. Wiedfelt, for speeding. The diplomat, with Consul Johannes Jantzen, Vice-Consul Baer, and Mrs. Jantzen, had left Washington for a recreation trip. While they were passing through Bolivar at high speed, they were stopped by Policeman Littleton. As the town's mayor could not be located then, the officer informed the foreigners that they would have to post $5.60 bond. Protests that the car belonged to a foreign representative and hence was entitled to certain privileges availed the Germans nothing. Reluctantly, they paid the money and were allowed to depart instead of being locked up in the town jail, the other alternative.

When Ambassador Wiedfelt returned to Washington, he laid the matter before Secretary of State, Charles E. Hughes. The latter communicated with Governor Ephraim F. Morgan, who, in turn, referred the problem to the State Road Commission. The road officials negotiated with the Bolivar authorities, who finally sent a check for $5.60. This was forwarded to the ambassador, and as Governor Morgan sent a note of apology through Secretary Hughes, the incident was closed.[23]

Reminiscences of Reconstruction days were brought to mind when on the night of December 1, 1923, several members of the Ku Klux Klan set fire to a cross in the public square of Charles Town. The cross blazed brilliantly for a few minutes and attracted much attention. As the perpetrators of this act were masked and drove away soon after they started the fire, their identity was not revealed.[24]

On December 20, 1930, announcement was made that the Federal Government would locate a $75,000 fish hatchery at Leetown. The plant was subsequently erected and is used to restock streams in this region and for experimental purposes.[25]

In the summer of 1933 it was announced that a group of Maryland race-track promoters had purchased the grounds of the Charles Town Horse Show Association. This syndicate was headed by Joseph B. Boyle of Baltimore and was incorporated as the Shenandoah Valley Jockey Club. Alleged reasons for the location of a track at Charles Town were the quality of the soil, slope of the ground, proximity to Washington and Baltimore, and nearness to the large horse-breeding farms of northern Virginia.

Work on the necessary buildings was soon begun and before long over $100,000 had been spent. Racing under the parimutuel system of betting started December 2, 1933, and continued for twenty days. Special busses and trains brought many fans to the meet, and Charles Town became known to followers of the turf sport.[26]

Dark days were, however, ahead for the Shenandoah Valley Jockey Club. Because it was unable to meet its financial obligations, creditors took over the plant. They effected a reorganization in which the Charles Town Jockey Club was formed and Albert J. Boyle, a brother of the former official, was made manager. Under his supervision the organization was placed on a paying basis and at the present time is prospering.

Jefferson County was visited in March, 1936, by one of the worst floods in its history. Both the Shenandoah and Potomac rivers went on a rampage and resulting property losses were great. Most of Harpers Ferry was inundated and the lower sections of Shepherdstown were flooded. On March 18 the highway bridge across the Potomac River at Shepherdstown was carried away. This bridge had been built in 1889-1890 to replace the one lost

The Charles Town Jockey Club

in the flood of 1889. A short time later both of the highway bridges at Harpers Ferry suffered a similar fate. The flood was said to be one of the greatest the Potomac has ever had.

The authorities of both Maryland and West Virginia were slow to restore the bridges. For several years nothing was done and then an agreement was reached with Baltimore and Ohio Railroad officials whereby the Valley Branch Railroad bridge across the Potomac at Harpers Ferry would be planked. Consequently, both trains and automobiles now use the same bridge. This arrangement is satisfactory except for the delay caused when a train crosses the bridge. The structure across the Shenandoah River at Harpers Ferry has not been replaced. Shepherdstown was forced to resort to ferry service in communicating with Maryland until a new bridge was opened on July 21, 1939.[27]

Census figures for 1940 showed increases over those of 1930. The population of Jefferson County in 1940 was 16,762, an excess of 982 over that of 1930. Charles Town boasted 2,926 inhabitants, the largest number in its history. Ranson was next with 1,171. Shepherdstown was third with 945, Harpers Ferry was fourth with 665, and Bolivar was fifth with 628. All of these towns showed gains over the 1930 figures, except Harpers Ferry which had forty less. This was no doubt due largely to damage caused by the flood of 1936, since many residents deserted the lower ground along the rivers and never went back. The trend of population there seems to be in the direction of Bolivar.[28]

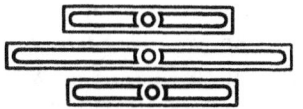

BIOGRAPHIES OF PROMINENT FORMER RESIDENTS

BAYLOR, GEORGE (Feb. 13, 1843—March 6, 1902). One of the county's gallant Confederate soldiers was Captain George Baylor of Charles Town, who was educated at Dickinson College, Carlisle, Pennsylvania. Graduating in 1860, he served as an instructor in the Episcopal High School in Fauquier County, Virginia, until the beginning of the Civil War. In April, 1861, he joined Company G, Second Virginia Infantry. During the first year of the war he was with the Stonewall Brigade, after which he joined Company B, Twelfth Virginia Cavalry, commanded by his father, Colonel Robert W. Baylor. He was made a second lieutenant in this organization, and after his father was captured, on April 27, 1862, he took command. In February, 1863, he, too, was taken prisoner and was sent to Fort McHenry. He was later transferred to Fort Delaware but was subsequently exchanged. Returning to his command, Captain Baylor was wounded but continued to take an active part in the various campaigns in Virginia. On April 5, 1865, he joined Colonel John S. Mosby and became captain of Company H in that daring leader's organization. He surrendered at Winchester on May 8, 1865.

When he returned to civil life, Captain Baylor studied law at Washington College, now Washington and Lee University. After graduating in 1867, he practiced five years in Kansas City, Missouri, and then returned to Charles Town. He was married April 30, 1872, to Lalla Louise Beatty of Maryland. Captain Baylor formed a law partnership with William L. Wilson, which lasted until the latter was elected president of West Virginia University. During the same period he served four years as prosecuting attorney of Jefferson County. In 1900 he published in book form an account of his Civil War experiences entitled, **Bull Run to Bull Run.**[1]

BEALL, JOHN YATES (Jan. 1, 1835—Feb. 24, 1865). John Yates Beall created much excitement by his exploits during the Civil War. Born at "Walnut Grove", about three miles northeast of Charles Town, he entered the University of Virginia at the beginning of the 1852-1853 session and studied law for three years. Although he completed his legal training, he never obtained a license to practice. The death of his father on August 21, 1855, compelled him to change his plans and to assume the management of the family farm.[2]

After the John Brown affair Beall became a member of one of the many volunteer military companies existing then. His company was organized by Captain Lawson Botts in Jefferson County and later became known as Company G, Second Virginia Infantry. Beall was wounded in an engagement at Bolivar Heights on October 16, 1861, and was brought to his home, where he recovered. After a number of varied experiences he conceived the idea of attempting to liberate the Confederate prisoners confined on Johnson's Island in southern Lake Erie.

Although the Confederate authorities at Richmond favored Beall's plan, they restrained him for fear of endangering neutral relations with England. However, the bold soldier was given official permission to privateer on the Chesapeake Bay. A medical examining board had discharged him from the army on the ground of disability caused by the wound received at Bolivar. A series of spectacular acts as a privateer resulted in his capture on November 10, 1863. He was exchanged on May 5, 1864.[3]

In pursuit of his plan to rescue the Confederates imprisoned on Johnson's Island, Beall reached Canada and on September 18, 1864, with a small group of picked men, he captured two vessels, the **Philo Parsons** and the **Island Queen.** He was prevented from accomplishing his real purpose, however, by a mutiny among his followers. As a result, he was forced to abandon his scheme. Several months later he gathered a few associates and tried to capture a military train on the New York and Erie Railroad. Failing in this mission, he was captured on December 16 by Niagara police who believed him to be an escaped prisoner. One of his party, in order to save himself, revealed Beall's true identity to the captors, and the Jefferson Countian was taken to New York City.

The unfortunate captive was tried before a military commission, found guilty of being a guerrilla and spy, and sentenced to be hanged. The Confederate Government assumed responsibility for his deeds, and influential friends intervened in his behalf, but all to no avail. He was removed to Governor's Island, New York, where on February 24, 1865, the grim sentence of death was carried out. His body was sent to Charles Town and was laid to rest in the northwest corner of Zion Episcopal Churchyard.[4]

An unusual story is sometimes told about a friendship alleged to have existed between Beall and John Wilkes Booth, the assassin of President Abraham Lincoln. According to the occount, Booth's anger toward Lincoln was caused by his resentment over the President's failure to pardon his friend, Beall. The writer is not in a position to pass judgment on the authenticity of this story, but as it is not backed with proof and there is considerable room for doubt, he has not thought it advisable to give it credence at present. In Beall's memoirs, edited by Judge Daniel B. Lucas, he makes no mention or suggestion that Beall's execution was in any way connected with Lincoln's assassination.[5]

BEDINGER, HENRY (1812—Nov. 26, 1858). Born at "Bedford", near Shepherdstown, Henry Bedinger was the son of Daniel Bedinger, a Revolutionary soldier, and Sarah Rutherford Bedinger. His mother was a daughter of Robert Rutherford, the Lower Valley's first representative in Congress. Daniel died when Henry was young, and when the son was about eighteen years old he was placed in the clerk's office at Romney, Hampshire County. He did not remain in this position long but left to join the family of his brother-in-law, William Lucas, near Charles Town. After reading law, he opened an office in Shepherdstown about 1838. In the meantime, he had married a daughter of General George Rust.

He entered a partnership with his brother-in-law at Charles Town, and in 1845 Bedinger succeeded William Lucas as the Lower Valley's representative in Congress. He served two terms in this capacity as a member of the Democratic party. As he had lost his first wife shortly after his removal to Charles Town, he married Caroline Lawrence, the daughter of a fellow-Congressman, John W. Lawrence of New York. Not long after the end of Bedinger's second term in Congress President Franklin Pierce appointed him charge d'affairs to Denmark. He was later commissioned minister to that country. When he returned home, he was on November 5, 1858, given a large reception by his Jefferson County friends. Less than a month later he died at his Shepherdstown residence.[6]

BOTELER, ALEXANDER ROBINSON (May 16, 1815—May 8, 1892). Born near Shepherdstown the son of Dr. Henry Boteler, Alexander R. Boteler was descended on his mother's side from Charles William Peale, the famous patriot and artist of the Revolutionary period. From him Boteler inherited artistic ability that enabled him to paint some excellent pictures. Graduating from Princeton College in 1835, Boteler the following year married Helen Stockton, the daughter of a Revolutionary army surgeon. Prior to 1850 he devoted his time to literary and agricultural pursuits. In that year he entered politics and obtained the Whig nomination for the State Senate but was defeated.[7]

In 1852 and again in 1856 Boteler was a Whig Presidential elector. After two defeats for Congress he was in 1859 successful over the Democratic candidate, Charles James Faulkner. At the assembling of the Thirty-Sixth Congress Boteler was nominated for the position of Speaker of the House of Representatives, an unusual compliment for a newcomer. However, he was defeated for this honor by William Pennington of New Jersey. In the Presidential contest of 1860 he served as chairman of the National Executive Committee of the Constitutional Union party.

Boteler was bitterly opposed to the disruption of the Union, but, when Virginia seceded, he resigned from Congress and threw his lot with the Confederacy. He was a member of its Provisional Congress and later served in the first regular Congress of the Confederate States. He was chairman of the House committee which designed the Confederate flag, and, he himself was the designer of the Confederate seal. The latter consisted of a picture of Washington on horseback, surrounded by a wreath composed of the South's agricultural products. Boteler had an artist draw a sketch of the statue of George Washington located in the capitol grounds at Richmond. This reproduction was then sent to England, where it was made into a seal. In the war Boteler served on the personal staff of General Thomas J. Jackson with the rank of colonel and later was on the staff of General J. E. B. Stuart.

Colonel Boteler's home, "Fountain Rock", was burned on July 19, 1864 by Federal soldiers, but after the war he returned to Shepherdstown to live. Appointed by President Ulysses S. Grant as a Centennial Commissioner from West Virginia, he was also made a member of the Tariff Commission by President Chester A. Arthur. At the request of his old friend and classmate, Arthur's Attorney General, B. H. Brewster, Boteler was made pardon clerk in the Department of Justice at Washington. Retaining this position through Grover Cleveland's first administration, he then returned to Jefferson County to spend his remaining days in peace and quiet.[8]

BROOKE, HENRY ST. GEORGE TUCKER (July 22, 1844— May 16, 1914). This distinguished educator and lawyer, the son of Henry Lawrence and Virginia (Tucker) Brooke, was born at the University of Virginia. He received his early education in the private schools of Winchester and Richmond and was in the latter city when the Civil War began. Enlisting in the Confederate Navy, he served until his health failed. When he recovered, he volunteered as a private in Company B, Second Virginia Cavalry Regiment, and remained in service until he received a serious wound on May 28, 1864, which ended his days as a soldier.

After the war was over Professor Brooke taught school at Salem, Virginia, and from 1867 to 1869 studied law at the University of Virginia. He practiced law at New Castle, Craig County, Virginia, in 1869-1870, after which he moved to Charles Town. He was a member of the Charles Town bar until 1878, when he accepted an appointment as the first professor of law in the newly established West Virginia University Law School. He taught there until 1909, when he retired because of ill health. Returning to Charles Town, he lived there until his death.

On August 15, 1882, he married Mary Harrison Brown of Charles Town.[9]

CHEW, ROGER PRESTON (April 9, 1843—March 15, 1921). Roger Preston Chew, the son of Roger and Sarah West (Aldridge) Chew, was born in Loudoun County, Virginia. In 1846 the family moved to Jefferson County where they made their home at the "Hermitage Farm", about three miles southeast of Charles

Town. The son attended school at the Charles Town Academy and later at Virginia Military Institute from which he was graduated in 1861. When the Civil War began, Chew entered the Confederate cavalry. In conjunction with classmates at the Lexington institution he organized a battery of horse artillery that later became famous. This was known as "Chew's Battery" and Roger Preston Chew was its captain. As the story of this organization has been narrated in the first chapter on the Civil War, repetition is unnecessary. It should be noted, however, that he was made chief of artillery of the Stuart cavalry, with the rank of lieutenant colonel. He was in command of all the horse artillery of the Army of Northern Virginia.

When hostilities ceased, Colonel Chew returned to Jefferson County and engaged in farming. In 1871 he married Louise Fontaine Washington, daughter of Colonel John Augustine Washington of "Blakeley", a descendant of George Washington's brother, John Augustine. From 1884 to 1890 Colonel Chew represented Jefferson County in the West Virginia Legislature. He was at the head of the Charles Town Mining, Manufacturing and Improvement Company, which promoted the subdivision that later became the town of Ranson. He took an active part in community affairs until his death.[10]

CRAIGHILL, WILLIAM PRICE (July 1, 1833—Jan. 15, 1909). William P. Craighill was a Charles Town man who later became one of the most brilliant engineers in the United States army. He was born at the county seat, the son of William Nathaniel and Sarah Elizabeth (Brown) Craighill. Receiving his early education at the Charles Town Academy, on July 1, 1849, he entered the United States Military Academy at West Point and was graduated in 1853. His scholastic ability was such that he ranked second in a graduating class of fifty-two. Among his classmates were Generals Sheridan, Schofield, McPherson, Sooy, Smith, and Vincent, on the Union side during the Civil War, and Generals Hood, Chambliss, and Walker, of the Confederacy. Upon his graduation he was attached to the engineering corps and in 1854-1855 he superintended the construction of Fort Sumter. In 1858 he assisted in the building of Fort Delaware.

During the ensuing four years Craighill was assistant professor of military and civil engineering at West Point. When the Civil War began, he was in a dilemma. Although he loved the Union, he did not want to fight against his own Southern people. General Winfield Scott is said to have told him that he could remain in the engineering corps of the Union army and thus not have to take up arms against the Confederacy. The Charles Town soldier agreed to this and for the next few years he was busy constructing harbor defenses for important American cities. His services were principally devoted to the harbors of San Francisco, New York, Baltimore, Norfolk, Philadelphia, Charleston, and Savannah. In recognition of his work at Baltimore a channel was named for him. He was active in the improvement of a large number of American rivers and directed the surveys for various ship canals.

General Craighill was twice sent to Europe on engineering missions for the Federal Government and five times to the Pacific coast on similar service. In 1881 he superintended the construction of the monument erected at Yorktown, Virginia, in memory of the surrender of Cornwallis. For many years he was a member of the American Society of Civil Engineers and became president of that organization in 1894. He declined the superintendency of the Military Academy at West Point and membership on the Nicaragua Canal Commission. As an author, he compiled **The Army Officers Pocket Companion** in 1863 and translated and published General Dupont's **Cours de Tactiques.** In connection with a Captain Mendell he translated General Jomini's **Precis de l'Art de la Guerra.**

General Craighill was first married on October 14, 1856, to Mary A. Morsell of the District of Columbia. On September 22, 1874, he was married to Rebecca C. Jones of Virginia. He died in Charles Town and was buried in Zion Episcopal Churchyard.[11]

CUTSHAW, WILFRED E. (1837—Dec. 19, 1907). Information concerning this Jefferson County native is meagre. He was born at Harpers Ferry about 1837 and received his education at Virginia Military Institute from which school he was graduated in 1858. At the outbreak of the Civil War he was made a first lieutenant and assigned to a battalion of artillery in the brigade of General Stonewall Jackson. In the spring of 1862 he became a major and in February, 1865, a lieutenant colonel. He was severely wounded in the battle of Winchester in May, 1862, and was captured by the enemy. He remained a prisoner of war until he was exchanged in April, 1863.

When Cutshaw returned to the Confederate army, he was pronounced by a medical examining board as unfit for active duty. Consequently, he was made acting commander of cadets at Virginia Military Institute. Serving in this position until September, 1863, he then applied for readmission into the army. Notwithstanding the fact that his wound was still unhealed, he was accepted. After the war Colonel Cutshaw lived in Richmond, where he served for a time as city engineer. He died there.[12]

DANDRIDGE, DANSKE BEDINGER (Nov. 19, 1854—June 3, 1914). Danske Bedinger was born in Copenhagen, Denmark, while her father Henry Bedinger, was United States minister to that country. The name of "Danske", meaning "Little Dane" in that language, was given her by her father. When she was three years old, her parents returned to America, where shortly afterwards they died. She was reared by her grandfather, John W. Lawrence of New York, and was educated in Staunton, Virginia. On May 3, 1877, she married A. S. Dandridge and went to "Rose Brake", near Shepherdstown, to live.

Mrs. Dandridge is distinguished chiefly as an author. She wrote a number of poems for **Harper's, The Century,** and the New York **Independent,** several volumes of which were later published in book form. The first of these books was **Joy and Other Poems.** She contributed to the historical information of Jefferson County by writing **George Michael Bedinger, a Kentucky Pioneer** and **Historic Shepherdstown,** each of which deals with the Revolutionary period. Another publication by the same author was **American Prisoners of the Revolution.**

Mrs. Dandridge died at her home near Shepherdstown.[13]

DARKE, WILLIAM (1736—Nov., 1801). One of the foremost Indian fighters of his time, William Darke was born in Bucks County, Pennsylvania, and was descended from John Rush, one of Oliver Cromwell's commanders, who emigrated to Pennsylvania in

1683. When William was only a few years old, his father, Joseph Darke, moved the family to Virginia and settled near Shepherdstown. The Darke residence is supposed to have been a log cabin located about four miles east of Shepherdstown. When William Darke first moved to the site along Elk Branch, near Duffields, is unknown.[14]

Darke's military career began when he served as a corporal in the Rutherford Rangers, which organization functioned in 1758-1759 as Indian fighters. The assertion that he was present at Braddock's defeat, apparently, lacks confirmation. At the beginning of the Revolution he received a commission as captain of a company raised among his friends and neighbors. Darke distinguished himself by his bravery at the battle of Germantown in October, 1777, but was there captured by the British and taken to a prison-ship at New York. Enduring all the horrors of prison life, he remained a captive until November, 1780, when he was exchanged.

In the spring of 1781 he was instrumental in organizing the Berkeley and Hampshire regiment which participated in the siege of Yorktown. Because of his distinguished service Darke was retired at the close of the Revolutionary War with the rank of lieutenant colonel. Returning to his home near Duffields, he resumed a civil life.

In 1788 William Darke and Adam Stephen were elected as Berkeley County's delegates to the Virginia Convention of that date called to accept or reject the Federal Constitution. Both of them voted for ratification. Darke then turned to politics and in 1791 made an unsuccessful attempt to be elected Congressman from the Lower Valley District. However, he was chosen to the Virginia General Assembly.

After serving only three days in Richmond, Darke resigned to accompany General Arthur St. Clair on the latter's punitive expedition against Indians in Ohio. The story of the defeat of this army on November 4, 1791, is well-known, and Darke is credited with saving the left wing from annihilation. Both he and his son, Joseph, were wounded in the fighting, the latter mortally. As a reward for his services the old soldier was given the rank of brigadier general and a tract of almost 8,000 acres of public land in Ohio.

BIOGRAPHIES

The remainder of General Darke's life was spent at his home on Elk Branch. Serving as a trustee for Charles Town, he also was a justice of the peace for Berkeley County. He is described as possessing a herculean frame, rough manner, and a fiery temper. His disposition, however, was frank and fearless. His wife was a widow named Sarah Delayea who bore him three sons and a daughter. All of the sons died in early manhood, but the daughter has left descendants. General Darke died at his home near Duffields and was buried in the Old Ronemous graveyard near that place.[15]

DOUGLAS, HENRY KYD (Sept. 29, 1838—Dec. 18, 1903). This soldier, who later became the youngest member of General Stonewall Jackson's staff, was born in Shepherdstown. His father, Robert Douglas, who was pastor of the Reformed Church there, came from Scotland, while his mother was a native of Ireland. Living on both sides of the Potomac River, the family later resided at the "Ferry Hill" place, in Maryland, directly across the river from Shepherdstown. Douglas was graduated from Franklin and Marshall College at Lancaster, Pennsylvania, in 1859 and then attended Judge John Brockenbrough's law school in Lexington, Virginia. In 1860 he was admitted to the bar and went to St. Louis to practice his profession. When the Civil War began, he hastened to Shepherdstown.

The military career of Henry Kyd Douglas began when he enlisted in Company B, Second Virginia Infantry, later a part of the Stonewall Brigade. His rise was rapid and in April, 1862, he was detailed by General Stonewall Jackson to carry important dispatches to General Richard S. Ewell. Performing the designated task in record time, he won Jackson's commendation. The Confederate general was so impressed with Douglas that he assigned him a position on his staff.

Douglas remained in this capacity until Jackson's death at the battle of Chancellorsville, after which he served on the staffs of Generals Edward Johnson, John B. Gordon, Jubal A. Early, John Pegram, and James A. Walker. He was seriously wounded at Gettysburg, captured by the enemy, and imprisoned for nine months at Johnson's Island. He was finally exchanged and in 1865 was appointed to command The Light Brigade. He had attained the rank of major and had been recommended by the Confederate Secretary of War for the position of brigadier general. Cessation of hostilities prevented the completion of this recognition.

When the war was over, Major Douglas returned to Shepherdstown, where he was arrested within a few weeks for having his picture taken in a Confederate uniform. Tried by a military commission, he was sentenced to serve three months at Fort Delaware. He served this term, after which he went to Winchester to practice law. Remaining there two years, he then moved to Hagerstown, Maryland. Entering politics, Douglas made unsuccessful efforts to obtain seats in the State Senate and in Congress. In 1891 he was appointed circuit judge, in which position he conducted himself creditably. His intimate knowledge of the war, added to his ability as a public speaker, caused his services to be in much demand throughout the countryside.

After his death his body was buried in Elmwood Cemetery at Shepherdstown. Many years later, in 1940, a nephew published a manuscript written by Major Douglas under the title, **I Rode with Stonewall.** In this interesting account of the Civil War the author drew upon his diary, letters, photographs, and reminiscences.[16]

GATES, HORATIO (1729—April 10, 1806). This unique figure in American history was born in England. Entering the army at an early age, Gates participated in many of the struggles between England and the continental powers. About 1772 he moved to the United States and took up his residence on a recently purchased farm located then in Berkeley County, Virginia. This was known as "Travelers Rest" and was a mile southwest of Kearneysville, later within the limits of Jefferson County. Aside from serving as a lieutenant colonel in the Virginia militia and as a justice of the peace, Gates lived a life of comparative inactivity.

When the Revolutionary War began, Gates remained true to the land of his adoption and offered his services to the American cause. This action was influenced in part by his hatred of the English caste system. It is perhaps needless to add that his services were gladly accepted and his appointment as adjutant general of the Continental army on June 17, 1775, was one of the first made by Congress. The position carried with it the rank of brigadier general. Gates assisted Washington at Cambridge in the work of organizing the untrained militia into an effective fighting force. After the evacuation of Boston he was commissioned a major general and in 1776 was appointed to take command of the American troops in the vicinity of Crown Point and Ticonderoga.[17]

General Gates remained in charge and was present at Burgoyne's surrender after the battle of Saratoga. The Continental Congress was so pleased with this important victory that it voted Gates its thanks and ordered a medal in commemoration of the success. An attempt to replace Washington as commander-in-chief, known in history as the Conway Cabal, failed and caused unfavorable criticism of the former Englishman. It has not been definitely proved that Gates participated in this plot, but it is known that he was favorable to it and allowed his friends in Congress to work for him. In April, 1778, he was placed in command of the northern army along the Hudson River and the next year he was sent to Boston to assist in obtaining supplies for the Continentals.

Although Gates wanted to retire from active fighting and had spent the winter of 1780 on his Virginia plantation, he was appointed by Congress in June of that year to take command of the American army in the South. Accordingly, he went to the Carolinas, where he fought with Cornwallis the disastrous battle of Camden. The defeat suffered there caused Congress to order an inquiry concerning the cause of the reverse. Being commanded to remove Gates, Washington did so and appointed General Nathaniel Greene in his stead. Gates retired to his farm and demanded that Congress either court-martial or exonerate him. Finally, in the fall of 1782 that body repealed the measure ordering the court of inquiry. Gates rejoined the army at Newburgh, where he aided Washington in quelling a mutiny among the dissatisfied Continentals.

After the war General Gates returned to "Travelers Rest" and lived there until 1790, when he sold his estate, moved to "Rose Hill", a country place near New York City, and served one term in the New York Legislature before death overtook him.[18]

GIBSON, JOHN THOMAS (Jan. 3, 1825—Jan 29, 1904). Although he was born in Hampshire County, Virginia, John Thomas Gibson was long associated with Jefferson County. In 1847 he was graduated from Jefferson College, in Pennsylvania, after which he completed the law course at the University of Virginia. Practicing for several years in Chicago, he came to Charles Town in the early 1850's, where on May 9, 1855, he was married to Frances Davenport. He served as a member of the General Assembly for four terms. As colonel of the Fifty-Fifth Regiment, Virginia Militia, he commanded this organization at the John Brown raid. The first official report of the first day's operations in that engagement was made by Colonel Gibson to Governor Henry A. Wise.

When the Civil War began, he remained in command of his militia regiment for a time. Later he resigned and joined the Rockbridge Artillery. His final service in the war was with the First Regiment of engineers. He was paroled at Appomattox when the Army of Northren Virginia surrendered.

Farming occupied Colonel Gibson's attention at the end of hostilities. Being active in local politics, he served as mayor of Charles Town and as a member of the County Court. His death occurred at his Charles Town home.[19]

GREEN, THOMAS CLAIBORNE (1820—Dec. 4, 1889). Thomas Claiborne Green, for years a member of the State Supreme Court of Appeals, was not a native of Jefferson County but of Fredericksburg, Virginia. He was one of the seven sons of a Virginia Supreme Court of Appeals judge, John W. Green. He began the practice of law at Charles Town in 1843 but, after remaining there a year, he moved to Romney. The occasion for the change was the offer of a law partnership at the Hampshire County town with Colonel Angus McDonald. He remained in Romney for seven or eight years in the course of which time he married his partner's oldest daughter, Mary Naylor McDonald. Shortly thereafter he returned to Charles Town.

Judge Green was mayor of Charles Town during the John Brown raid and, as such, found himself confronted with new responsibilities. He also served as one of Brown's defense attorneys until that fanatic declared he had no confidence in his counsel. After this insult Green and the other defense attorney, Lawson Botts, declined to continue in the case, and Brown obtained out-of-state lawyers. When the Civil War began, Green enlisted as a private in Company B, Second Virginia Infantry Regiment. When he was elected to the House of Delegates in the autumn of 1861, he divided his time between that work and the army. In 1863 President Davis appointed him chief collector of Confederate taxes in Virginia, which position he held until the close of the war.

Green then retired to Charles Town and attempted to begin life anew. In 1876 he was appointed by Governor John J. Jacob to the West Virginia Supreme Court of Appeals. He was subsequently elected and continued on the bench until his death.[20]

GWYNN, WALTER (1802—Feb., 1882). Born in Jefferson County, Walter Gwynn received the ordinary common school education of his day, after which he entered the United States Military Academy at West Point. Upon his graduation from there in 1822, he became a lieutenant of engineers, and, after serving ten years in the army, he resigned in 1832 to accept a position as civil engineer for the Baltimore and Ohio Railroad Company. He later became one of the leading civil engineers in the South and was made chief engineer of the James River and Kanawha Canal. When the Civil War began, he was appointed a brigadier general and was made chief of the Confederate engineering corps. He died in Baltimore.[21]

HAGAN, HENRY (1821—June 18, 1895). Coming to Shepherdstown early in life and later moving to Cumberland, Maryland, Henry Hagan returned to Jefferson County when the Civil War began. He enlisted as a corporal in Company F, First Virginia Cavalry, and at the First Battle of Bull Run displayed such courage that General J. E. B. Stuart had him detailed to serve at headquarters. Promoted to the rank of major, he remained on Stuart's staff until the chieftain's death at Yellow Tavern in May, 1864. After that Major Hagan was transferred to the staff of General Wade Hampton, where he served until the close of the war. Returning then to Shepherdstown, he became superintendent of the Potomac Cement Mill, in which capacity he served for a number of years. Ill health finally caused his retirement.[22]

HAMTRAMCK, JOHN FRANCIS (April 17, 1798—April 21, 1858). John Francis Hamtramck was born at Fort Wayne, Indiana, the son of Colonel J. F. Hamtramck, a daring Indian fighter. When his father died in 1803, Hamtramck was left under the guardianship of General William Henry Harrison, the later Hero of Tippecanoe. At the age of twelve young Hamtramck fought Indians with the command of Captain Zachary Taylor, a future Mexican War officer.

Through the influence of General Harrison and his own stepfather, Senator Jesse B. Thomas of Illinois, Hamtramck obtained an appointment in 1815 to the United States Military Academy at West Point. Graduating from that institution four years later, the young officer served with the artillery. He was stationed at Fort McHenry until March, 1822, when he resigned his commission. Three years later he was appointed United States Indian Agent, with the rank of major. Remaining in this position until 1832, he then moved from St. Louis to Shepherdstown. Prior to this change of residence he had been married in Jefferson County.

When war with Mexico began and volunteers were sought, Governor William Smith of Virginia placed Hamtramck in command of the state's regiment and the Jefferson Countian was made a colonel. While in Mexico Colonel Hamtramck was for a part of the time Governor of Saltillo and in command of about 4,000 troops. When the war was over, the Virginia regiment in August, 1848, disbanded and its leader returned to Shepherdstown.

Colonel Hamtramck organized a company of riflemen in his community which was known as the "Hamtramck Guards". When the Civil War began, this organization entered the Confederate army as Company B, Second Virginia Infantry Regiment. Hamtramck's public service was completed by being mayor of Shepherdstown for several years and a justice of the peace for Jefferson County.[23] His death occurred in Shepherdstown.

HAWKS, WELLS J. (1814—May 28, 1873). Although a native of Massachusetts, Wells J. Hawks came to Winchester,

BIOGRAPHIES

Virginia, about 1843. Moving to Charles Town, he bought an old church and turned it into a carriage factory. He so completely identified himself with the interests and people of his adopted community, that he became successful. In 1855 and 1857 he was sent to the Virginia General Assembly. He was also chosen mayor of Charles Town and was selected as a school commissioner in the county. His record in these various capacities was one of great credit to himself.

When the Civil War began, Wells Hawks threw his lot with the Stars and Bars. Going to Harpers Ferry with the Second Virginia Regiment, he received a commission as captain and was made its commissary. Although beyond the age for military service, he determined to help in this capacity. From the position of regimental commissary he gradually rose until he became a member of General Stonewall Jackson's staff as chief commissary, with the rank of major.

Major Hawks remained on Jackson's staff until the leader fell at Chancellorsville. While Jackson was slowly dying his thoughts wandered to the field of battle, and, among his last words, he said, "Tell Major Hawks...." Leaving the sentence unfinished, he then stopped but later cried, "Let us cross over the river and rest under the shade of the trees." After the death of his chief Hawks was transferred successively to the staffs of Generals Richard S. Ewell, Jubal A. Early, and, in Pennsylvania, to that of Robert E. Lee.

After the surrender at Appomattox Major Hawks returned to Charles Town to repair his shattered health and fortune. He had married three times. His first two wives were daughters of a Dr. Smith of Massachusetts, and his last wife was Sarah Worthington. One of his sons, Arthur "Sunshine" Hawks, later became a noted lecturer. Major Hawks died in Charles Town and was buried in Edge Hill Cemetery.[24]

HOOFF, JAMES LAWRENCE (Oct. 2, 1825—Sept. 24, 1887). Although details about this person's early life are scarce, he was a native of Jefferson County. When the Civil War commenced, he was serving as major in the Second Virginia Regiment, a volunteer organization, and he continued in this position until his regiment was attached to the Confederate army. He then enlisted in the Botts Greys, remained about twelve months, and was afterwards promoted to the rank of major in the Eleventh Virginia Regiment. From this position he was later detailed as quartermaster in Rosser's Brigade, where he served until the close of the war.

On his return home Major Hooff entered the mercantile business in Charles Town. In 1875 he was elected to the West Virginia Legislature, and several years afterward he became president of the Jefferson County Court. His death occurred at his home near the county seat.[25]

HOPKINS, ABNER CRUMP (Oct. 24, 1835—Dec. 4, 1911). Although a native of Powhatan County, Virginia, Abner C. Hopkins resided in Jefferson County for forty-five years. He was graduated from Hampden-Sydney College in 1855, taught school for two years, and then studied at Union Theological Seminary. Licensed to preach in April, 1860, he was in the fall of that year called to be pastor of the Martinsburg Presbyterian Church. On May 16, 1861, he was married to Anne Pleasants Atkinson.

The Rev. Abner Hopkins's ministry at Martinsburg was interrupted in the spring of 1862 when the town was entered by hostile troops and the congregation scattered. Compelled to leave, he entered the Confederate army as a chaplain. At first he was attached to the Stonewall Brigade under General Jackson, but he later served as chaplain in the Second Corps, Army of Northern Virginia. For a time he was on the staff of General John B. Gordon.

When hostilities ceased, Dr. Hopkins became pastor of the Willis Presbyterian Church for a few months. In 1866 he received a call to Charles Town to succeed the Rev. Dr. W. B. Dutton as pastor of the Presbyterian Church. Installed on December 9 of that year, he continued to serve the pastorate until his death in 1911.

For twenty-two years Dr. Hopkins was a director of Union Theological Seminary. He was seven times chosen a commissioner to the general assembly of his church and in 1903 was made moderator. He was one of the principal organizers and for many years was president of the Lee Memorial Association, which organization was chartered to erect a monument to the Confederate dead in Edge Hill Cemetery, Charles Town.

Upon the death of Dr. Hopkins his remains were buried in Edge Hill Cemetery. A monument at his grave was erected by former friends with whom he had served in the Confederate army.[26]

HUMPHREYS, DAVID (May 2, 1832—July 5, 1905). Born in Charles Town the son of John and May (Davis) Humphreys, David attained the rank of major in the Confederate army during the Civil War. He entered the service as a private in Company G, Second Virginia Infantry, and after being promoted several times, he was placed in charge of the quartermaster's department. He remained in this position until the end of the war when he returned home and engaged in business. In 1869 he moved to Norfolk, Virginia, where he died.[27]

HUNTER, ANDREW H. (March 22, 1804—Nov. 21, 1888). Andrew Hunter, a distinguished lawyer who assisted in the prosecution of John Brown, was born in Berkeley County, the son of Colonel David H. and Elizabeth Pendleton Hunter. After graduating from Hampden-Sydney College, he studied law. He first went to Harpers Ferry but soon after settled in Charles Town to practice. In 1840 he was a Whig Presidential elector and six years later he declined a nomination to Congress. In 1850 he served as a member of the Virginia Constitutional Convention. On October 18, 1859, a few hours after the capture of John Brown at Harpers Ferry Governor Henry A. Wise met Hunter and engaged him to assist Charles B. Harding, the county's commonwealth attorney, in the prosecution of the raiders. Hunter performed this duty in a creditable and thorough manner.

During the Civil War he was at times the trusted friend and adviser of General Robert E. Lee. On July 17, 1864, his home at Charles Town was ruthlessly destroyed by order of his first cousin, General David Hunter of the Union army. Although no charges were preferred against him, Andrew Hunter was kept in custody for a month. When the war was over, he was one of Virginia's lawyers in the suit to regain the lost counties of Jefferson and Berkeley.

After his death in Charles Town his daughter, Florence, received a letter from United States Senator from Indiana, Daniel W. Voorhees. This distinguished personage had met Hunter in Charles Town when the John Brown raiders were being tried. Although Voorhees had attempted to defend one of Brown's men, John E. Cook, and had lost, he bore no malice toward the prosecution. On the contrary, he regarded Hunter with much respect and in the letter to the Charles Town attorney's daughter Voorhees paid him praise.[28]

LEE, CHARLES (1731—Oct. 2, 1782). One of the most unusual characters in American history was Charles Lee. He was born in England, the youngest son of General John Lee, and was educated in his own country and in Switzerland. Becoming interested in a military career at an early age, he was in 1751 commissioned a lieutenant. His regiment accompanied General Edward Braddock on the ill-fated expedition against Fort Duquesne in 1755, after which Lee was sent to the Mohawk Valley, New York.

Lee bought a captaincy for 900 pounds in 1756 and was stationed near Schenectady when he was adopted into the tribe of Mohawk Indians. Although he married a daughter of an Indian chief, he did not remain long with the redskins. His regiment was ordered to assist in the attack on Fort Ticonderoga in July, 1758, and in the ensuing engagement he was so severely wounded that he was sent to Albany and from there to Long Island. Later he joined the force besieging Fort Niagara and at its capture he departed for Fort Duquesne. He was also present when Montreal surrendered on September 8, 1760.[29]

When the French and Indian War was over, Lee returned to England. Becoming a lieutenant colonel and wandering over most of Europe, he was from then until 1771 a soldier of fortune. He came to America again in 1773 and two years later, at the suggestion of his friend, Horatio Gates, bought a large estate in Berkeley County, Virginia. He named his home "Prato Rio" and located it on the southwestern outskirts of the present village of Leetown, now Jefferson County. He lived in an old shell of a house which did not have any partitions except lines of chalk on the floor.

Lee actively supported the American colonies in their struggle against British tyranny. When hostilities commenced, he offered his services to Congress and, because of his previous military experience, was appointed a major general. After serving at the siege of Boston, he was ordered to the South, where he supervised the defense of South Carolina and Georgia. As the enemy withdrew from this region, he returned north to join the main army. Unfortunately, having an exaggerated opinion of his own ability and being susceptible to flattery, Lee began to criticize his superiors on all occasions. When the Americans were forced to surrender Fort Washington to overwhelming numbers of British, he censured General Washington severely in a letter to Gates.

Shortly afterwards General Lee was captured by the enemy at his headquarters in New Jersey and was taken to New York, where he was kept in close confinement for a year. While he was a prisoner, he is supposed to have given the British General Howe information how the Americans could be defeated. A document in Lee's handwriting endorsed "Mr. Lee's Plan, 29th March 1777", was found among the papers of Henry Strachey, who had been with Howe. As a result of this, Lee has been denounced as a traitor by many historians.

However that may be, he was exchanged for a British officer and later joined the American army at Valley Forge at the beginning of the Monmouth campaign. In the ensuing battle he ordered a retreat at a critical time and almost caused the Continentals to lose the day. Washington severely censured Lee for this apparently cowardly retreat. Lee replied by writing an insulting letter to his commander.

General Washington was willing to forget the whole matter, but Lee's pride had been hurt and he demanded a court-martial to decide on his conduct. The trial was held and Lee was found guilty of disobedience of orders, misbehavior before the enemy, and disrespect to the commander in chief. He was suspended from the army for twelve months and, being unable to control his anger, he wrote numerous letters criticizing both Congress and Washington. His connection with the American army was officially severed when, on January 10, 1780, Congress voted his dismissal after it had received an insulting letter from him. In an effort to sell his Berkeley County estate in the fall of 1782 Lee went to Baltimore and from there to Philadelphia. In the Quaker City he was seized with an ague which resulted in a fever and caused his death. He was buried in Christ Church graveyard there.[30]

LEE, EDWIN GRAY (May 25, 1835—Aug. 24, 1870). Edwin Gray Lee, one of the few Jefferson County residents who reached the rank of brigadier general in the Confederate army, was born at "Leeland", near Shepherdstown, the son of Edmund Jennings and Henrietta Bedinger Lee. His early education was obtained at Hallowell's School at Alexandria, Virginia, and at the College of William and Mary. He also studied law under Judge John Brockenbrough at Lexington and began practicing, but his work was interrupted by the Civil War.

Entering the Confederate service as a second lieutenant in the Second Virginia Infantry, Lee won rapid promotions. In May, 1861, he was appointed a first lieutenant and aide to General Stonewall Jackson, and he advanced in rank so that in August, 1862, he became a colonel. Ill health forced him to resign from the army early in 1863, but he returned to active duty that fall. In May, 1864, he served on the staff of General Robert Ransom and in October he was appointed a brigadier general. He continued to serve the Confederacy by making a secret mission to Canada.

General Lee was married on November 17, 1859, to Susan Pendleton of Lexington, Virginia. His health had become so bad that the close of the war found him ill and he died a few years later at the Yellow Sulphur Springs, Montgomery County, Virginia. In addition to his military record, he achieved distinction as the author of a number of poems.[31]

LUCAS, DANIEL BEDINGER (March 16, 1836—June 24, 1909). Daniel Bedinger Lucas, one of the county's ablest lawyers, was born near Halltown and was descended from a number of prominent statesmen. His father, William Lucas, and his uncles, Edward Lucas and Henry Bedinger, at various times represented the Lower Valley in Congress. His great uncle, Robert Lucas, was one of the four governors Jefferson County furnished to the State of Ohio. His mother was Virginia Bedinger, a daughter of

Captain Daniel Bedinger, a Revolutionary soldier.[32]

After attending several private academies, Daniel Lucas entered the University of Virginia for the 1851-1852 session. While a student there, he excelled in oratory and was the valedictorian of the Jefferson Society of the University in 1856. Upon his graduation from this institution he entered the law school of Judge John W. Brockenbrough at Lexington, Virginia. Completing the law course there, he began to practice at Charles Town in the spring of 1859. As he moved the next year to Richmond, he was in that city when the Civil War began. Joining the staff of General Henry A. Wise in June, 1861, Lucas served with him in the Kanawha Valley campaign until October of that year. He left Richmond in January, 1865, for Canada to assist in the defense of his friend, John Yates Beall, charged with being a guerrilla and a Confederate spy. He was not permitted to defend Beall, however, before the military authorities.

Lucas remained in Canada for the next few months and then returned to Jefferson County. He was barred from practicing law until 1870 because of the test oath required by West Virginia of attorneys after the war. When he was allowed to practice, he formed a partnership with Thomas C. Green, a later judge of the State Supreme Court of Appeals. In the Presidential elections of 1872 and 1876 he was Democratic elector for his Congressional district. In 1884 he was elector-at-large on the Cleveland ticket. Although unanimously chosen a professor of law at West Virginia University in 1876, he declined the honor. He did serve for eight years on the school's Board of Regents, however. In 1884 the University awarded him the honorary degree of Doctor of Laws.

Lucas was elected to the West Virginia Legislature in 1884 and was re-elected two years later. When the Legislature was unable to decide on a United States Senator in 1887, Governor E. Willis Wilson on March 5 appointed Lucas. However, the state's lawmakers met in special session the next month and elected Charles James Faulkner. When the United States Senate was called upon to determine which one was to represent the state, it decided in favor of Faulkner. Upon the death of his former law partner, Judge Thomas C. Green, in 1889, Lucas was appointed to succeed him on the State Supreme Court of Appeals. He was re-elected by a handsome majority in 1890 and served on this tribunal until 1902.

In addition to being a lawyer of outstanding ability, Judge Lucas was also an able writer. In 1865 he published the memoirs of his friend, John Yates Beall, which included Beall's life and diary. Most of his other writings were poems. He was known as the Poet of the Shenandoah Valley. In 1865 he published **The Land Where We Were Dreaming**, in 1869 **The Wreath of Eglantine and Other Poems**, in 1879 **The Maid of Northumberland**, and in 1884 **Ballads and Madrigals**.

His daughter, Virginia, was also a writer of ability.

Judge Lucas was married in 1869 to Lena Tucker Brooke, a great niece of John Randolph of Roanoke. He died at his home "Rion Hall", near Halltown.[33]

LUCAS, EDWARD (1788—March 5, 1858). Edward Lucas, statesman and uncle of Daniel B. Lucas, was born in Jefferson County. He served in the War of 1812 as a lieutenant in the battle of North Point and in the fight at Crany Island. In 1819 he was one of Jefferson County's delegates to the Virginia General Assembly. Re-elected in 1821, he was chosen for a third term in 1830. From 1833 to 1837 he represented the Valley District in Congress and from 1837 to 1841 he was superintendent of the Harpers Ferry Armory and Arsenal. In 1847 he was its paymaster, which position he filled until his death in 1858.[34]

LUCAS, WILLIAM (Nov. 30, 1800—Aug. 29, 1877). William Lucas, the third member of this outstanding family and the father of Daniel B. Lucas, was born at the family homestead, "Cold Spring", near Shepherdstown. He made the most of his academic training but was unable to complete his education at college. After teaching school for a short time at Harpers Ferry, he entered the law office of Henry Berry of Shepherdstown. Later he attended the law school of Judge Henry St. George Tucker at Winchester.

Although Lucas began practicing law at Shepherdstown, he later moved to Charles Town. He was elected to the General Assembly for the 1837-1838 session and in 1839 was chosen a representative in Congress. Two years later his Whig opponent,

BIOGRAPHIES 299

Richard W. Barton, was successful, but Lucas came back and won a seat for the 1843-1845 term. He was on board the **Princeton** when a gun exploded on February 28, 1844, and killed several prominent politicians, among whom were two members of President John Tyler's cabinet.

William Lucas acquired an estate near Halltown which he named "Rion Hall". He took much pleasure in adding to his holdings and at one time owned nearly two thousand acres. His intense love for his home is revealed in the following conversation in Richmond, when his name was mentioned for that of governor:

> I am here, gentlemen, with Hunter and Faulkner, at the Constitutional Convention, to do what I may for the old state, but no office for me. I have possessed me of a goodly home on the banks of the Shenandoah, in the Valley of Virginia, with the Blue Ridge stretching away to the East and the Alleghany to the West of my estate. In the morning as I stand on my portico I can behold the sun rising through the Gap at Harpers Ferry, where the marriage of the waters of the Shenandoah and Potomac takes place. Thanks, gentlemen, but no office. I wouldn't swap my curtilage and acres for your whole city of Richmond.

The wife of William Lucas was Virginia A. Bedinger, a sister of another famous Jefferson Countian, Henry Bedinger, who preceded her husband in death by a number of years. Lucas died at "Rion Hall".[35]

McDONALD, EDWARD ALLEN HITCHCOCK (Oct. 26, 1832—Sept. 17, 1912). Born in Romney, Virginia, Edward Allen H. McDonald did not move to Jefferson County until after the Civil War had ended. At the beginning of the war he was colonel of the Seventy-Seventh Regiment, Virginia Militia, in Hampshire County. After the battle of Brandy Station in 1863 he became major of the Eleventh Virginia Cavalry Regiment in the regular Confederate army. Major McDonald participated in a number of battles until the end of the war and served with great credit to himself. About 1870 he engaged in business in Louisville, Kentucky, and in 1890 he moved to "Media", near Shenandoah Junction, in Jefferson County. On October 12, 1869, he married Julia Yates Leavell. One of the children resulting from this union,

Julia Terrell McDonald, married John W. Davis, Democratic Presidential nominee in 1924.

At Major McDonald's death the remains were interred in the cemetery of Zion Episcopal Church, Charles Town.[36]

MORGAN, WILLIAM AUGUSTINE (March 30, 1831—Feb. 14, 1899). William A. Morgan was born in Fairfax County, Virginia, but his family moved to Jefferson County about 1837 and resided at the famous old estate on which was located the "Morgan's Spring" of Revolutionary fame. In 1854 he married Anna J. Smith, daughter of Colonel Augustine Charles Smith of Winchester.

When the Civil War began, Morgan entered the Confederate service as captain of a cavalry company which had been previously organized at Shepherdstown. This became Company F, First Virginia Cavalry Regiment, and Morgan was afterwards promoted to be colonel of the regiment. At the same time he was advancing in rank, a fellow-countian, Milton J. Billmyer, was made captain of Company F. Colonel Morgan participated in a number of battles and skirmishes and had fourteen horses killed and wounded under him. His military record was so outstanding that toward the end of the war he was slated to be appointed a brigadier general. However, this promotion was interrupted by the surrender at Appomattox.

When hostilities were over, Colonel Morgan set out for his Jefferson County home. While crossing New Canton Ferry, he was robbed of his saber and, when almost in sight of Shepherdstown, he was forced to relinquish his pistols to a party of Federal soldiers. The loss of his horse that night by theft deprived him of every memento of the war, except his bullet-pierced suit of rusty gray. He spent most of his later years in managing his estate and serving as a deputy sheriff of the county. He was a member of the Constitutional Convention of 1872 which framed the document West Virginia now uses.

Colonel Morgan died at his home near Shepherdstown.[37]

PORTERFIELD, GEORGE ALEXANDER (Nov. 24, 1822—Feb. 27, 1919). Born in Berkeley County, the son of George and Mary Tabb Porterfield, George A. Porterfield served in both the

Mexican and Civil wars. His military training was obtained at Virginia Military Institute, from which school he was graduated in 1844. During the two succeeding years he taught school in Richmond.

When the Mexican War began, Porterfield and two of his former classmates organized the Richmond company of a Virginia regiment. Becoming a first lieutenant in this body, he was later appointed adjutant of the whole regiment. He subsequently succeeded Captain Irwin McDowell as assistant adjutant general of the whole American division, then stationed at Buena Vista. He held this position from October, 1847, to the end of the war. On his return from Mexico he was for a while in the employ of the United States Coast Survey.

At the beginning of the Civil War he was appointed a colonel in the Confederate army and assigned to duty in northwestern Virginia. Colonel Porterfield first went to Grafton, but when he learned that the enemy greatly outnumbered him, he retreated to Philippi. He was expecting reinforcements but, while waiting for them, he was suddenly attacked on June 3, 1861, by two Federal detachments. In the ensuing contest he was defeated and in the "Philippi Races" withdrew to Beverly, where on June 8 he was superseded by Brigadier General Robert S. Garnett. He later served on the staff of General W. W. Loring but retired from the service in 1862.

Colonel Porterfield came to Charles Town after the war and in 1870 was made secretary of the Valley Fire Insurance Company. At his suggestion this was reorganized as the Bank of Charles Town, which he served as cashier for a number of years. He died at the county seat in his ninety-seventh year, and his remains were taken to Martinsburg for burial.[38]

QUICK, JOHN (June 20, 1870—Sept. 9, 1922). John Quick was a Charles Town native who served in the Marine Corps for twenty-six years and was awarded a Congressional medal and the Distinguished Service Cross. He rose to the position of sergeant major.

His first citation for bravery occurred in 1898 in the Spanish-American War. In the fighting around Guantanamo Bay it was necessary to signal an American warship to ask it to shell the enemy. Sergeant Major Quick volunteered to communicate with the vessel, but after a trial of twenty minutes he found the officers on board were unable to read his signals. Realizing that the cause of this was the poor background, he stood on the crest of a hill so that the signalling flag would show against the sky. Three times he stood in this exposed position with bullets flying all about him and coolly wig-wagged the information to the warship which proceeded to fire upon the Spaniards, in accordance with orders. After this he helped put down the Philippine insurrection and in 1914 participated in the occupation of Vera Cruz, Mexico.

In the World War Sergeant Major Quick went to France, where he won his second honor. On June 16, 1918, he volunteered and assisted in taking a truckload of ammunition and material into the town of Bouresches, France, over a road swept by artillery and machine gun fire and thereby relieved a critical situation. For this service he was later awarded the Distinguished Service Cross and was commended by General John J. Pershing.

Sergeant Major Quick died in St. Louis, Missouri.[39]

REYNOLDS, JOHN (March 31, 1817—Jan. 2, 1891). Dr. John Reynolds, who was born in Shepherdstown, is said to have performed the first operation in this section with the use of chloroform. He administered the anaesthetic on March 1, 1848, to an Irish workman at the Virginia Ore Bank, near Bakerton. The cholroform was obtained from Baltimore by another physician, a Dr. Taylor, and with his assistance and that of Dr. Vincent M. Butler, Dr. Reynolds successfully amputated the man's leg.

Dr. Reynolds prepared himself for his chosen profession by reading medicine under Thomas Hammond and then by attending the state universities of Virginia, Maryland, and Pennsylvania. He was graduated in medicine from the University of Pennsylvania in 1841 and, forming a partnership with Dr. Hammond, he began practicing at Shepherdstown in April of that year. He relieved the sufferings of his friends and neighbors for almost fifty years.

He was married to Kate Witherow on June 21, 1854, in Shepherdstown. He died at his home there.[40]

RUTHERFORD, ROBERT (1728—Oct., 1803). This statesman had the distinction of being the first member from beyond the Blue Ridge Mountains elected to Congress. He served from 1793 to 1799, when he was defeated by General Daniel Morgan. Prior to this, he had been active as a statesman in other ways.

Robert Rutherford is supposed to have been born in Scotland. His father, Thomas Rutherford, bought land along Bullskin Run in present Jefferson County from Lord Fairfax and shortly thereafter moved his family to this location. Thomas was appointed on November 11, 1743, the first high sheriff of Frederick County and Robert assisted him as a deputy. In 1750 Robert helped George Washington survey land on the Shenandoah River for Edward Musgrove and the same year he opened a store in Winchester.

There seems to be a mistake in the record concerning the date of his marriage, but it is known that his wife was Mary Daubigny Howe, the widow of Viscount George Augustus Howe. The latter was an English army officer killed at Ticonderoga in 1758. Some years after his marriage Robert left Winchester and moved to his farm, "Flowing Springs", in present Jefferson County.

After the defeat of General Braddock in 1755 the Indians became so bold that it was necessary for the frontiersmen to defend themselves. For this Robert Rutherford organized a company known as the "Rutherford Rangers", which later gave a good account of itself in fighting the redskins. From 1758 until after the Revolution Rutherford served in the House of Burgesses. He was one of the delegates to a convention held in Richmond and later at Williamsburg, 1775, which resolved itself into a committee to take into its future consideration the state of the colony. Rutherford was one of the seven delegates chosen to reply to the orders of Lord Dunmore for Virginians to join the British army or be held as rebels. On December 13 the answer severing relations between Virginia and England was announced.

The next year Robert Rutherford, together with George Mason, Edmund Randolph, and Patrick Henry, drafted the Declaration of Rights and framed a plan of government for Virginia. He did not fight in the Continental army but supported the cause for liberty by doing what he could at home. His subsequent terms in Congress from 1793 to 1799 afforded valuable experience but did not add much to his material means. Consequently, upon his retirement he was heavily in debt. His vast holdings in Jefferson County, as well as his western lands, were all sacrificed in an effort to meet his obligations. He died at his home and was buried in an unmarked grave at "Flowing Springs", a mile and a half northeast of Charles Town.[41]

STEPHEN, ADAM (?—1791). Although information about Adam Stephen is scarce, apparently, he was born in Scotland. He studied medicine and served as physician on board several ships before he came to America. Accounts concerning his arrival in this country differ, as they vary from 1738 to 1748, but they agree that he first settled at Fredericksburg, Virginia. Practicing medicine with success, Stephen was in 1754 induced to enter the army with a commission as captain. He raised a company from the neighborhood of Winchester and led it in engagements of the French and Indian War.

Adam Stephen's military ability earned him an appointment as major in June, 1754, and one as lieutenant colonel a short while later. He was with George Washington at the battle of Great Meadows and was included in the capitulation of Fort Necessity to the French. The following year he was wounded at Braddock's defeat. When an Indian outbreak occurred in 1763, he commanded a regiment in the ensuing struggle.

When the Revolutionary War began, Stephen offered his services to his adopted country and in 1777 rose to the rank of major general in the American army. His conduct in the battle of Germantown on October 4, 1777, was severely censured by General Washington and led to his eventual dismissal. Charged with intemperance, he was blamed when his troops collided in a fog with those of General "Mad Anthony" Wayne. Historians have risen to his defense and have claimed that the court-martial which dismissed him from the army was too severe.

General Stephen then returned to his Berkeley County home, said to have been "The Bower" near Leetown, in present Jefferson County. He laid out the town of Martinsburg in 1778. Together with William Darke, he was elected a delegate to the Virginia Convention of 1788 for the purpose of ratifying or rejecting the new Federal Constitution. Like Darke, he voted in favor of the document.

After the death of Stephen his body is supposed to have been buried within the present limits of Martinsburg on the grounds of the "Boydville" estate.[42]

STEPHENSON, HUGH (?—1776). Hugh Stephenson lived on Bullskin Run in present Jefferson County. His father, Richard Stephenson, came to this vicinity early in the eighteenth century. Not much is known about Hugh except his military activities. He commanded a company of riflemen in the French and Indian War, served in Dunmore's War, and upon the recommendation of George Washington headed one of the two rifle companies raised in 1775 in Virginia. Stephenson's part in this venture and his rivalry with Daniel Morgan have been described in the chapter on the Revolutionary War.

The following year, 1776, Stephenson was promoted to the rank of colonel in the American army. He was engaged in the task of raising a rifle regiment when he became ill with camp fever. His death occurred shortly after at his home on Bullskin Run.[43]

STEPHENSON, JAMES (March 20, 1764—August 27, 1833). Born in Adams County, Pennsylvania, Stephenson at an early age moved to what is now Jefferson County. Commanding a company at St. Clair's defeat in 1791, he was three years later among those ordered to quell the Whiskey Rebellion, which occurred when western Pennsylvania farmers attempted to evade a Federal tax. The date of his appointment as major is not known.

In civil life Major Stephenson served as a magistrate and later as one of Berkeley County's delegates in the Virginia General Assembly from 1800 to 1802. He was chosen a representative in Congress three times and served from 1803 to 1805, 1809 to 1811, and 1822 to 1825. Retiring from Congress in 1825, he continued to live at Charles Town until his death a few years later.[44]

WASHINGTON, CHARLES (May 2, 1738—1799). Charles Washington, the founder of Charles Town, was born at Hunting

Creek, now Fairfax County, Virginia. He was the youngest full brother of General George Washington. In the fall of 1738 the family moved to the Ferry Farm, opposite Fredericksburg, and in that locality Charles spent his childhood. Active in church affairs, he served as a member of the vestry of St. George's Church at Fredericksburg. By 1761 he had become a prominent landholder and figured in a number of real estate deals. On February 27, 1766, he was one of the signers of the Westmoreland Resolutions, a spirited declaration against the British Stamp Act of 1765.[45]

Charles Washington came to present Jefferson County some time between April 20 and October 6, 1780. He had been bequeathed land in this region by the will of his half-brother, Lawrence, who had accumulated vast holdings in what was then Frederick County, Virginia. Charles resided on a hill on the southern outskirts of present Charles Town and is said to have lived in a log cabin before beginning the construction of his new house, which he named "Happy Retreat".

Charles Washington married Mildred Thornton, a first cousin of his brother Samuel's second wife of the same name. They became the parents of four children, George Augustine, Samuel, Frances, and Mildred Washington. In General George Washington's will he remembered the children of Charles. He had visited at "Happy Retreat" on some of his numerous journeys into this part of the country.

Charles Town was laid out in 1786 by Charles Washington and was incorporated in January, 1787, by the Virginia General Assembly. It was named for its founder, who donated the four corner lots at the intersection of George and Washington streets for the public buildings of the town and county. Eighty acres of Washington's land were divided into half-acre lots as the site of the town. Additional information concerning the establishment of Charles Town is given in the chapter on early days.

Charles Washington's health declined in later years and his death occurred between July 25 and September 23, 1799, only a short while before that of his brother, George. He was buried in the family plot at his home near Charles Town.[46]

WASHINGTON, JOHN AUGUSTINE (May 3, 1821—Sept. 13, 1861). John Augustine Washington, the great grandson of George's brother, John Augustine, was born at his father's home, "Blakeley", three miles southwest of Charles Town. John Augustine's father, who had the same name, inherited Mount Vernon upon the death of Judge Bushrod Washington, to whom the General had left it. The new owner moved his family from "Blakeley" to the home on the Potomac River and continued to live there until his death in 1832. The son, John Augustine, who is the subject of this biography, inherited the Mount Vernon estate from his father and was its last Washington owner. He sold it to the Mount Vernon Ladies Association, the organization which now has charge of it.

John Augustine Washington was graduated in 1840 from the University of Virginia. When the Civil War began, he entered the Confederate army and served as aide-de-camp on the staff of General Robert E. Lee in the campaign in western Virginia. In this capacity he was given the rank of colonel. He was killed while on duty near Cheat Mountain, in present West Virginia.[47]

WASHINGTON, JOHN THORNTON AUGUSTINE (Jan. 22, 1826—July 10, 1894). A great grandson of Colonel Samuel Washington, John Thornton Augustine Washington was born at "Cedar Lawn", near Charles Town. His early education was received at the Charles Town Academy and from a private tutor. Being graduated from Princeton College, he entered the United States Military Academy at West Point and in 1849 was graduated from that institution. He was instructor of tactics there when Jefferson Davis was Secretary of War. He saw service with the American army on the frontier, but, when the Civil War began, he resigned his commission and joined the Confederate troops.

President Davis appointed him a captain in the Confederate army, and the young officer was acting adjutant general and chief of staff of General Robert E. Lee, when the latter organized the Southern Atlantic states. Washington was promoted to the rank of major in June, 1862, and was later sent to the Trans-Mississippi department. He was later made a colonel. After the war he continued to reside in the West.

Colonel Washington was married on March 8, 1860, to Olive Ann Jones of San Antonio, Texas. He died in Washington, D. C.[48]

WASHINGTON, SAMUEL (Nov. 16, 1734—1781). Born at Pope's Creek, Westmoreland County, Virginia, Samuel Washington was the second full brother of General George Washington to settle within the limits of present Jefferson County. Most of his boyhood was spent on the Ferry Farm, opposite Fredericksburg. He moved across the Rappahannock River to that town about 1754 and six years later changed his residence again, this time to the Chotank community, now part of northern King George County, where he had inherited 600 acres from his father. Like his brother, Charles, Samuel was one of the signers of the Westmoreland Resolutions in February, 1766. These were a formal protest against the Stamp Act of the preceding year.[49]

Samuel Washington's first important public office came to him in November, 1766, when his name appears among the twenty-seven justices of Stafford County. On April 11, 1767, he is again named as a justice, but on July 27, 1767, he is noted as "removed". However, as he is again mentioned on May 26, 1768, it is probable that he was temporarily absent from the county for about a year. He was, no doubt, looking after his lands in Frederick County, to which he was planning to move. The last date on which he is listed as a justice in Stafford County is July 18, 1769. The fact that he had visited in Frederick County before taking his family there is proved by the appearance of his name among the justices of Frederick on May 10 and again on October 23, 1769. At that time Frederick included the present counties of Jefferson and Berkeley. By the will of Lawrence, his half-brother, Samuel was left a tract of 230 acres on Evitt's Marsh, a few miles west of present Charles Town.

Although the exact date of the construction of Samuel Washington's new home in present Jefferson County has not been definitely established, it was probably between the years 1767 and 1770. He did not move his family there until September, 1770.[50] Doubt exists concerning the builder of "Harewood", as the new home was named, but it is said that George Washington had it built for his brother. The mansion, located about three miles west of present Charles Town, is declared to be one of the first houses in the Shenandoah Valley of native limestone construction. There was formerly another wing on the north with the entrance facing east, but the present mansion and small office facing it are all that remain of the original buildings. The marble mantel in the paneled room on the first floor is declared by Samuel's descendants to have been presented to General George Washington by the Marquis de Lafayette. The finer parts of the woodwork, pilasters, wainscoting, and cornice were brought from England to Alexandria and thence carted to "Harewood".

Among prominent visitors to this home were George Washington, Louis Philippe, later King of France, and his two brothers, the Duke de Montpensier and the Count de Beaujolais. The young son of Lafayette was also entertained here. In 1794 the house witnessed the wedding of James Madison to Mrs. Dolly Payne Todd. Mrs. Todd's sister, Lucy, had previously married George Steptoe Washington, one of Samuel's sons.

After Samuel Washington had been at his new home a comparatively short time he began to accumulate real estate. The result of his activities in this regard is attested by the fact that when he died, he owned more than 4,000 acres of land, most of which was located within the limits of present Jefferson County. He took a prominent part in public affairs, for, in addition to serving as a magistrate, he was on February 5, 1771, commissioned a colonel of the Frederick County militia. About the same time he became a vestryman of Norborne Parish, later St. George's Chapel. When Berkeley County was formed from Frederick in 1772, Samuel was made a justice of the peace for the new county. He was appointed to this position by Governor Dunmore on April 17, 1772. A year later he was appointed sheriff, and in 1776 he was reappointed. Because of ill health he was compelled to resign from his position as county lieutenant on April 3, 1777. This reference to the state of his health offers a possible explanation why he did not take a more active part in the Revolutionary War then waging.

Colonel Samuel Washington was married five times. His wives were Jane Champe, Mildred Thornton, Lucy Chapman, Anne Steptoe, and the Widow Perrin. He was the father of the following children: Thornton, Tristam, Frederick or Ferdinand,

George Steptoe, Lawrence Augustine, Harriet, and John Perrin Washington.

Colonel Samuel Washington died at "Harewood" and was buried in the family plot there.[51]

WETZEL, CHARLES McCLUER (Aug. 17, 1850—June 8, 1929). Charles McCluer Wetzel, who became speaker of the West Virginia House of Delegates, was not a native of Jefferson County. He was born in Knox County, Indiana, the son of Solomon and Eliza Burriss Wetzel. He practiced law for a while at Vincennes, Indiana, in the course of which time he married Margaret A. Beck. In 1885 he was appointed to a position in the customs service by President Grover Cleveland, which necessitated his moving to Washington. Remaining in this work for twelve years, he served under Presidents Benjamin Harrison and Cleveland.

Charles Wetzel's connection with Jefferson County began in 1895 when he purchased the old Vestal home near the site of Keyes's Ferry in the Millville region. He was interested in apple-growing and farming but in 1901 entered politics when he was chosen at a special election to succeed R. W. Morrow as the county's member of the House of Delegates. His friends reelected him in 1902, 1904, 1906, 1910, and 1912. In January, 1911, he was nominated by the Democratic caucus for speaker of the House of Delegates, to which office he was later elected. He continued active in county and state politics and at one time was mentioned as a candidate for governor. Under President Woodrow Wilson he served in both administrations as chief deputy collector of internal revenue, with headquarters at Parkersburg.

He died at his Jefferson County home.[52]

WILSON, EMANUEL WILLIS (Aug. 11, 1844—May 28, 1905). Emanuel Willis Wilson, born at Harpers Ferry, was Jefferson County's sole native to be elected Governor of West Virginia. The son of James Fitzgerald and Maria Spangler Wilson, he was educated in the common schools and then spent a year and a half at a business college. In 1866 he began the study of law without an instructor. In spite of this handicap he obtained a legal knowledge sufficient to enable him in 1869 to be admitted to practice in Jefferson County.

Entering politics in 1870, Wilson was elected to represent his native county in the House of Delegates. Two years later he was chosen to the State Senate. In the upper branch of the West Virginia Legislature he spoke so long against one bill that he received the nickname of "Windy".

In April, 1874, he married Henrietta S. Cotton, the daughter of a prominent Charleston physician, and in September of that year moved to the capital city. In 1876 and 1880 he was chosen to represent Kanawha County in the State Legislature and in 1880 he was elected speaker of the House of Delegates. Wilson's advocacy of reform legislation, added to his outstanding ability, caused him to be chosen Democratic Governor of West Virginia for the term beginning on March 4, 1885.

Although he was a Democrat, Governor Wilson supported the Populists in their desire to eliminate various abuses. A dispute concerning the outcome of the gubernatorial race in 1888 caused him to remain in office until February 5, 1890, when the Legislature declared Judge A. B. Fleming the victor. The popular result had showed the Republican, General Nathan D. Goff, to be elected, but irregularities in the voting caused a contest that was determined by the Legislature.

Ex-Governor Wilson was the Democratic nominee for Congress in 1896 but was defeated by his Republican opponent, Charles P. Dorr. His death occurred a few years later.[53]

WILSON, WILLIAM LYNE (May 3, 1843—Oct. 17, 1900). William Lyne Wilson, who was born on a farm near Middleway, was Jefferson County's most prominent son in national affairs since the Civil War and possibly since the county was formed. His parents were Benjamin and Mary Lyne Wilson. Although the father died when William was only four years old, he provided in his will that the son be thoroughly educated. William entered the Charles Town Academy, where he was noted for his quick mind and studious habits. It was said that at fifteen he had read more Latin, Greek, and French than was required for college graduates. This was declared true notwithstanding the fact that mathematics was his favorite study. Entering Columbian College, Washington, D. C., he was graduated from that institution in 1860 with the degree of Bachelor of Arts. He then attended the University of Virginia until the Civil War interrupted his studies.[54]

In the ensuing struggle William L. Wilson fought as a private in Company B, Twelfth Virginia Cavalry. When hostilities ceased, he accepted a position as assistant professor of ancient languages in Columbian College. While so engaged he took the degree of Master of Arts from Columbian and, in addition, was graduated from there in 1867 in law. Because the lawyer's test oath prevented him from practicing his profession, he continued teaching at Columbian until 1871. By that time the test oath had been annulled and he returned to Charles Town, where he formed a partnership with his cousin, Captain George Baylor. Meanwhile, he had married in 1869 Nannie Huntington, the daughter of the president of Columbian College.

Wilson's first venture in politics was in 1880 when he was elected a delegate to the Democratic National Convention. He made a canvass of the state that year as an elector-at-large on the Hancock ticket. Two years later, in 1882, by the unanimous vote of the Board of Regents he was asked to accept the presidency of West Virginia University. Although beginning his duties in this capacity on September 6, he was on September 20 nominated by acclamation as the Democratic candidate for Congress from the Second District. He was elected the following October and resigned from his university position with the beginning of his Congressional term on March 4, 1883. However, on being petitioned by the regents, faculty, and students, he remained at Morgantown until the school session ended in June.

Congressman Wilson's tenure of office in the House of Representatives lasted until 1894, when he was defeated by Judge Alston G. Dayton, his Republican opponent. Thus he was elected and reelected for six terms. His career in Congress was brilliant. In his second term he was made a member of the Committee on Appropriations, the chairman of which, Samuel J. Randall, frequently sought his counsel. Becoming an advocate of tariff reform, Wilson in 1887 was made a member of the powerful Ways and Means Committee. He was one of the fathers of the Mills Bill, a piece of legislation designed to reduce the tariff. The speech which he made in its behalf gave him a national reputation.

In 1892 William L. Wilson was the permanent chairman of the Democratic National Convention which renominated Grover Cleveland for President. He was also chosen to inform the Democratic candidate of his selection, which he did in an able address at Madison Square Garden, New York. He prepared and introduced the bill to repeal the Sherman Silver Purchase Act in a special session of Congress. Speaker of the House Crisp appointed him chairman of the Ways and Means Committee, and Wilson began work on his tariff bill. By this time he was generally regarded as the country's foremost authority on the vexing tariff question.

The strain of framing this important piece of legislation, coupled with the task of promoting its passage, caused him to seek a rest in Mexico. He was stricken with typhoid fever the evening he crossed the Rio Grande and for weeks he lay ill in Mexico. Returning home in May, 1893, he was unable to prevent the Senate a month or two later from amending his tariff bill so that he hardly recognized it. The resulting Wilson-Gorman Tariff Act, of which he was co-author, did little to reduce the tariff.

Before his last term was over Wilson was appointed Postmaster General by his friend, Grover Cleveland. The part he played in making the first experiment with rural free delivery in his native county of Jefferson has been related in the chapter on that subject. When Cleveland's second administration retired in 1897, William L. Wilson became president of Washington and Lee University at Lexington, Virginia. Entering upon his duties there in the fall of that year, he continued in this position until his death. His remains were brought back to Charles Town and buried in Edge Hill Cemetery. Ex-President Cleveland was present at the funeral.

William L. Wilson was a born orator and was called upon to deliver a number of speeches throughout the country. He was also an able writer and contributed many articles to leading newspapers and magazines of his day. For several years he was a regent of the Smithsonian Institute at Washington and was selected to represent that organization at the meeting of the Royal Institute of England to be held in June, 1899, in London. He was unable to accept, however, because of the commencement exercises at Washington and Lee. Nevertheless, the Royal Institute made him a fellow of that body. The degree of Doctor of Laws was awarded him by Hampden-Sydney College and Columbian College at Washington. Other honors which came his way but were declined were offers of the presidency of the University of Missouri in 1890 and that of Richmond College, Virginia, the following year.[55]

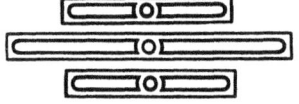

FOOTNOTES

CHAPTER ONE
NATURAL FEATURES

1. G. P. Grimsley, West Virginia Geological Survey for Jefferson, Berkeley, and Morgan Counties, p. 22.
2. Ibid., p. 38.
3. Ibid., pp. 120, 121.
4. Geologic Atlas of the United States, Harpers Ferry Folio [U. S. Geological Survey].
5. Grimsley, Geological Survey, pp. 31, 32.
6. Ibid., pp. 82, 83.
7. Ibid., p. 602; Virginia Free Press, Aug. 23, 1838; March 25, 1858; June 12, 1902; Farmer's Repository, Aug. 4, 1824; Sept. 8, 1824; Spirit of Jefferson, Nov. 9, 1909.
8. Grimsley, Geological Survey, p. 494. Many of the quarries furnish fluxing stone for iron and steel industries and, in addition, produce marl and rock wool.
9. Ibid., pp. 585, 586; Virginia Free Press, July 11, 1839.
10. T. Jefferson, Notes on the State of Virginia. Second American Edition. pp. 23, 24.

CHAPTER TWO
EARLY DAYS

1. Samuel Kercheval, A History of the Valley of Virginia. Fourth Edition. pp. 35, 36.
2. Clarence W. Alvord and Lee Bidgood, The First Explorations of the Trans-Allegheny Region by the Virginians, 1650-1674, pp. 64-69.
3. The Official Letters of Alexander Spotswood (Virginia Historical Society Collection). Vol. I, pp. 152, 153. De Graffenreid later founded the settlement of New Bern,

North Carolina, which was destroyed by Indians.
4. Leonidas Dodson, **Alexander Spotswood, Governor of Colonial Virginia, 1710-1722,** pp. 238, 239.
5. **Records of the Presbyterian Church in the United States of America,** p. 58.
6. Donegal Presbytery, **Records; The Independent,** Shepherdstown, W. Va., Oct. 10, 1934.
7. **Records of the Presbyterian Church,** pp. 58-60; **The Independent,** Oct. 3, 1934; Dec. 4, 1935; Dec. 11, 1935.
8. Secretary of the Commonwealth of Virginia, **Land Records;** C. H. Ambler, **West Virginia The Mountain State,** pp. 48, 49.
9. Carl Wittke, **We Who Built America, The Saga of the Immigrant,** pp. 66-70; Hermann Schuricht, **History of the German Element in Virginia.** Vol. I, pp. 60, 61, 85.
10. **Executive Journals of the Council of Colonial Virginia,** Oct. 25, 1721; Oct. 28, 1739. Vol. 4, p. 223.
11. Papers in **Hite, Duff, et al. vs. Fairfax** suit.
12. Kercheval, **History of the Valley,** p. 50.
13. Virginia Land Office Records, **Patent Book No. 15,** p. 279; Robert L. Bates, **The Story of Smithfield, Jefferson County, W. Va.** (MS.), p. 7.
14. John W. Wayland, **Hopewell Friends History, 1734-1934,** pp. 183, 184.
15. Joseph Barry, **The Strange Story of Harper's Ferry,** p. 14; **The Shepherdstown Register,** Feb. 9, 1933.
16. **Ibid.** One account states that Harper paid Stephens fifty British guineas for 125 acres and the ferry privilege, while another account states the sum was sixty guineas.
17. Joseph Barry, **Harpers Ferry,** p. 14; **The Shepherdstown Register,** Feb. 9, 1933.
18. George Washington, **Diaries** (ed. Fitzpatrick). Vol. I, pp. 3, 4.
19. Virginia General Assembly, **Acts,** 1850-1851 Session, p. 176; T. K. Cartmell, **Shenandoah Valley Pioneers and Their Descendants,** p. 67.
20. Barry, **Harpers Ferry,** pp. 14, 15.
21. **The Shepherdstown Register,** Jan. 20, 1910; May 19, 1910.
22. **Journals of the House of Burgesses of Virginia, 1761-1765,**

FOOTNOTES—EARLY DAYS 317

pp. 90, 106, 110, 114, 120, 165; W. W. Hening, **The Statutes at Large; Being a Collection of All the Laws of Virginia.** Vol. 7, p. 600.
23. **Journals of the House of Burgesses,** pp. 100, 105, 144, 154, 164.
24. Kercheval, **History of the Valley,** p. 50; Federal Writers Project of the Works Progress Administration, **Historic Romney, 1762-1937,** p. 45.
25. Secretary of the Commonwealth of Virginia, **Land Records;** Frederick County, **Deed Book No. 9,** p. 374; C. S. Musser, **Two Hundred Years' History of Shepherdstown,** pp. 7, 8.
26. Secretary of the Commonwealth of Virginia, **Land Records;** Samuel Shepherd, **The Statutes at Large of Virginia,** Vol. II, p. 139; Musser, **History of Shepherdstown,** pp. 8, 21.
27. Secretary of the Commonwealth of Virginia, **Land Records**: Musser, **History of Shepherdstown,** pp. 11, 12.
28. Spotsylvania County, **Deed Book J,** p. 538; **Deed Book A,** pp. 9, 315; Jefferson County, **Deed Book No. 22,** p. 320.
29. **Journal of the House of Delegates of the Commonwealth of Virginia, 1786-1790,** pp. 56, 68, 83, 84, 86, 150; **Journal of the Senate of the Commonwealth of Virginia for Oct. 16, 1786 to Jan. 11, 1787 Session,** pp. 40, 41, 46, 47, 77.
30. Hening, Statutes, Vol. 12, pp. 370, 371. As a matter of fact, the House did not obtain a quorum until October 23, 1786. The Senate was delayed for the same reason until November 7 and hence could not transact any business until then. See **House Journal,** pp. 3, 4 and **Senate Journal,** pp. 3-6.
31. Hening, **Statutes.** Vol. 12, pp. 370, 371.
32. Shepherd, **Statutes.** Vol. II, pp. 120, 121.
33. R. B. Woodworth, **Presbyterian Churches in Jefferson County, West Virginia** (MS.), p. 1.
34. Ibid.; The Martinsburg Journal, Oct. 24, 1940.
35. Donegal Presbytery, **Records;** The Shepherdstown Register, Sept. 19, 1929.
36. St. Peter's Lutheran Church, **Records,** Shepherdstown, W.

Va.; The Independent, June 19, 1940.
37. The Independent, June 27, 1934.
38. Ibid.
39. The Shepherdstown Register, April 27, 1916; Musser, History of Shepherdstown, p. 14.
40. The Shepherdstown Register, Aug. 30, 1934.
41. Christ Reformed Church, Records, Shepherdstown, W. Va.; The Shepherdstown Register, Dec. 22, 1898; The Independent, July 11, 1934; Musser, History of Shepherdstown, p. 14.
42. James Rumsey, A Plan Wherein the Power of Steam is Fully Shewn, p. 12; Danske Dandridge, Historic Shepherdstown, pp. 49, 53.
43. Spirit of Jefferson, April 10, 1900.
44. Jefferson County Historical Society Magazine for December, 1938, pp. 10, 11.
45. Berkeley County, Order Book No. 1, p. 339; The Independent, July 18, 1934; Jefferson County Historical Society Magazine for December, 1937, pp. 15-18; Statement of Colonel B. D. Gibson of Charles Town, W. Va., to author on June 10, 1941.

CHAPTER THREE
THE REVOLUTION

1. Francis B. Heitman, Historical Register of Officers of the Continental Army during the War of the Revolution, pp. 96, 117, 493, 518; Danske Dandridge, Historic Shepherdstown, pp. 88, 152, 176, 216, 229, 240.
2. Spirit of Jefferson, Jan. 29, 1850.
3. Dandridge, Historic Shepherdstown, p. 77.
4. Ibid., p. 79.
5. Farmer's Repository, June 22, 1825.
6. Dandridge, Historic Shepherdstown, p. 81.
7. Morris H. Hancock, Washington's Life and Military Career, p. 198.
8. Spirit of Jefferson, Nov. 26, 1901.
9. Heitman, Historical Register, p. 518; Dandridge, Historic Shepherdstown, p. 151.

10. Dandridge, **Historic Shepherdstown**, pp. 152, 160.
11. **Ibid.,** pp. 176-181.
12. **Ibid.,** pp. 216, 229.
13. **Ibid.,** pp. 228, 240, 241.
14. Heitman, **Historical Register,** pp. 244; **Dictionary of American Biography** (eds. Johnson and Malone). Vol. VII, pp. 187, 188.
15. **Ibid.**
16. Heitman, **Historical Register,** pp. 344, 345; **Dictionary of American Biography.** Vol. XI, pp. 99, 100.
17. **Virginia Free Press and Farmer's Repository,** Feb. 14, 1850.
18. Berkeley County, **Will Book No. 1,** p. 309.
19. Heitman, **Historical Register,** p. 519; **Virginia Free Press,** Nov. 29, 1860.
20. **Scrap Book** belonging to Mrs. J. M. Miller of Charles Town, W. Va.
21. Heitman, **Historical Register,** p. 519; **Richmond Enquirer,** Sept. 1, 1820; Statement of Colonel B. D. Gibson of Charles Town, W. Va., to author on May 3, 1941.

CHAPTER FOUR
JAMES RUMSEY AND THE STEAMBOAT

1. Ella May Turner, **James Rumsey, Pioneer in Steam Navigation,** pp. 3-5.
2. **Ibid.,** pp. 6, 7.
3. George Washington, **Writings** (ed. Ford). Vol. X, p. 402.
4. George Washington, **Diaries** (ed. Fitzpatrick). Vol. 2, pp. 282-284; George Washington, **Writings** (ed. Fitzpatrick). Vol. 29, p. 319; James Rumsey, **A Plan Wherein the Power of Steam is Fully Shewn,** p. 2.
5. Rumsey, **A Plan,** etc., p. 3.
6. Turner, **James Rumsey,** p. 203.
7. **Ibid.,** pp. 30, 31, 37, 52.
8. Rumsey, **A Plan,** etc., p. 13.
9. **Ibid.,** p. 17.
10. **Ibid.,** p. 15.
11. Turner, **James Rumsey,** pp. 74, 75.
12. Rumsey, **A Plan,** etc., pp. 15, 16.

13. J. E. Norris, A History of the Lower Shenandoah Valley, pp. 412-415.
14. Ibid., p. 416.
15. Rumsey Papers, Virginia State Library.
16. Turner, James Rumsey, pp. 141, 142, 153, 156.
17. Rumsey Papers, Aug. 4, 1789, Virginia State Library.
18. Turner, James Rumsey, pp. 170, 175, 176.
19. Rumsey Papers, Aug. 23, 1791, Virginia State Library.
20. Turner, James Rumsey, pp. 198, 199. His best friend, Captain Charles Morrow, had died the preceding month in America, but Rumsey had not received word of this misfortune at the time of his death.
21. The Gentleman's Magazine, Feb., 1793, p. 182.
22. The Shepherdstown Register, Sept. 16, 1887.
23. John Fitch, The Original Steam-Boat Supported, p. 3.
24. George M. Beltzhoover, Jr., James Rumsey, The Inventor of the Steamboat, pp. 6-8.
25. Fitch, The Original Steam-Boat Supported, pp. 4, 6.
26. Ibid., Turner, James Rumsey, p. 113.
27. Turner, James Rumsey, pp. 123, 124.
28. Ibid., pp. 125-128, 135.
29. Richmond Times-Dispatch, Aug. 3, 1930. Fitch acquired exclusive privileges in Virginia in October, 1787, according to his own statement.
30. Turner, James Rumsey, pp. 114, 132, 133; Rumsey, A Plan, etc., pp. 10-12. Anyone desirous of acquiring a more detailed account of the Rumsey-Fitch controversy is referred to James Rumsey, Pioneer in Steam Navigation by Ella May Turner. In this exhaustive study of Rumsey and his claim to fame the author quotes from many source materials.
31. Matthew Page Andrews, Virginia the Old Dominion, pp. 373, 374.
32. The Shepherdstown Register, March 1, 1906; March 4, 1909; Feb. 27, 1913; May 27, 1915.
33. Ibid., July 26, 1939.

CHAPTER FIVE

ASPIRATIONS AND INCIDENTS, 1790-1800

1. The West Virginia Review, Vol. XI, No. 5 (Feb., 1934), p. 134; The Shepherdstown Register, Sept. 14, 1932; The American Boy, Feb., 1941.
2. The West Virginia Review, Vol. XI, No. 5 (Feb., 1934), p. 134; The Shepherdstown Register, Sept. 14, 1932.
3. George Washington, Papers, Oct. 25, 1790—Jan. 11, 1791, Vol. 248.
4. Clifford S. Musser, Two Hundred Years' History of Shepherdstown, p. 19.
5. Dictionary of American Biography (eds. Johnson and Malone), Vol. V, p. 75.
6. The Shepherdstown Register, April 21, 1910.
7. American State Papers, Military Affairs, I, pp. 65, 66.
8. The Public Statutes at Large of the United States, Vol. I, p. 352; Charles W. Sawyer, Firearms in American History, p. 202.
9. George Washington, Writings (ed. Fitzpatrick), Vol. 34, pp. 308, 318, 465.
10. Sawyer, Firearms, pp. 203, 204.
11. Joseph Barry, The Strange Story of Harper's Ferry, p. 20; The Shepherdstown Register, March 20, 1885.
12. Virginia Free Press, April 15, 1858.
13. Charles Town Methodist Church, Records; Jefferson County, Deed Book No. 3, p. 339.
14. Robert L. Bates, The Story of Smithfield, Jefferson County, W. Va. (MS.), p. 27.
15. Mrs. V. S. Milbourne, Sketch of Charles Town Baptist Church (MS.), pp. 1, 2; Robert B. Semple, History of the Rise and Progress of the Baptists in Virginia, p. 322.
16. R. B. Woodworth, The Charles Town Presbyterian Church, Its Origin and Antecedents (MS.), pp. 3-6.
17. Ibid.
18. St. Peter's Lutheran Church, Records, Shepherdstown, W. Va.; Berkeley County, Petitions, Dec. 4, 1798, No. 3840; The Independent, Shepherdstown, W. Va., June 19, 1940.

19. Virginia Free Press, Feb. 19. 1857.
20. Ibid., Feb. 19, 1857; Feb. 26, 1857.
21. Ibid., Feb. 26, 1857; July 29, 1858; Berkeley County, Petitions, Dec. 13, 1797, No. 3771; Samuel Shepherd, The Statutes at Large of Virginia, Vol. II, p. 110; Thomas Brown, An Account of the Lineage of the Brown Family (MS.), Vol. I, p. 34.
22. Mynna Thruston, The Washingtons and Their Colonial Homes in West Virginia, p. 17; The Shepherdstown Register, March 19, 1928.

CHAPTER SIX

THE JEFFERSONIAN ERA

1. Jefferson County, **Deed Book No. 1,** p. 116.
2. Berkeley County, **Petitions,** Dec. 5, 1800, No. 4176.
3. Samuel Shepherd, **The Statutes at Large of Virginia,** Vol. II, pp. 271, 272.
4. W. W. Hening, **The Statutes at Large; Being a Collection of All the Laws of Virginia,** Vol. 1, p. 224; **Virginia State Library Bulletin** for January, April, July, 1916, Vol. 9, Nos. 1, 2, 3, p. 168.
5. Jefferson County, **Minute Book No. 0,** p. 1.
6. Ibid., pp. 1, 2.
7. Ibid., p. 3.
8. Ibid., pp. 31, 33.
9. Ibid., pp. 135, 136.
10. Ibid., pp. 100, 119, 139, 146, 170; **Minute Book No. 1,** pp. 194, 311, 332.
11. Jefferson County, **Minute Book No. 1,** p. 366.
12. J. E. Norris, **A History of the Lower Shenandoah Valley,** p. 343.
13. **Farmer's Repository,** Sept. 2, 1808.
14. Ibid., Oct. 21, 1808; Oct. 12, 1810.
15. **The Shepherdstown Register,** Sept. 15, 1898; April 29, 1920; May 6, 1920.
16. **Farmer's Repository,** April 1, 1808.
17. Ibid., Nov. 11, 1808.
18. Ibid., March 3, 1809.

FOOTNOTES—THE NEW NATIONALISM 323

19. Ibid., April 14, 1809; April 13, 1810; April 26, 1811; May 1, 1812.
20. Ibid., Nov. 13, 1812; Spirit of Jefferson, Oct. 19, 1880.
21. Farmer's Repository, Feb. 5, 1817.
22. Ibid., March 19, 1813.
23. Spirit of Jefferson, Jan. 14, 1873.
24. Virginia Free Press, Sept. 3, 1868.
25. Ibid.
26. Ibid., Oct. 22, 1870.
27. Ibid., Sept. 3, 1868; Farmer's Repository, Sept. 29, 1814.
28. The Shepherdstown Register, Dec. 7, 1872.

CHAPTER SEVEN

THE NEW NATIONALISM, 1815 TO 1840

1. Jefferson County, Petitions, Nov. 18, 1816, No. 6734.
2. Farmer's Repository, April 30, 1817.
3. Virginia Free Press and Farmer's Repository, April 21, 1830.
4. Virginia Free Press, Nov. 8, 1832.
5. Ibid., Jan. 24, 1833.
6. Ibid., Jan. 23, 1834; April 24, 1834.
7. Ibid., April 23, 1835.
8. Ibid., April 28, 1836; Nov. 10, 1836.
9. Arcadi Gluckman, United States Martial Pistols and Revolvers, pp. 119, 120; Spirit of Jefferson, March 28, 1905.
10. Farmer's Repository, June 27, 1821.
11. Virginia Free Press and Farmer's Repository, Feb. 3, 1830.
12. Ibid., Feb. 10, 1830; Virginia Free Press, Jan. 19, 1837; April 13, 1837; Oct. 19, 1837.
13. R. B. Woodworth, The Charles Town Presbyterian Church, Its Origin and Antecedents (MS.), p. 7.
14. The Shepherdstown Register, April 27, 1916.
15. St. Peter's Lutheran Church, Records, Shepherdstown, W. Va.; The Shepherdstown Register, Oct. 11, 1906.
16. Farmer's Repository, June 17, 1818.
17. The Shepherdstown Register, Sept. 19, 1929.
18. Farmer's Repository, April 28, 1819; The Shepherdstown Register, Dec. 17, 1936.
19. The Shepherdstown Register, Dec. 4, 1930.

20. Farmer's Repository, Oct. 22, 1823; Nov. 12, 1823; Nov. 19, 1823.
21. Ibid., May 18, 1825.
22. Jefferson County, Petitions, Jan. 14, 1830, No. 9440; Virginia General Assembly, Acts, 1829-1830 Session, p. 86; The Shepherdstown Register, April 29, 1920.
23. Virginia Free Press and Farmer's Repository, June 24, 1829.
24. Virginia Free Press, Nov. 14, 1833; Dec. 5, 1833; Sept. 18, 1834.
25. Ibid., Dec. 4, 1834.
26. Ibid., March 17, 1836.
27. Ibid., April 7, 1836; Robert L. Bates, The Story of Smithfield, Jefferson County, W. Va. (MS.), p. 57.
28. Virginia Free Press, Sept. 19, 1833; Nov. 28, 1833; June 15, 1837.
29. Ibid., July 11, 1839.
30. Farmer's Repository, July 28, 1819; Aug. 4, 1819.
31. Jefferson County, Petitions, Jan. 13, 1835, No. 10819; Virginia General Assembly, Acts, 1834-1835 Session, pp. 161-165.
32. Virginia Free Press, June 18, 1835.
33. Jefferson County, Petitions, Dec. 8, 1819, No. 7368; Virginia General Assembly, Acts, 1820-1821 Session, p. 110; The Shepherdstown Register, Jan. 9, 1919.
34. Farmer's Repository, Nov. 30, 1825.
35. Jefferson County, Petitions, Dec. 7, 1825, No. 8338; Virginia General Assembly, Acts, 1825-1826 Session, p. 94.
36. Jefferson County, Petitions, Dec. 11, 1826, No. 8691; Virginia General Assmebly, Acts, 1826-1827 Session, pp. 109. 110.
37. United States Census, Reports.
38. Jefferson County Historical Society Magazine for December, 1937, pp. 13-15; Notes belonging to Colonel B. D. Gibson of Charles Town, W. Va.
39. Ibid., pp. 34-36.

CHAPTER EIGHT
THE EVENTFUL FORTIES

1. **Virginia Free Press,** April 30, 1840; Nov. 5, 1840.
2. **Spirit of Jefferson,** Nov. 8, 1844; April 25, 1845.
3. **Ibid.,** Nov. 14, 1848.
4. **Virginia Free Press,** June 17, 1841; **Spirit of Jefferson,** Nov. 15, 1844; Joseph Barry, **The Strange Story of Harper's Ferry,** pp. 34-37.
5. Virginia General Assembly, **Acts,** 1845-1846 Session, pp. 37-41; **Spirit of Jefferson,** May 1, 1846.
6. Virginia General Assembly, **Acts,** 1846-1847 Session, pp. 29-34; **Spirit of Jefferson,** June 11, 1847; **The Shepherdstown Register,** July 22, 1937.
7. **Spirit of Jefferson,** Jan. 16, 1849.
8. **Ibid.,** Nov. 27, 1846.
9. **Ibid.,** Nov. 27, 1846; Dec. 11, 1846; Dec. 18, 1846.
10. **Ibid.,** Dec. 18, 1846; Dec. 25, 1846; Jan. 1, 1847.
11. **Ibid.,** Jan. 1, 1847; Jan. 8, 1847.
12. **Ibid.,** Jan. 15, 1847; Feb. 5, 1847; Feb. 26, 1847.
13. **Ibid.,** Feb. 26, 1847; March 5, 1847; April 9, 1847; June 4, 1847.
14. **Ibid.,** Aug. 8, 1848; Aug. 22, 1848; **Virginia Free Press,** Sept. 9, 1858.
15. **Spirit of Jefferson,** Jan. 30, 1849.
16. **Ibid.,** Feb. 13, 1849; Feb. 20, 1849.
17. **Ibid.,** March 6, 1849; June 19, 1849; **The Shepherdstown Register,** Jan. 31, 1901.
18. **Spirit of Jefferson,** June 19, 1849; Nov. 20, 1849; **The Shepherdstown Register,** Feb. 14, 1901.
19. **Spirit of Jefferson,** July 17, 1844; **The Shepherdstown Register,** Dec. 4, 1849.

CHAPTER NINE
ANTE BELLUM DAYS, 1850-1861

1. United States Census, **Reports.**
2. **Virginia Social Statistics for 1850,** p. 591.
3. Virginia General Assembly, **Acts,** 1830-1831 Session, pp. 6-8;

C. H. Ambler, Sectionalism in Virginia from 1776 to 1861, p. 253.
4. The Shepherdstown Register, Aug. 20, 1850; Aug. 27, 1850.
5. Virginia General Assembly, Acts, 1852 Session, pp. 325-331; C. H. Ambler, West Virginia The Mountain State, pp. 285-287.
6. Spirit of Jefferson, Oct. 28, 1851; Nov. 3, 1852.
7. The Shepherdstown Register, June 2, 1855; Virginia Free Press, Nov. 6, 1856; June 4, 1857.
8. Virginia Free Press, June 2. 1859.
9. Ibid., Nov. 15, 1860.
10. Ibid., Dec. 20, 1860.
11. Ibid., Feb. 7, 1861.
12. Ambler, The Mountain State, pp. 313, 314, 317.
13. Virginia Republican, June 1, 1861; Ambler, The Mountain State, p. 320.
14. Virginia Free Press, June 13, 1861.
15. Spirit of Jefferson, March 2, 1852.
16. Ibid., Feb. 8, 1853; May 24, 1853; July 4, 1854; July 25, 1854; Aug. 8, 1854; Jan. 2, 1855; The Shepherdstown Register, March 11, 1854.
17. Virginia Free Press, Dec. 30, 1858.
18. Mrs. V. S. Milbourne, Sketch of Charles Town Baptist Church (MS.), pp. 3, 4.
19. The Shepherdstown Register, Aug. 26, 1897.
20. Jefferson County, Petitions, March 13, 1850, No. 17183; Virginia Free Press, April 3, 1856; Sept. 11, 1856; Spirit of Jefferson, Jan. 16, 1849.
21. Robert L. Bates, The Story of Smithfield, Jefferson County, W. Va. (MS.), p. 58.
22. Jefferson County, Petitions, Feb. 6, 1858, No. 19667.
23. Ibid., Feb. 8, 1858, No. 19668; Virginia Free Press, April 15, 1858.

CHAPTER TEN

THE JOHN BROWN RAID

1. Oswald Garrison Villard, John Brown, 1800-1859, a Biography Fifty Years After, p. 344; Thomas Dixon, The Man in

FOOTNOTES—THE JOHN BROWN RAID

Gray, pp. 216-218.
2. Virginia Free Press, May 5, 1859; Dixon, The Man in Gray, pp. 218, 219.
3. Baltimore Weekly Sun, Nov. 12, 1859.
4. Boyd B. Stutler, Captain John Brown and Harper's Ferry, pp. 9, 13, 18.
5. Baltimore Weekly Sun, Nov. 19, 1859; Villard, John Brown, pp. 159, 160; Dixon, The Man in Gray, pp. 169, 170, 175, 177.
6. Baltimore Weekly Sun, Nov. 19, 1859; Richmond Daily Enquirer, Nov. 21, 1859; Villard, John Brown, pp. 368, 369; Dixon, The Man in Gray, p. 224.
7. Stutler, John Brown, p. 19; Henry Kyd Douglas, I Rode with Stonewall, p. 2.
8. Stutler, John Brown, p. 19.
9. Baltimore Weekly Sun, Oct. 22, 1859.
10. Stutler, John Brown, p. 19.
11. Joseph Barry, The Strange Story of Harper's Ferry, pp. 55, 56.
12. Baltimore Weekly Sun, Oct. 22, 1859.
13. Baltimore Weekly American, Nov. 5, 1859.
14. Independent Democrat, Oct. 25, 1859; Diary of Capt. V. M. Butler, under date of Oct. 17, 1859.
15. Barry, Harper's Ferry, pp. 64, 65.
16. Baltimore Weekly American, Nov. 5, 1859; Independent Democrat, Oct. 25, 1859.
17. Baltimore Weekly Sun, Oct. 22, 1859; Independent Democrat, Oct. 25, 1859.
18. Baltimore Weekly American, Nov. 5, 1859.
19. Visit of author to residence of Mrs. William B. Packette of Charles Town, W. Va., on March 1, 1941.
20. Villard, John Brown, pp. 330-333; Statement of Col. B. D. Gibson of Charles Town, W. Va., to author on March 2, 1941.
21. Baltimore Weekly American, Nov. 5, 1859.
22. Baltimore Weekly Sun, Nov. 12, 1859; Dec. 3, 1859.
23. The Shepherdstown Register, Feb. 5, 1886.
24. Ibid.
25. Ibid., Baltimore Weekly Sun, Oct. 22, 1859.
26. Baltimore Weekly Sun, Oct. 22, 1859; Stutler, John Brown, p. 23.

27. Baltimore Weekly Sun, Oct. 22, 1859.
28. Independent Democrat, Nov. 1, 1859.

CHAPTER ELEVEN
THE JOHN BROWN TRIAL AND EXECUTION

1. Independent Democrat, Nov. 1, 1859; Oswald Garrison Villard, John Brown, 1800-1859, a Biography Fifty Years After, p. 444; Daniel C. Draper, "Legal Phases of the Trial of John Brown", in West Virginia History, A Quarterly Magazine for Jan., 1940, pp. 87-103.
2. John Brown Papers, Circuit Clerk's Office, Charles Town, W. Va.; Independent Democrat, Nov. 1, 1859.
3. Ibid.
4. Ibid.
5. Baltimore Weekly American, Nov. 5, 1859.
6. John Brown Papers; Baltimore Weekly American, Nov. 5, 1859.
7. Baltimore Weekly Sun, Nov. 12, 1859.
8. Ibid., Nov. 26, 1859; Villard, John Brown, p. 570; Thomas Dixon, The Man in Gray, pp. 298, 299.
9. Baltimore Weekly Sun, Nov. 19, 1859; Nov. 26, 1859; Dec. 3, 1859.
10. Ibid.; Dec. 3, 1859.
11. Shepherdstown Register, Nov. 19, 1859; Spirit of Jefferson, Dec. 24, 1901.
12. Baltimore Weekly Sun, Dec. 3, 1859; Dec. 10, 1859.
13. Ibid., Dec. 10, 1859.
14. Jefferson County, Will Book No. 16, p. 143.
15. Virginia Free Press, Dec. 22, 1859; Villard, John Brown, p. 571.
16. Baltimore Weekly Sun, Dec. 17, 1859; Dec. 24, 1859.
17. Ibid., Jan. 14, 1860; Feb. 4, 1860; Feb. 11, 1860; Feb. 18, 1860; Spirit of Jefferson, July 18, 1929.
18. The Shepherdstown Register, Aug. 11, 1893; Boyd B. Stutler, Captain John Brown and Harper's Ferry, pp. 25, 26.
19. The Shepherdstown Register, Aug. 3, 1899; Spirit of Jefferson, Sept. 5, 1899.
20. Independent Democrat, April 10, 1860.

FOOTNOTES—THE CIVIL WAR 329

CHAPTERS TWELVE AND THIRTEEN

THE CIVIL WAR AND THE CIVIL WAR (CONCLUDED)

1. Sam M. Hendricks, Military Operations in Jefferson County, Virginia (and West Virginia), 1861-1865, p. 1.
2. Ibid., William N. McDonald, A History of the Laurel Brigade, pp. 31, 32.
3. Ibid.,
4. Spirit of Jefferson, Sept. 22, 1903.
5. Barton H. Wise, The Life of Henry A. Wise of Virginia, 1806-1876, pp. 275-278.
6. The War of the Rebellion: A Compilation of the Official Records of the Union and Confederate Armies, Series I, Vol. II, p. 4; The Shepherdstown Register, April 27, 1911.
7. J. E. Norris, History of the Lower Shenandoah Valley, p. 511; The Shepherdstown Register, April 27, 1911.
8. Official Records, I, Vol. II, pp. 809, 810; Mary Anna Jackson, Memoirs of Stonewall Jackson, p. 155.
9. Official Records, I, Vol. II, pp. 871, 872; Joseph E. Johnston, Narrative of Military Operations, p. 14.
10. Official Records, I, Vol. II, p. 472; Jackson, Memoirs, p. 160.
11. Festus P. Summers, The Baltimore and Ohio in the Civil War, p. 65.
12. Official Records, I, Vol. II, p. 32; Summers, Baltimore and Ohio, pp. 66, 67.
13. Official Records, I, Vol. LI, pt. 1, pp. 7, 8.
14. Ibid., I, Vol. V, pp. 8, 240-248; Joseph Barry, The Strange Story of Harper's Ferry, pp. 132, 133.
15. Official Records, I, Vol. XII, pp. 738, 739.
16. The Shepherdstown Register, Feb. 9, 1922.
17. The Virginia Free Press, Jan. 7, 1871; Spirit of Jefferson, May 7, 1889.
18. George Baylor, Bull Run to Bull Run, pp. 55-58.
19. Ibid., pp. 58-60; Official Records, I, Vol. XII, pt. 3, pp. 650, 652.
20. Baylor, Bull Run to Bull Run, pp. 60-62.
21. Jackson, Memoirs, p. 335.

22. Ibid., pp. 335, 337; Official Records, I, Vol. XIX, pt. 1, pp. 147, 953, 954.
23. Official Records, I, Vol. XIX, pt. 1, pp. 528, 955.
24. Ibid., I, Vol. XIX, pt. 1, p. 955.
25. Ibid., pp. 583, 584.
26. Baylor, Bull Run to Bull Run, p. 72.
27. The Shepherdstown Register, July 16, 1886.
28. Ibid., Sept. 22, 1921; July 16, 1886.
29. Official Records, I, Vol. XIX, pt. 1, p. 982.
30. Ibid., pp. 204, 348, 349.
31. Hendricks, Military Operations, p. 8.
32. Official Records, I, Vol. XIX, pt. 2, pp. 8, 9, 85-88.
33. Ibid., pp. 90-93, 97.
34. Ibid., I, Vol. XXI, pp. 7, 8; The Shepherdstown Register, June 7, 1934.
35. Official Records, I, Vol. XIX, pt. 2, pp. 160, 161.
36. Ibid., I, Vol. XXI, pp. 30-35; Baylor, Bull Run to Bull Run, pp. 74-77.
37. Official Records, I, Vol. XXI, p. 704.
38. Ibid., I, Vol. XXV, pt. 1, p. 15; Baylor, Bull Run to Bull Run, pp. 82-84.
39. Official Records, I, Vol. XXV, pt. 1, p. 15; Baylor, Bull Run to Bull Run, pp. 84, 85.
40. Official Records, I, Vol. XXV, pt. 1, pp. 138, 145; The Shepherdstown Register, Sept. 26, 1890.
41. Official Records, I, Vol. XXVII, pt. 2, p. 766; Baylor, Bull Run to Bull Run, p. 150.
42. Official Records, I, Vol. XXVII, pt. 2, pp. 204, 205, 767; Baylor, Bull Run to Bull Run, p. 151.
43. Official Records, I, Vol. XXVII, pt. 1, pp. 978, 980.
44. Ibid., pp. 972, 978, 981; Hendricks, Military Operations, p. 11.
45. Official Records, I, Vol. XXIX, pt. 1, p. 102.
46. Ibid., p. 210; Harry Gilmor, Four Years in the Saddle, pp. 107-111.
47. Official Records, I, Vol. XXIX, pt. 1, pp. 487-491; Spirit of Jefferson, Sept. 15, 1903; The Shepherdstown Register, Sept. 19, 1884.
48. Ibid.
49. Official Records, I, Vol. XXIX, pt. 1, pp. 1010, 1011.

FOOTNOTES—THE CIVIL WAR (CONCLUDED) 331

50. Ibid., I, Vol. XXXIII, p. 151; Gilmor, Four Years in the Saddle, pp. 144-146.
51. Official Records, I, Vol. XXXIII, pp. 152-154, 223; Gilmor, Four Years in the Saddle, p. 146.
52. Official Records, I, Vol. XXXIII, pp. 247-249.
53. Ibid., Vol. XXXVII, pt. 1, pp. 3, 692-695.
54. Ibid., pp. 175, 176; Ibid., I, Vol. XXXVII, pt. 2, p. 20.
55. Ibid., I, Vol. XXXVII, pt. 1, pp. 184-186.
56. Shepherdstown Register, Oct. 13, 1866.
57. Ibid.
58. Henry Kyd Douglas, I Rode with Stonewall, p. 380.
59. Official Records, I, Vol. XXXVII, pt. 2, pp. 367, 368, 394; Matthew Page Andrews, The Women of the South in War Times, pp. 196, 197; The Shepherdstown Register, July 27, 1899; Douglas, I Rode with Stonewall, p. 297.
60. Andrews, The Women of the South in War Times, pp. 197-201; The Shepherdstown Register, July 27, 1899; July 16, 1914.
61. Ibid.
62. Ibid.
63. Andrews, The Women of the South in War Times, pp. 201-204; The Shepherdstown Register, July 27, 1899.
64. Douglas, I Rode with Stonewall, p. 303.
65. Official Records, I, Vol. XLIII, pt. 1, pp. 874, 875.
66. Ibid., pp. 155, 156, 570.
67. Hendricks, Military Operations, pp. 35, 36.
68. Official Records, I, Vol. XLIII, pt. 1, p. 570; Gilmor, Four Years in the Saddle, pp. 231-234.
69. Official Records, I, Vol. XLIII, pt. 1, p. 425; George E. Pond, The Shenandoah Valley in 1864, pp. 137, 138.
70. Official Records, I, Vol. XLIII, pt. 1, pp. 440, 570.
71. Ibid., pp. 21, 399, 400, 571.
72. Official Records, I, Vol. XLIII, pt. 1, pp. 440, 441, 571; Robert L. Bates, The Story of Smithfield, Jefferson County, W. Va. (MS.), p. 98.
73. Official Records, I, Vol. XLIII, pt. 1, pp. 489, 571; Gilmor, Four Years in the Saddle, pp. 244, 245.
74. Official Records, I, Vol. XLIII, pt. 2, pp. 876, 878; Pond,

Shenandoah Valley, pp. 144, 147, 148.
75. Official Records, I, Vol. XLIII, pt. 1, pp. 615, 616, 634.
76. Official Records, I, Vol. XLIII, pt. 2, pp. 368, 372; Virginia Free Press, Jan. 12, 1898; The Shepherdstown Register, Aug. 19, 1909; Summers, Baltimore and Ohio, pp. 174, 175.
77. Ibid.
78. Ibid.
79. Official Records, I, Vol. XLIII, pt. 2, pp. 648, 650; Spirit of Jefferson, Aug. 3, 1897; The Shepherdstown Register, Nov. 27, 1919.
80. Ibid.
81. Official Records, I, Vol. XLIII, pt. 1, pp. 673, 674; Baylor, Bull Run to Bull Run, pp. 265-267.
82. Official Records, I, Vol. XLVI, pt. 1, p. 455.
83. D. B. Lucas, Memoir of John Yates Beall, pp. 11-14, 23-29, 40, 50, 81.
84. Baylor, Bull Run to Bull Run, pp. 310, 311.
85. Official Records, I, Vol. XLVI, pt. 1, p. 526; pt. 3, p. 617; Baylor, Bull Run to Bull Run, pp. 311, 312.
86. The Shepherdstown Register, Nov. 24, 1921; June 7, 1934.
87. Baylor, Bull Run to Bull Run, pp. 341, 342.

CHAPTER FOURTEEN

VIRGINIA OR WEST VIRGINIA

1. C. H. Ambler, West Virginia The Mountain State, pp. 325, 326.
2. Ibid., p. 321.
3. Ibid., pp. 323, 327, 329, 330; Joseph Barry, The Strange Story of Harper's Ferry, p. 113; Statement of Attorney D. K. Koonce of Charles Town, W. Va., to author on March 3, 1941.
4. Ambler, The Mountain State, pp. 332-337.
5. Ibid., pp. 371, 374, 375; Edward H. Phillips, The Transfer of Jefferson and Berkeley Counties to West Virginia (MS.), pp. 58, 86.
6. Ambler, The Mountain State, pp. 382, 383, 389, 395, 398.
7. Ibid., p. 399.

FOOTNOTES—RECONSTRUCTION

8. Virginia General Assembly, Acts, Reorganized Gov't. Extra Session, 1862-1863, p. 66; Ambler, The Mountain State, p. 405; Festus P. Summers, The Baltimore and Ohio in the Civil War, p. 201.
9. Shepherdstown Register, Nov. 25, 1865.
10. Virginia, Executive Papers (Pierpont).
11. Alexander R. Boteler Papers, belonging to Miss Helen Pendleton, Shepherdstown, W. Va.
12. Ambler, The Mountain State, p. 405.
13. West Virginia Legislature, Acts, 1863 Session, pp. 103, 104; Virginia Free Press, Aug. 24, 1865.
14. Virginia Free Press, Aug. 24, 1865.
15. Ibid., Aug. 31, 1865.
16. Ibid., Sept. 7, 1865.
17. Shepherdstown Register, Jan. 27, 1866.
18. Ibid., Nov. 25, 1865.
19. Ibid., Dec. 2, 1865.
20. Ibid., Dec. 9, 1865; Virginia Free Press, Dec. 14, 1865.
21. Shepherdstown Register, Dec. 16, 1865; Feb. 10, 1866; March 10, 1866; Virginia Free Press, Dec. 28, 1865; Jan. 18, 1866; March 15, 1866.
22. The Virginia Free Press, May 9, 1867.
23. Ibid., May 2, 1867; May 16, 1867; Jan. 30, 1868.
24. Ibid., Feb. 11, 1871.
25. Ibid., Feb. 18, 1871; March 11, 1871; Summers, Baltimore and Ohio, p. 201.

CHAPTER FIFTEEN

RECONSTRUCTION

1. The Shepherdstown Register, July 29, 1865.
2. Ibid., July 22, 1865; Virginia Free Press, Aug. 24, 1865; Spirit of Jefferson, Jan. 9, 1866.
3. West Virginia Legislature, Acts, 1865 Session, p. 3; 1866 Session, p. 22; Spirit of Jefferson, Jan. 24, 1871; Virginia Free Press, Aug. 24, 1865; Shepherdstown Register, July 29, 1865.
4. Shepherdstown Register, July 15, 1865.
5. Ibid., July 29, 1865.

6. The Virginia Free Press, May 9, 1867; Jefferson County, Deed Book No. 5, p. 333; Charles Town Methodist Church, Records.
7. The Virginia Free Press, April 18, 1867.
8. Shepherdstown Register, Oct. 28, 1865; Nov. 11, 1865.
9. Ibid., Nov. 11, 1865; July 22, 1865.
10. Ibid., June 2, 1866; Virginia Free Press, May 31, 1866; June 7, 1866.
11. Shepherdstown Register, July 22, 1865; March 24, 1866; June 9, 1866.
12. The Virginia Free Press, May 9, 1867, May 23, 1867; C. H. Ambler, West Virginia The Mountain State, p. 430.
13. The Virginia Free Press, Feb. 13, 1868.
14. Ibid., Sept. 10, 1868; Oct. 8, 1868; Oct. 15, 1868.
15. Ibid., Nov. 12, 1868.
16. Ibid., Nov. 26, 1868.
17. West Virginia Legislature, Acts, 1868 Extra Session, pp. 93, 94; The Virginia Free Press, Jan. 14, 1869; Jan. 21, 1869.
18. Spirit of Jefferson, June 8, 1869; Jefferson County, Deed Book No.1, pp. 116, 117.
19. The Virginia Free Press, Oct. 28, 1869; Nov. 11, 1869.
20. Ibid., Nov. 5, 1870; Spirit of Jefferson, Aug. 22, 1893; Thomas Brown, An Account of the Lineage of the Brown Family. (MS.), Vol. I, p. 1.
21. Spirit of Jefferson, Dec. 13, 1870.
22. Ibid., Jan. 3, 1871.
23. West Virginia Legislature, Acts, 1871 Session, pp. 123, 124; Spirit of Jefferson, Feb. 14, 1871; Feb. 28, 1871; The Virginia Free Press, Feb. 25, 1871.
24. West Virginia Legislature, Acts, 1871 Session, pp. 123, 124; Spirit of Jefferson, Feb. 28, 1871; The Virginia Free Press, March 4, 1871.
25. West Virginia Legislature, Acts, 1871 Session, pp. 153, 154; The Virginia Free Press, March 4, 1871.
26. The Virginia Free Press, March 18, 1871; Spirit of Jefferson, March 7, 1871.
27. The Virginia Free Press, March 18, 1871; Spirit of Jefferson, March 21, 1871.

28. The Virginia Free Press, April 1, 1871.
29. Ibid., April 8, 1871; April 15, 1871; Spirit of Jefferson, April 4, 1871.
30. The Virginia Free Press, April 29, 1871.
31. Ibid., May 13, 1871; May 20, 1871.
32. Spirit of Jefferson, Aug. 22, 1871.
33. The Virginia Free Press, Sept. 2, 1871; Sept. 16, 1871; Dec. 21,1872; July 26, 1873; The Shepherdstown Register, Nov. 28, 1874.
34. The Virginia Free Press, Sept. 23, 1871; Oct. 7, 1871.
35. Ibid., Oct. 10, 1867.
36. Joseph Barry, The Strange Story of Harper's Ferry, p. 173; Morris P. Shawkey, West Virginia in History, Life, and Industry, Vol. I, p. 395.
37. The Virginia Free Press, Dec. 2, 1869.
38. Ibid., Feb. 28, 1870; Barry, Harper's Ferry, pp. 198-200.
39. The Shepherdstown Register, Oct. 24, 1884; Barry, Harper's Ferry, pp. 200-204.
40. The Virginia Free Press, April 11, 1870; April 6, 1872.
41. Barry, Harper's Ferry, pp. 175-180.

CHAPTER SIXTEEN
NEW INTERESTS AND OUTLOOKS

1. West Virginia Legislature, Acts, 1872-1873 Session, pp. 34-36; The Virginia Free Press, Aug. 31, 1872; Nov. 2, 1872; The Shepherdstown Register, Jan. 11, 1873.
2. The Virginia Free Press, Nov. 9, 1872.
3. Ibid., Feb. 15, 1873; Feb. 22, 1873.
4. West Virginia Legislature, Acts, 1872-1873 Session, p. 51; The Virginia Free Press, Jan. 18, 1873; June 21, 1873.
5. The Virginia Free Press, June 21, 1873; Aug. 9, 1873.
6. Spirit of Jefferson, Dec. 10, 1889.
7. Mervin R. Shirey, "The Granger Movement in West Virginia" (Master's Thesis, W. Va. Univ., 1933), pp. 7, 8, 12; Jefferson County Historical Society Magazine for December, 1939, pp. 4-6.
8. The Shepherdstown Register, Aug. 26, 1876; Nov. 11, 1876; Aug. 18, 1877.

9. Ibid., Nov. 13, 1880.
10. The Shepherdstown Register, Nov. 15, 1894; The Virginia Free Press, Feb. 17, 1897.
11. West Virginia Legislature, Acts, 1872 Session, p. 148; 1872-1873 Session, p. 79; The Virginia Free Press, Aug. 3, 1872; Morris P. Shawkey, West Virginia, in History, Life, Literature, and Industry, Vol. I, p. 369.
12. The Virginia Free Press, Feb. 15, 1873.
13. West Virginia Legislature, Acts, 1875 Session, p. 346.
14. Ibid., 1877 Session, pp. 72, 73; The Shepherdstown Register, March 27, 1875; Spirit of Jefferson, April 13, 1875; Jan. 23, 1877; Jefferson County Historical Society Magazine for December, 1939, pp. 4-6.
15. The Shepherdstown Register, April 2, 1881; Sept. 10, 1881; April 1, 1882; Oct. 2, 1885.
16. Ibid., July 28, 1883; July 15, 1887.
17. Ibid., July 22, 1887; C. H. Ambler, West Virginia The Mountain State, p. 446.
18. Statement of Miss Laura W. Campbell of Charles Town, W. Va. to author on February 27, 1941.
19. The Shepherdstown Register, Feb. 10, 1893; July 14, 1893.
20. Ibid., March 30, 1899.
21. Ibid., Sept. 28, 1872; July 2, 1914.
22. Ibid.
23. Ibid.
24. Ibid., June 13, 1874; July 25, 1874.
25. Ibid., Feb. 21, 1890.
26. Ibid., May 16, 1890; May 30, 1890; Nov. 28, 1890.
27. Ibid., Dec. 5, 1890; Statement of J. Frank Turner of Charles Town, W. Va. to author on May 5, 1941.
28. The Shepherdstown Register, Dec. 12, 1890.
29. Ibid.
30. Ibid., March 13, 1891.
31. Ibid., Dec. 12, 1890; Jan. 30, 1891.
32. Ibid., May 1, 1891; June 26, 1891; Dec. 21, 1911.
33. Ibid., July 4, 1874.
34. Ibid., Jan. 4, 1879; Jan. 11, 1879; Sept. 19, 1907.
35. Ibid., Feb. 2, 1899; June 4, 1903; Jefferson County Historical Society Magazine for December, 1936, p. 32.

FOOTNOTES—THE RURAL FREE DELIVERY

36. The Shepherdstown Register, Dec. 15, 1898.
37. The Virginia Free Press, May 4, 1898.
38. Ibid., June 1, 1898; The Shepherdstown Register, June 2, 1898; June 30, 1898.
39. The Shepherdstown Register, Aug. 18, 1898; Dec. 15, 1898; April 13, 1899.

CHAPTER SEVENTEEN
THE RURAL FREE DELIVERY

1. Cushing Marshall, The Story of the Post Office, The Greatest Government Department in All Its Phases, p. 1004.
2. Ibid.
3. Herbert A. Gibbons, John Wanamaker, Vol. I, p. 278.
4. Ibid., p. 281.
5. United States Post Office Department, Records; C. H. Greathouse, "Free Delivery of Rural Mail", in United States Department of Agriculture, Yearbook for 1900, pp. 513-528.
6. Ibid.; The Baltimore Sun, Sept. 18, 1896; Spirit of Jefferson, Sept. 22, 1896.
7. Spirit of Jefferson, April 20, 1938.
8. Post Office Department, Records; Spirit of Jefferson, April 20, 1938; The Shepherdstown Register, Feb. 4, 1926.
9. The Virginia Free Press, Nov. 4, 1896.
10. Post Office Department, Records; Greathouse, "Free Delivery of Rural Mail", p. 517.
11. Greathouse, "Free Delivery of Rural Mail", pp. 518-520.
12. Ibid., p. 520.
13. Ibid., pp. 527, 528.
14. The Shepherdstown Register, Sept. 4, 1902; July 30, 1903.
15. Post Office Department, Records.

CHAPTER EIGHTEEN
THE NEW CENTURY

1. The Shepherdstown Register, Nov. 15, 1900.
2. Ibid., Sept. 18, 1902; Sept. 25, 1902.
3. Ibid., Oct. 9, 1902; Nov. 6, 1902.

4. Ibid., Jan. 12, 1911.
5. Ibid., Nov. 14, 1912; July 17, 1913.
6. Ibid., Oct. 22, 1914; Nov. 5, 1914.
7. Ibid., Nov. 16, 1916.
8. Ibid., May 9, 1901; March 13, 1902.
9. Ibid., March 13, 1902; March 27, 1902; July 10, 1902.
10. Ibid., Aug. 28, 1902; Sept. 4, 1902; Nov. 22, 1906.
11. The Shepherdstown Register, Nov. 13, 1902; June 4, 1903.
12. Ibid., Dec. 2, 1909; March 24, 1910; June 1, 1911.
13. Ibid., July 31, 1919; Jefferson County Historical Society Magazine for December, 1936, p. 32.
14. The Shepherdstown Register, Oct. 20, 1910; Jefferson County, Law Order Book No. 1, pp. 96-99.
15. The Shepherdstown Register, March 24, 1910.
16. Ibid., June 25, 1914.
17. Ibid., March 13, 1919.
18. Ibid., May 5, 1904.
19. Ibid., July 7, 1904.
20. Ibid., July 6, 1905.
21. Ibid., March 9, 1911.
22. Ibid., Feb. 29, 1912; March 14, 1912; Jan. 16, 1913.
23. Statement of Miss Laura W. Campbell of Charles Town, W. Va. to author on February 27, 1941.
24. The Shepherdstown Register, Jan. 11, 1906; Jan. 25, 1906; Feb. 1, 1906.
25. Ibid., May 6, 1909.
26. Ibid., May 11, 1911; June 8, 1911.
27. Ibid., June 8, 1911; Jan. 9, 1913.
28. Ibid., March 23, 1916; Spirit of Jefferson, March 21, 1916.
29. The Shepherdstown Register, June 14, 1917; July 5, 1917; July 26, 1917; Sept. 19, 1918.
30. Ibid., July 11, 1918.
31. Spirit of Jefferson, Jan. 20, 1920; Feb. 24, 1920; The Shepherdstown Register, Sept. 30, 1920.
32. The Shepherdstown Register, Oct. 25, 1917; May 9, 1918; May 30, 1918; May 15, 1919.
33. Ibid., Jan. 10, 1918.
34. Ibid., Oct. 2, 1919.
35. Ibid., Feb. 6, 1902; Statement of City Attorney Lee Bushong,

FOOTNOTES—RECENT YEARS

Jr., of Charles Town, W. Va. to author on March 3, 1941.
36. Ella May Turner, Stories and Verse of West Virginia, pp. 248-250.
37. The Shepherdstown Register, April 19, 1902.
38. United States Census, Reports.

CHAPTER NINETEEN
RECENT YEARS

1. The Shepherdstown Register, June 23, 1921.
2. Ibid., July 21, 1921; Aug. 2, 1923; Jan. 31, 1924.
3. Spirit of Jefferson, March 28, 1922.
4. Ibid.
5. Ibid., April 25, 1922; May 2, 1922; May 30, 1922.
6. Ibid., June 13, 1922; June 27, 1922; Aug. 15, 1922; Aug. 22, 1922; Sept. 5, 1922; Sept. 19, 1922.
7. Ibid., Oct. 24, 1922; Nov. 7, 1922; Nov. 21, 1922; Nov. 28. 1922; March 17, 1926.
8. The Shepherdstown Register, June 2, 1921.
9. Ibid., March 26, 1925; April 15, 1926.
10. Ibid., Nov. 6, 1924; Nov. 22, 1928.
11. Ibid., Nov. 17, 1932.
12. Ibid., June 29, 1933.
13. Farmers Advocate, Nov. 8, 1940.
14. The Shepherdstown Register, April 13, 1922.
15. Ibid., April 27, 1922; May 11, 1922.
16. Ibid., July 17, 1924; Sept. 18, 1924; Nov. 10, 1927; Nov. 22, 1928.
17. Ibid., Nov. 15, 1928.
18. Minutes of Harpers Ferry District Board of Education at a meeting on June 19, 1929, pp. 337-339, 381.
19. The Shepherdstown Register, Nov. 20, 1930.
20. L. V. Cavins and David Kirby, A Study of the Clientele of the Institutions of Higher Education in West Virginia, pp. 4, 5.
21. Jefferson County Selective Service, Records.
22. The Shepherdstown Register, Sept. 30, 1920.
23. Ibid., Oct. 4, 1923.
24. Ibid., Dec. 6, 1923.

25. Ibid., Dec. 25, 1930.
26. Ibid., Aug. 3, 1933; Dec. 7, 1933.
27. Ibid., March 19, 1936; July 26, 1939.
28. United States Census, **Reports.**

BIOGRAPHIES OF PROMINENT FORMER RESIDENTS

1. George Baylor, **Bull Run to Bull Run,** pp. 408-411; Spirit of Jefferson, March 11, 1902.
2. D. B. Lucas, **Memoir of John Yates Beall,** pp. 1, 4, 7-10.
3. **Ibid.,** pp. 11-29.
4. **Ibid.,** pp. 40, 50-57, 81.
5. The Shepherdstown Register, Nov. 28, 1929.
6. Virginia Free Press, Dec. 2, 1858; Ella May Turner, **Stories and Verse of West Virginia,** p. 70.
7. The Shepherdstown Register, May 13, 1892.
8. **Ibid.,** Sept. 24, 1886; May 13, 1892; Virginia Free Press, May 11, 1892.
9. **Notes** belonging to Mrs. Anne Brooke Harold of Charles Town, W. Va.
10. Spirit of Jefferson, Oct. 14, 1890; March 22, 1921.
11. **Ibid.,** March 6, 1894; Jan. 16, 1909.
12. **Ibid.,** Dec. 24, 1907.
13. The Shepherdstown Register, June 4, 1914; Turner, **Stories and Verse,** pp. 178, 179.
14. Dictionary of American Biography, Vol. V, p. 74.
15. **Ibid.,** pp. 74, 75; Francis B. Heitman, **Historical Register of Officers of the Continental Army during the War of the Revolution,** p. 185; The Shepherdstown Register, April 21, 1910.
16. The Shepherdstown Register, Dec. 24, 1903; Henry Kyd Douglas, **I Rode with Stonewall,** pp. 1, 5, 46, 239, 330.
17. Heitman, **Historical Register,** p. 244; Dictionary of American Biography, Vol. VII, pp. 184, 185.
18. Heitman, **Historical Register,** p. 244; Dictionary of American Biography, Vol. VII, pp. 186-188.
19. Spirit of Jefferson, Feb. 2, 1904.
20. **Ibid.,** Dec. 28, 1875; Jan. 14. 1890.
21. **Ibid.,** Feb. 14, 1882.

FOOTNOTES—BIOGRAPHIES

22. The Shepherdstown Register, June 20, 1895.
23. Ibid., May 1, 1858; Virginia Free Press, April 29, 1858.
24. The Virginia Free Press, May 31, 1873;Spirit of Jefferson, Aug. 29, 1911; Sept. 15, 1926.
25. Spirit of Jefferson, Sept. 27, 1887.
26. Ibid., Dec. 5, 1911; Notes belonging to Miss Amelia Hopkins of Charles Town, W. Va.
27. Spirit of Jefferson, Aug. 1, 1905.
28. Spirit of Jefferson, June 19, 1930; The Shepherdstown Register, Nov. 30, 1888; J. E. Norris, A History of the Lower Shenandoah Valley, pp. 634, 635.
29. Dictionary of American Biography, Vol. XI, p. 98.
30. Heitman, Historical Register, pp. 344, 345; Virginia Free Press and Farmer's Repository, Feb. 14, 1850; Dictionary of American Biography, Vol. XI, pp. 98-100.
31. Turner, Stories and Verse, pp. 144, 145.
32. Norris, Shenandoah Valley, p. 598.
33. Ibid., pp. 599-601; Spirit of Jefferson, June 27, 1909.
34. Virginia Free Press, March 11, 1858; Norris, Shenandoah Valley, p. 598.
35. Spirit of Jefferson, Oct. 9, 1877.
36. Ibid., Sept. 21, 1912.
37. The Shepherdstown Register, Feb. 16, 1899; The Virginia Free Press, Feb. 22, 1899.
38. Spirit of Jefferson, March 4, 1919; C. H. Ambler, West Virginia The Mountain State, pp. 350, 351.
39. Spirit of Jefferson, Sept. 19, 1922; The Shepherdstown Register, July 11, 1918.
40. The Shepherdstown Register, Jan. 9, 1891.
41. Spirit of Jefferson, Nov. 26, 1901; Jefferson County Historical Society Magazine for December, 1939, pp. 10-15.
42. Heitman, Historical Register, p. 517; Virginia Free Press, Nov. 29, 1860; Danske Dandridge, Historic Shepherdstown, p. 348; Hardesty's Geographical and Historical Encyclopedia (History of Berkeley County), p. 10.
43. Heitman, Historical Register, p. 518; Dandridge, Historic Shepherdstown, p. 349.
44. Virginia Free Press, Sept. 5, 1833; Spirit of Jefferson, March 13, 1883.

45. John W. Wayland, Samuel Washington (MS.), p. 2; Notes belonging to Miss Laura Mitchell of Charles Town, W. Va.; Bishop Meade, Old Churches and Families of Virginia, Vol. II, p. 296.
46. Spotsylvania County, Deed Book J, p. 538; Deed Book A, pp. 9, 315; Albert Welles, The Pedigree and History of the Washington Family, pp. 187, 188; Millard K. Bushong, "The Washingtons of Jefferson County, West Virginia" (Master's thesis, W. Va. Univ., 1937), pp. 21-24.
47. The South in the Building of the Nation, Vol. XII, pp. 528, 529.
48. Spirit of Jefferson, July 17, 1894; Welles, The Washington Family, pp. 241, 242.
49. Welles, The Washington Family, p. 115.
50. Bushong, "The Washingtons of Jefferson County" pp. 30-32.
51. Ibid., pp. 33-35, 37-43, 45; Heitman, Historical Register, p. 573.
52. The Shepherdstown Register, Nov. 6, 1902; Nov. 17, 1904; Nov. 8, 1906; Nov. 10, 1910; Jan. 12, 1911; Nov. 14, 1912.
53. George W. Atkinson and Alvaro F. Gibbens, Prominent Men of West Virginia, pp. 262-267; C. H. Ambler, The Mountain State, pp. 461, 462; The Shepherdstown Register, June 1, 1905.
54. Virginia Free Press, Feb. 17, 1897; Spirit of Jefferson, Oct. 23, 1900.
55. Ibid.

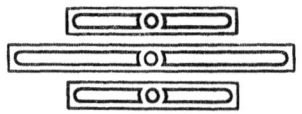

BIBLIOGRAPHY

PRIMARY SOURCES

MANUSCRIPT MATERIALS

The Papers of Alexander R. Boteler. In possession of Miss Helen Pendleton of Shepherdstown, W. Va.
Diary of Captain Vincent Moore Butler. In possession of Mrs. George Moore of Charles Town, W. Va.
The Papers of James Rumsey. Virginia State Library, Richmond, Va.
Notes belonging to Colonel B. D. Gibson of Charles Town, W. Va.
Notes belonging to Mrs. Anne Brooke Harold of Charles Town, W. Va.
Notes belonging to Miss Amelia Hopkins of Charles Town, W. Va.
Notes belonging to Miss Laura Mitchell of Charles Town, W. Va.
Notes belonging to Mrs. S. W. Washington of Charles Town, W. Va.
Scrap Book belonging to Mrs. J. M. Miller of Charles Town, W. Va.

PUBLIC RECORDS

American State Papers, 1794, Washington, D. C.
Berkeley County, Petitions, Virginia State Library, Richmond, Va.
Berkeley County, Records, Martinsburg, W. Va.
Cavins, L. V. and Kirby, David, A Study of the Clientele of the Institutions of Higher Education in West Virginia, Charleston, W. Va.: Hood-Hiserman-Brodhag Co., 1938.
Charles Town Methodist Church, Records, Charles Town, W. Va.
Christ Reformed Church, Records, Shepherdstown, W. Va.
Confederate Rosters, Virginia State Library, Richmond, Va.
Donegal and New Castle Presbyteries, Records, Presbyterian Historical Society Library, Philadelphia, Pa.
Executive Journals of the Council of Colonial Virginia, Virginia

State Library, Richmond, Va.
Frederick County, **Records**, Winchester, Va.
Grimsley, G. P., **West Virginia Geological Survey for Jefferson, Berkeley, and Morgan Counties.** Wheeling: Wheeling News Litho. Co., 1916.
Hening, W. W., **The Statutes at Large: Being a Collection of All the Laws of Virginia, 1619-1792,** 13 vols., New York, Philadelphia, and Richmond: 1819-1823.
Jefferson County Board of Education, **Records,** 1929-1932, Charles Town, W. Va.
Jefferson County, **Petitions,** Virginia State Library, Richmond, Va.
Jefferson County, **Records,** Charles Town, W. Va.
Jefferson County Selective Service, **Records,** Charles Town, W. Va.
The Papers of John Brown, Circuit Clerk's Office, Charles Town, W. Va.
Journals of the House of Burgesses of Virginia, 1761-1765, Richmond, Va.
Journals of the House of Delegates of the Commonwealth of Virginia, 1786-1790, Richmond, Va.
Journals of the Senate of the Commonwealth of Virginia, 1786-1787, Richmond, Va.
Records of the Presbyterian Church in the United States of America, Philadelphia: Presbyterian Board of Publication, 1841.
Secretary of the Commonwealth of Virginia, **Records,** Richmond, Va.
Shepherd, Samuel, **The Statutes at Large of Virginia,** 3 vols., Richmond: 1835, 1836.
Spotsylvania County, **Records,** Spotsylvania, Va.
Statutes at Large of the United States, 1794, Washington, D. C.
St. Peter's Lutheran Church, **Records,** Shepherdstown, W. Va.
The War of the Rebellion: A Compilation of the Official Records of the Union and Confederate Armies. 70 vols. in 128 books. Washington: Government Printing Office, 1881-1901.
United States Census, **Reports,** 1810-1940. Washington, D. C.
United States Department of Agriculture, **Yearbook,** 1900, Washington, D. C.
United States Post Office Department, **Records,** Washington, D. C.

United States War Department, **Records,** Washington, D. C.
Virginia Executive Papers, Virginia State Library, Richmond, Va.
Virginia General Assembly, **Acts,** 1786-1869.
Virginia Land Office, **Records,** Richmond, Va.
Virginia Social Statistics, **Reports,** Virginia State Library, Richmond, Va.
West Virginia Legislature, **Acts,** 1863-1912.
West Virginia State Department of Archives and History, **Records,** Charleston, W. Va.

NEWSPAPERS

Baltimore Weekly American, 1859-1860, Baltimore, Md.
Baltimore Weekly Sun, 1859-1860, Baltimore, Md.
Farmers Advocate, 1940, Charles Town, W. Va.
Farmer's Repository, 1808-1827, Charles Town, W. Va.
Independent Democrat, 1859, Charles Town, W. Va.
Richmond Daily Enquirer, 1859, Richmond, Va.
Richmond Times-Dispatch, 1930, Richmond, Va.
Spirit of Jefferson, 1844-1857, 1865-1930, Charles Town, W. Va.
The Independent, 1933-1940, Shepherdstown, W. Va.
The Martinsburg Journal, 1940, Martinsburg, W. Va.
The Shepherdstown Register, 1849-1860, 1865-1940, Shepherdstown, W. Va.
Virginia Free Press, 1831-1861, 1865-1900, Charles Town, W. Va.
Virginia Free Press and Farmer's Repository, 1827-1831, Charles Town, W. Va.
Virginia Republican, 1861, Martinsburg, W. Va.

DIARIES, MEMOIRS, AND WRITINGS OF PUBLIC MEN

Baylor, George, **Bull Run to Bull Run or Four Years in the Army of Northern Virginia.** Richmond, Va.: B. F. Johnson Publishing Co., 1900.
Brown, Thomas, **An Account of the Lineage of the Brown Family** (MS.). 2 vols.
Douglas, Henry Kyd, **I Rode with Stonewall,** Chapel Hill, N. C.: The Univ. of N. C. Press, 1940.
Fitch, John, **The Original Steamboat Supported, or, a Reply to Mr. James Rumsey's Pamphlet, Shewing the True Priority of John Fitch, and the False Datings, &c. of James**

Rumsey, Philadelphia: 1788.

Fitzpatrick, John C. (ed.), **George Washington's Diaries.** 4 vols. Boston and New York: Houghton, Mifflin Co., 1925.

——— **The Writings of George Washington, from the Original Manuscript Sources, 1745-1799.** Washington, D. C.: Government Printing Office.

Ford, Worthington C. (ed.), **The Writings of George Washington.** New York and London: G. P. Putnam's Sons, 1889-1893.

Gilmor, Harry, **Four Years in the Saddle.** New York, 1866.

Jackson, Mary Anna, **Memoirs of Stonewall Jackson.** Louisville, Ky.: 1895.

Johnston, Joseph E., **Narrative of Military Operations.** New York: 1874.

Lucas, D. B., **Memoir of John Yates Beall.** Montreal: John Lovell, 1865.

McIlhany, Edward, **Recollections of a Forty-Niner.** Kansas City, Mo.: Hailman Printing Co., 1908.

Rumsey, James, **A Plan Wherein the Power of Steam is Fully Shewn.** Berkeley County, Va.: 1788.

The Official Letters of Alexander Spotswood (Virginia Historical Society Collection) 2 vols. Richmond, Va.: 1882.

The Papers of George Washington. Library of Congress, Washington, D. C.

MISCELLANEOUS

The Gentleman's Magazine, 1793, London, England.

SECONDARY SOURCES

Alvord, Clarence W. and Bidgood, Lee, **The First Explorations of the Trans-Allegheny Region by the Virginians, 1650-1674.** Cleveland: The Arthur H. Clark Co., 1912.

Ambler, Charles H., **Francis H. Pierpont Union War Governor of Virginia and Father of West Virginia.** Chapel Hill, N. C.: Univ. of N. C. Press, 1937.

——— **Sectionalism in Virginia from 1776 to 1861.** Chicago. Univ. of Chicago Press, 1910.

——— **West Virginia The Mountain State.** New York: Prentice-Hall, 1940.

Andrews, Matthew Page, **The Women of the South in War Times.** Baltimore: The Norman, Remington Co., 1920.

———— **Virginia the Old Dominion.** New York: Doubleday, Doran & Co., 1937.

Atkinson, George W. and Gibbens, Alvaro F., **Prominent Men of West Virginia.** Wheeling: 1890.

Barry, Joseph, **The Strange Story of Harper's Ferry.** Martinsburg, W. Va.: Thompson Brothers, 1903.

Bates, Robert L., **The Story of Smithfield, Jefferson County, W. Va.** (MS.).

Beltzhoover, George M., Jr., **James Rumsey, the Inventor of the Steamboat.** Charleston, W. Va.: W. Va. Historical and Antiquarian Society, 1900.

Bushong, Millard K., "The Washingtons of Jefferson County, West Virginia" (Master's Thesis, W. Va. Univ., 1937).

Cartmell, T. K., **Shenandoah Valley Pioneers and Their Descendants.** Winchester, Va.: The Eddy Press Corp., 1909.

Dandridge, Danske, **Historic Shepherdstown.** Charlottesville, Va.: The Michie Co., 1910.

Dictionary of American Biography (edited by Allen Johnson and Dumas Malone). 20 vols. New York: Charles Scribner's Sons, 1928-1936.

Dixon, Thomas, **The Man in Gray.** New York: Grosset & Dunlap, 1921.

Dodson, Leonidas, **Alexander Spotswood, Governor of Colonial Virginia, 1710-1722.** Philadelphia: Univ. of Penna. Press, 1932.

Draper, Daniel C., "Legal Phases of the Trial of John Brown." **West Virginia History, A Quarterly Magazine** for January, 1940. Charleston, W. Va.

Federal Writers Project of the Works Progress Administration, **Historic Romney, 1762-1937.** 1937.

Gibbons, Herbert A., **John Wanamaker.** 2 vols. New York: Harper & Brothers, 1926.

Gluckman, Arcadi, **United States Martial Pistols and Revolvers.** Buffalo, N. Y.: 1939.

Hancock, Morris H., **Washington's Life and Military Career.** Chicago: Thompson & Thomas, 1902.

Heitman, Francis B., **Historical Register of Officers of the Continental Army during the War of the Revolution.** Washington, D. C.: The Rare Book Shop Pub. Co., 1914.

Hendricks, Sam M., **Military Operations in Jefferson County, Virginia (and West Virginia), 1861-1865.** Charles Town, W. Va.

Historical Hand Atlas (History of Jefferson and Berkeley Counties), Chicago & Toledo: H. H. Hardesty & Co., 1883.

Jefferson, Thomas, **Notes on the State of Virginia.** (Second American Edition). Philadelphia: 1794.

Jefferson County Historical Society, **Magazines, 1936-1940.** Shepherdstown, W. Va.

Kercheval, Samuel, **A History of the Valley of Virginia.** (Fourth Edition). Strasburg, Va.: Shenandoah Publishing House, 1925.

McDonald, William N., **A History of the Laurel Brigade; Originally the Ashby Cavalry of the Army of Northern Virginia and Chew's Battery.** Baltimore: Sun Job Printing Office, 1907.

Marshall, Cushing, **The Story of the Post Office, the Greatest Government Department in All Its Phases.** Boston: A. M. Thayer & Co., 1893.

Meade, Bishop, **Old Churches and Families of Virginia.** 2 vols. Philadelphia: J. P. Lippincott Co., 1857.

Milbourne, Mrs. V. S., **Sketch of Charles Town Baptist Church** (MS.).

Musser, Clifford S., **Two Hundred Years' History of Shepherdstown.** Shepherdstown, W. Va.: 1931.

Norris, J. E., A History of the Lower Shenandoah Valley. Chicago: A. Warner & Co., 1890.

Phillips, Edward H., **The Transfer of Jefferson and Berkeley Counties to West Virginia** (MS.).

Pond, George E., **The Shenandoah Valley in 1864** (Vol. XI of Campaigns of the Civil War). New York: 1884.

Sawyer, Charles W., **Firearms in American History.** Boston, 1910.

Schuricht, Herman, **History of the German Element in Virginia.** 2 vols. Baltimore: Theo. Kroh & Sons, 1898.

Semple, Robert B., **History of the Rise and Progress of the Bap-

tists in Virginia. Richmond: John Lynch, 1810.
Shawkey, Morris P., **West Virginia in History, Life, Literature, and Industry.** 5 vols. Chicago & New York: The Lewis Publishing Co., 1928.
Shirey, Mervin R., "The Granger Movement in West Virginia". (Master's Thesis, W. Va. Univ., 1933).
Stutler, Boyd B., **Captain John Brown and Harpers Ferry.** Charleston, W. Va.: 1926.
Summers, Festus P., **The Baltimore and Ohio in the Civil War.** New York: G. P. Putnam's Sons, 1939.
The South in the Building of the Nation (J. A. C. Chandler et al. eds.). 12 vols. Richmond: The Southern Publication Society, 1909.
Thruston, Mynna, **The Washingtons and Their Colonial Homes in Virginia.** Charles Town, W. Va.: Jefferson Publishing Co.
Turner, Ella May, **James Rumsey, Pioneer in Steam Navigation.** Scottdale, Pa.: Mennonite Publishing House, 1930.
—————— **Stories and Verse of West Virginia.** Scottdale, Pa.: Mennonite Publishing House, 1940.
Villard, Oswald Garrison, **John Brown, 1800-1859, a Biography Fifty Years After.** New York and Boston: Houghton Mifflin Company, 1910.
Virginia State Library, **Bulletins,** 1908-1912, Richmond, Va.
Wayland, John W., **Hopewell Friends History, 1734-1934.** Strasburg, Va.: Shenandoah Publishing House, 1936.
—————— **Samuel Washington** (MS.).
—————— **The German Element of the Shenandoah Valley.** Charlottesville, Va.: The Michie Co., 1907.
Welles, Albert, **The Pedigree and History of the Washington Family.** New York: 1879.
Wise, Barton H., **The Life of Henry A. Wise of Virginia, 1806-1876.** New York: The Macmillan Co., 1899.
Wittke, Carl, **We Who Built America, The Saga of the Immigrant.** New York: Prentice-Hall, 1939.
Woodworth, R. B., **Presbyterian Churches in Jefferson County, West Virginia** (MS.).
—————— **The Charles Town Presbyterian Church, Its Origin and Antecedents** (MS.).

APPENDIX A

ROLLS OF SOLDIERS

REVOLUTIONARY WAR

CAPTAIN HUGH STEPHENSON'S COMPANY.[1]
1775-1776

OFFICERS

Hugh Stephenson, capt.
William Henshaw, 1st lieut.
George Scott, 2nd lieut.
Thomas Hite, 3rd lieut.
Abraham Shepherd, 4th lieut.
William Pyle, ensign
Samuel Finley, 1st serg.
William Kelly, 2nd serg.
Josiah Flagg, 3rd serg.
Henry Bedinger, 4th serg.
John Crawford, 1st corp.
David Miller, 2nd corp.
Henry Barrett, 3rd corp.
George M. Bedinger, 4th corp.
Garrett Tunison, surgeon.
Stephen Vardine, drummer

PRIVATES

Aldridge, Benjamin
Allen, Ebenezer
Anderson, William
Bennet, Edward
Blackhead, Anthony
Blair, William
Bodine, John
Brady, Christopher
Butcher, Richard
Carter, Joseph
Cole, John
Curry, John
Davis, William
Eakins, Robert
Engle, Michael
English, William
Fink, Jacob
Graham, William
Gray, David
Green, William
Hamilton, James
Harrison, Battaille
Haynes, or Hanes, Peter
Hickman, Francis
Hickman, William
Higgins, James
Hill, Peter
Howard, Robert

APPENDIX A

Hulse, Peter
Hunter, William
Kearney, or Kerney, James
Kelly, William
Keys, John
Knox, Thomas
Logan, William
McCann, Robert
McCartney, Henry
McCord, Arthur
McCue, William
McDead, John
McGarah, John
Mange, Peter
Makin, Nicholas
Medcalf, John
Miller, David
Mulliken, John
Murray, Charles
Neal, Richard
Neilson, James
Nelson, Thomas
Oldham, Conway
Pendleton, Nathaniel
Prime, Benjamin
Rider, Adam

Roberts, James
Sheetz, Adam
Shepherd, William
Smith, David
Smoote, John
Steadman, David
Steer, Thomas
Stewart, John
Swearingen, Joseph
Swearingen, Josiah
Tabb, George
Tabb, William
Taylor, George
Tingle, George
Tullis, Aaron
Tullis, Michael
Vaughan, Patrick
Wagoner, Philip
Wallace, James
Waller, William
White, Robert
Williams, Thomas S.
Wright, James
Wysong, Jacob
Yancey, James

CAPTAIN ABRAHAM SHEPHERD'S COMPANY[2]
1776
OFFICERS

Abraham Shepherd, capt.
Samuel Finley, 1st lieut.
William Kelly, 2nd lieut.
Henry Bedinger, 3rd lieut.
John Crawford, 1st serg.
John Kerney, 2nd serg.
Robert Howard, 3rd serg.

Dennis Bush, 4th serg.
John Seaburn, 1st corp.
Evert Hoglant, 2nd corp.
Thomas Knox, 3rd corp.
Jonathan Gibbons, 4th corp.
Stephen Vardine, drummer
Thomas Cook, fifer

PRIVATES

Aitken, James
Anderson, William
Barger, John
Beatty, Thomas
Bedinger, Daniel
Bevins, Samuel
Blackhead, Anthony
Blake, John
Blount, Samuel
Boulden, John
Boyle, William
Brown, George
Brown, James
Brown, Samuel
Bryan, Timmons
Bush, Conrad
Butts, Zechariah
Cabbage, Conrad
Case, William
Cassody, John
Collins, Charles
Connell, Patrick
Cummins, John
Davis, Samuel
Donnelly, William
Fox, James
Fritz, Valentine
Gilmore, David
Good, Peter
Gray, John
Green, William
Griffith, James
Hamilton, James
Hanes, Peter
Harmon, David
Helm, George
Hickman, William

Hicks, William
Hill, Peter
Holmes, John
Hughes, Benjamin
Jones, Charles
Larkin, Anthony
Lewis, John
McComesky, Moses
McKnight, Benjamin
McSwayne, John
Malcher, John
Mitchell, Thomas
Moredock, William
Mountsfield, Thomas
Murphy, Patrick
Myers, Caspar
Neal, Richard
Nixon, John
Peninger, Christian
Pollock, Thomas
Price, Isaac
Rider, Adam
Roberts, James
Rush, Conrad
Russell, Nicholas
Seaman, William
Sheetz, Adam
Snowden, Charles
Snyder, Peter
Stevens, Gabriel
Taylor, George
Vaughan, Patrick
Waller, William
Wilson, William
Wine, Jacob
Wolf, Michael

APPENDIX A 353

CAPTAIN WILLIAM MORGAN'S COMPANY[3]
1776
OFFICERS

William Morgan, capt.

William Lucas, 1st lieut.
Edward Lucas, 2nd lieut.
George M. Bedinger, 3rd lieut.
Cato Moore, 4th lieut.

PRIVATES

Kearsley, John
Morgan, George
Randall, John
Reynolds, George
Robb, Philip
Shaner, George
Staley, Peter
Turner, Thomas

MISCELLANEOUS[4]

Ambrose, ———
Anderson, ———
Angel, John
Arters, ———
Avis, George
Basil, John
Baylor, Robert
Beall, Capt. Isaac
Beeson, William
Bell, Daniel
Bell, Hugh
Beller, H. E.
Bener, George
Bennett, Lieut. William
Beverley, John
Blue, John
Blue, Michael
Boltz, John Jacob
Boltz, John Michael, Sr.
Bowers, George
Boyer, Capt. John
Brady, James
Brady, Capt. William
Breedin, John
Breedin, Richard
Briscoe, Dr. John H.
Briscoe, Capt. Reuben
Broaddus, Lieut. William
Bryan, Daniel
Buckles, Robert, Jr.
Butts, Baruch
Byers, Conrad
Byrnes, Thomas
Cameron, Daniel
Campbell, ———
Chapline, Capt. Abraham
Chapline, Isaac, Sr.
Cherry, Capt. William
Cloak, Capt. ———
Cole, Joseph
Cole, Robert
Cookus, Michael
Copenhover, Joseph
Cowing, James
Crawford, Valentine
Crawford, Col. William

APPENDIX A

Crim, Peter
Crutcher, James
Dandridge, Capt. A. S.
Darnheffer, John
Davenport, Abraham, Sr.
Davenport, Abraham, Jr.
Davenport, John
Davenport, Samuel
Davis, Joseph
Davis, Michael
Delrock, Michael
Duke, Capt. Francis
Duke, George
Duke, James
Duke, John
Duke, Matthew
Eckhart, John
Engle, Philip
Entler, Adam, Sr.
Entler, Adam, Jr.
Entler, Michael
Entler, Philip
Ernst, Martin
Fackler, Jacob
Filch, Daniel
Fisher, Peter
Folk, Daniel
Forman, Capt. William
Frank, Valentine
Freese, John
Gates, Maj. Gen. Horatio
Gerard, ———
Gilbert, Nathan
Gilpin, William
Glenn, James
Goodman, Capt. William
Guseman, Abraham
Halpenny, Thomas
Harkwheimer, John

Harper, James
Hatthiver, George
Haynes, Capt. Jacob
Haynes, or Hanes, John
Hedges, ———
Hendricks, Col. James
Hite, Lieut. George
Hixon, John
Hoffman, John
Hoffman, Robert
Hough, Jacob
Husband, James
Israel, Lieut. ———
Jewett, Matthew
Jewett, Robert
Johnson, Thomas
Jones, Harrison
Kearney, or Kerney, Anthony
Kirby, Patrick
Kremer, or Creamer, ———
Kretzer, James
Lafferty, Thomas
Langham, Lieut. Elias
Lee, Maj. Gen. Charles
Lemon, Lieut. James
Lemon, Capt. John
Levick, Caleb
Lewis, Andrew
Likens, Jacob A.
Linder, ———
Loar, John
Loar, Philip
Lucas, Job
Lyle, ———
McCarty, Andrew
McCormick, Moses
McDonald Hugh
McDonald, John
McGill, Maj. Charles

APPENDIX A

McGuire, James
McIntire, Capt. John
McIntire, William
McKnight, Lieut. John
Market, Jonathan
Mathenger, William
Medlar, Boston
Millan, John
Miller, John
Moler, Adam, Sr.
Moore, Lieut. Cato
Mordand, Michael
Morgan, Dr. Abel
Morgan, Abraham
Morgan, William, Jr.
Morrow, Capt. Charles
Morrow, Col. John
Morrow, Capt. Thomas
Myers, Capt. Ludwig
Nelson, Capt. John
Noble, ———
Nourse, James
Oldham, William
Oliver, Thomas
Orndorff, Capt. Christian
Osborn, Samuel
Ox, George
Peacock, James
Pendleton, Col. Philip
Pierce, John, Sr.
Piper, Jacob
Powell, George
Randall, John
Reynolds, George
Riger, Capt. Burkitt
Riger, Lieut. Leonard
Rion, John
Robb, Philip
Ronemous, Andrew

Ronemous, Conrad
Ronemous, Lewis
Rumsey, James
Rutherford, Robert
Sappington, Thomas
Scott, William
Seaton, James
Shaner, George
Shell, Dr. Nicholas
Shepherd, Col. David
Shepherd, John
Smith, William
Spang, David
Spohn, ———
Staley, Peter
Stephen, Maj. Gen. Adam
Stevens, Gen. Edward
Stephenson, Maj. David
Stephenson, William
Strode, Samuel
Swan, John
Swearingen, Benoni
Swearingen, Hezekiah
Swearingen, Maj. Thomas
Swearingen, Col. Van, Sr.
Swearingen, Van, Jr.
Thornburg, Lieut. Thomas
Turner, Joseph
Unseld, Henry
Vancliff, ———
VanMetre, Isaac
VanMetre, Capt. John
Vining, William
Wallace, Col. George B.
Walls, Maj. George
Washington, Col. Charles
Washington, Col. Samuel
Washington, Thornton
Williams, Henry

Willis, Maj. Francis
Willis, John
Wolf, George
Worthington, ———
Wright, George

Wysong, Fayette
Yeasley, Michael
Young, Charles
Young, Chrisley

WAR OF 1812

CAPTAIN GEORGE W. HUMPHREYS'S COMPANY[5]
August 26, 1814

OFFICERS

George W. Humphreys, captain

Thomas Griggs, 1st lieut.
James L. Ranson, 2nd lieut.
Joseph Blackburn, 3rd lieut.
Samuel Russell, ensign
David Humphreys, serg.
William Gray, serg.
Isaac Keyes, serg.

Elias Shope, serg.
John Bowley, serg.
John Rice, serg.
John B. Shope, corp.
John Kelley, corp.
James McClain, corp.
Daniel W. Griffith, corp.

PRIVATES

Adamson, J.
Avis, James
Avis, Joseph
Avis, Samuel
Bowley, George
Briscoe, Samuel
Britton, Jesse
Brouer, William
Bryson, William
Buckmaster, Theo.
Carson, John
Carter, George
Clarke, James
Conrad, Dan. Pey
Conway, John
Crain, Peter
Crooks, Job

Crow, William
Davis, Samuel
Downey, Edmund R.
Fetzer, Ben
Fielding, Richard
Fouke, Jacob
Fulton, John
Gaither, John
Gallaher, John S.
Gilman, Joshua
Goff, Charles P.
Grove, William
Harris, David
Harrison, Seth
Hawkey, Jacob
Heafer, John
Henderson, Carlton

APPENDIX A

Henderson, Samuel
Huston, Thomas
Hyatt, John
Isler, George
Jett, William
Johnson, John
Keyes, Humphrey
Koontz, Jacob
Little, Charles
McClellan, John
McDonald, Hugh
McKinney, Thomas
McSherry, Richard
Malone, William
Marley, Francis
Mellon, Joseph
Moler, Richard
Moler, Samuel
Newman, Christ.

Paul, Lewis
Roberts, Elias C.
Sands, George
Serrenger, George
Smith, Mathew
Smith, Seth
Spangler, John
Speaks, John
Spots, David
Steadman, Thomas
Stephenson, James
Strider, Samuel
Strider, William
Tabler, John
Taylor, David
Taylor, James
Whaley, James
Wilson, Mathew
Young, Daniel

CAPTAIN JOSEPH GRANTHAM'S COMPANY, 55TH REGIMENT, VIRGINIA MILITIA[6]
March 31, 1814

OFFICERS

Joseph Grantham, captain
Braxton Davenport, 1st lieut.   Thomas Briscoe, 1st ensign
Richard Williams, 2nd lieut.   George Fayman, 2nd ensign

PRIVATES

Alexander, Joseph
Arvin, George
Atwell, Samuel
Avis, John
Barr, James
Beasley, Cornelius
Beasley, William
Beller, Ephraim
Bradshaw, Uriah

Brawner, William
Brown, Elias
Brown, John
Bruce, George
Burnett, Thomas
Cage, William
Callahan, William
Carr, William
Carven, Eden

Colbreth, John
Cole, Abram
Columber, Mathew
Cornicle, John
Dillow, David
Dodenhaver, John
Drew, Daniel
Duke, James
Duke, Samuel
Duke, Thomas
Edmondson, James
Ervin, Lewis
Farman, David
Feagans, Joseph
Fitzgerald, Thomas
Games, Benjamin
Games, Robert
Grove, Jacob
Grove, John
Haines, Philip
Hall, Thomas
Hawkins, John
Hedges, Raleigh T.
Heskitt, James
Howell, John
Hummer, Jacob
Jacobs, Rudolph
James, William
Johnson, John
Johnson, Richard
Johnston, Benjamin
Jordan, Thomas
Lancaster, Samuel
LaRue, William
Lucas, Ashel
McClanahan, Thomas
McCloy, John
McClure, James
McCormick, George L.

McCormick, Joseph
McFallin, John
McKnight, John
Mappins, William
Marmaduke, Jesse
Mercer, Jesse
Mercer, William
Merchant, James
Milburn, James
Mustin, John
Newman, Christian
Novis, James
O'Ferrel, Nathan
Oldfield, James
O'Neill, Robert
O'Neill, Thomas
Park, Elisha
Parmer, William
Poland, Samuel
Price, George
Quingley, William
Sagle, Philip
Shirley, Timothy
Snyder, George
Southerns, William
Staley, Daniel
Sufferans, Daniel
Tansberry, Benjamin
Tarr, Levi
Taylor, John
Tellers, John
Thompson, Cary
Toul, Andrew
Toul, Thomas
Trope, Jacob
VanMetre, Jonathan
VanMetre, Solomon
Vanzant, John L.
Waggoner, Elias

APPENDIX A

Watson, John
Wilhelms, Philip

Young, John C.

CAPTAIN JAMES CONN'S COMPANY OF INFANTRY, 2ND BATTALION, 55TH REGIMENT, 16TH BRIGADE, VIRGINIA MILITIA.[7]
April 16, 1814

Addy, William
Aucheart, Hugh
Basel, Richard
Brenton, William
Brisco, Samuel
Burnett, William
Cochran, William
Conner, Charles
Conner, William
Cooper, Jonah
Cousin, James
Craighill, William P.
Crusin, Levy
Dillow, David
Dillow, James
Dillow, Joseph
Dillow, Peter
Dillow, William, Jr.
Dillow, William, Sr.
Ford, Joseph
Fulton, James
Garison, Washington
Goldsberry, Cornelius
Harris, David
Heath, Jonah
Heskett, Abraham
Heskett, David
Heskett, Evert
Heskett, James
Heskett, John
Heskett, Solomon

Heskett, Thomas
Heskett, William
Howell, James
Howell, John
Hummer, Jacob
Koover, Solomon
Lang, Thomas
Lansbury, William
Lewis, James
Little, William
McKee, James
McWilliams, William
Mackintree, William
Matheny, Jonah
Melton, Robert
Musselman, Daniel
Musselman, Mull
Panter, Jacob
Panter, William
Parmer, William
Patridge, John
Piles, John
Right, Isaac
Roley, William
Saunders, William B.
Slip, John
Steadman, James
Steadman, John
Stewart, Archibald
Taylor, James
Thomas, James

Tracy, Everet
Vestal, David
Walraven, Jonah

Weldon, John
Whitson, John
Yountus, John

CAPTAIN PRESLEY MARMADUKE'S COMPANY OF INFANTRY, 1ST BATTALION, 55TH REGIMENT, VIRGINIA MILITIA.[8]
April 27, 1814

Bagan, William
Beall, George R.
Beall, William
Beller, Ephraim
Boteler, Henry
Bovey, Henry
Briscoe, John
Broome, John M.
Buckles, Daniel
Buckles, William
Busey, Edward
Cameer, John
Cameron, Daniel
Cameron, John
Carr, William
Creamer, Philip
Cressinger, George
Crowl, John
Daugherty, John
Dowden, Thomas
Entler, Daniel
Entler, George
Entler, Joseph
Entler, Martin
Entler, Solomon
Ernst, Jacob
Fayman, Jacob
Fee, Samuel
Ferrell, Nathan O.
Flagg, John R.

Fleming, James
Folk, Fred
Foster, Seth B.
Foulk, Harvey
Grove, William
Hamilton, James
Henry, John B.
Hiser, John
Ingles, Thomas
Jackson, John
James, Thomas
Lafferty, David
Lafferty, Isaac
Laley, Michael
Lane, James T.
Leighliter, Conrad
Line, George
McCormick, John
McFarland, John
Mason, Enoch
Middlecalf, Jacob
Miller, John
Morgan, Daniel
Morgan, Joel
Nicholson, Thomas
Park, William C.
Pascue, Charles
Perry, George
Perry, Jacob
Piper, George

Shepherd, Abraham
Shindler, Conrad
Snider, John
Snyder, George
Spangler, George V.
Sprunkle, Anthony
Staley, Daniel, Jr.
Stokes, John
Sugars, John
Swearingen, Thomas V.
Tapscott, Baker
Toul, Thomas
Towner, Benjamin T.
Wisenall, Henry
Wisenall, Lewis
Worthington, Robert
Wysong, Jacob
Wysong, John

MEXICAN WAR
COMPANY K, 2ND BATTALION, VIRGINIA REGIMENT, UNITED STATES ARMY[9]

OFFICERS

John W. Rowan, capt.
John Avis, 1st lieut.
L. B. Washington, 2nd lieut.
W. McCormick, 2nd lieut.
G. W. Fairfax, 1st serg.
John W. Gallaher, 2nd serg.
L. D. Ball, 3rd serg.
J. M. English, 4th serg.
J. W. Duke, 1st corp.
J. R. Copeland, 2nd corp.
J. Jones, 3rd corp.
W. McClure, 4th corp.
J. Cunningham, fifer
T. H. Douglass, drummer

PRIVATES

Baker, J. H.
Baker, W. A.
Ball, J. B.
Barr, C. P.
Bateman, J. A.
Beam, E.
Birkit, W.
Bougher, P.
Bradford, B. H.
Bragg, W. F.
Brock, J. P.
Bryant, W.
Bush, V. W.
Cable, H. L.
Carlin, C.
Cole, Fayette
Copenhafer, A. J.
Davy, H.
Ellius, S.
Evans, J. L.
Everett, J. L.
French, C.
Galleman, H.
Gibson, C.
Glasscock, D. B.
Gover, W. C.
Granberry, J.
Hafer, R.

Hampton, J. L.
Harding, J. A. B.
Hart, J.
Heflin, J. F.
Henning, J.
Herrington, D.
Hilliard, W.
Hogan, J.
Howell, J. M.
Howell, M. B.
Hurst, S. D.
Kendall, W.
Kile, G. W.
King, J. W.
Kirk, W.
Lancaster, B.
McCrong, T.
McKay, P.
McKinney, J. H.

Mack, G. W.
Mendenall, P.
Miller, P.
Myers, J.
Polard, J. S.
Satterfield, T. R.
Seabright, J.
Sheetz, J. W.
Shelling, B.
Shipman, W. P.
Shryock, J.
Thompson, C. M.
Thomson, J.
Vonreason, H.
Waddle, C.
Wall, T. S.
Watson, D.
Wood, A. J.

REGIMENTAL AND COMPANY OFFICERS OF THE 55TH REGIMENT, VIRGINIA MILITIA, AT THE BEGINNING OF THE CIVIL WAR[10]

John T. Gibson, colonel
J. J. Grantham, lieut. colonel
W. H. T. Lewis, major
R. V. Shirley, major

COMPANIES

The Jefferson Guards, Charles Town, John W. Rowan, capt.
The Botts Greys, Charles Town, Lawson Botts, capt.
The Hamtramck Guards, Shepherdstown, Vincent M. Butler, capt.
The Letcher Riflemen, Duffields, J. H. L. Hunter, capt.
The Floyd Guards, Harpers Ferry, George W. Chambers, capt.
The Shepherdstown Troop, Jacob Reinhart, capt.

The first five were infantry companies, whereas the sixth, The Shepherdstown Troop, was a cavalry organization. Letters were not used to designate these companies until after they had been absorbed into the Confederate army. Becoming part of

APPENDIX A

the famous Stonewall Brigade, these troops saw much fighting. One of the members of the Jefferson Guards was Wells J. Hawks, who later served on General Stonewall Jackson's staff with the rank of major and had charge of the commissary department.

CIVIL WAR
CHEW'S BATTERY, ROSSER'S BRIGADE, ARMY OF NORTHERN VIRGINIA[11]

OFFICERS

R. Preston Chew, capt.
James W. Thomson, 1st lieut.
James H. Williams, 2nd lieut.
John W. Carter, 3rd lieut.
E. L. Yancey, 4th lieut.
A. J. Souder, orderly serg.
George Phillips, 1st serg.
John Kagey, 2nd serg.
Stephen Miller, 3rd serg.
George Everley, 4th serg.
George M. Neese, 1st corp.
Carthage Kendall, 2nd corp.
Gregory Britner, 3rd corp.
Newton Keyes, 4th serg.
Samuel Williams, 5th serg.
Frank Riely, 6th serg.
Samuel Everley, 7th serg.
Mark Rodeffer, 8th serg.
Wm. Shaffer, commissary serg.
John Chew, quartermaster serg.

PRIVATES

Ainsworth, T.
Allen, James
Ambler, John
Anderson, George
Anderson, William
Asberry, Frank
Atkinson, R. C.
Baker, Samuel
Baker, S.
Bird, Derrick
Blair, James
Bliss, A.
Bliss, Thos.
Boston, ———
Bowley, E. Devereaux
Boyd, Philip W.
Brady, Louis
Brady, George
Brook, J. A.
Brooks, E. C.
Brown, Bailey
Brown, Charles
Brownough, J. W.
Buck, Willie
Bull, Americus
Burgess, A. Bealle
Butts, Samuel
Callahan, George
Carpenter, Charles
Carr, J. B.
Cline, Samuel
Conrad, Charles F.
Conrad, Frank E.
Cooper, George

Crawford, ———
Dabney, Basil G.
Dash, George
Davis, George
Davis, Henry
Davis, Thomas
Dawson, George E.
Deahl, Henry
Deck, J.
Deck, Morgan
Deck, William
Dennis, Alfred I.
Dingledine, Jacob
Edmunds, Joseph A.
Everly, Amos F.
Farris, Moses
Few, Samuel
Fiser, Jacob
Fisher, Isaac
Fitzsimmons, Matthew
Fravel, Henry
Fravel, Kyte
Fravel, J. W.
Fravel, John H.
Frazier, William
Fry, Jesse
Fultz, Joe
Fultz, Reuben
Furry, Robert
Furry, William
Furry, Van
Gillock, John
Golladay, Perry
Good, Anthony
Green, John
Haas, Isaac
Hammer, Junius B.
Hare, John
Hattle, H. H.

Helsley, ———
Henkel, Al
Henry, J. W.
Hetzall, ———
Hicklin, George W.
Higgs, John
Hill, William
Holliday, B. T.
Homan, Hiram C.
Homrick, James
Hoofmaster, George
Hoshour, Robert
Huff, George
Huff, H.
Johnson, T. D.
Jolliffe, John
Jones, Thomas
Kagey, Benjamin
Kagey, Joseph
Kapeharte, ———
Kerr, Upsher
Knisely, G.
Knisely, H.
Kolhenhousen, Luther
Lakin, Charles
Landon, ———
Lewis, John
Lindsay, John
Long, Benjamin
Longerbeam, Abe
Longerbeam, Charley
Longerbeam, George
Longerbeam, John
Loveday, John
Lyman, William R.
Lyon, John D.
McGuire, William P.
McVicar, Charles W.
McWilliams, George

APPENDIX A

Magruder, William
Markell, Samuel
Marstella, William
Matheny, Randolph
Miller, A.
Miller, Cal
Miller, F. Thomas
Miller, William
Morrill, Louis D.
Mosher, Frank
Myers, P. H.
Nelson, D.
Nicely, George
Nicely, H.
Nisewander, Abe
Nisewander, George
Noland, C. C.
Noland, L.
Oakes, R.
O'Roark, J.
O'Roark, J. C.
Page, John B.
Painter, George
Phillips, Reuben
Pierce, John
Pifer, Jacob
Powell, P.
Powell, Raleigh
Procter, John
Procter, Noah
Purl, ———
Ramey, W. H.
Reed, Edward
Richard, George W.
Rinker, Fenton
Rivercomb, H.
Rivercomb, W.
Roberts, John
Roberts, Stephen

Rodeffer, John
Rodeffer, Samuel
Rodeffer, Theodore
Roderick, Philip
Ruffin, W. N.
Shaffer, Amos
Shaffer, Ferd
Shaffer, J.
Shaffer, William
Sheetz, John
Shell, George
Stickley, Laban
Stribbling, Frank
Stuart, George
Stuart, John
Suddith, Edward
Supinger, C. B.
Supinger, Lemuel B.
Taylor, J. W.
Teawalt, William
Thompson, Pem. B.
Thompson, William
Thornton, J. R.
Thornton, R. A.
Thuma, Chap.
Venable, James
Vorhees, George
Ware, Nimrod
Weymer, John
Wharton, Isaiah
Wheeler, Mack
Whitaker, F. B.
White, ———
Wickes, William
Williams, Andy
Williams, James H.
Williams, John
Williams, John J.
Williams, Samuel

Williams, T. Clayton
Williamson, Levi
Wiltshire, James G.
Wooton, John R.
Wright, James
Wright, S.
Wunder, J. C.
Wunder, Reuben
Zea, Martin
Zirkle, A. P.

COMPANY A (JEFFERSON GUARDS), 2ND VIRGINIA INFANTRY REGIMENT, STONEWALL BRIGADE, ARMY OF NORTHERN VIRGINIA[12]
(Mustered into service at Harpers Ferry, May 13, 1861)

OFFICERS

John W. Rowan, capt.
Henry B. Davenport, 1st lieut.
David H. Cockrill, 2nd lieut.
George A. S. Davis, 2nd lieut.
Edward R. Harrell, 3rd lieut.
Frank A. Simpson, 4th lieut.
Berkeley W. Moore, serg. major
M. S. B. Robertson, comp. serg.
Dolphin T. Rawlins, 1st serg.
Henry D. Rust, serg.
Thomas B. McIntyre, serg.
Charles W. Trussell, serg.
James W. Myers, serg.
Smith Murphy, serg.
Thomas B. Young, serg.
Randolph K. Ogden, serg.

Charles W. Spates, 1st corp.
James N. Gallaher, 2nd corp.
George W. Noland, 3rd corp.
Albert J. Pendleton, 4th corp.
William H. Moore,
    1st sharpshooter
Henry Cline, 2nd sharpshooter
John H. Leemaster,
    3rd sharpshooter
C. Frank Gallaher,
    4th sharpshooter
George W. Henson, drummer
John F. Webster, tenor horn
Hense Butler, capt's. cook
Robert Ford, Jr., Lieut.
    Davenport's orderly

PRIVATES

Arrington, William H.
Ashbaugh, Jos. H.
Backhouse, Edward C.
Backhouse, George H. C.
Baker, William H.
Bantz, Frederick
Bantz, W. F., Jr.
Barr, Thomas S.
Beall, Benjamin F.

Bolling, James B.
Bowers, John B.
Brown, William J.
Byrd, Lewis F.
Campbell, E. H.
Campbell, James W.
Campbell, John A.
Chapman, John W.
Clarke, George W.

APPENDIX A

Clemens, Francis
Cline, Parron B.
Cockrill, Jos. H.
Coffelt, A.
Coghill, George E.
Coleman, John W.
Conrad, Alexander
Copeland, Philip D.
Cowley, Samuel T.
Craig, William
Crist, Ephraim B.
Cromwell, John O.
Cromwell, Richard H.
Daugherty, Charles A.
Daugherty, James
Davis, George A. S.
Davis, Henry C.
Dorsey, Edward W.
Easterday, John S.
Edmunds, Jos. A.
Faughender, Jos. A.
Gallaher, Wm. W. B.
Garber, Jacob
Gardner, Gervis S.
Gatewood, Robert
Gentry, Eli
Hackley, William F.
Hannah, Thomas W.
Harrell, Edward R.
Harrell, E. S.
Harris, Frank T.
Hartman, P.
Hodges, Benjamin
Hunsicker, Jas. W.
Hunter, Henry C.
Hurst, James A.
Hurst, John H.
Hurst, Manny
Hurst, Thomas G.

Isler, William
Jeter, Jesse
Jeter, R. H.
Jones, James K. P.
Jones, John W.
Kane, William W.
Kanode, Blackford W.
Kimes, William
Kline, H. J.
Kline, Richard P.
Lawrence, John W.
Layman, N.
Lewis, Abram
Lowry, C. B.
Luck, E. W.
McDonough, Chas. F.
McDonough, James
McIntyre, Richard W.
McKinney, Francis E.
Magaha, Wilson H.
Milburn, Henry W.
Mitchell, Burrell D.
Moler, Raleigh
Moore, Albert L.
Moore, Fonrose
Mosley, W. H.
Myers, George N.
Myers, Samuel B.
Nichols, Francis M.
Noel, W. L.
Noland, Samuel C.
O'Bannon, Geo. M. D.
O'Bannon, Henry C.
O'Bannon, William A.
Overton, James W.
Phillips, Wm. T.
Pope, Washington
Pope, William H.
Rawlins, Joseph E.

APPENDIX A

Roby, John
Rodeffer, Henry
Rust, Thomas G.
Rutherford, Gerard D.
Sadler, Leonard L.
Sampson, D.
Shepherd, James W.
Showalter, Robinson
Small, James M.
Smith, George W.
Souders, Fayette B.
Spotts, Joseph B.
Stewart, Charles A.
Stubbs, Lewis
Suddith, George E.
Swartz, James
Thomas, R. N.

Thompson, Charles E.
Triplett, James W.
Trussell, Edward C.
Trussell, James T.
Tutwiler, Jacob O.
Vanvacter, Jos.
Watson, Orsen
Watts, Thomas D.
Weller, William M.
Welsh, George W.
Wheat, F. D.
Whittington, John N.
Whittiker, Fred B.
Wilkerson, W. O.
Wingfield, Thomas H.
Wooddy, W. P. C. S.

COMPANY B (HAMTRAMCK GUARDS), 2ND VIRGINIA INFANTRY REGIMENT, STONEWALL BRIGADE, ARMY OF NORTHERN VIRGINIA[13]
(Mustered into service at Harpers Ferry, May 11, 1861).

OFFICERS

Vincent M. Butler, capt.

Edmund J. Lee, 1st lieut.
John H. Zittle, 2nd lieut.
L. C. Heskitt, 3rd lieut.
Lee H. Moler, 1st serg.
George R. Staley, 2nd serg.
George M. Bast, 2nd serg.
Joseph S. Fleming, 3rd serg.

Henry F. Cameron, 3rd serg.
Henry F. Barnhart, 4th serg.
David H. Hout, 1st corp.
L. M. Taylor, 2nd corp.
John W. Walters, 3rd corp.
William Butler, 4th corp.
Henry Cameron, ensign

PRIVATES

Acton, William
Adams, George E.
Allen, William
Arthur, William L.
Athey, George W.

Bailey, J. G.
Bailey, Nathaniel
Baker, Harrison
Baldwin, John R.
Ball, Nathan

APPENDIX A

Barnhart, Daniel
Barnhart, George W.
Baylor, John T.
Beadle, Samuel
Bedinger, B. P.
Bedinger, George R.
Bell, J. M.
Bellhamer, John
Boteler, A. R., Jr.
Bowers, William
Branscome, Edmond
Brower, J. D.
Callahan, W. M.
Cameron, A. B.
Clem, Noah
Clem, Remington
Clem, William
Coffelt, Israel
Coleman, Seaton
Conley, James B.
Conley, William B.
Cookus, George W.
Cookus, Jacob
Cookus, J. H.
Creasy, Cusbert
Creasy, William E.
Cross, W. T.
Crow, Jacob B.
Culp, John W.
Daniels, B. F.
Davis, C.
Dellinger, A
Dellinger, W. L.
Dick, William R.
Dillinger, Daniel H.
Dillinger, Thomas
Dinwiddie, John W.
Douglas, Henry Kyd
Douglas, John B.

Dowdy, James
Dudley, C.
Entler, Cato M.
Entler, Charles E.
Entler, Daniel M.
Entler, John P.
Ernst, John M.
Ernswiller, F.
Ernswiller, S.
Feaman, John S.
Feaman, W. A.
Feather, P. W.
Fennils, Jacob
Ferrell, Charles F.
Fiser, Eli L.
Folek, George
Frieze, William
Garrison, Louis
Gibson, Booker
Greenwood, James W.
Grove, Frank T.
Grove, W. H.
Gune, William
Hamtramck, S. M.
Hawn, John
Hawn, William C.
Helsey, William
Hensell, William
Hepig, Charles E.
Hessey, Charles E.
Hessey, Edward H.
Hessey, Richard A.
Hoffman, Robert N.
Holtzman, J. W.
Hooks, J. L.
Hout, George W.
Hudson, Samuel
Humrickhouse, G. W.
Humrickhouse, Samuel P.

Hutson, Jacob
Hutson, Robert
Hutson, W. S.
Irvin, H. S.
Jaycox, J. J.
Jones, Henry
Jones, John A.
Kaufman, Jacob
Kaufman, Robert
Kaufman, William
Kerr, John
Keyes, William
Keyser, Charles A.
Kimes, Henry
Kimes, William
Lambert, Charles V.
Lambright, George W.
Lee, Edwin G.
Licklider, George W.
Line, Thomas R.
Little, Columbus M.
Long, Cernad
Lucas, Benjamin F.
Lucas, Edward D.
Lucas, J. T.
Lutz, Mars
McDonald, J. P.
McEndree, Daniel M.
McEndree, William H.
McGlensey, R. R.
McWilliams, William
Magaha, Jacob
Magaha, John W.
Magill, Dr. Charles
Marmaduke, A.
Marmaduke, Jasper
Marmaduke, Luther
Martin, John
Miller, **Ben**

Miller, Jacob G.
Miller, John H.
Miller, William
Moler, Clay
Morgan, William M.
Musgrove, John H.
Nicewarner, J. B.
Osbourn, Nathan
Padgat, I.
Parmell, G. W.
Pendleton, Benj. S.
Peregory, W. R.
Phillips, J.
Poindexter, J. W.
Printz, Gideon
Ray, John
Ray, Samuel H.
Reed, John J.
Rickard, James R.
Rightstine, Adam
Ritter, James
Sandy, John H.
Sandy, Tilman R.
Scheffler, Jerry B.
Secrist, Charles W.
Seibert, Joseph W.
Shaders, ———
Shaner, W. J.
Sheets, Joseph L.
Shepherd, Clarence
Shepherd, J. Smith
Shultz, William M.
Small, James Newton
Smith, Abraham
Smith, Conrad
Snyder, John
Spotts, G. W.
Staley, William H.
Stonebraker, Dr. A. S.

APPENDIX A 371

Tappy, Simon
Tapscott, Samuel
Taylor, J. W.
Taylor, L. T.
Thomas, Robert
Thurston, P. L.
Towner, James L.
Towner, Harris
Unseld, John G.
Vorhees, Jacob F.
Walters, Joseph W.
Weis, James E.
Weis, William
Whitsel, Simon C.

Whitton, William H.
Willingham, James
Willis, J. K.
Wintermoyer, Henry
Wintermoyer, Jacob
Wintermoyer, Jeptha
Wintermoyer, John
Wintermoyer, Thomas
Wintermoyer, William
Wright, John
Yontz, George W.
Yontz, Joseph E.
Yontz, Martin

COMPANY G (BOTTS GREYS), 2ND VIRGINIA INFANTRY REGIMENT, STONEWALL BRIGADE, ARMY OF NORTHERN VIRGINIA[14]
(Mustered into service at Harpers Ferry, May 11, 1861)

OFFICERS

Lawson W. Botts, captain

Edmund L. Moore, capt.
Richard Henry Lee, 1st lieut.
Robert M. English, 2nd lieut.
W. H. T. Lewis, 3rd lieut.
S. Howell Brown, 1st serg.
William C. Sheerer, 2nd serg.

John A. Chew, 3rd serg.
Henry D. Middlekauff, 4th serg.
John E. Hilbert, 1st corp.
James Frazier, 2nd corp.
B. C. Washington, 3rd corp.
Thomas D. Burnett, 4th corp.

PRIVATES

Aisquith, A. H.
Aisquith, Charles W.
Aisquith, William T.
Alexander, Thomas
Alexander, William F.
Annan, Roberdeau
Annan, Robert
Backhouse, Harry
Baird, A. S.

Baylor, George
Beall, John Y.
Beall, William
Beard, Alex
Bennick, J. S.
Bennick, W. S.
Berry, Charles J.
Berry, Lawrence
Biller, ———

Briscoe, James H.
Briscoe, Thomas
Briscoe, William D.
Brown, Daniel
Brown, James
Buck, ———
Burks, Hiram C.
Burnett, William
Butler, Frank G.
Campbell, E. H.
Carrier, Samuel
Chapman, John
Chapman, Joseph
Clarke, F. B.
Colbert, George W.
Colbert, John
Cooke, Bushrod W.
Craighill, Edward A.
Craighill, James B.
Crane, Joseph
Donnelly, John
Douglas, J. A.
Douglas, James T.
Eichelberger, Daniel
Eichelberger, George F.
Emswiler, Wesley
Flagg, George H.
Fry, Solomon
Gaddy, Bat.
Gallaher, C. Horace
Gibson, Gregg
Gibson, Moses
Good, John
Green, Thomas C.
Hatcher, George W.
Hatcher, John E.
Heiskell, Henry Lee
Henderson, David E.
Henderson, Richard

Hewett, R. D.
Hewitt, David
Hicks, James H.
Hite, ———
Hogan, Y. Q.
Hooff, Francis R.
Hooff, James L.
Hooff, William A.
Howell, David
Humphreys, David
Hunter, Thomas
Isler, Charles H.
Jenks, J. A.
Johnson, ———
Keerl, John D.
Keerl, Robert
Keerl, William L.
Larue, Gilbert B.
Lewis, John
Lindamood, John
Lindsay, George
Lippitt, Charles E.
Locke, William M.
McDonald, William N.
McWilliams, Joseph
Mason, J. J.
Manning, Charles J.
Manning, Upshur
Manning, William P.
Maury, Magruder
Maury, Thompson
Medler, Napoleon B.
Moler, Daniel
Moler, David
Moore, Cleon
Moore, George B.
Moore, Vincent B.
Mowry, Ephraim
Noland, J. Henry

APPENDIX A 373

Oglesby, Joshua B.
Padgett, William A.
Page, Lute
Painter, James
Perrow, F. C.
Perry, Dr. Van Lear
Propst, Joel
Puller, William G.
Ranson, Thomas D.
Rawlins, Fayette W
Rector, Edward H.
Redman, Thomas B.
Reid, John W.
Rider, J. William
Rissler, George L.
Rissler, Samuel L.
Robinson, Fred M.
Russell, John
Sadler, J. Newton
Sanborn, John
Selden, John
Sheetz, Samuel
Sheetz, William M.
Sheetz, W. W.
Shrout, Shadrack
Slifer, George
Sly, Silas
Smith, John W.
Sprigg, R. Lamar
Straith, Dr. John A.

Tabb, Charles
Terrill, John
Thomas, James
Thompson, W. T.
Thomson, A. S.
Timberlake, Benj.
Timberlake, D. W.
Timberlake, George
Timberlake, James
Timberlake, Joseph
Timberlake, Seth M.
Timberlake, Thomas
Tucker, William M.
Turpin, G. W.
Turpin, R. G.
Washington, George
Washington, Richard B.
Washington, Thomas B.
Watson, James
Watson, Samuel
Watson, Thomas
Watson, William
Weller, William
White, Benjamin S.
Wilkerson, Ned
Willis, W. Beale
Wiltshire, Charles
Wiltshire, James
Wright, Samuel W.

COMPANY H (LETCHER RIFLEMEN), 2ND VIRGINIA INFANTRY REGIMENT, STONEWALL BRIGADE, ARMY OF NORTHERN VIRGINIA[15]
(Mustered into service at Harpers Ferry, May 12, 1861).

OFFICERS

James H. L. Hunter, capt.
James A. Hurst, 1st lieut.

Thomas Link, 2nd lieut.
J. S. Melvin, 2nd lieut.

James E. Maddox, 1st serg.
John F. Bane, 2nd serg.
Joseph J. Jenkins, 3rd serg.
James W. Chapman, 4th serg.

Alexander L. Osburn, 1st corp.
G. W. Sappington, 2nd corp.
Charles A. Nicely, 3rd corp.
Charles W. Hess, 4th corp.

PRIVATES

Allen, James W.
Allen, John W.
Ashby, George W.
Ashby, John W.
Bales, David
Barringer, Frank
Barringer, George W.
Barringer, James W.
Bell, Henry
Bennett, Mason
Billings, Henry M.
Bonavita, F. W.
Bowers, Samuel
Brantner, George W.
Brown, Joseph W.
Clanahan, Samuel
Colbert, Joseph
Colbert, Richard
Conner, John
Conner, Morris
Craley, Edward
Crim, George
Crisfield, John W.
Crown, F. N.
Currie, Charles
Currie, George E.
Day, John
Deck, Edward C.
Delwin, Patrick
Develine, Giles
Eichelberger, H.
Eichelberger, L.
Eichelberger, S.

Engle, B. F.
Engle, George W.
Engle, John M.
Enos, ———
Eskridge, John W.
Estes, Jackson
Feller, Samuel
Fender, F. L.
Fiery, E.
Foley, John F.
Fraley, Edward
Fraley, G.
Frieze, G. W.
Gageby, David B.
Gall, George
Gall, William
Getts, Joseph
Gibson, S. J.
Gibson, William
Gillock, David
Gollada, Samuel
Greenwood, J. W.
Gruber, A.
Gruber, Benjamin
Gruber, D.
Harding, Charles B.
Harding, S. D.
Harp, John W.
Harvey, Simon W.
Hastings, David B.
Henderson, Richard
Hendricks, Daniel W.
Hendricks, James M.

APPENDIX A

Hendricks, William
Henkle, ———
Hensell, R. S.
Hicks, Joseph
Higgins, Edward
Hill, John
Hodges, John
Hoffman, Thomas
Hogg, T. R.
Horn, George
Hoskin, A.
Howe, George W.
Hunter, J. S.
Jackock, J. J.
Jenkins, Fount.
Jenkins, William
Keigle, B. F.
Kephart, Jacob M.
King, John
Kirkner, J. W.
Knott, E. J.
Lambright, George
Licklider, George
Link, A. Cruzin
Link, Adam
Link, John Allen
McCabe, James
McCormic, W. S.
McWilliams, J. G.
Maddox, James S.
Maddox, R. P.
Marcus, James
Melvin, William
Morison, B.
Padgett, James
Padgett, Joseph
Pitts, John L.
Reed, William
Riley, James

Robinson, James
Robinson, John
Ronemous, Lewis
Ronemous, William
Rowe, Edward
Rutherford, J. T.
Rutherford, John D.
Rutherford, W. T.
Sharff, Jacob
Shepherd, A. H.
Shepherd, James T.
Shepherd, Robert
Shepherd, W. H.
Shire, G. M.
Shirley, G.
Shirley, John
Smith, Thomas
Smith, W. R.
Snyder, John
Snyder, Henry M.
Stephens, Ambrose
Sweeney, C. H.
Thacker, S. E.
Thompson, Robert
Thompson, R. W.
Thomson, P.
Tribby, James
Trussell, James
Weaver, Michael
Webster, R.
Whittington, C.
Whittington, James
Whittington, Neal
Widemyer, ———
Willingham, J. W.
Wintermoyer, John
Winters, Samuel
Wright, D. B.

COMPANY K (FLOYD GUARDS), 2ND VIRGINIA INFANTRY REGIMENT, STONEWALL BRIGADE, ARMY OF NORTHERN VIRGINIA[16]

(Mustered into service at Harpers Ferry, May 17, 1861)

OFFICERS

Charles H. Stewart, capt.

Berkeley W. Moore, capt.
George W. Chambers, capt.
John Avis, 1st lieut.
William Eagle, 1st lieut.
John B. Davis, 2nd lieut.
William F. Engle, 2nd lieut.
Randolph Barton, 2nd lieut.

Charles W. Pope, 1st serg.
John W. Sturdy, 2nd serg.
Palatine Decker, 3rd serg.
Marcellus C. Gompf, 1st corp.
John R. Burke, 2nd corp.
John N. Legg, 3rd corp.
Henry H. Forsythe, 4th corp.

PRIVATES

Allstadt, J. T.
Argenbright, James M.
Arvin, Thomas E.
Ashby, G.
Ashby, William F.
Baker, James
Barr, Thomas O.
Baugher, Isaac N.
Blanchfield, Owen
Bremmerman, John L.
Bull, J.
Burke, Matthew P.
Buzzard, Albert
Callan, Owen
Carr, William
Coakley, John
Colbert, Richard W.
Collis, Joseph W.
Dailey, William
Davis, J. B.
Dixon, Robert W.
Doll, Joseph
Doyle, Garrett

Emerson, Ridgeley
Ferguson, H.
Fishbach, George
Fleming, Jesse A.
Foley, John
Furr, John
Furth, John
Hamilton, Edwin R.
Hays, William
Higgins, Andrew
Hudson, Samuel
Jones, William
Kennedy, William
Kibler, William
Lantz, Nicholas
Leavett, Charles P.
McCabe, James
McCardle, Owen
McCormick, Philip J.
Mackin, Patrick
Miller, Noah
Moore, Cleon
Moore, V. G.

APPENDIX A

Phillips, William
Sale, L. E.
Saunders, John P.
Scott, Michael
Shay, William
Sheetz, George W.
Singleton, J. L.
Skinner, Willis
Slaughtery, John
Smith, Daniel C.
Staples, Walter

Staton, J. N.
Steinecker, Henry Von
Strider, John S.
Terry, Lawrence
Thornton, J. P.
Trail, Charles H.
Trainor, Bernard
Troy, Larry
Vellers, W. F.
Zane, Noah

COMPANY A, 12TH VIRGINIA CAVALRY REGIMENT, ROSSER'S BRIGADE, ARMY OF NORTHERN VIRGINIA[17]

OFFICERS

———— Isabel, first capt.
John H. Henderson, 2nd capt.
James W. Glenn, 3rd capt.
William H. Morrow, 4th capt.
Jacob Engle, 1st lieut.
Samuel M. Engle, 2nd lieut.
Charles Owen, 3rd lieut.
James Osborn, ————
James A. Langdon, 1st serg.
J. Corbin Blackford, corp.
Joseph T. Wright, corp.

PRIVATES

Ashby, G. H.
Ashby, John
Barrett, Charles
Barringer, Frank
Belt, Adam S.
Billmyer, William
Blake, George V.
Blue, John
Blue, Joseph G.
Bolus, Thomas
Boyer, George
Briscoe, William
Brown, Joe
Brown, Thomas
Burner, C. Eldrige

Burns, Isaac
Butt, J. W.
Cameron, William H.
Cincindiver, George
Cincindiver, James
Cincindiver, John
Cincindiver, Samuel
Cockrill, Thomas
Colbert, John
Coleman, John
Coyle, I. M.
Coyle, Jerome B.
Coyle, Joseph H.
Cramer, Robert
Dailey, John

APPENDIX A

Dailey, Richard
Dillow, Joe
Dixon, George
Dooley, Lewis
Doran, J. W.
Doran, Matthew
Doran, James
Dorsey, Patrick
Driscol, Daniel
Engle, Benjamin
Engle, Brent
Engle, Henry
Engle, William
Foreman, Charles
Foreman, Perry
Fraley, David
Fritts, John
Gainor, Patrick
Garrison, Lewis
Geisling, Harrison
Gheisling, James
Glassford, Alexander
Grove, Henry
Harrold, Elihu
Hawthorn, J. J.
Hess, J. Frank
Hicks, John
Hiser, John
Homer, Sandy
Homer, Thomas
Homer, William
Hosier, James
Hughes, Thomas
Jones, George
Jones, James
Jones, John
Kane, Maurice
Keller, John
Kerfott, P.

Kimmell, Isaac
Kimmell, John
Lance, James
Lattimer, T.
Lyons, Jeff
McCann, Patrick
McGarry, James W.
McGlone, Edward
McSherry, William
McWinkle, J.
Manuel, Columbus
Manuel, Jasper
Manuel, John
Manuel, Lucien
Manuel, Thornton
Mercer, Fenton
Miller, James
Moore, Albert
Moore, A. L.
Moore, Vincent
Morgan, Samuel
Nelson, Isaac
Niceley, A. D.
Noland, Charles
O'Bannon, Alfred
O'Bannon, Hiram
O'Connell, Patrick
Painter, Jacob
Painter, James
Painter, Lewis
Pearl, Burt
Piper, James
Piper, William
Ramey, Isaac
Ramey, Michael
Reed, Benjamin
Roberts, Samuel
Roberts, William
Rockenbaugh, John W.

APPENDIX A

Sager, John
Seldon, Carey
Sencindiver, G. W.
Shepherd, William
Shipway, Thomas
Skinner, William
Small, A. S.
Souders, F. B.
Spates, Charles
Staley, Parin
Staub, Jesse
Staub, Lewis
Taylor, John
Thompson, Charles
Thompson, Josiah
Trist, John
Vaughan, S.
Wageley, William
Way, Harrison A.
Webster, Dallas
Webster, Thomas D.
Whittington, Daniel
Whittington, James C.
Whittington, James W.
Whittington, John N.
Wiltshire, Charles B.
Wiltshire, James G.
Wright, W. H.
Yoll, Stephen
Zombro, George

COMPANY B, 12TH VIRGINIA CAVALRY REGIMENT, ROSSER'S BRIGADE, ARMY OF NORTHERN VIRGINIA[18]

OFFICERS

Robert W. Baylor, capt.

William S. Thompson, capt.
Milton Rouss, 1st lieut.
George Rowland, 2nd lieut.
B. C. Washington, 2nd lieut.
George Baylor, 3rd lieut.
S. W. Timberlake, orderly serg.
J. H. Conklyn, 2nd serg.
C. W. Trussell, 3rd serg.
W. C. Frazier, 4th serg.
George M. Lewis, 4th serg.
William J. Roberts, 5th serg.
John W. Smith, 1st corp.
Joseph A. Bartlett, 2nd corp.
Lucien Chamberlain, 3rd corp.
James L. Timberlake, 3rd corp.
Robert W. North, 4th corp.

PRIVATES

Abrill, Robert P.
Aisquith, E. M.
Aisquith, William
Alexander, Charles
Alexander, Herbert
Allen, William
Anderson, Isaac
Averill, William
Baker, William H.
Baney, Thaddeus
Barringer, James
Baylor, Richard C.
Baylor, Robert W., Jr.
Beall, H. D.
Bell, Daniel
Berry, Charles

APPENDIX A

Boley, Frank
Bonham, Edward
Butler, J. D.
Callahan, Ferdinand
Cameron, William H.
Castleman, Robert
Chew, John
Clapsaddle, William
Colbert, Joseph
Coleman, John
Conklyn, C. C.
Conrad, J. M.
Conrad, Morris
Cooke, B. W.
Cookus, Robert
Copeland, Philip D.
Coyle, James W.
Craighill, Robert
Crane, Charles L.
Crane, James C.
Crane, Joseph
Creaton, George
Dovenberger, Daniel
Easterday, John S.
Easterday, Joseph H.
Eastham, Jackson
Eddins, H. C.
English, W. D.
Faughnder, Daniel
Faughnder, Fenton
Fry, Jesse P.
Fry, Joseph D.
Furley, John
Gallaher, Edward
Gallaher, James N.
Gallaher, J. H.
Gallaher, J. S.
Garrison, Thomas
Gibson, William H.

Gordon, Abraham
Grantham, John S.
Hardesty, Charles R.
Harvey, William
Hatcher, William R.
Henderson, Charles E.
Henderson, Robert
Heskitt, William
Hesser, C. F.
Hilbert, George
Hilbert, John E.
Hoffmaster, John W.
Howell, John M.
Hunter, H. C.
Hutchinson, Julian
Huyett, R. D.
Isler, C. H.
Johnson, Charles G.
Jordan, M. F.
Kanode, B. W.
Lackland, E. M.
Lewis, B. F.
Lewis, David
Lewis, Elisha
Lewis, F. J.
Lewis, John L.
Locke, William F.
McCluer, John
McDonough, James
McKown, Warner
Manning, Addison D.
Manning, Charles J.
Manning, F. J.
Manning, George U.
Manning, William P.
Mason, William S.
Moore, Monrose
Mumaw, W. H.
Myers, Thomas

APPENDIX A

Neill, Samuel B.
Nicely, Charles
Noland, Samuel C.
Partlow, E. L.
Randall, James
Ranson, B. B.
Ranson, Thomas D.
Redman, Thomas B.
Rickamore, George C.
Ridgway, Josiah
Rouss, Charles B.
Rowland, J. H.
Rucker, S.
Ryman, F.
Sadler, L. L.
Selden, W. C.
Shewbridge, J. H.
Smith, John W.
Starry, Tustin
Strider, Isaac H.
Tearney, George
Tearney, Leonidas
Terrill, John U.
Terrill, Philip
Thomson, William S.
Timberlake, George
Timberlake, Harry
Timberlake, James H.
Timberlake, Joseph E.
Timberlake, T. W.

Timberlake, Richard
Timberlake, Stephen
Trussell, E. C.
Trussell, J. T.
Trussell, Moses E.
Wade, Algernon S.
Walker, George
Walker, John
Washington, George
Washington, James C.
Watkins, John
West, A. J.
Whittington, Benjamin
Whittington, James
Willis, Albert
Willis, Frank
Willis, W. Beale
Wilson, William L.
Wiltshire, J. C.
Wingard, George
Wolfe, John W.
Workman, John
Wright, Samuel
Wysong, R. L.
Yates, John O.
Young, Mason E.
Zombro, James W.
Zombro, John D.
Zombro, Thomas B.

COMPANY D, 12TH VIRGINIA CAVALRY REGIMENT, ROSSER'S BRIGADE, ARMY OF NORTHERN VIRGINIA[19]

OFFICERS

John L. Knott, major
H. W. Kearney, capt.
George Engle, 1st lieut.
John W. James, 2nd lieut.

Benjamin Lucas, 3rd lieut.
Charles R. Haines, 1st serg.
John Allen, 2nd serg.
J. W. McCleary, 3rd serg.

APPENDIX A

G. W. Watson, 4th serg.
Andrew Higgins, 5th serg.
James Allen, 1st corp.

J. W. Coffinbarger, 2nd corp.
E. C. Deck, 3rd corp.
A. L. Osbourn, 4th corp.

PRIVATES

Adams, W. A.
Andrews, Daniel
Andrews, John
Athey, James
Backus, H. C.
Badger, John
Bane, Garrett
Banks, Washington
Barnhart, George
Berlin, Charles
Beyer, Gus
Bowers, George W.
Brantner, George
Brubaker, Isaac
Burley, P.
Caton, George W.
Chambers, I. M.
Chambers, M.
Chambers, T. T.
Claw, A. J.
Clymer, Dan
Clymer, Frank
Colbert, Richard
Conrad, Alexander
Conrad, Nathaniel
Cook, George
Cook, James
Currie, Charles
Day, Samuel
Deck, Fred
Dickson, J. C.
Dodson, Thomas
Doran, W.
Elliott, Charles

Engle, Benjamin
Engle, H. C.
Eskridge, Thomas
Farnsworth, John B.
Fincham, H.
Flanagan, William
Fraley, Dave
Fraley, James
Frazier, James
Furrey, John
Furrey, Martin
Gall, George
Gay, James
Goodwin, Charles
Hagley, George H.
Halpin, Robert
Hanby, William
Hartman, George
Hastings, Daniel
Hayslett, John
Hayslett, William
Heckroach, William
Hendricks, Daniel W.
Hendricks, J. M.
Hendricks, Tobias
Henkle, D. Grove
Henry, William
Herr, E. G. W.
Hess, Charles
Hicks, J. W.
Higgins, Owen
Hipsley, Thomas P.
Hoffman, David
Hoffman, George

APPENDIX A

Hoffman, John
Holmes, David C.
Hough, Mason
House, Samuel
Hudson, Charles
Johnson, E. C.
Johnson, George
Johnson, William
Kephart, Jacob
Kephart, W. H. H.
Keys, James
Keys, J. Richard
Kilmer, Harry
Kirby, T. L.
Kisner, Joseph
Knott, Charles H.
Knott, George S.
Knott, Samuel M.
Lambert, Charles
Leopold, Andrew
Lewis, John
Lewis, David
Licklider, Frank
Licklider, John
Licklider, Joseph S.
Loudon, John
McBee, William
McGarry, James W.
Mackin, Patrick
Melvin, James
Melvin, William
Merritt, Henry
Minghinni, Joseph
Moler, D. Griff
Moler, George
Moler, H. Clay
Moler, Jacob
Moler, Newton
Moler, Raleigh

Moler, Rollin
Moler, Sanders
Moler, William J.
Moore, Bart
Moore, George
Moore, Hedley
Morgan, Frank
Morningstar, Charles
Nichols, Lewis
Ogden, John J.
Osbourn, George W.
Osbourn, James B.
Osbourn, Robert L.
Patten, James
Polly, Samuel
Prather, Charles
Prather, Denton
Pretzman, Wallace
Reed, Samuel
Reinhart, A. Philip
Reinhart, William
Ritter, James
Roberts, James
Roberts, Robert
Roe, George
Ronemous, George
Rowdan, John
Rutherford, Thomas
Shewbridge, John H.
Shirley, James
Show, Collin
Simpson, John T.
Slavin, John
Smith, George
Smith, William
Snyder, James
Snyder, John
Staley, William
Strider, Howard

Swimley, H. Harrison
Swimley, J. Samuel
Walker, T. L.
Ware, Richard
Watson, Bart
Watson, Eph
Watson, William

Welch, Michael
Whittington, James
Wilson, John
Wintermoyer, William
Wright, James
Yates, John R.
Zombro, Isaac

COMPANY F, 1ST VIRGINIA CAVALRY REGIMENT, WICKHAM'S BRIGADE, ARMY OF NORTHERN VIRGINIA[2d]

OFFICERS

William A. Morgan, capt.
Milton J. Billmyer, 1st lieut.
J. S. Tanner, 2nd lieut.
John A. Jones, 2nd lieut.
Joseph Reinhart, 2nd lieut.
J. M. Billmyer, 1st serg.

W. N. Lemen, 2nd serg.
John T. Billmyer, 3rd serg.
T. W. Latimer, 1st corp.
J. S. Stonebraker, 2nd corp.
William Hunter, 3rd corp.
Henry Hagan, 4th corp.

PRIVATES

Andrews, George
Baker, N. D.
Billmyer, R. L.
Bledsoe, James
Brown, A. J.
Burk, F. W.
Burk, George
Burk, John
Burk, Polk
Butler, William
Conley, James P.
Daniels, W. Benjamin
Davidson, John
Deck, William
Driscoll, John
Eakle, John
Ellis, Benjamin M.
Ellis, E.
Engle, William

Evans, A. Mason
Feaman, W.
Ford, James P.
Ford, T.
Fryatt, J. W.
Gall, Christian
Grove, F. T.
Grove, J. S.
Hamil, James
Hammond, J. T.
Harnick, Harvey
Harnick, Jesse
Harris, George
Hawn, David
Hensell, Edward L.
Hensell, Scott
Hensell, William
Herron, David
Hill, George

APPENDIX A

Hill, John P.
Hipsly, Thomas
Hite, Cornelius
Hite, Fontaine
Holliday, John W.
James, Peyton
Johnson, William C.
Jones, Frank
Jones, Isaac
Jones, Reynolds
Jones, Samuel
Jones, Thomas F.
Jones, W. T.
Kearfoot, John P.
Kearney, J. Briscoe
Kearney, W. A.
Keplinger, J. F.
Keys, William
Kimes, Newton
Knott, C. O.
Koontz, Thornton
Kimes, George H.
Lease, G. W.
Lee, A. F.
Lemen, John J.
Lemen, Thomas T.
Leopold, Andrew
Lincoln, Abraham
Lucas, Frank
Lucas, George R.
Lucas, Louis C.
Lucas, R. R.
Lucas, William
McMullen, Charles
McQuilken, W. H.
Marshall, J. J.
Marshall, Mason
Marshall, P. P.
Martin, Saron

Mash, Joe
Miller, William
Morgan, Daniel H.
Morgan, J. S.
Morrison, William
Mugler, D.
Mugler, P.
Myers, David
Myers, John W.
Nottingham, David
Nottingham, Joseph
O'Brien, Nathan
O'Brien, W.
Osbourn, Robert L.
Payne, Abner
Payne, G. W.
Perry, L. C.
Peyton, E. B.
Peyton, James
Peyton, Thomas
Powell, H. P.
Randall, A. W.
Reynolds, Henry C.
Reynolds, J. C.
Roberts, J. W.
Roberts, Daniel
Rodgers, Thomas
Ronemous, John
Rowsy, A.
Rush, Jacob
Sanford, Van L.
Sanford, William
Seibert, John
Seibert, Oliver
Shafer, Edward
Shepherd, W. M.
Showman, Oliver
Small, David
Small, James H.

Small, Mack
Small, M. B.
Smith, A. Magill
Smith, B. F.
Smith, James
Smith, John
Spotts, George
Spotts, Jacob
Spotts, John W.
Spotts, William
Taylor, David
Taylor, J. F.
Tice, John
Turner, Magill
VanMeter, A. M.

VanMeter, Joseph B.
VanMeter, M. S.
Walters, James
Walters, John
Warner, George
Weaver, John
Welsh, Clinton
Welsh, William
Williamson, M. W.
Williamson, Thomas
Williamson, White
Wilson, E.
Wysong, R. L.
Yontz, George
Yount, Nathan

SPANISH-AMERICAN WAR

COMPANY G (NATIONAL GUARD), 1ST WEST VIRGINIA INFANTRY REGIMENT, UNITED STATES ARMY[21]
(Mustered into service in April, 1898).

OFFICERS

James M. Pyne, capt.

Noah H. Hale, 1st lieut.
Oscar A. Price, 2nd lieut.
Thomas P. Earnshaw, serg.
John Strother, serg.
Andrew C. Glaize, serg.
Amos F. Dunlap, serg.
James M. Moore, serg.
John R. Burr, serg.
William S. Stillwell, corp.
Howard J. Smith, corp.

Andrew F. Wait, corp.
Joseph B. Scott, corp.
Ferd W. Snyder, corp.
John W. Howard, corp.
Dallas C. Painter, corp.
George W. T. Ware, corp.
Guy W. Lynn, corp.
Clinton O. Lemon, corp.
Edward F. Pollock, corp.
Matthew J. Dunahue, corp.

PRIVATES

Ayers, John C.
Ayers, Thomas E.

Bayard, Samuel
Beckner, Blanchard

APPENDIX A

Bickley, Richard
Black, Charles E.
Brown, Thomas F.
Clayton, John R.
Combs, Lion H.
Condran, James H.
Cox, John L.
Crond, John
Davis, James S.
Dolan, Frank W.
Dolan, Henry W.
Ewing, William H.
Fetty, Lloyd
Gillison, William L.
Glaize, Clifton B.
Grim, William J.
Grimes, Charles H.
Hatfield, John S.
Horbarger, Joseph
Johnston, Frank C.
Jolliffe, Jacob C.
Linsley, Walter
Livesay, Jesse J.
Lownes, Leon H.
Lynn, Bernard A.
McCloy, Glen C.
Martin, John W.
Midkiff, Harry C.
Milbee, Charles

Miller, William G.
Moody, Benjamin R.
Moore, Orson A.
Moore, W. L.
Morgan, Whitner R.
Mosi, Wilmer
Murray, Joseph
Myers, Robert P.
Nutter, James
Nuzum, Harry E.
Parsons, Jefferson
Patton, George S.
Raimine, William
Roach, William H.
Rutherford, Charles
Seese, Amidee
Shanklin, William C.
Shumaker, Charles
Toothman, E. B.
Vanmeter, Benjamin F.
Viands, Robert L.
Vincent, Delmore L.
Walters, Herbert
Ware, Edward
White, John W.
Willis, John W.
Wilson, Charles H.
Zane, Harry M.

COMPANY M, 2ND WEST VIRGINIA VOLUNTEER INFANTRY REGIMENT, UNITED STATES ARMY[22]
(Mustered into service July 9, 1898)

OFFICERS

Henry Clay Getzendanner, capt.

Kemble White, 1st lieut.
John Henshaw, 2nd lieut.
Frank J. Manning, 1st serg.

Spalding Winchester, 2nd serg.
Archibald Morgan, 3rd serg.
Willie F. Patton, 4th serg.

Paul Gassman, 5th serg.
Albert Chapline, 6th serg.
David S. Brown, corp.
Harry R. Fayman, corp.
William H. Wilson, corp.
Wilber F. Crutchley, corp.
Jacob A. Kidwiler, corp.

Thomas N. Shewbridge, corp.
George F. Whitmore, corp.
Daniel L. Moler, corp.
John P. Thompson, corp.
Samuel F. Pierson, corp.
Thomas R. Rodgers, corp.
Frank L. Billmyer, corp.

PRIVATES

Alkire, William E.
Anthony, William H.
Arbogart, Owen
Arvin, Robert L.
August, Louis
Barton, Harry I.
Beaver, Robert M.
Bledsoe, Champion T.
Board, Charles
Brinkley, James E.
Burkhardt, William
Burkholder, Ferdinand
Burns, William D.
Casto, James T.
Connely, Franklin
Connors, George W., Jr.
Davis, James L.
Dorr, Harry F.
Duff, Reuben D.
Ehrhart, James A.
Ellis, George M.
Exline, Edward
Fidinger, Christian
Frederick, John D.
Gray, William C.
Greathouse, Oscar
Green, Philip
Grubb, John N.
Hansel, James
Harris, William M.

Johnston, John H.
Justice, Walter
Leonard, Clyde C.
Lovejoy, Ferdinand
McDonough, John A.
McElwain, Samuel L.
McLain, Pearl
Mace, John H.
Marlatt, Harry D.
Maroney, Stephen
Marrow, Percy H.
Martin, Walter F.
Mills, John E.
Mollihan, William
Morris, George W.
Mose, Richard
Myers, Columbus J.
Myers, John H.
Myers, William R.
Nordeck, William D.
O'Hare, Edwin
Phillips, Melvin
Pierson, Daniel D.
Plant, Marshall
Racer, Benjamin B.
Saunders, Charles
Schwarz, Benjamin C.
Sears, Benjamin C.
Shipes, William S.
Sisler, John H.

APPENDIX A 389

Smith, Andrew J.
Smith, Ira O.
Smith, Lothrom R.
Spralding, Calvin F.
Stump, Okey M.
Summers, Ronnie
Swain, Newton A.
Thomas, Thomas B.
Tuaning, Arthur B.

Updegrove, John E.
Walker, Charles
West, Albert
Williams, Albert L.
Wolfe, Absalom M.
Wood, Arthur B.
Workman, Frederick
Workman, William W.
Zeiher, Henry H.

WORLD WAR[23]
1917—1918
WHITE

Alexander, Charles Nelson
Alfriend, John S., Jr.
Allen, Howard
Ambrose, David Henry
Anderson, Perry Albert
Anderson, William Neill
Bagent, Daniel Howard
Bagent, James Edward
Baker, Courtland Darke
Baker, Henry S., Jr.
Baker, Samuel H.
Ballinger, Lewis C.
Bane, Frank
Banks, Horace McMurran
Banks, Washington Grover
Barnes, John Hughson
Barnhart, James Edward, Jr.
Barron, Lloyd E.
Bates, Harry H.
Bates, Lieut. Robert Lee
Beckwith, Frank J.
Bell, Lieut. Ellis Clifton
Bell, Marion Border
Bell, Royal Austin

Beltzhoover, Lieut. Geo. M., Jr.
Benner, Grover C.
Best, William Elliott
Biller, Harry Walton
Bishop, John Peale
Black, Lieut. Col. Hanson B.
Black, John K.
Blackford, Henry J.
Blackford, William B.
Blake, Walter Garry
Blessing, Herbert S., Jr.
Bowers, Lester Lee
Boyd, Elic McDaniel
Boyd, Woodford Lee
Boyer, Lucas
Bradley, William Franklin
Bragonier, Arthur Taylor
Bready, Gordon
Breeden, Herbert
Brooke, Francis John T.
Brown, Forrest A.
Brown, Harry Leonard
Brown, Lee William
Brown, S. Howell

APPENDIX A

Burleigh, Thomas J., Jr.
Butts, James Charles
Byers, Raymond Hendricks
Cain, Ashby Francis
Campbell, William C.
Carper, Wilbur Lee
Casey, Earl DeWitt
Chinto, Bassie
Clipp, Ernest Andrew
Clipp, Roger A.
Cockrell, John David
Colston, Randolph C., Jr.
Colston, Robert Dean
Conrad, Harry
Cooke, Henry Harrison
Cooke, Roy E.
Cookus, John Wm. S.
Cornwell, Leslie K.
Coyle, George Snyder
Crabbe, Ray W.
Crawford, George W.
Cromwell, Rudolph E.
Crowl, Robert Lee
Dailey, Jesse S.
Daniel, Francis W.
Darr, Harry Hudson
Davidson, Hugh E.
Davis, Edward N.
Davis, Harvey Frank
Davis, Norvel Reed
Decker, Edward F.
Denny, George H.
Dillow, Charles F.
Dillow, George W.
Dodson, Gilbert Lee
Donley, Raleigh A.
Dorsey, Robert Earl
Drish, Frank H.
Dunn, James Robert

Dunn, Perry
Eaton, Clarence Benjamin
Eby, Cecil D.
Eddy, Thomas Milton
Edmonds, John H.
Edwards, Ivan Bates
Elliott, Roy D.
Engle, C. Preston
Feagans, Harry R.
Fellers, Charles R.
Field, Rodney H.
Flaherty, Hubert B.
Flanagan, Oscar S.
Fleming, John C.
Folk, David
Foster, Cleveland Lee
Fry, Edgar Neill
Furr, Harry S.
Furr, Wilbur J.
Furr, Willie Lee
Galli, Ernidio
Gardner, Glenn G.
Geary, John Patrick
Getzendanner, W. J.
Giogtra, Vincenzo
Golady, Claude
Gordon, G. T. W.
Gore, Charles E.
Gore, John W.
Gravatt, W. Loyall
Gray, James Lawrence
Green, Bedford B.
Grey, Charles Samuel
Grey, Ellesey Linden
Grove, Clarence C.
Grove, Dearl Armistead
Grove, Frank J.
Grove, George M.
Guiseppe, Moietti

APPENDIX A

Hahn, Benjamin F.
Hall, Capt. Baker
Harder, Samuel Henry
Hardin, James Thomas
Hardy, Clarence E.
Hardy, Elmer Bryan
Hawk, John Lewis
Hawk, William E.
Heafer, Oliver Victor
Heinz, Samuel C.
Hendricks, Garland W.
Hendricks, John W.
Henkle, Edward Earl
Henry, Albert Lloyd
Henry, Marvin Wharton
Herr, Walter Edward
Higgs, Benjamin F.
Higgs, Ernest E.
Hill, Charles Edgar
Hill, Karl Ellsworth
Hill, Walter Hugh
Hirshman, Charles
Hirshman, Kirby Lee
Hoffman, Benjamin
Hoffman, Orland E.
Hoffman, Oscar L.
Hoffman, Raleigh P.
Hoffman, Robert L.
Hoffmaster, Louis A.
Hoffmaster, Roy H.
Hoke, Bernard B.
Hooe, Franklin
Hooe, Garland H.
Hooe, Oscar Lucas
Hostler, John W.
Houser, George S.
Humrickhouse, Davis B.
Hyatt, William L.
Jackson, Robert Lee

Jackson, Wade H.
Jacobs, Edgar F.
Jenkins, Rodney
Jenkins, Walter E.
Johnson, Garland H.
Johnson, Harrison W.
Johnson, Obie
Johnston, George W.
Johnston, Norman E.
Jones, Charles N.
Jones, David T.
Jones, George W.
Jones, John F.
Jones, Paxton
Kelly, Martin, Jr.
Kidwell, Clarence
Kidwell, Robert
Kirby, Norval C.
Kline, John William
Knight, Henry Clay
Knight, Thomas R.
Knott, Edgar S.
Knott, Robert M.
Knott, Walter
Koonce, Charles H., Jr.
Koonce, George S.
Lancaster, Edgar E.
Landis, Wilbur H.
Langdon, Harry B.
Latimer, Capt. Julian B.
Lee, John Pitt, Jr.
Lemen, Willoughby M.
Lewis, John F.
Lewis, John R.
Lilla, Vincenzo
Link, Dennis D.
Link, William H.
Lloyd, Capt. William W.
Locke, James Strider

Long, Charles Raymond
Longerbeam, J. William
Longerbeam, Thomas J.
Louden, Norman S.
Lowe, Ira Titus
Lowe, John S.
Lucas, Maj. John
Luckett, George N.
Luckett, Stephen L.
Luke, John W.
Luke, Richard T.
Lynch, Charles I.
Lynch, James M.
Lyne, Mason E.
McCarty, Robert W.
McCauley, James H.
McCormack, Harry
McDonald, Carroll E.
McDonald, Charles W.
McDonald, E. A.
McDonald, Frank A.
McDonald, Gloyd A.
McDonald, James W.
McDonald, Lieut. Marshall W.
McGarry, Jesse
McKee, George R.
McKee, Kirkland S.
McKee, Robert B.
McNamara, Ira J.
McSherry, Joseph W.
Maddex, Grover
Mahoney, Wesley
Mansfield, Elsworth C.
Mansfield, Robert S.
Manuel, Roger
Marcus, Raymond L.
Marlatt, George E.
Mater, Oscar B.
Mauzy, Joseph K.

Mercer, Harry B.
Merchant, Marion G.
Milbourne, D. Fairfax
Milbourne, Harvey Lee
Miller, Clyde P.
Miller, James E.
Miller, Raymond W.
Miller, William L.
Miller, Wilmer B.
Milton, James W.
Mitchell, William
Mock, Granville A.
Moler, Hugh S.
Moler, James B.
Moler, Marshal C.
Moler, Raleigh M.
Moler, Robert C.
Moler, Wallace M.
Moore, Robert T.
Morgan, William A.
Morrow, Joseph W.
Morrow, Lyndon T.
Morrow, William H.
Myers, Donald H.
Myers, Roy V.
Nicewarner, William P.
Nichols, D. Shirley
Nichols, Joseph
Nichols, Lewis Duke
O'Bryan, Emmett J.
Oden, Raymond S.
Osbourn, Lieut. Cleon S.
Ott, Frank S.
Ott, George E.
Ott, Grover E.
Ott, Lawrence F.
Ott, Raymond D.
Painter, Harry E.
Peer, Charles O.

APPENDIX A

Pendleton, John H.
Penwell, Bushrod
Perks, Joseph Ward
Perry, John Leonard
Perry, William M.
Perry, William P. C.
Phillips, Gerard D.
Phillips, Harry R.
Piper, Garland W.
Piper, Lawrence W.
Porterfield, John T.
Price, Jesse Edward
Price, J. Levering
Pyles, Norman L.
Quick, Sgt. Maj. John H.
Racey, Walter Boyd
Ramey, Ensign Arthur G.
Ramey, Walter Carson
Reek, Charles Henry
Reinhart, Henry B.
Reinhart, Thomas C.
Riddleberger, Fred M.
Ridgeway, Allen Leon
Ridgeway, Robert Neal
Rightstine, Joseph W.
Rinaldi, Enrico
Rissler, Brown L.
Ritenour, Claude D.
Roberts, John A.
Rockenbaugh, Carroll C.
Rockenbaugh, E. Glenn
Rockenbaugh, William D.
Rodeffer, Earl H.
Roderick, Edgar D.
Roderick, Elmer E.
Roeder, Harry R.
Romine, Cecil E.
Rouzee, James H.
Rouss, Lieut. Alex. H. S.

Russell, Joseph A.
Russell, Willard C.
Sager, Allen T.
Sager, Charley L.
Sager, Eutaw F.
Sampson, Arthur N.
Scarlett, Oscar M.
Scarlett, Walter F.
Schell, Thomas E.
Schley, John E.
Sechrist, Howard L.
Shaffer, Raleigh Boyd
Shanholtzer, James C.
Shawen, Edgar A.
Shepherd, Henry
Shipley, R. D.
Shipley, Stephen B. E.
Shirley, John T.
Shreck, Howard E.
Shugart, Benjamin R.
Shugart, Leland F.
Shull, Ernest Lee
Sibert, Daniel H.
Siford, William
Sigler, Henry M.
Simpson, James C.
Skinner, John M.
Slusher, James E.
Snowden, Herman W.
Snowden, John L.
Snyder, Luther D.
Snyder, Nelson T., Jr.
Snyder, William B.
Souders, Fayette
Sponsler, B. C.
Springer, Charles A.
Springer, George S.
Staubs, Earl William
Swann, Hunter F.

Tabb, C. Creighton
Tabler, D. Harvey
Taylor, Edmund R.
Tearney, Edward
Tennant, Elmer C.
Tharp, Harry R.
Thomas, Roy Earl
Thomas, Wilbur Bushrod
Thompson, Joe
Triplett, Charles C.
Trundle, Mason N.
Trussell, Charles F.
Underwood, Harry T.
Venning, Edward W.
Wageley, Arthur C.
Walker, George W.
Walker, Harry Neill
Wall, C. Fred
Walper, Golden H.
Walper, Harry H.
Walraven, John G.
Ware, James Howard
Watson, Forrest E.
Watson, Robert S.
Weaver, Frank R.
Webb, Joseph Edgar
Webster, Frank E.
Webster, Gordon
Webster, John Lacey
Weller, Franklin J.
Weller, Henry W.

Whittington, John W. F.
Whittington, Lester B.
Wheatley, Walter
Wheaton, Earl
Whipp, Charles Roland
Whitacre, Andy N.
White, Charles Conrad
White, Harry S.
White, Leon
Whiting, H. Wilmer
Williams, Cornelius C.
Williamson, Samuel G.
Willingham, Thomas L.
Willis, George Henry
Wilt, George W.
Wiltshire, Louis E.
Wiltshire, Robert E.
Winters, Paul E.
Wire, Milton M.
Wolf, Jacob
Womack, John E.
Wood, Lewis L.
Woodward, Wade H.
Wooddy, J. Campbell
Wooddy, Stanley L.
Wright, Charles H.
Wynkoop, Adrian G., Jr.
Wysong, William S.
Yates, Frank L.
Zombro, William E.

NEGROES

Adams, John
Baltimore, Frank
Beaner, Daniel L.
Beard, Levi
Blackburn, Shady M.

Boyd, William
Briscoe, Thomas A.
Brown, Harley C.
Brown, James A.
Burke, John W.

APPENDIX A

Campbell, Thomas
Carr, George H.
Carter, Henry T.
Clark, Alexander
Clark, Hubert
Clay, Lige
Clinton, Charles W.
Clinton, James N.
Cole, Charles C.
David, Jentres James
Dennis, Bernard M.
Dennis, Carroll L.
Devonshire, Thomas R.
Doleman, George
Douglas, George
Douglas, William
Drew, Charles F.
Enicks, Olive Willis
Ferguson, John
Fields, John Henry
Fox, James H. T.
Gillison, Huel Bert
Goens, James E.
Good, Charles
Gore, Rodney D.
Green, Walter M.
Hall, James Wilmer
Hallman, John W. C.
Harris, Harry A.
Hester, Alfred R.
Houke, James H.
Jackson, Lincoln
Jackson, Walter
Johnson, Arthur B.
Johnson, Charles H.
Johnson, Forrest G.
Johnson, Harvey
Johnson, Henry
Johnson, Isaac J.

Johnson, James E.
Johnson, Thomas C.
Johnson, William
Jones, James R.
King, George F.
Lee, Josias
Lewis, John Henry
Lowery, Harry W.
Lucas, Marion Hite
McCann, Dennis
McCann, George
McDaniel, Charles F.
Mitchell, Albert T.
Mitchell, Elder Young
Mitchell, Mathew
Mitchell, Samuel J., Jr.
Moore, Richard H.
Morgan, Edward O.
Moten, Clifton
Napper, Clarence T.
Newman, Batley
Newman, James
Page, Freddie J. W.
Page, Gouverneur M.
Parker, Charles
Payne, Charles F.
Payne, George A.
Payne, William H., Jr.
Pendleton, James
Puller, Eugene
Puller, Howard
Reed, Oscar
Reed, Roy
Reeler, Francis B.
Rideout, James H.
Rideout, Raymond W.
Robinson, Carl F.
Robinson, Frank
Robinson, Luther

Robinson, Thornton
Robinson, Washington
Russ, Franklin L.
Scott, Gilmore
Smith, Albert R.
Smith, John H.
Snowden, Charles N.
Snyder, Martin
Spriggs, David T.
Staley, George W.
Staley, John W.
Striblen, Isaac
Strother, Albert
Strother, Arthur W.
Strother, George
Stubbs, Daniel C.
Talbott, Edward D.
Talbott, Robert C.
Thomas, Frank
Thomas, Thomas M.
Thornton, James E.
Thornton, James W.
Turner, Bernard
Twyman, George
Walker, John T.
Washby, Matthew
Washington, Henry
Washington, Henry A.
Washington, James
Washington, W. N.
Weathers, Charles H.
Weaver, Roy
Weaver, Samuel C.
White, Armistead M.
White, Earl
Whiting, Benjamin O.
Williams, David
Williams, Van Perry
Williams, Walker L.
Yates, Raymond

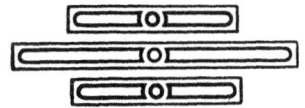

APPENDIX B

THE FORTY-NINERS[24]

OFFICERS

Benjamin F. Washington, president
Robert H. Keeling, first commander
Smith Crane, second commander
Joseph E. N. Lewis, third commander
E. M. Aisquith, treasurer
Nat Seevers, quartermaster
J. Harrison Kelly, secretary
Dr. Wake Bryarly, surgeon

MEMBERS

Allen, James R.
Barley, Richard
Bender, Jacob
Boley, John L.
Bowers, John W.
Bradley, Thornton C.
Brakmore, R. M.
Burwell, Walter J.
Clevenger, Asa
Cockrell, Daniel
Comegys, G. W.
Conway, Hugh
Cribs, James S.
Cunningham, Charles
Cunningham, George
Cunningham, James
Daugherty, Enos
Davidson, James
Davidson, Samuel

Davis, Jos. C.
Donelly, Daniel
Duke, F. W.
Engle, Jacob H.
Engle, Joseph
Fagan, Daniel
Ferrill, Milton
Gallaher, John W.
Garnhart, John H.
Gieger, Vincent E.
Gittings, Charles F.
Harrison, Ham. C.
Hayden, Charles
Hoffman, Ben
Hooper, Edward
Hubbert, Noble T.
Humphrey, J. T.
Humphreys, Dr. J. D.
Locke, Elisha

Lupton, John M.
McCurdy, James
McIlhany, Edward W.
Mackaran, William H.
Manning, James M.
Marmaduke, A. J.
Marshall, George
Miller, Andrew R.
Miller, Morgan
Milton, Taliaferro
Moore, H. H.
Moore, James H.
Moore, John, Jr.
Moore, Thomas C.
Murphy, John H.
Poland, John T.
Purcell, John
Riely, Edwin A.
Rissler, William

Rohrer, Elisha
Seevers, Ben F.
Showers, John S.
Showman, P. B.
Simpson, Francis R.
Slagle, Charles S.
Small, James B.
Stonebraker, G. C.
Strider, Isaac Keys
Strider, Jesse A. S.
Tavenner, Newton
Thomas, Charles C.
Waner, Andrew
Walper, John C.
Washington, Lawrence
Washington, T. F.
Washington, Thomas
Young, Joseph C.

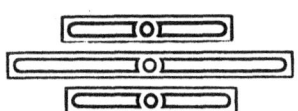

APPENDIX C

AFFIDAVIT OF CAPTAIN JOHN AVIS, THE JAILER, AS TO ASSOCIATION WITH JOHN BROWN AND CONCERNING TAKING BROWN FROM THE JAIL TO THE SCAFFOLD ON THE DAY OF HIS EXECUTION[25]

From original that was preserved by the late Rev. Abner C. Hopkins, and now in the possession of Col. Braxton D. Gibson, Charles Town, West Va.

I, John Avis, a Justice of the Peace of the County of Jefferson, State of West Virginia, under oath do solemnly declare that I was Deputy Sheriff and Jailor of Jefferson County, Virginia, in 1859 during the whole time that Captain John Brown was in prison and on trial for his conduct in what is familiarly known as the Harper's Ferry Raid; that I was with him daily during the whole period; that the personal relations between him and me were of the most pleasant character; that Sheriff James W. Campbell and I escorted him from his cell the morning of his execution one on either side of him; that Sheriff Campbell and I rode with Captain Brown in a wagon from the jail to the scaffold one on either side; that I heard every word that Captain Brown spoke from the time he left the jail till his death; that Sheriff Campbell (now deceased) and I were the only persons with him on the scaffold.

I have this day read, in the early part of chapter 8 of a book styled 'The Manliness of Christ', by Thomas Hughes, Q. C., New York: American Book Exchange, Tribune Building, 1880, the following paragraph, to-wit:

"Now I freely admit that there is no recorded end of a life that I know of more entirely brave and manly than the one of Captain John Brown, of which we know every minutest detail, as it happened in the full glare of our modern life not twenty years ago. About that I think there could scarcely be disagreement anywhere. The very men who allowed him to lie in his bloody clothes till the day of his execution, and then hanged him, recognize this. 'You are a game man, Capt. Brown', the Southern Sheriff said in the wagon. 'Yes', he answered, 'I was so brought up. It was one of my Mother's lessons. From infancy I have not suffered from physical fear. I have suffered a thousand times more from bashfulness;' and then he kissed a negro child in its mother's arms, and walked cheerfully on to the scaffold, thankful that he was 'allowed to die for a cause and not merely to pay the debt of nature as all must."

Respecting the statements contained in the above paragraph quoted from the book above mentioned, I solemnly declare:

First, that Captain John Brown was not "allowed to lie in his bloody clothes till the day of his execution," but that he was furnished with a change of clothing as promptly as prisoners in such condition usually are; that he was allowed all the clothing he desired and that his washing was done at his will without any cost to himself. As an officer charged with his custody, I saw that he was at all times and by all persons treated kindly properly and respectfully. I have no recollection that there was ever any attempt made to humiliate or maltreat him. Captain Brown took many occasions to thank me for my kindness to him and spoke of it to many persons including his wife. In further proof of the kindness he received at my hands I will state that Captain Brown in his last written will and testament bequeathed to me his Sharpe's Rifle and a pistol. Furthermore, on the night before the execution Captain Brown and his wife, upon my invitation, took supper with me and my family at our table in our residence which was a part of the jail building.

2. I have no recollection that the Sheriff said to Captain Brown, "You are a game man," and received the reply quoted in the above paragraph, or that any similar remarks were made by either parties. I am sure that neither these remarks nor any like them were made at the time. The only remarks made by Captain Brown between his cell and the scaffold were commonplace remarks about the beauty of the country and the weather.

3. The statement that "he kissed a negro child in his mother's arms" is wholly incorrect. Nothing of the sort occurred. Nothing of the sort could have occured, for his hands, as usual in such cases, were confined behind him before he left the jail; he was between Sheriff Campbell and me, and a guard of soldiers surrounded him, and allowed no person to come between them and the prisoner, from the jail to the scaffold, except his escorts.

4. Respecting the statement that he "walked cheerfully to the scaffold," I will say that I did not think his bearing on the scaffold was conspicuous for its heroism, yet not cowardly.

5. Whether he was "thankful that he was allowed to die for a cause and not merely to pay the debt of nature as all must," or not, I cannot say what was in his heart; but if this clause means, as the quotation marks would indicate, that Captain Brown used any such language or said anything on the subject, it is entirely incorrect. Captain Brown said nothing like it.

APPENDIX C

The only thing that he did say at or on the scaffold was to take leave of us and then just about the time the noose was adjusted he said to me: "Be quick."

(Signed) John Avis.

Charlestown, West Virginia.
April 25, 1882.

State of West Virginia, County of Jefferson SS:

I, Cleon Moore, a notary public in and for the County of Jefferson, State aforesaid, hereby certify that John Avis whose name is signed to the foregoing affidavit this day personally appeared before me in my county aforesaid and made oath that the statements contained in said affidavit are true to the best of his knowledge and belief.

Given under my hand and notarial seal at Charlestown, West Virginia, this 25th day of April, 1882.

(SEAL) Cleon Moore,
Notary Public.

APPENDIX D
LIST OF JEFFERSON COUNTY OFFICIALS

SHERIFFS

1801-1803, William Little
1803-1805, Joseph Swearingen
1805-1807, Alexander White
1807-1809, John Briscoe
1809-1811, George North
1811-1813, Daniel Collett
1813-1815, Abraham Davenport
1815-1817, Van Rutherford
1817-1819, John Packett
1819-1821, Daniel Morgan
1821-1823, Jacob Bedinger
1823-1826, David Humphreys
1826-1828, James Hite
1828-1830, William P. Flood
1830-1832, Carver Willis
1832-1834, Richard Williams
1834-1836, John T. A. Washington
1836-1838, John Packett
1838-1840, George W. Humphreys
1840-1842, Sebastian Eaty
1842-1844, Richard Duffield
1844-1846, David Sniveley
1846-1848, John Moler
1848-1850, George Reynolds
1850-1852, Fontaine Beckham
1852-1855, John W. Moore
1855-1858, Robert Lucas

APPENDIX D

1858-1860, James W. Campbell
1860-1861, Joseph Crane
1861-1865, The Civil War
1865-1867, William Rush
1867-1870, T. W. Potterfield
1870-1873, George W. Chase
1873-1876, Edward Tearney
1877-1880, Eugene Baker
1880-1881, John S. Moore
1881-1884, George W. Moore
1885-1888, J. Garland Hurst
1889-1892, Eugene Baker
1893-1896, Albert F. Davis
1897-1900, Eugene Baker
1901-1904, J. Davis Billmyer
1905-1908, J. W. Gardner
1909-1912, Charles D. Wysong
1913-1916, J. W. Gardner
1917-1920, Charles T. Engle
1921-1924, W. O. Macoughtry
1925-1928, J. Strider Moler
1929-1932, M. S. R. Moler
1933-1936, G. K. Wysong
1937-1937, William C. Moore
1937-1944, R. J. Madison

COUNTY CLERKS

1801-1817, George Hite
1817-1823, Robert G. Hite
1823-1840, Dr. Samuel J. Cramer
1840-1889, Thomas A. Moore
1889-1896, Gerard D. Moore
1897-1908, W. F. Alexander
1909-1934, Charles A. Johnson
1934-   , Emily A. M. Stanley

CIRCUIT CLERKS

1831-1861, Robert T. Brown
1861-1865, The Civil War

1865-1872, William A. Chapline
1872-1877, Robert T. Brown
1877-1878, Bushrod C. Washington
1879-1886, Frank P. Lynch
1887-1894, T. W. Latimer
1895-1913, John M. Daniel
1913-1936, Charles W. Conrad
1936-1936, Frank J. Beckwith
1936-   , William M. Jones

SURVEYORS

1801-1832, William McPherson
1832-1852, James M. Brown
1852-1856, George Mauzy
1856-1861, John Hess
1861-1865, The Civil War
1865-1902, S. Howell Brown
1902-1912, James K. Hendricks
1912-1917, Marshall McDonald
1917-1920, A. S. Dandridge
1920-1924, J. James Skinner
1924-1932, Marshall McDonald
1932-   , J. James Skinner

HOUSE OF DELEGATES (Virginia)

1802.	James Crane, Jacob H. Manning
1803.	George Tate, Abram Morgan
1804.	George Tate, Abram Morgan
1805.	Daniel Morgan, James Crane
1806.	Daniel Morgan, James Hite
1807.	Smith Slaughter, Carver Willis
1808.	Smith Slaughter, Carver Willis
1809.	Abram Morgan, William Tate
1810.	Daniel Morgan, Rawleigh Morgan
1811.	Thomas Griggs, Rawleigh Morgan
1812.	Rawleigh Morgan, William Tate
1813.	George W. Humphreys, George Reynolds
1814-15.	George W. Humphreys, George Reynolds
1816-17.	George W. Humphreys, George Reynolds

APPENDIX D

1818.	Daniel Morgan, Braxton Davenport
1819-20.	Edward Lucas, Braxton Davenport
1821-22.	Edward Lucas, Smith Slaughter
1823.	Braxton Davenport, Smith Slaughter
1824.	T. A. Washington, Daniel Morgan
1825-26.	Daniel Morgan, Carver Willis
1827-28.	Daniel Morgan, Carver Willis
1829.	B. C. Washington, Daniel Morgan
1830.	Edward Lucas, John S. Gallaher
1831-32.	Henry Berry, John S. Gallaher
1833.	G. B. Wager, John S. Gallaher
1834.	Henry Berry, John S. Gallaher
1835.	Henry Berry, Thomas Griggs
1836.	John Davenport, John Peter
1837-38.	William Lucas, John Peter
1839.	William C. Worthington, Anthony Kennedy
1840.	William C. Worthington, George B. Stevenson
1841.	John Moler, Anthony Kennedy
1842.	William C. Worthington, John S. Gallaher
1843.	William F. Turner, John S. Gallaher
1844-45.	William F. Turner, Benjamin T. Towner
1846.	Andrew Hunter, William B. Thompson
1847.	John A. Thomson, Joseph McMurran
1848.	John A. Thomson, William C. Worthington
1849.	William C. Worthington, T. S. Duke
1850.	John M. Jewett, T. S. Duke
1851-52.	Benjamin Moore, John T. Gibson
1853-54.	James D. Gibson, C. W. Button
1855-56.	Wells J. Hawks, T. H. Towner
1857-58.	Wells J. Hawks, Logan Osburn
1859-60.	John T. Gibson, John J. Lock
1861-65.	The Civil War.

HOUSE OF DELEGATES (West Virginia)

1865.	George Koonce, Joseph A. Chapline
1866.	George Koonce, Charles H. McCurdy
1867.	David Billmyer, George Koonce
1868.	David Billmyer, Edmund H. Chambers
1869.	Benjamin F. Harrison, E. Willis Wilson

1870.	George M. Beltzhoover, Jacob J. Miller
1871.	E. Willis Wilson, C. E. Stubbs
1872.	G. F. Cross, John W. Grantham
1872-73.	R. Hume Butcher, J. W. Shirley
1875.	James M. Mason, Isaac S. Tanner
1877.	G. F. Cross, James Lawrence Hooff
1879.	W. H. T. Lewis, J. S. Melvin
1881.	Frank Beckwith, John W. Grantham
1883.	Isaac Fouke, John W. Rider
1885.	R. Preston Chew, Daniel B. Lucas
1887.	R. Preston Chew, Daniel B. Lucas
1889.	R. Preston Chew, Braxton D. Gibson
1891.	A. S. Dandridge, Braxton D. Gibson
1893.	A. S. Dandridge
1895.	A. S. Dandridge
1897.	J. Garland Hurst
1899.	J. Garland Hurst, R. W. Morrow
1901.	C. M. Wetzel
1903.	C. M. Wetzel
1905.	C. M. Wetzel
1907.	C. M. Wetzel
1909.	John P. Kearfott
1911.	C. M. Wetzel
1913.	C. M. Wetzel
1915-16.	Milton W. Burr
1917.	Milton W. Burr
1919-20.	Milton O. Rouss
1921.	Frank J. Beckwith
1923.	J. Strider Moler
1925.	E. E. Cooke
1927.	Robert L. Withers
1929.	U. S. Martin
1931.	Clayton L. Haines
1933.	U. S. Martin
1935.	U. S. Martin
1937.	John C. Skinner
1939.	W. F. Alexander
1941.	W. F. Alexander

APPENDIX D

WEST VIRGINIA STATE SENATORS
FROM JEFFERSON COUNTY

1866-69.	Joseph A. Chapline
1870-71.	George Koonce
1872.	E. Willis Wilson
1872-77.	John W. Grantham
1877-79.	C. T. Butler
1883-85.	Jacob S. Melvin
1889-91.	Charles H. Knott
1893-95.	Robert Earl
1897-99.	Harry C. Getzendanner
1901-07.	William Campbell
1915-17.	Frank Beckwith
1919-21.	Milton Burr
1927-29.	Frank B. Robinson
1935.	Milton O. Rouss
1937.	Clayton L. Haines

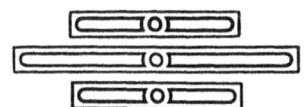

FOOTNOTES FOR APPENDICES

1. Danske Dandridge, **Historic Shepherdstown,** pp. 88, 89, 298-359.
2. **Ibid.,** pp. 154, 298-359.
3. **Ibid.,** pp. 176, 298-359.
4. **Ibid.,** pp. 298-359; Jefferson County Historical Society Magazine for December, 1938, pp. 38-46.
5. **Virginia Free Press,** Sept. 3, 1868.
6. **Spirit of Jefferson,** Jan. 14, 1873; Jefferson County Historical Society Magazine for December, 1940, p. 11.
7. **Jefferson County Historical Society Magazine for December,** 1940, p. 12.
8. **Ibid.,** pp. 12, 13.
9. **Spirit of Jefferson,** Feb. 5, 1847; June 4, 1847.
10. West Virginia State Department of Archives and History, **Records.**
11. **Confederate Roster,** Vol. 18, pp. 164-171; William N. McDonald, **A History of the Laurel Brigade,** pp. 496-499.
12. **Confederate Roster,** Vol. 1, pp. 65-69; **Spirit of Jefferson,** Feb. 16, 1904.
13. **Confederate Roster,** Vol. 1, pp. 70-74; **The Shepherdstown Register,** Feb. 6, 1936.
14. **Confederate Roster,** Vol. 1, pp. 93-97; **Spirit of Jefferson,** Dec. 21, 1909.
15. **Confederate Roster,** Vol. 1, pp. 98-102; **The Shepherdstown Register,** July 27, 1933.
16. **Confederate Roster,** Vol. 1, pp. 108-111.
17. **Ibid.,** Vol. 10, pp. 107-114; McDonald, **Laurel Brigade,** pp. 450-454.
18. **Confederate Roster,** Vol. 10, pp. 117-124; McDonald, **Laurel Brigade,** pp. 454-458; **Spirit of Jefferson,** April 24, 1888.
19. **Confederate Roster,** Vol. 10, pp. 139-145; **The Shepherds-**

town Register, Feb. 6, 1936.
20. Confederate Roster, Vol. 8, pp. 53-58; The Shepherdstown Register, Feb. 6, 1936.
21. Spirit of Jefferson, May 17, 1898; The Shepherdstown Register, April 28, 1898.
22. Spirit of Jefferson, July 21, 1926; The Shepherdstown Register, July 14, 1898.
23. Officers and Enlisted Men from Jefferson County in the World War, County Clerk's Office, Charles Town, W. Va., pp. 1-15; Spirit of Jefferson, Jan. 20, 1920.
24. Edward McIlhany, Recollections of a Forty-Niner, pp. 13, 14; The Shepherdstown Register, Jan. 31, 1901; Spirit of Jefferson, Feb. 13, 1849.
25. Copy in possession of Col. B. D. Gibson of Charles Town, W. Va.

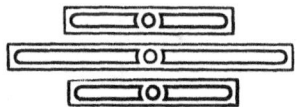

INDEX

A

Abolitionist, 112, 123, 133
Academy, Charles Town, 60, 161, 162, 225, 251, 281, 307, 311
Academy, Shepherdstown, 24, 106
Accawmack County, Va., 65
Adams, F. C., 217
Adams, John, 57
Adams County, Pa., 305
Adams Express Company, 154
Adelphi Hotel, 47
African Colonization Society, 85
Aisquith, Edward M., 94, 96
Albany, N. Y., 294
Albemarle Old Court House, Va., 31
Alburtis, E. G., 93, 118
Aldrich, J. W., 183
Aldridge, W. Va., 83, 177
Alexander, Archibald, 59, 60
Alexander, Mrs. D., 93
Alexander, William F., 124
Alexandria Artillery, 131
Alexandria Riflemen, 131
Alexandria, Va., 24, 72, 73, 296, 309
Allegheny Mountains, 299
Allen, Arthur M., 108
Allen, Benjamin, 79, 80
Allen, Howard, 257
Allen, Walter, 264
Allstadt, Mrs. Elizabeth, 58
Allstadt, Jacob, 68
Allstadt, John, 116, 121, 122

"American Boy, The", 53
American Party, 99
American Philosophical Society, 48
American Sunday Schools, 80
Anderson, Jeremiah G., 112, 122
Anderson, John, 68
Anderson, Osborn P., 119, 122
Anderson, R. H., 177, 179-181
Andrews, Charles W., 189
Antietam, Md., 228
Antietam, Battle of, 157-159
Antietam City, 231
Antietam Creek, 157
Antietam Manufacturing & Land Improvement Company, 231
Appomattox, Va., 145, 195, 201, 288, 291, 300
Armory & Arsenal, Harpers Ferry, 55, 56, 72, 77, 78, 89, 90, 102, 103, 109, 115-121, 123, 142, 145, 201, 217, 298
Army of Northern Virginia, 281, 288, 292
Arthur, Chester A., 280
Asbury, Francis, 58
Ashby, Turner, 144, 145, 152, 153
Ashby, Richard, 145
Ashby's Brigade, 144
Askew, William, 50
Atkinson, Anne P., 292
Atkinson, George W., 235
Atterbury, William, 150
Averill Township, 203, 207, 209
Avis, John, Jr., 92, 134, 136, 138
Avis, Robert, 87

INDEX

B

Back Alley, 16
Baer, 273
Bailey, Edward, 23
Bailey, Robert, 75
Baker, James H., 93
Baker, John, 66
Bakerton, W. Va., 4, 230, 302
Balch, Rev., 20
Ball, Armistead, 121
Balmaine, Alexander, 63
Baltimore and Ohio Railroad, 5, 82-84, 117, 118, 142, 150, 160, 168, 169, 181, 182, 187, 193, 196, 197, 202, 217, 230, 231, 246, 275, 289
Baltimore, Md., 13, 37, 41, 54, 82, 83, 94, 115, 120, 122, 273, 274, 282, 289, 296, 302
Banks, N. P., 152
Baptist Church, 58, 97, 217
Barbour, Alfred M., 101, 102, 105, 145, 146
Barbour, John A., 145
Barclay, 46
Bardane, W. Va., 242
Barnes, Joseph, 215
Barry, 208
Barry, Joseph, 215
Barton, Richard W., 299
Bath, (Berkeley Springs), W. Va., 37, 38, 40
Baner, Rev., 21, 23
Baylor, George, 153, 154, 163-165, 186-188, biog. 276, 312
Baylor, Richard, 66
Baylor, Robert W., 66, 67, 117, 144, 221, 223, 276
Baylor, Robert W., Jr., 186
"Beall Air", 110
Beall, Frank, 206
Beall, John Yates, 187, biog. 277, 278, 297, 298
Beall, William, 238
Beatty, Lalla Louise, 276
Beaujolais, Count de, 309
Beauregard, P. G. T., 102
Beck, Margaret A., 310
Beckford Parish, 22
Beckham, Fontaine, 87, 118, 122
Beckwith, Frank, 230, 253, 255
"Bedford", 174, 278
Bedinger, Daniel, 278, 297
Bedinger, Edward W., 233
Bedinger, George M., 27, 28, 31, 32, 37, 40, 55, 283
Bedinger, Henry, 16, 27, 28, 30-32, 42, 43, 45, 49, 54, biog. 278, 283, 296, 299
Bedinger, Jacob, 66
Bedinger, Sarah R., 278
Bedinger, Virginia, 296, 299
Belcher, A. M., 262
Bell, Col., 178
Bell, John, 100
Bell, Major, 105
Beller, James W., 96
Beltzhoover, George M., 232
Beltzhoover, George M., Jr., 50, 262
Berkeley, Norborne, 22
Berkeley, Sir William 7
Berkeley Church, 22
Berkeley Circuit, 23, 58, 202
Berkeley County, W. Va., 17, 19, 24, 26, 27, 31, 32, 34, 36, 40, 64-66, 68, 93, 148, 155, 191, 196, 198-200, 206, 247, 257, 269, 284-286, 293-295, 300, 305, 308, 309
Berkeley Springs, W. Va., 37, 38, 40, 41, 264
Berry, Henry, 77, 298
Berryville, Va., 59, 108, 162, 163, 167, 168, 177, 247
Beverly, W. Va., 301
Billmyer, J. Davis, 243, 244
Billmyer, Milton J., 300
Bissell, W. S., 237
Blackburn, H. H., 211-213
Blackford, Joseph, 72, 73

Blackford's Ford, 6, 159
Bladensburg, Md., 72
Bladensburg Races, 72
Blagrove, Charles, 53, 54
Blair, Montgomery, 172
Blair Mountain, 262
"Blakeley", 281, 307
Blakeley Howitzer, 144
Blazer, Richard, 181, 185, 186
Blazer's Scouts, 182, 184-186
Blizzard, William, 263
Bloomery, The, 30, 244
Bloomfield, Va. 184
Blue Ridge Mountains, 1, 7, 24, 75, 108, 299, 303
Boerly, Thomas, 116, 122
Boggerson, Barbour, 257
Bogges, Robert, 58
Bohemia Manor, Md., 37
Boiler, Vertical Tubular, 50
Boiler, Water-Tube, 50
Bolivar, Simon, 87
Bolivar, W. Va., 56, 57, 87, 97, 107, 110, 165, 201, 203, 207, 218, 221, 232, 251, 258, 273, 275, 277
Bolivar Heights, W. Va., 146, 148, 152, 155, 156, 162, 165, 170, 187, 277
Bolivar Township, W. Va., 207, 209, 211
Boone County, W. Va., 262
Booth, John Wilkes, 131, 278
Boreman, Arthur I., 195, 197, 206
Boston, Mass., 28, 30, 54, 287, 294
Boston Neck, 30
Boston Tea Party, 53
Boteler, Alexander R., 100, 166, 173-176, 195, 280, biog. 279, 280
Boteler, Helen, 173
Boteler, Henry, 279
Boteler's Ford, 6
Botts, Lawson, 125, 126, 144, 277, 289
Botts Greys, 142, 292

Bougher, Peter, 93
Boulton, Matthew, 45, 46
Bouresches, France, 302
"Bower, The", 36, 160, 304
Bowden, Thomas R., 198
Bowie, Washington, 72
Bowman, Clinton, 122
Bowman, George, 11
Boyd, Elisha, 61, 66
Boyd, Samuel J., 238
'Boydville", 305
Boyer, George W., 126
Boyle, Albert J., 274
Boyle, Joseph B., 273
Brackett, N. C., 217
Braddock, Sir Edward, 24, 25, 32, 284, 294, 303, 304
Bradley, Joseph, 199
Brady, Christopher, 30
Brady, William, 27, 30
Brandy Station, Battle of, 299
Brandywine, Battle of, 31, 36
Brazos River, 93
Breckinridge, John C., 100, 101
Brewster, B. H., 280
Brice, William, 43
Bridesburg, 145
Bridge, James Rumsey, 52
Bridgeport, Md., 229
Bridges, Thomas, 59
Briscoe, John, 66
Briscoe, Thomas, 71
Broaddus, Andrew, 59
Brockenbrough, John, 285, 296, 297
Brooke, Henry Lawrence, 280
Brooke, Henry St. George T., 224, biog. 280
Brooke, Virginia Tucker, 280
Brooke County, W. Va., 269
Brooks, Shepherd, 222
Brown, Annie, 114
Brown, Forrest A., 271
Brown, Forrest W., 230, 253, 255, 261, 262
Brown, Frederick, 112

INDEX 413

Brown, Gustav, 238
Brown, James M., 81
Brown, John, 84, 109, 110, 112-114, 116-122, 123-126, 128-134, 136, 141, 172, 201, 244, 249, 277, 288, 289, 293, 294
Brown, Mary A., 133, 136
Brown, Mary Harrison, 280
Brown, Oliver, 112, 114, 122
Brown, Owen, 112, 114, 119, 122
Brown, Robert T., 87
Brown, S. Howell, 238
Brown, Thomas, 208
Brown, Watson, 122
Brown, William, 69
Brown, John, Fort, 140
Brown's Shop, 168
Brownville, Pa., 95
Bruce, John, 83
Bruce's Mills, Va., 88
Brucetown, Va., 88, 180
Bryan, Morgan, 19
Bryan, William J., 243
Bryant, William, 93
Bryarly, Wake, 94
Buchanan, James, 99, 100, 112, 120, 124
Buckles, Edward, 11
Buck Marsh Baptist Church, 58
Buckmaster, Zacariah, 67
Buck's County, Pa., 12, 15, 283
Budinger, Henrich, Sr., 20
Buena Vista, Battle of, 94, 301
Bull Run, Battle of, 155, 289
Bullskin Church, 8, 19, 20, 60
Bullskin Run, 3, 19, 28, 60, 108, 303, 305
Bunker Hill, W. Va., 9, 21, 30, 159, 163, 177, 179, 180, 182
Bunn, S., 80
Burgoyne, 34
Burke, Redmond, 162
Burnett, Alexander, 67
Burnett, Mary, 58
Burnett, Sarah, 58
Burr, Aaron, 62

Burr, Moses W., 124
Burr, M. W., 221
Burwell, W. J., 96
Bush, Lester L., 271
Bushong, Frank L., 255
Bushong, Lee, Jr., 271
Butcher, R. Hume, 108
Butler, Ormond, 110
Butler, Vincent M., 117, 142, 302
Butler, William, 81
Butler's Hill, 160
Butler's Woods, 166
Butt, James D., 229
Byers, Conrad, 16
Byrd, Richard E., 81
Byrne, James, 119
Byrne, Terrence, 119

C

Cahongaroota River, 11
Cairo, Ill., 95
Calhoun, John C., 3
California, 94
Callis, Otho W., 71
Camargo, 93
Cambridge, Mass., 29, 287
Camden, Battle of, 34, 36, 287
Cameron, Daniel, 204
Cameron, Samuel, 77
Cameron's Depot, 83, 177
Campbell, Charles N., 225, 226
Campbell, James W., 124, 134, 136
Campbell, Laura W., 226
Campbell, William, 232, 255
Campbell County, Va., 7
Camp Hill, 57, 170, 215, 217
Carlile, John S., 191, 192
Carlisle, Pa., 56, 146, 276
Carr, George, 257
Carter, J. W., 144, 145, 160, 161
Carter, Robert, 11
Carter House, 164, 196, 213
Cass, Lewis, 89
Castleman, David, 19

Castleman, H. W., 108
Castleman's Ferry, 182
Catawba Indians, 6, 7
Caven, Samuel, 8
"Cedar Lawn", 178, 307
Cedar Lick, 11
Cement Mill, Battle of, 159
Cerro Gordo, Battle of, 94
Chafin, Don, 262
Chafin, John, 262
Chambers, George W., 144
Chambersburg, Pa., 113, 176
Chambliss, John R., 166, 281
Champe, Jane, 309
Chancellorsville, Battle of, 285, 291
Chapel, St. George's, 21, 22, 79, 80
Chapline, Joseph A., 204, 208
Chapline, William, 16
Chapline, W. A., 206
Chapline City, 198
Chapline Precinct, 203
Chapline Township, 207, 209
Chapman, Lucy, 309
Chapman, William H., 185, 189
Chapultepec, Battle of, 94
Charity Lodge, 88
Charles City, 265
Charles City County, Va., 65
Charles River County, Va., 65
Charleston, S. C., 282
Charleston, W. Va., 221, 222, 233-235, 265, 311
Charles Town, W. Va., 3, 11, 17, 20-25, 27, 30, 58, 59, 62, 64, 65, 68, 70, 71, 72, 76, 78, 80-82, 86-89, 92-97, 107, 108, 116, 118, 119, 121, 122, 124, 125, 130, 131-134, 142, 144, 152, 157, 159, 160, 162-170, 177-182, 186-188, 196, 197, 201, 203-215, 218, 220, 221, 225, 230, 232, 233, 238, 239, 244, 247-249, 251, 253, 255, 257, 258, 260-262, 264, 269, 271, 273, 274-277, 278, 280-282, 285, 288, 289, 291-294, 297, 298, 301, 304-309, 312, 313
Charles Town Academy, 60, 161, 162, 225, 251, 281, 307, 311
Charles Town Baptist Church, 105
Charles Town, Berryville & Winchester Street Railway Company, 246
Charles Town Graded School, 227
Charles Town High School, 267, 269
Charles Town Horse Show Association, 260, 273
Charles Town Jockey Club, 69, 274
Charles Town Manufacturing & Developing Company, 232, 281
Charles Town Mining, Manufacturing & Improvement Company, 230, 232-234, 264, 281
Charles Washington Hall, 233
Charlottesville, Va., 190
Chase, Salmon P., 199, 200
Chasteen, Lewis, 58
Chatham, Can., 119
Chatham Constitution, 119, 123
Cheat Mountain, Battle of, 307
Cherry Run, 246
Cherry Run & Potomac Valley Railroad, 246
Chesapeake Bay, 187, 277
Chesapeake & Ohio Canal, 4, 5, 81, 82, 142, 181
Chew, John, 163
Chew, Robert, 238
Chew, Roger, 280
Chew, R. Preston, 144, 145, 152, 164, 230, 235, 238, 247, biog. 280, 281
Chew, Sarah West, 280
Chew's Battery, 144, 145, 160, 281
Chicago, Ill., 140
Chicago World's Fair, 140

INDEX 415

Chickacoan District, 65
Chickamauga, Ga., 235
Chillicothe, Ohio, 53
Chilton, Samuel, 128
China, 94
Chotank, 308
Chrisman, Jacob, 11
Christ Church, 296
Christ Reformed Church, 23
Christian, Edward, 66
"Christian Panoply", 54
Churubusco, Battle of, 94
Cincinnati, Ohio, 55, 95, 113
Clarke County, Va., 13, 107, 108, 148, 174, 247
Clarksburg, W. Va., 107, 108, 191, 222
Classical and Scientific Institute, 222
Clay, Henry, 76, 89
Clay County, W. Va., 257
"Claymont Court", 258
Clegg, J. W., 235
"Clermont", 37, 48
Cleveland, Grover, 236, 237, 280, 310, 313
Clifford, Nathan, 199
Clowe, Henry W., 105
Cockburn, Robert, 24
Cockrell, J. G., 210
Cockrell, John D., 256,
Cogswell, William, 162
Colburn & Pike's Arithmetic, 91
"Cold Spring", 12, 298
Coleman, John, 163, 164
Colgrove, Silas, 162
Cole's Battalion, 163
Collett, Daniel, 66
Collins, Angelica, 62
Collins, Ann, 59
Collins, Christopher, 58, 59, 61, 62
Colston, Edward, 75
Columbian College, 311, 312, 314
"Columbian Maid", 46, 47
Comley's Spelling Book, 91

Committee of Correspondence, 45
Committee of Safety, 28, 32
Conaway, John, 68
Confederate Seal, 279
Conn, Hugh, 9
Conn, James, 70, 71
Connecticut, 48
Connecticut Cavalry, 165
Connell, Rev., 20
Connogocheague, 54
"Constitution", 71
Constitutional Convention, 190, 293, 299, 300
Constitution, John Brown, 118, 123
Constitutional Union Party, 100, 255, 279
Continental Congress, 27, 34, 287
Conway Cabal, 34, 287
Cook, John Edwin, 109, 110, 114, 119, 120, 122, 123, 130, 131, 136, 138, 294
Cook, Valentine, 58
Cooke, H. Harrison, 271
Cooke, John R., 77
Coolidge, Calvin, 266
Cooper, Robert, 20
Copeland, John, 117, 122, 124, 130, 134, 138
Coppoc, Barclay, 114, 120, 122
Coppoc, Edwin, 122, 124, 130, 136, 138
Corn Exchange Regiment, 159
Cornwallis, Lord, 32, 34, 36, 282, 287
Cotton, Henrietta, S., 311
Council of Virginia, 15
Cowman, Anna, 37
Cox, Ebenezer, 78
Craig, Henry K., 89, 90
Craighead, Rev., 20
Craighill, Nathaniel, 85
Craighill, Sarah E., 281
Craighill, William Nathaniel, 281
Craighill, William P., biog, 281, 282

Cramer, S. J., 80, 85
Crane, Charlie, 163
Crane, James, 17
Crane, Joe, 163
Crane, Smith, 94
Crany Island, Battle of, 298
Crayton, George, 163
Crisp, Speaker, 313
Cromwell, Oliver, 283
Cromwell, Rudolph, 257
Croner, D. L., 261
"Croquette", 184
Crook, George, 180
Cross, Rezin D., 117, 119, 211, 213
Crow, William, 208
Crowl, William, 153
Crown Point, 287
Cruise, David, 112
Culpeper County, Va., 36
Cumberland, Fort, 25
Cumberland, Md., 82, 95, 289
Cummings, Edward C., 271
Cunningham, James, 93
Curry, Linn, 119
Curtis, Benjamin R., 198-200
Custer, George A., 179
Cutshaw, George W., 116
Cutshaw, Wilfred E., 181, biog. 282, 283

D

Dandridge, A. S., 160, 245, 246, 283
Dandridge, Danske Bedinger, biog. 283
Dangerfield, John E. P., 121
Daniel, Mrs., 178
Darke, Joseph, 15, 55, 284
Darke, William, 15, 17, 25, 32, 42, 55, 66, biog. 283-285, 304, 305
Darrell, James, 116
Daugherty, Harry M., 260
Davenport, A. B., 58
Davenport, Abraham, 66
Davenport, Braxton, 71, 75, 81, 124
Davenport Family, 22
Davenport, Frances, 288
Davenport, H. B., 238
Davenport, John, 76
Davidson, James, 96
Davis, 26
Davis, B. F., 157
Davis, David, 199
Davis, Jefferson, 153, 289, 307
Davis, J. Lucius, 131
Davis, John W., 266, 299, 300
Davis, Mrs. Martha N., 108
Dawes, Henry L., 196
Dayton, Alston G., 312
Dear, Charles H., 183
Debuler, Micajah, 23
De Graffenreid, Baron, 7
Delaware, Fort, 164
Delaware Indians, 6
Delayea, Sarah, 285
Democratic Party, 70, 75-77, 89, 96, 97, 99, 100, 278, 279
Denny, Wright, 226
Derr, Ira M., 257
Dickinson College, 276
Dickinson, Jonathan, 9
Dilbard, G. W., 123
Dinwiddie, Gov., 25
Distinguished Service Cross, 256
Dittmeyer's Drug Store, 14
Dixon, John, 61, 66
Domer, Raleigh, 229
Donegal Presbytery, 8, 19, 20
Donohoo, John, 121
Dorr, Charles P., 311
Dorsey, Evan, 122
Douglas, Henry Kyd, 113, biog. 285, 286
Douglas, Robert, 285
Douglas, Stephen A., 100
Douglas Hill, The, 158
Douglass, 58
Douglass, Frederick, 123
Douglass, Isaac, 17
Dover, 46

INDEX 417

Downer, Joel, 87
Downey, O. D., 204
Downing, James, 94
Doyle, Drury, 112
Doyle, John, 112
Doyle, John, Jr., 112, 132
Doyle, Mahala, 112, 132
Doyle, William, 112
Draper Manuscript, 29
Dred Scott Decision, 100
Duffie's Brigade, 178
Duffields, W. Va., 15, 55, 59, 144, 160, 167-170, 174, 182, 227, 266, 267, 284, 285
Duke, Peter T., 94
Dunbar, Col., 24
Dunlap, A. F., 235
Dunmore, Lord, 30, 303, 309
Dunmore Proclamation, 30
Dunmore's War, 28, 305
Dunn, Perry, 257
Dunn, Thomas B., 78
Dupont, Gen., 282
Duquesne, Fort, 24
Dushane, Jerome, 153
Dust, Isaac, 126
Dutton, W. B., 292
Duval, Maria P., 251

E

Early, Jubal A., 92, 170, 172, 176-181, 285, 291
Earnshaw, T. P., 235
Eastern Panhandle, 1, 193,
Eaty, Sebastian, 81
Eby, John J., 178
Edge Hill Cemetery, 291, 293, 313
Eichelberger, D. S., 234
Eichelberger, George W., 124
Eichelberger, Webster, 107
Elizabeth City County, Va., 65
Elk Branch, 15, 19, 20, 60, 80, 284, 285
Elkins, Stephen B., Jr., 235

Elsey, Lewis, 66
Ellsworth, Alfred M., 119
Elmwood Cemetery, 286
Embargo Act, 70
Emmert, H. H., 235
Endler, Martin, 20
Engle, J. F., 233
Engle, Melchior, 15
Engle, W. Va., 4
Engle's Hill, 160
English Church, 22, 23
English, "Duck", 163
Entler Hotel, 69, 234
Entler Tavern, 27
Episcopal Church, 21, 79, 85, 97, 188, 249
Episcopal High School, 276
Essex County, Va., 65
Euphrates River, 7
Eureka Lodge, 88
Evitts Marsh, 12, 308
Evitts Run, 3
Ewell, Richard S., 285, 291
"Exact", 93
Eyster, George S., 247

F

Fagan, Daniel, 95, 96
Fairfax Circuit, 23
Fairfax County, Va., 300
Fairfax, Ferdinando, 61, 66
Fairfax, George William, 14
Fairfax, Lord, 3, 13-16, 303
Fairview High School, 107
"Falkland", 172
"Farmers Advocate", 234, 255
Farmers Alliance, 234, 237
"Farmers Repository", 69, 80, 87, 255
Farnsworth, Charles, 165
Faulkner, Charles J., 100, 105, 125, 200, 212, 213, 215, 279, 297, 299
Fauquier Cavalry, Lower, 131
Fauquier Cavalry, Upper, 131

418 INDEX

Fauquier County, Va., 7, 164, 276
Fayetteville, N. C., 145, 146
Fayman, H. R., 235
Feagans, Harry, 257
Feaman, George, 71
Feaman, James D., 208
Featherstonhaugh, Thomas R., 141
Federal Fugitive Slave Law, 86
Federalist Party, 57, 70, 75
Ferguson, Syd, 185, 186
Ferry Farm, 306, 308
Ferry Hill, 285
Field, Kate, 140
Field, Stephen J., 199
Fielding, Richard, 73
Fillmore, Millard, 3, 99
Finley, Samuel, 28, 30
Fish Hatchery, 273
Fitch, John, 37, 41, 47-49
Flagg, George H., 238, 239
Flagg, John R., 177
Flagg, Josiah, 28
Fleming, A. B., 311
"Flowing Springs", 25, 91, 303, 304
Floyd Guards, 144
Floyd, John B., 113, 114
Force Bill, 77
Ford, Thomas H., 155
Forester, Thomas, 11
Forester, William, 11
Forks, The, 160
Fort Cumberland, 25
Fort Delaware, 164, 276, 281, 286
Fort Duquesne, 24, 294
Fort Jefferson, 55
Fort Lee, 31
Fort McHenry, 164, 276, 290
Fort Necessity, 304
Fort Niagara, 294
Fort Shepherd, 16
Fort Sumter, 102, 281
Fort Ticonderoga, 294
Fort Washington, 31, 55, 295

Fort Wayne, 290
Forty-Niners, 94
Fossett, Alexander, 204
Fouke, Charles, 61
Fouke, Christian, 68
Fouke, Christina, 118
Fouke's Hotel, 115, 117
"Fountain Rock", 173, 174, 280
Frame, Matthew, 67
Franklin, Benjamin, 45
Franklin and Marshall College, 285
Frederick, Md., 13, 21, 22, 24, 28, 29, 41, 119, 120, 136, 155, 156
Frederick County, Va., 13, 19, 25, 28, 32, 65, 88, 108, 148, 191, 303, 306, 308, 309
Frederick, Parish of, 22
Frederick The Great, 110
Fredericksburg, Va., 288, 304, 306, 308
Free Schools, 90, 91, 106
Free Soil Party, 112
Fremont, John C., 152
French and Indian War, 24, 32, 294, 304, 305
French Revolution, 60
Friend, Israel, 11
Friends, Society of, 11, 13
Fritchie. Barbara, 136
Froman, James, 11
Froman, Paul, 11
Front Royal, Va., 163
Fry, John 58
Fry, Leodoric, 67
Fulton, L. F., 262
Fulton, Robert, 37, 41, 47, 48
Funsten, Oliver, 145
Furnace Run, 3, 4, 84
Furtney, George H., 95

G

Gallaher, John S., 87, 93, 255
Gallaher, W. W. B., 225

INDEX

Garfield, James A., 222
Garnett, Robert S., 301
Garney, A. Vernon, 239
Garnhart, Henry, 68
Garretson, Freeborn, 23
Gates, Horatio, 32, 34, 36, 39, 42, 43, biog. 286, 287, 294, 295
Gault House, 117
Geary, John W., 152, 162, 163
Geary, William J., 256
Genn, James, 14
George I, 7
Georgetown, D. C., 72, 82
Germantown, Battle of, 36, 284, 304
General Assembly, Va., 16, 17, 19, 38, 49, 60, 61, 64, 70, 71, 75-77, 81, 85-87, 89, 90, 91, 98, 99, 101, 106, 107, 138, 190, 192, 193, 197-199, 284, 288, 290, 291, 298, 305, 306
German Reformed Church, 60, 80, 97
Gettysburg, Battle of, 165, 285
Getzendanner, H. C., 235, 256
Ghent, Treaty of, 73
Gibbs, Charles, 80
Gibson, Billy, 163
Gibson, B. D., 232
Gibson, Harry C., 238, 239
Gibson, John T., 100, 116, 119, 134, 238, biog. 288
Gibson, Susan G., 119
Gilbert, Henry, 68
Gill, George B., 119
Gilmer County, W. Va. 271
Gilmor, Harry, 166-169, 178, 180
Glaize, A. C., 235
Glaize, C. B., 235
Glenn, James W., 210
Glover, Arthur, 271
Goetz, A. D., Harness Factory, 260
Goff, Nathan D., 311
Goldsborough, Robert, 58
Golden Horseshoe, Knights of the, 8
Gooch, Gov., 11
Good, William, 54
Gordon, John B., 180, 285, 292
Gore, Howard M., 264
Governor's Island, N. Y., 187, 278
Graffenreid, Baron de, 7
Grafton, W. Va., 301
Graham, John, 87
Grange, 221, 223, 224, 234, 237
Grant, U. S., 181, 188, 189, 195, 199, 207, 219, 280
Grant Township, 207-209, 211
Grantham, James, 58
Grantham, John, 66
Grantham, John, Jr., 19
Grantham, Joseph, 19, 70, 71
Gray, David, 43
Great Bridge, Battle of, 36
Great Falls, 40, 41
Great Meadows, Battle of, 304
Greeley, Horace, 219
Green, Duff, 3
Green, Israel, 120, 121
Green, John W., 288
Green, Nathaniel, 34, 287
Green, Shields, 122, 124, 130, 134, 138
Green, Thomas C., 126, 132, 209, 210, 212, 215, 221, 223, 230, biog. 288, 289, 297
Greenback Labor Party, 222
Greenback Raid, 182-184
Greenbrier County, W. Va., 264
Greenleaf's Point, 73
Greenville, S. C., 235
"Greenway Court", 13
Grier, Robert C., 199
Griffith, Miss, 175
Griggs, John, 81
Griggs, Thomas, 58, 61, 71, 72, 77
Griswold, Hiram, 128
Grove, Clarence C., 256
Grove, James H., 223
Grubb, Curtis, 68
Guadalupe-Hidalgo, Treaty of, 94

Guantanamo Bay, 301
Guard, Tom, 138
Guild, Lieut., 187
Guilford Court House, Battle of, 36
Gwynn, Walter, biog. 289

H

Hafer, Nathan, 94
Hagan, Henry, biog. 289
Hager, L. P., 262
Hagerstown, Md., 21, 286
Hagerty, John, 23
Hahn, Nicholas, 20
Haines, Clayton L., 255
Haines, George W., 238
Haines, Henry, 68
Haines, J. H., 209, 211, 213
Haines, Jacob, 67
Halket, Sir Peter, 24
Hall, Ephraim B., 204, 207, 212-214
Hall, E. P., 141
Hall, Jesse, 59
Hall, John H., 77
Hall, Mary, 58
Hallowell's School, 296
Hall's Rifle works, 78, 115, 117, 217
Halltown, W. Va., 58, 110, 152, 157, 165-166, 177-179, 221, 238, 247, 296, 298, 299
Hamilton, Alexander, 54
Hamilton, Squire, 13
Hammon, S., 165
Hammond, G. N., 122
Hammond, Thomas, 67, 302
Hammond's Hotel, 86
Hampden-Sydney College, 292, 293, 314
Hampshire County, W. Va., 7, 32, 211, 278, 288, 299
Hampton, George, 19
Hampton, Wade, 160, 289
Hamtramck Guards, 117, 142, 290
Hamtramck, J. F., 290
Hamtramck, John F., 92, 93, biog. 290
Hancher, William, 22
Hancock, W. S., 159-160, 162, 222, 312
"Happy Retreat", 17, 306
Hardesty, F., 58
Hardesty, Richard, 67
Harding, Charles B., 93, 125, 128, 293
Harding, Warren G., 260
"Harewood", 62, 178, 308, 309
Harman, A. W., 165, 166
Harman, John A., 145
Harmer, Gen., 55
Harney, William S., 150
Harper, Kenton, 148, 150
Harper, Robert, 13, 14, 56
Harpers Ferry, 2-5, 12-14, 28, 55-57, 72, 76-83, 86-90, 92, 93, 95, 97, 100, 102, 103, 109, 113-115, 118-120, 122, 124, 132, 133, 136, 140-142, 145, 146, 148, 150, 152, 154-157, 159, 160, 162, 163, 165-168, 170, 172, 191, 194, 198, 201, 203, 207, 208, 211, 213, 215, 217, 218, 221, 225, 228-230, 246-247, 251, 253, 255, 258, 269, 271, 274, 275, 282, 291, 293, 298, 299, 310
Harpers Ferry Armory and Arsenal, 55, 56, 72, 77, 78, 89, 90, 102, 103, 109, 145, 201, 217, 298
Harpers Ferry District, 269
Harpers Ferry Mining, Manufacturing and Improvement Company, 230
Harpers Ferry Water Power and Manufacturing Company, 217
Harris, David, 73
Harris, George, 185

INDEX

Harrison, Battail, 30
Harrison, Benjamin, 236, 310
Harrison, F. S., 247
Harrison, William Henry, 89, 290
Harrisonburg, Va., 163, 164
Hart, Edwin, 108
Hartford Convention, 75
Hatcher, Harry, 185
Hatton, S. P., 249
Hawks, Arthur "Sunshine", 291
Hawks, Wells J., biog. 290, 291
Hayes, Rutherford B., 221
Haymond, Alpheus F., 220
Haymond, Thomas, 58
Haynes, J. A., 105
Haynes, Jacob, 16
Hazen's Speller, 91
Hazlett, Albert, 122, 138, 140
Heath, Perry S., 240
Heath, William, 22
Heflebower, Daniel, 186
Henderson, Charlie, 163
Henderson, John H., 144
Hendricks, James, 15
Hening's Statutes, 17
Henrico County, Va., 65
Henry, Capt., 57
Henry, Patrick, 29, 303
Henry, Marvin W., 257
Henshaw, William, 28
Herbert, Noble, 95
Hermitage Farm, 280
Herr, A. H., 152
Heyden, John R., 87
Higgins, Patrick, 115
Hill, A. P., 155, 157, 159
Hill, William, 60-62
Hillsboro, Va., 182
Hipsley, 162
Hite, George, 58, 61, 66
Hite, Jacob, 11
Hite, James, 81
Hite, Jost, 11
Hite, Thomas, 28
Hitler, Adolph, 271
Hodges, G. T., 232

Hoffman, John S., 220
Hoffman, Peter, 13, 14
Hoge, Moses, 20, 43, 45, 59
Hoke, Bernard B., 257
Hoke, Judge, 212
Hole, The, 12, 13
Holl, Samuel, 68
Holmes, Hugh, 66
Holmes, Joseph, 69
Holmes, Oliver Wendell, 71
Hood, Charles T., 231
Hood, John, 281
Hooff, James L., biog. 291, 292
Hooff's Hall, 212, 213
Hooper, Wilson, 122
Hoover, Herbert C., 266
Hopewell Church, 19
Hopkins, Abner C., biog. 292, 293
House of Commons, 47
House of Delegates, Va., 49, 98, 108
Houston, H. W., 262
Howe, Gen., 295
Howe, George Augustus, 303
Howe, Mary Daubigny, 303
Howell, David, 208
Howell, David, Jr., 210
Howitzer Battery, 92
Hoyt, George H., 126, 128
Hudgin, 186
Hudson, Ohio, 112
Hudson River, 287
Huey, Pennock, 166
Huger, Benjamin, 103, 105
Hughes, Mrs. Ariana, 180
Hughes, Charles E., 273
Hulse, William, 28
Humphreys, A. A., 159, 160
Humphreys, David, 67, 73, biog. 293
Humphreys, George W., 70, 72, 73, 75, 80, 85
Humphreys, John, 293
Humphreys, May Davis, 293
Humphries, Thomas, 23
Humrickhouse, Albert, 153

Hunter, Andrew, 76, 98, 101, 125, 128, 131, 132, 136, 163, 172, 173, 176, 197, 198, 200, 211-213, 215, 299, biog. 293, 294, 299
Hunter, David, 171-174, 176
Hunter, David H., 293
Hunter, Elizabeth Pendleton, 293
Hunter, Florence, 293
Hunter, James H. L., 144
Hunter, Moses, 43
Hunter, Rebecca, 134
Hunter, R. M. T., 192
Hunter, Rev., 20
Hunter's Row, 213
Hunting Creek, Va., 305
Huntington, Nannie, 312
Hurley, Dwight P., 269
Hurt, John, 22
Hutchcraft, B. R., 231

I

Imboden, John D., 145, 150, 167, 168
"Imperial Observer", 53
Independent Grays, 122
Independent Scouts, 181, 184-186
"Independent, The", 255
Indian Campaign, 31
Iron Industry, 84
Irvin, William R., 244
Isabel, Tex., 93
Isbell, Thomas M., 108
"Island Queen", 277
Island of Virginius, 83

J

Jackson, Andrew, 3, 76, 101, 243
Jackson, Thomas J., 113, 146, 148, 150, 152, 155-157, 159, 279, 283, 285, 291, 292, 296
Jackson, Wade H., 256
Jackson's Valley Campaign, 144, 152
Jacob, John J., 289

Jail, Jefferson County, 81, 249
James City County, Va., 65
James, John, 68
James River and Kanawha Canal, 289
Jantzen, Johannes, 273
"Java", 71
Jefferson, Thomas, 5, 49, 54, 57, 62, 65, 70, 76, 243
Jefferson Academy, 251
Jefferson College, 288
Jefferson County Agricultural College, 223, 224
Jefferson, Fort, 55
Jefferson Guards, 116, 117, 142
Jefferson Hotel, 262
Jefferson's Rock, 4, 5, 57
Jefferson Society, 297
Jessie Scouts, 164
Jockey Club, Charles Town, 69
John Stephenson Seminary, 226
Johnson, Andrew, 195, 198
Johnson, Charles A., 239
Johnson, Edward, 285
Johnson, Oakey, 210
Johnson, Reverdy, 199, 200
Johnson, Solomon, 256
Johnson, Thomas, 38
Johnson's Island, 187, 277, 285
Johnston, Joseph E., 145, 148, 189
Jomini, Gen., 282
Jones, Abram, 166
Jones, Alexander, 87
Jones, Olive Ann, 308
Jones, Rebecca C., 282
Jones, Roger, 146
Jones, William E., 163
Justices of the Peace, 65, 66

K

Kabletown, W. Va., 169, 185, 203, 208, 218, 225, 247
Kagi, John H., 118, 119, 122
Kanawha County, W. Va., 257, 262

INDEX

Kanawha, State of, 192
Kanawha Valley Campaign, 297
Kansas, 100, 109, 112, 113, 130, 132, 138
Kansas Legislature, 112
Kearneysville, W. Va., 4, 159, 160, 166, 168, 179, 182, 188, 230, 241, 258, 286
Kearsley, John, 40, 43, 66
Keedysville, Md., 228
Keeling, Robert H., 94
Keeney, Frank, 262, 264
Keller, Philip, 20
Kelly, J. Harrison, 94
Kelly, William, 28
Kennedy, Andrew, 81, 87
Kennedy, Booth, 113
Kennedy Farm, 113, 119, 123, 129
Kennedy, John W., 204, 208
Kennedy, Mary Virginia, 109, 110
Kennedy, Widow, 109
Kern, J. J., 213
Kershaw, Joseph B., 181
Keyes, Thomas, 58
Keyes's Ferry, 58, 68
Keyes's Ford, 24, 186-188
Keyes's Gap. 24, 81
Keyes's Switch, 188
King George County, Va., 308
Kirk, W., 93
Kitzmiller, Archibald M., 117, 119
Knights of the Golden Horseshoe, 8
Knott, C. H., 221
Knott, John L., 144, 166
Know Nothing Party, 99, 100
Knox, Henry, 49
Knoxville, Tenn., 235
Knutti, J. G., 249
Knutti Hall, 249
Koonce, George, 191, 192, 204, 210, **211**
Kramle, 24

Krauth, C. P., 79
Kuchas, Henrich, 20
Ku Klux Klan, 273

L

Lafayette, Marquis de, 88, 110, 309
Lake Erie, 187, 277
Lakeland Caverns, 258
Lamar, R. D., 230, 231
Lamb, Daniel, 192
Lancaster County, Va., 65
Landaff, Lord Bishop of, 54
Lang, Rev., 20
Larew, Isaac, 19
Lawrence, Caroline, 278
Lawrence, John W., 278, 283
Lawyer's Row, 249
Leach, W. H., 235
Lear, Tobias, 56
Leary, Lewis S., 122
Leavell, Julia Yates, 299
Lederer, John, 7
Lee, Charles, 32, 34, 36, biog. 294, 295
Lee, Edmund J., 174, 176, 296
Lee, Edwin Gray, biog. 296
Lee, E. I., 232
Lee, Fitzhugh, 160, 166, 180
Lee, Harry, 174
Lee, Henrietta, B., 174, 176, 296
Lee, John, 294
Lee, Light Horse Harry, 62
Lee, Nettie, 174
Lee, Richard Henry, 175
Lee, Robert E., 120, 145, 148, 155, 156, 158, 159, 162, 165, 167, 168, 172, 175, 181, 188, 189, 291, 293, 307
Lee, Fort, 31
Lee Hall, 209
Lee Memorial Association, 292
"Leeland", 296
Leeman, William H., 118-120, 122
Leesburg, Va., 23, 82, 155

INDEX

Leetown, W. Va., 34, 36, 80, 160, 170, 178-180, 221, 241, 242, 245, 273, 294, 304
Lemen, W. N., 232
Lemon, John, 11, 67
Lenhart, Charles, 138
Leopold, 162
Letcher, John, 148, 172
Letcher Riflemen, 144
Lettsom, John, 45
Lewis, Charles H., 124
Lewis, James B., 108
Lewis, John L., 264
Lewis, Joseph E. N., 94
Lexington, Battle of, 27
Lexington Presbytery, 59, 60
Lexington, Va., 153, 172, 281, 285, 296, 297, 313
Liberal Republicans, 219
"Liberty or Death", 29
Liberty Loan, 257
Library Society of Harpers Ferry, 86
Licklider, George, 106
Light Brigade, The, 285
Likens, James, 67
Likens, Thomas, 79, 80
Lincoln, Abraham, 100, 102, 131 192, 193, 195, 278
Line, Henry, 16
Link, Adam, 106
Link, William H., 256
Link Spring, 20
Lippitt, W. F., 230
Liquor Saloons, 253, 255
Little, George, 68
Little Timber Creek, 95
Little, William, 17, 66
Little, William, Jr., 66
Littleton, Arthur, 273
Livingston Lodge, 88
Lock, John J., 124
Lock, William, 80
Locke, John J., 100, 210
Locke's Shop, 164
"Locust Hill", 177

Logan County, W. Va., 261-263
Logan Lodge, 88
Logie, James, 204
Lomax, L. L., 178, 180
London, Eng., 45-47
Long, Jacob, 66
Long Island, N. Y., 294
Long Marsh Run, 108
Longstreet, James, 157
Loring, W. W., 301
Loudoun County, Va., 68, 78, 81, 93, 188, 280
Loudoun Heights, 148, 152, 155, 156
Loudoun Rangers, 188
Louis Philippe, 309
Lovell, C. S., 160
Lower Fauquier Cavalry, 131
Lowery, William R., 66
Lucas, Daniel Bedinger, 12, 50, 221, 223, 224, 278, biog. 296-298
Lucas, Edward, 11, 12, 31, 76-78, 90, 296, biog. 298
Lucas, John W., 238
Lucas, Robert, 12, 70, 208, 296
Lucas, Virginia, 163, 298
Lucas, William, 12, 31, 76, 89, 98, 101, 278, 296, biog. 298, 299
Lunford, Lewis, 59
Luray, Va., 163
Luther Chapel, 106
Lutheran Church, 19, 20, 23, 60, 79, 80, 97, 105
Lutheran Church, Uvilla, 105
Lyall, Thomas, 58

M

McAllister, James, 20
McCabe, Edward, 118, 122
McCarty, J. W., 144
McCarty, W. F. M., 231
McClellan, George B., 156, 157, 159, 160, 162
McCausland, John, 176

INDEX 425

McClure, John C., 126
McConnell, Rev., 20
McCormick, Francis, 23
McCormick, William, 19, 92
McCrea, Rebecca, 58
McCurdy, Charles H., 204
McCurdy, John W., 204
McDonald, Angus W., 230, 288
McDonald, Edward A. H., biog. 299, 300
McDonald, Henry T., 217
McDonald, Hugh, 73
McDonald, Julia, 266, 300
McDonald, Mary N., 288
McDowell, Irvin, 152, 301
McGanis, Rev., 8
McGill, Daniel, 9
McGuffey's Reader, 91
McGuire, William, 66
McHenry, Fort, 164
McIntire, B. S., 230
McKee, George, 271
McKinley, William, 240, 243
McKnight, John, 20
McLaws, Lafayette, 155, 156
McLenahan, William, 58
McMechen, James, 39, 43
McMurran, Joseph, 222
McMurran Hall, 16
McPherson, Gen., 281
McPherson, William, 66
McPherson's Mill, 108
Macoughtry, William O., 180
Madison, Dolly, 62, 309
Madison, James, 54, 62, 63, 70, 309
Madison County, Va., 7
Madison, W. Va., 262
Madison Square Garden, 313
Maine Cavalry, 166
Mallorie, T. Percy, 233
Malta Lodge, 88
Manning, Billy, 163
Manning, Frank, Jr., 235
Manning, Upshur, 163, 164

Marche, Thomas B., 238
Mark, Ann, 43
Mark, John, 45
Mark, Mrs., 43
Marker, Jacob, 229
Marmaduke, Presley, 70, 71
Marmaduke, Samson, 59
Marmet, W. Va., 262
Marquis de Lafayette, 309
Marseilles, France, 60
Marsh Creek, 20
Marshall, Cushing, 236
Marshall, John, 85
Marshall, Robert, 59
Martin, Peter, 66
Martin, William A., 126
Martindale, William F., 172, 173-175
Martinsburg, W. Va., 8, 24, 30, 36, 55, 58, 64, 65, 88, 116, 118, 150, 155, 156, 163, 170, 213, 222, 246, 261, 263, 292, 301, 304, 305
Maryland Heights, 5, 110, 120, 148, 155, 156, 165, 170
Maryland Telephone Company, 234
Mason, George, 303
Mason, Gerard F., 126
Mason, James M., 192
Mason, James M., Jr., 262
Mason, James M., Sr., 234
Mason and Dixon's Line, 133
Masonic Cave, 25
Masons, 25, 26, 87, 88
Massanutten Mountain, 163
Matamoros, 93
Matthews, J., 80
Maxwell, Edwin, 212, 214
Mealey, Edward M., 231
Mechanicstown, W. Va., 169
"Media", 299
Medler, Henry, 117
Melvin, Thayer, 214, 215
Mendell, Capt., 282

Mercer, Richard, 11
Merriam, F. J., 114, 122
Merritt, Wesley, 177, 179, 180
Methodist Church, 23, 58, 97, 115, 202, 203
Metropolitan Turf Exchange, 253
Mexican War, 91, 290, 301
Mexico, 92, 313
Mexico City, 94
Michel, Louis, 7
Middletown, Md., 155
Middletown, Pa., 235
Middleway, W. Va., 11, 12, 19, 76, 77, 81, 82, 84, 87-89, 97, 154, 160, 163, 166, 177, 178, 180, 203, 218, 221, 225, 251, 258
Middleway Blues, 88
Miles, Dixon, S., 156, 157
Mill Creek, 9
Miller, Jacob, 126
Miller, Samuel F., 199
Miller, Wilmer, 257
Mills, Benjamin F., 121
Mills Bill, 312
Mills Gap, 81
Millville, W. Va., 4, 188, 247
Milton, Thomas, 96
Mineral County, W. Va., 7
Miners' Trials, 261-265
Mines, John, 62, 65
Mingo County, W. Va., 261, 262
Mississippi River, 93
Missouri, 112
Missouri, University of, 314
Mohawk Indians, 294
Mohawk Valley, 294
Moler, Hugh S., 256
Moler, Jacob, 67
Moler's Cross Roads, W. Va., 144, 159, 166, 230
Molino del Rey, Battle of, 94
Money Tree, The, 227-229
Monmouth, Battle of, 34, 295
Monocacy, Battle of, 172
Monongalia County, W. Va., 271

Monroe, James, 3, 65, 66, 70
Montgomery, Samuel, 263
Montgomery, Ala., 148
"Montpelier", 63
Montpensier, Duke de, 309
Montreal, Can., 294
Moore, Ann, 59
Moore, Cato, 17, 31, 43
Moore, Charles P. T., 220
Moore, David, 59
Moore, Gen., 183
Moore, Gerard D., 233
Moore, James H., 210
Moore, Mary, 180
Moore, Thomas A., 87, 106, 153
Moore, Thomas C., 96
"Mordington", 17
Morgan, Abraham, 67
Morgan, Daniel, 28, 29, 66, 70, 75, 81, 303, 305
Morgan, Ephraim F., 264, 273
Morgan, Jacob, 77
Morgan, Morgan, 9
Morgan, Raleigh, 70
Morgan, Richard, 24
Morgan, William, A., 144, biog. 300
Morgan, William, 27, 28, 31
Morgan Continentals, 131
Morgan County, W. Va., 37, 264, 265, 269
Morgan's Grove Fair Grounds, 173, 243, 235
Morgan's Spring, 300
Morris, A. J. & Company, 230
Morris, Edward, 23
Morristown, N. J., 31
Morrow, Charles, 43, 45, 46, 49
Morrow, Jeremiah, 208
Morrow, John, 16, 43, 45
Morrow, Mrs., 43
Morrow, R. W., 234, 310
Morse's Geography, 91
Morsell, Mary A., 282
Mosby, John S., 169, 181-184, 187, 189, 276

INDEX

Mosby's Greenback Raid, 182, 183
Mosby's Rangers, 181, 184, 187
Mt. Hope, 266
Mt. Jackson, Va., 153
Mt. Nebo Lodge, 87
Mt. Parvo Institute, 225
Mt. Vernon, 73, 307
Mt. Vernon Guards, 131
Mt. Vernon Ladies Association, 307
Mt. Zion Church, 65
Mountain Mission, 251
Mud Fort, 87
Mulligan, James A., 170
Munford, Thomas T., 145, 160
Murphy, Dr., 121
Murphy, George H., 122
Musgrove, Edward, 303
Musser, Clifford S., 255
Myers, Joseph, 126
Myers, Wesley, 227, 228
Myers's Ford, 181, 182, 185
Myerstown, W. Va., 181, 185

N

National Farmers' Congress, 237
National Republican Party, 76
Naval Observatory, 73
Navy Yard, 120
Neely, M. M., 266
Neil, 229
Neill, William, 256
Nelson, Joseph, 181, 182
Nelson, Samuel, 199
Newburgh, 287
Newby, Dangerfield, 122
Newcomer, Daniel, 257
Newspapers, 53, 96
New Canton Ferry, 300
New Castle Presbytery, 8, 20
New Castle, Va., 280
New Deal, 267
New England, 112
New Jersey, 258, 279
New Market, Va., 163

New Mecklenburg, 9, 11, 12, 15
New York City, N. Y., 31, 54, 277, 282-284, 287
New York & Erie Railroad, 277
Niagara, 187, 277, 294
Nicaragua Canal Commission, 282
Nichols, 84
Nicodemus, Rev., 21
Norborne Chapel, 22, 309
Norborne Parish, 22, 309
Norfolk, Va., 36, 282, 293
Norfolk & Western Railroad, 16, 218, 231
Norris, Uncle Jordan, 188
Norris, W. O., 247
North, George, 61, 66
North Elba, N. Y., 136, 141
North Mountain, 1, 81, 160, 161, 246
North Point, Battle of, 298
Northumberland County, Va., 65
Northwest Territory, 55, 92
Nourse, James, 22
Nullification, 76, 101

O

Oak Grove Schoolhouse, 230
Oatlands, Va., 184
O'Brien, 162
Odd Fellows' Hall, Shepherdstown, 157
O'Donnell, James, 237
Ohio, 55, 82, 112, 284
Ohio County, W. Va., 247, 269
Ohio, River, 82
Ohio, Territory of, 53
Oil Boom, 230
Old Dominion, 1, 92, 190, 194, 196-198, 200
Old Fair Grounds, Charles Town, 160
"Old Ironsides", 71
Old Hickory, 77
Old Point Comfort, Va., 93
Old Rappahannock County, Va.,

65
Old Ronemous Graveyard, 285
Old Sheriffalty Party, 243
Oliver, John, 19
Olliman, Christian, 67
Opeckon Church, 8
Opequon Creek, 1-3, 8, 11, 36, 64, 65, 68, 106, 177, 179-181, 198
Opie, Hierome, 81
Orange County Court, 19, 65
Orebank, Virginia, 4, 230, 302
Orme, John, 9
Orrick, Nicholas, 40
Osawatomie, 110, 112, 116, 133
Osborn Township, 203, 207, 210, 211, 221
Osbourn, Thomas, 126
Osburn, Logan, 101-103, 210, 211, 213, 215, 221
Oxford University, 271
Ozenton, C. W., 262

P

Packett, 66
Packett, John, 19, 66, 71
Packett, John B., 177
Pack Horse Ford, 6, 8, 9, 158, 159, 179
Page, Bernard, 22
Page, Mann, 11
Paine, Thomas, 54
Painter, D. A., 235
Paley, William, 54
Palm Hotel, 262
Panhandle District, 193
Park, Moses, 23
Parker, Daniel, 47
Parker, Richard, 125, 128
Parkersburg, W. Va., 261, 310
Parley's & Morse's Geography, 91
Partridge, William, 23
Patrons of Husbandry, 221
Patterson, S. M., 247
Patuxent River, 71

Paull, James, 220, 221
Payne, Nathaniel, 186
Payne's Ford, 65
Peale, Charles William, 279
Pegram, John, 285
Pendleton, E, 207
Pendleton, Gordon H., 108
Pendleton, Hugh N., 108
Pendleton, Philip, 31, 43, 61
Pendleton, Susan, 296
Pendleton, W. N., 158
Pennington, William, 279
Pennsylvania, University of, 302
Pennsylvania Volunteers, 159
Perdue, 84
Perkins, 57, 78
Perks, Joseph W., 256
Perrin, Widow, 309
Perry, Gilbert, 271
Pershing, John J., 302
Peter, John, 81
Peterkin Hall, 251
Petersburg Artillery, 131
Petersburg Grays, 131
Petersburg Guards, 131
Petersburg, Va., 181, 188
Phelps, Conductor, 115, 120
Phelps, Eli, 67
Philadelphia, Pa., 45, 46, 48, 54, 63, 80, 282, 296
Philadelphia Presbyterian Synod, 8
Philippi, W. Va., 93
Philippi Races, 301
"Philo Parsons", 277
Philpott, G. B., 164, 165
Pickering, Timothy, 56
"Piedmont", 12
Piedmont, Va., 102, 164
Pierce, Franklin, 99, 105, 278
Pierpont, Francis H., 192-195, 198, 199
Pigman, Ignatius, 23
Pike's Arithmetic, 91
Pinckney, C. C., 70
Pinkney, Gen., 57

INDEX

"Pioneer, The", 83
Piscataway, Battle of, 31
Pittsburg, Pa., 15, 95
Pleasant Valley, 155
Pleasants County, W. Va., 271
Pocomoke, 8
Point of Rocks, Md., 82, 150, 156
Polk, James K., 89
Pony Express, 73
Poolesville, Md., 95
Pope, John, 154, 155
Pope's Creek, Va., 308
Populist Party, 311
Porter, David, 3, 73
Porterfield, George A., 73, 93, biog. 300, 301
Porterfield, John T., 262
Porterfield, Mary Tabb, 300
Portsmouth, Va., 93
Potato Hill, 152
Potomac Cement Company, 4
Potomac Cement Mill, 159, 228, 289
Potomac Company, 39
Potomac District, 221
Potomac River, 1, 3, 4, 6-9, 12, 14, 24, 29, 39, 41-43, 49, 50, 52, 54, 56, 65, 69, 70, 72, 73, 78, 81, 82, 110, 115-119, 142, 145, 146, 148, 150, 152, 155-159, 165, 170, 171, 179, 228, 229, 247, 274, 275, 285, 299 307
Potomack, 8
Potomoke, 8, 9
Potomoke Presbyterian Church, 19
Potowmac Guardian & Berkeley Advertiser, 53
Potowmack, 8
Pottawatomie Creek, 112
Potterfield, Truman W., 204, 213
Powhatan Band, 257
Powhatan College, 249, 251
Powhatan County, Va., 292
'Prato Rio", 34, 294

Presbyterian Church, 59, 79, 80, 97, 292
Presbytery, Donegal, 19, 20
Presbytery, Lexington, 59, 60
Presbytery, New Castle, 20
Presbytery, Winchester, 19, 60, 79, 80
Price, Jesse, 257
Price, John, 22
Prier, O. A., 235
Princeton College, 279, 307
"Princeton, The", 299
Prince William County, Va., 14
Prohibition Amendment, 244, 266
Prohibition Party, 244
Pyle, William, 30
Pyne, J. M., 235

Q

Quaker State, 86
"Quarry Banks", 12
Quick, John H., 256, biog. 301, 302
Quinn, Luke, 121, 122

R

Rabb, John, 108
Race Track, 68
Rainfall, 2
Raleigh, Sir Walter, 47
Ramsburg, J. J., 209, 211, 213
Ramseur, Stephen, 180
Randall, Samuel J., 312
Randolph, Edmund, 49, 303
Randolph, John, 298
Rankin, Benjamin, 17
Rankin, William, 19
Ransom, Robert, 170, 296
Ranson, James L., 72, 81
Ranson, W. Va., 4, 233, 248, 260, 281
Ransone, Richard, 17
Rappahannock County, Va., 7
Rappahannock River, 308

Rattling Springs Hotel, 253
Rawlings, Moses, 30
Ray, John R., 209
Realf, Richard, 119
Red Cross, 257
Reed, Samuel, 66, 67
Reese, Jacob, 19
Reformed Church, 23, 60, 80, 285
Reinhart, Thomas C., 257
Reno, M. A., 187
Rentch, 162
Rentch, Daniel S., 153
Reorganized Government of Virginia, 192-194, 198
Republican Party, 57, 70, 75-77
Revolutionary War, 27, 36
Reynolds, A. S., 232
Reynolds, George, 75
Reynolds, John, biog. 302
Rhea, Rev., 20
Rhine Valley, 9
Richards, Adolphus, 185, 186
Richards, A. E., 169
Richardson, G. W., 122
Richland, 64
Richmond, Va., 70, 75, 93, 97, 101-103, 132, 133, 145, 148, 150, 182, 184, 188, 191, 198, 277, 279, 280, 283, 284, 297, 299, 301, 303
Richmond College, 314
Richmond Greys, 131
Richmond Howitzer, 131, 160
Ridenour, Samuel, 208
Rider, J. W., 256
Ridgway, Mary, 59
Riely, William A., 108
Riflemen, Alexandria, 131
Rightstine, William, 126
Riley, Elizabeth, 59
Riley, John, 19
Ringer, Mrs. Ruth, 180
Rio Grande River, 313
"Rion Hall", 298, 299
Rippon, W. Va., 108, 162, 185, 186, 221

Rissler, R. C., 255
Roads, 247
Robinson, Luther, 257
Rockingham County, Va., 7, 167
Rock's Ferry, 108
Rockbridge Artillery, 288
Rocket Battery, 92
Rockville, Md., 72
Rocky Lane, 16, 160
Rocky Marsh Run, 1, 65
Roderick, Hezekiah, 117, 209. 211, 213
Rodes, Robert E., 178
Rogers, Coleman, 231
Rogers, Samuel, 47
Roman Catholic Church, 97
Romney, 15, 278, 280, 288, 299
Ronemous Graveyard, 285
Ronemous, John, 106
Roosevelt, F. D., 266, 267
Roosevelt, Theodore, 244
Rootes, Philip, 53, 54
"Rose Brake", 283
"Rose Hill", 287
Ross, Horatio, 54
Rosser's Brigade, 144, 292
Rouss, Milton, 144, 153, 154, 163, 164
Rouss Memorial Hall, 238
Rowan, John W., 92-94, 116, 142
Rowland, George, 154
Rowles, George, 87
Roxbury, 29, 30
Royal Institute of England, 313
Ruggles, Gen., 183
Rumsey, Edward, 37, 39
Rumsey, James, 37-43, 45-50, 52
Rumsey, Mrs. James, 43
Rumseian Society, 45, 47, 49
Rumseyan Society, 50
Rupert, Private, 121, 122
Rural Free Delivery, 236
Rush, Benjamin, 45
Rush, John, 283
Rush, William, 202, 204
Russel, Israel, 119

INDEX

Russell, Samuel, 72
Rust, George, 78, 278
Rutherford, 56
Rutherford, Robert, 17, 25, 30, 278, biog. 303
Rutherford, Thomas, 303
Rutherford, Thomas, Sr., 61
Rutherford, Van, 66
Rutherford Rangers, 25, 284, 303

S

Sabbath School Union, 80
Sacramento, Calif., 96
Sadler, George, 134
Safety, Committee of, 28, 32
Salem, Va., 280
Saloons, 229, 253, 255
Saltillo, 290
Sample's Manor, 113
Sampson's Ford, 169
Sanborn, John J., 205
Sanders, Cyrus, 66
Sanders, John, 66
Sands, Joseph, 233
Sandy Hook, Md., 110, 112, 115, 120, 150
San Francisco, Calif., 96, 282
Sappington's Hotel, 95
Saratoga, Battle of, 34, 287
Savannah, Ga., 282
Savory, Thomas H., 218
Schaff, J. G. Company, 246
Schenectady, N. Y., 294
Schofield, Gen., 281
Schools, 60-62, 90, 91, 97, 106, 215, 222-227, 267-271
School Teachers' Salaries, 224, 225
"Scioto Gazette", 53
Scott, Dred Decision, 100
Scott, George, 28
Scott, Thomas, 58
Scott, Winfield, 94, 99, 282
Scrabble, W. Va., 198
Secession, 101
Secession Convention, 191

Secession Ordinance, 101-103, 145, 191
Seevers, Nathaniel, 94
Selective Service Act, 256, 271
Seneca Creek, 72
Seneca Falls, 40
Seymour, Horatio, 207
Shall, Nicholas, 67
Shannondale Springs, 3, 4, 84
Sharples, W. Va., 1, 262
Sharpsburg, Md., 49, 54, 156, 157, 160, 162, 170, 171
Sharp's Rifles, 113, 118, 123, 136
Sheeler, Billy, 13
Sheeley, John, 67
Sheler's Spring, 58
Shenandoah Falls, 14, 40, 41
Shenandoah Junction, W. Va., 59, 182, 221, 231, 299
Shenandoah River, 2, 3, 7, 11, 12, 14, 56, 58, 78, 84, 87, 108, 117, 141, 145, 152, 156, 160, 167, 169, 182, 184, 187, 218, 244, 247, 274, 275, 299, 303
Shenandoah Valley, 1, 6, 7-9, 76, 98, 102, 170, 172, 176, 184, 196, 278, 284, 298, 309
Shenandoah Valley Jockey Club, 273, 274
Shenandoah Valley Railroad, 218, 231, 233
Shepherd, Abraham, 16, 27, 28, 30, 31, 43, 45, 70
Shepherd, Amos, 108
Shepherd, Mrs. David, 173
Shepherd, Elizabeth, 16
Shepherd, Hayward, 115, 116, 122
Shepherd, Henry, 234
Shepherd, Mrs., 43
Shepherd, Rezin D., 205
Shepherd, Thomas, 11, 15, 16, 23
Shepherd, T. R., 105
Shepherd College, 16, 222, 249, 267
Shepherd County, 197

432 INDEX

Shepherd District, 221
Shepherd, Fort, 16
Shepherd Precinct, 203
Shepherd State Teachers' College (See Shepherd College)
Shepherd Township, 209
Shepherdstown Academy, 24, 106
"Shepherdstown, Charles-town and County Advertiser", 53
Shepherdstown High School, 267
Shepherdstown Mining, Manufacturing, and Improvement Company, 232
"Shepherdstown Register, The", 96, 97, 234
Shepherdstown, W. Va., 4, 6, 8, 9, 11, 15, 16, 19, 20, 22-25, 27-29, 31, 32, 41, 46, 49, 50, 52-55, 59, 60, 65, 69, 70, 71, 76, 79, 80, 82, 87-91, 96, 97, 106, 116, 117, 123, 133, 144, 153, 157-160, 162, 166, 170, 171, 173, 173, 179, 180, 188, 189, 194, 195, 197, 198, 202, 203, 205, 206, 209-214, 218, 222, 225, 227-230, 232-235, 246, 247, 253, 258, 266, 267, 269, 271, 274, 275, 278-280, 283-286, 289, 290, 296, 298, 300, 302
Sherando River, 11
Sheridan, Philip H., 172, 176-179, 181, 182, 184, 187, 281
Sheriffalty Party, Old, 243
Sherman, Henry, 112
Sherman, William, 112
Sherman Silver Purchase Act, 313
Shields, James, 152
Shirley, James, 81
Shoe Lane, 16
Shope, William, 66
Short, William, 81
Showman, Hiram, 223
Shriver, Colonel, 119

Sigel, Franz, 170
Simmons, J. V., 210
Simpson, Benjamin L., 167, 168
Simpson, Sarah, 59
Sinn, Capt., 119
Slaughter, Michael, 23
Slavery, 67, 85, 97, 99, 100, 112, 122, 190, 193, 202, 219
Sleepy Creek, 37
Slemons, Rev., 20
Smeltzer, Rev., 106, 107
Smith, Alfred E., 265, 266
Smith, Anna J., 300
Smith, Augustine Charles, 300
Smith, B. H., 160
Smith, C. H., 166
Smith, Charles E., 240, 241
Smith, Isaac, 110
Smith, John, 11, 19
Smith, Mrs. John, 58
Smith, John, Jr., 19
Smith, John F., 88, 124
Smith, Moses, 19
Smith, Paul, 108
Smith, Peter, 106, 107
Smith, Peyton, 69
Smith, Rees, 11
Smith, Walter, 72
Smith, William, 19, 91, 290
Smithfield, W. Va., 12, 19, 58, 69, 87, 154
Smithsonian Institution, 313
Smurr, Jacob, 67
Snickersville, Va., 187
Snyder, Harry L., 50, 96
Snyder, Martin, 256
Snyder, William B., 96
Society of Friends, 11, 13
Society of Mechanic Arts, 47
Solomon's Gap, 155
Sooy, Gen., 281
Souders, F. B., 256
South Carolina, 101
South Mountain, Battle of, 156, 157
Sowders, Captain, 171

INDEX

Sowders's Battery, 171
Spanish-American War, 234, 301
Spencer Rifles, 184
"Spirit of Jefferson", 92, 96, 97, 255
Spotswood, Alexander, 7
Spotsylvania County, Va., 17, 64, 65
Springfield, Mass., 56, 145
Stafford County, Va., 308
Staley, John D., 211, 213, 214
Stamp Act, 306
Stanton, Benjamin H., 199, 200
Stanton, E. M., 192
Starry, Joseph, 210
Staunton River, 145
Staunton, Va., 283
St. Clair, Arthur, 55, 284, 305
St. George's Chapel, 21, 22, 79, 80, 309
St. George's Church, 306
St. Hilda's Hall for Girls, 251
St. Joseph, Mo., 95
St. Louis, Mo., 95, 285, 290
St. Margaret's Churchyard 47
St. Peter's Lutheran Church, 60
Steadman, Harold W., 257
Steadman, Thomas, 73
Stephen, Adam, 32, 36, 284, biog. 304, 305
Stephens, Peter, 12-14
Stephens City, Va., 31
Stephenson, Benjamin, 66
Stephenson, Hugh, 27-30, biog. 305
Stephenson, James, biog. 305
Stephenson, John, 226
Stephenson, Richard, 305
Stephenson's Depot, Va., 180
Stephenson's Seminary, 226
Steptoe, Anne, 309
Stevens, Aaron D., 122, 124, 138, 140
Stevens, Edward, 36
Stevens, Thaddeus, 195
Stewart, Juliana, 40

Stewart, Richardson, 40
Stewart, William, 9
Stockton, Frank R., 258
Stockton, Helen, 279
Stonewall Brigade, 144, 148, 178, 276, 285, 292
Stony Lick, 11
Storer, John, 217
Storer College, 141, 217
Strachey, Henry, 295
Strider, I. Keyes, 238
Strider, Isaac, 221
Strider, Melvin T., 238
Strong, William, 199
Stroop, William, 11
Strother, David H., 175
Strother, John, 80, 244-246
Stuart, J. E. B., 120, 160, 167, 279, 289
Stuart, Judge, 214
Stuart's Horse Artillery, 144, 145, 281
Stubblefield, James, 72, 73, 78
Stubbs, C. E., 211
Stubbs, Robert, 23, 24, 43, 45
Sturgiss, Daniel, 22, 23
Suffrage, Woman's, 246
"Sulgrave", 178
Sullivan, Hannah, 59
Sullivan, Jerry A., 169
Summers, George D., 164, 166, 167
Summers, William W., 257
Summit Point, W. Va., 19, 60, 81, 84, 108, 153, 154, 163, 164, 166, 167, 177, 221, 247
Summit Point and Berryville Railroad Company, 232
Sumner, Charles, 195
Sunday School Union, 80
Susquehanna River, 6
Swayne, Noah H., 199
Swearengen, Benoni, 45
Swearengen, Thomas, 11
Swearengen, Van, 11, 31
Swearengen's Spring, 43

Swearingen, Henry, 71
Swearingen, Joseph, 42, 45, 66, 70
Swift Run Gap. 7
Swiss, 7
Switzerland, 294
Symington, John, 90, 92, 103

T

Tabb, George W., 126
Taft, William H., 244
Talbot, William, 59
Taliaferro, William B., 134
Tate, George, 164
Tate, Magnus, 17
Tate, William, 66
Tavener, Noah, 96
Taylor, Atty. Gen'l., 200
Taylor, Dr., 302
Taylor, J. Alfred, 266
Taylor, John, 11
Taylor, Samuel, 11
Taylor, Stewart, 122
Taylor, Zachary, 89, 92, 94, 290
Taylor County, W. Va., 257
Tazewell, Littleton W., 88
Teachers, Salaries of, 224, 225
Telford, 82
Texas Rangers, 95
Thames River, 47
"The Bower", 36, 160, 304
"The Pioneer", 83
"The Tennessee", 83
"The Thomas Jefferson", 83
"The Virginia", 83
Thomas, Jesse B., 290
Thomas, Philip E., 84
Thompson, Dauphin, 118-120, 122, 257
Thompson, John A., 76
Thompson, Rev., 20
Thompson, William, 122
Thomson, James, 144, 145
Thornton, James, 257
Thornton, Mildred, 306, 309
Throckmorton Family, 22

Throgmorton, Robert, 37
Ticonderoga, Fort, 287, 294, 303
Tidd, Charles P., 122
Tidewater, 102
Tiffin, Edward, 61, 208
Tilden, Samuel J., 221
Tippecanoe, 290
Timber, 2
Timberlake, Richard, 126
Timberlake Building, 267
Todd, Dolly Payne, 62, 309
Todd, Lucy, 62, 309
Toler, Henry, 59
Tomahawk Titles, 14
Torbert, T. A., 179
Torrington, Conn., 112
Towner, Benjamin T., 89
Townsend, George Alfred, 157
Townsend, T. C., 262
Trans-Allegheny Region, 38, 102
Trapnell, Richard, 251
"Travelers Rest", 32, 286, 287
Travers, W. H., 197, 210, 212, 214
Trayor, C. H., 211
Triluminar Lodge, 88
Trinity Chapel, 22
Trinity Episcopal Church, 22, 79, 188
Tubular Boiler, 50
Tucker, Henry St. George, 71, 280, 298
Tunnel, John, 23
Turkey Run, 11
Turner, Ehud, 204, 209, 211, 213
Turner, George H., 207, 212, 213
Turner, George W., 118, 122
Turner, Henry S., 81, 85
Turner, Nat, 22
Turner, William H., 89
Tuscarora Church, 8
"Tuscawillow", 178
Twelfth Pennsylvania Cavalry, 163, 178, 186
Twelfth Virginia Cavalry, 144, 157, 160, 162, 163, 165, 166,

INDEX 435

186, 276, 312
Tyler, John, 90, 299

U

"Uncle Tom's Cabin", 258
Underwood, H. T., 256
Underwood's Farm, 132
Union Conservative Party, 101
Union Hotel, 93
Union Theological Seminary, 292
Unionville, 106
United Mine Workers of America, 262, 264
United States Bank, 76
United States Harness Company, 260, 261
United States Military Academy, 281, 282, 289, 290, 307
Unseld, John G., 68, 87
Upper Fauquier Cavalry, 131
Uvilla, 160, 238
Uvilla Lutheran Church, 105

V

Valley Fire Insurance Company, 301
Valley Forge, Pa., 295
Valley of Virginia, 142
Valley Pike, 163
Van Buren, Martin, 3, 77, 89
Vance, Rev., 20
Van Fleet, Charles J., 262
Van Metre, Isaac, 11
Van Metre, John, 11
Van Swearengen, Joseph, 23, 31, 42
Van Swearingen, Thomas, 211-213
Vaughan, Benjamin, 45, 46
Veasey, Rev., 22
Vera Cruz, 94, 302
Vermilyea, I. D., 163
Vertical Tubular Boiler, 50
"Vestal Hall", 310
Victory Loan, 257

Vincent, Gen., 281
"Virginia, The", 83
Virginia, Army of Northern, 281, 288, 292
Virginia Battalion, 55
Virginia Convention, 30, 102, 103, 190, 284, 293, 299, 304
Virginia, Council of, 15
"Virginia Free Press", 87, 97, 107, 255
"Virginia Free Press and Farmer's Repository", 87
Virginia General Assembly, 16, 17, 19, 37, 39, 49, 60, 61, 64, 70, 71, 75-77, 81, 85-87, 89, 90, 91, 98, 99, 101, 103, 106, 107, 138, 190, 192, 193, 197, 198, 199, 284, 288, 290, 291, 298, 305, 306
Virginia House, 84
Virginia Military Institute, 131, 144, 148, 172, 271, 281, 282, 283, 301
Virginia Orebank, 4, 230, 302
Virginia, Reorganized Government of, 192-194, 198
Virginia Rifles, 131
Virginia Secession Ordinance, 191
Virginia Slave Insurance Company, 86
Virginia, University of, 277, 280, 297, 302, 307, 312
Virginius, Town of, 87
Voorhees, Daniel W., 130, 131, 294

W

Wade, A. L., 225
Wade's Depot, 154
Wageley, Roy, 256
Walker, James A., 281, 285
Walker, Harry N., 256
Walker, J. D., 235
Walker, John G., 155, 156

Walker's Dictionary, 91
Wallace, Lew, 172
Waller, Absalom, 59
Wallingford's Tavern, 65
"Walnut Grove", 91, 277
Walper, Casper, 68
Walper's Cross Roads, 188
Walsh, Chief Clerk, 120
Walton, W. C., 80
Wanamaker, John, 236, 237
Warner, Charles, 205
War of 1812, 70
Warren County, Va., 7
Warrick River County, Va., 65
Warrior's Path, 6
Warrosquyoake County, Va., 65
Washington and Lee University, 276, 313
Washington, Anne Steptoe, 309
Washington, Benjamin, 94
Washington, Bushrod C., 81, 85, 220, 230, 258, 307
Washington, Charles, 17, 59, 64, 208, biog. 305, 306, 308
Washington, Fairfax, 61
Washington, Ferdinand, 309
Washington, Frances, 306
Washington, Frederick, 309
Washington, George, 3, 4, 17, 25, 28-31, 34, 36, 38, 39, 41, 49, 54-56, 62, 67, 81, 88, 110, 238, 258, 279, 287, 295, 303-306, 308, 309
Washington, George Augustine, 306
Washington, George Steptoe, 61, 62, 309, 310
Washington, George W., 238
Washington, Harriet, 310
Washington, Jane Champe, 309
Washington, John Augustine, 17, 281, biog. 307
Washington, John T. A., 85, biog. 307, 308
Washington, John Perrin, 310
Washington, Lawrence Augus-tine, 310
Washington, Lawrence, 67, 92, 306
Washington, Lewis, 110, 116, 119, 121, 122
Washington, Louise Fontaine, 281
Washington, Lucy Chapman, 309
Washington, Martha, 62
Washington, Mildred, 306
Washington, Mildred Thornton, 309
Washington, R. B., 208
Washington, Samuel, 22, 26, 31, 61, 62, 64, 208, 271, 306, 307, biog. 308-310
Washington, S. W., 271
Washington, Thomas, 96
Washington, Thornton, 17, 309
Washington, Tristam, 309
Washington, Widow Perrin, 309
Washington Building and Lime Company, 230
Washington, Charles Hall, The, 233
Washington, D. C., 71, 72, 81, 82, 85, 90, 128, 141, 145, 170, 172, 181, 182, 223, 230, 242, 246, 260, 271, 273, 308, 310, 311, 313, 314
Washington, Fort, 31, 55, 295
Water-Tube Boiler, 50
Watson, Thomas E., 237
Watson, Thomas, Jr., 126
Watson, R., 54
Watt, James, 45, 46
Wayne, Anthony, 36, 304
Wayne, James M., 199
Weaver, Adam, 85
Weaver, James B., 222
Webb, James C., 257
Weber, Max, 170
Welch's Spring, 177
Wernwag, Lewis, 87
Westminster Abbey, 47, 97
Westminster, Md., 240

INDEX 437

Westmoreland Resolutions, 306, 308
West Point, 118, 281, 282, 289, 290, 307
W. Va. Constitutional Convention, 192
"W. Va. Democrat", 234
W. Va. University, 224, 276, 280, 297, 312
Wetzel, Charles M., 244, biog. 310
Wetzel, Eliza Burriss, 310
Wetzel, Solomon, 310
Wheeling Convention, 191, 192
Wheeling Rifles, 131
Wheeling State Fencibles, 131
Wheeling, W. Va., 81, 115, 132, 168, 191-193, 206, 214, 221
Whelan, Daniel, 115
Whig Party, 75, 77, 89, 97, 99, 100, 255, 279, 293, 298
Whiskey Rebellion, 305
White, Alexander, 17, 61, 66
White House, 73
White House Farm, 166
White, John, 20
White, Julius, 154, 156
White, Robert, 28
White, Thomas, 45
White, W. H. S., 222
Whiting, 46
Whiting, Beverly, 67
Whiting, Col., 95
Whiting, Matthew, 66
Whittier, John Greenleaf, 134, 136
Wickham's Brigade, 144
Wiedfelt, Otto L., 273
Wilburn, James E., 263, 264
Wilburn, John, 264
Wildbahm, Rev., 21
Wild Goose Farm, 234
Wilkinson, Henry, 112
Willard, Ashbel P., 130, 136
Willey, W. T., 192
William and Mary College, 296

Williams, A., 80
Williams, I. I., 108
Williams, James W., 144
Williams, Richard, 69, 71, 80
Williams, Samuel, 58, 115
Williams, William, 19, 115
Williamsburg, Va., 7, 30, 303
Williamson, W. Va., 262
Williamson, Basil, 65, 68
Williamsport, Md., 24
Willis, Nathaniel, 53, 54
Willis, Nathaniel, Jr., 53
Willis, Robert Carter, 31
Willis, Thomas H., 124
Willis Presbyterian Church, 292
Willkie, Wendell L., 267
Wilmer, Emanuel, 22
Wilson, Benjamin, 311
Wilson, E. W., 208, 297, biog. 310, 311
Wilson, Henrietta S., 311
Wilson, James F., 310
Wilson, J. H., 177, 179
Wilson, John, 22, 40
Wilson, Maria S., 310
Wilson, Mary L., 311
Wilson, William L., 222, 223, 236, 237, 239, 276, biog. 311-313
Wilson, Woodrow, 244, 256, 310
Wilson-Gorman Tariff Act, 313
Wiltsheiner, Katherine, 68
Wiltshire, 222
Wiltshire, James G., 182
Wiltshire, John C., 126
Winchester, Va., 6, 11, 21, 28, 32, 53, 63, 69, 71, 83, 93, 116, 125, 148, 152-154, 163, 172, 189, 196, 276, 280, 283, 286, 290, 300, 303, 304
Winchester and Potomac Railroad, 83, 84, 153, 154
Winchester Presbytery, 19, 60, 79, 80
Winchester Telephone Company, 234

Winder, Charles S., 152
Winder, W. H., 72
Winston, Charles, 31
Wise, Henry A., 124, 125, 131-133, 145, 288, 293, 297
Witherow, Kate, 302
Wohlfarth, Martin, 20
Wollett, George, 122
Woman's Suffrage, 246
Woods, J. M., 261, 263, 264
World's Fair, Chicago, 140
World War, 256, 257, 260, 271
Worthington, Robert, Jr., 21, 22, 80, 85
Worthington, Robert, Sr., 11, 12
Worthington, Sarah, 291
Worthington, Thomas, 12, 208
Wright, John, 11, 20
Wright, Samuel, 67
Wyman, B. C., 123
Wynkoop, Cornelius, 45
Wynkoop's Spring, 65

Y

Yancey, E. L., 144
Yarmouth, Maine, 77
Yates, John, 87, 91, 163
Yellow Sulphur Springs, Va., 296
Yellow Tavern, Va., 289
York, 72
Yorktown, Va., 32, 36, 282, 284
Young, Captain, 93
Young, Daniel J., 201
Young, David, 60
Young, Frank, 238
Young, John, 61, 67
Young, Joseph C., 95, 96
Young, Samuel C., 118, 122
"Youth's Companion", 53

Z

Zion Episcopal Church, 79, 187, 278, 282, 300
Zittle, John H., 96
Zoar Baptist Church, 58, 59, 105